D1436068

THE
PAUL HAMLYN
LIBRARY

DONATED BY
THE PAUL HAMLYN
FOUNDATION
TO THE
BRITISH MUSEUM

opened December 2000

The Rise of the Greeks

THE RISE OF
THE GREEKS

Michael Grant

Weidenfeld & Nicolson
LONDON

Published in Great Britain in 1996 by
Weidenfeld & Nicolson

The Orion Publishing Group Ltd
Orion House
5 Upper Saint Martin's Lane
London WC2H 9EA

First published in Great Britain in 1987 by
Weidenfeld and Nicolson Ltd

All rights reserved. No part of this publication may be reproduced,
stored in a retrieval system, or transmitted, in any form or by any
means, electronic, mechanical, photocopying, recording or
otherwise, without the prior permission of the copyright owner.

Copyright © 1987 Michael Grant Publications Ltd

Michael Grant has asserted his right to be identified as the author of
this work in accordance with the Copyright, Designs and
Patents Act 1988

ISBN 0 297 81768 x

A catalogue record for this book is available
from the British Library

Printed and bound in Great Britain by
Butler & Tanner Ltd, Frome and London

938.01 GRA

THE
BRITISH
MUSEUM
THE PAUL HAMLYN LIBRARY

WITHDRAWN

CONTENTS

938 OL

ILLUSTRATIONS

Neck of terracotta storage jar showing the 'Trojan Horse', made perhaps on Tenos, *Archaeological Museum, Myconos* (Print: German Archaeological Institute, Athens)

Neck of a bronze mixing-bowl made either in Laconia or southern Italy, showing soldiers and a chariot, *Archaeological Museum, Châtillon-sur-Seine* (Print: Ancient Art and Architecture Collection)

Cypriot flask found at Lefkandi in Euboea (Print: M. R. Popham, British School at Athens)

Vase found at Lefkandi in Euboea (Print: M. R. Popham, British School at Athens)

Protogeometric amphora from Athens, *National Archaeological Museum, Athens* (Print: Mansell Collection)

Geometric jar from Thera, *National Museum, Copenhagen*

Protocorinthian aryballos, *National Museum, Naples*

Earthenware jar with griffin head spout from one of the Cyclades islands, *British Museum*

Wine-jug from Corinth, *British Museum*

Handle of the François vase from Clusium showing Ajax carrying the body of Achilles, *Museo Archeologico, Florence*

The François vase from an Etruscan tomb at Clusium, *Museo Archeologico, Florence* (Print: Archivi Alinari)

Handle of the François vase from Clusium, showing Artemis, *Museo Archeologico, Florence* (Print: Archivi Alinari)

Attic black-figure amphora showing Achilles slaying Penthesilea, *British Museum*

Attic black-figure perfume-bottle showing a wedding procession, *Metropolitan Museum of Art, New York*

Attic black-figure amphora illustrating the olive-harvest, *British Museum*

Attic black-figure cup showing 'long ships' and 'round ships', *British Museum* (Print: Mansell Collection)

Attic red-figure plate depicting a Scythian archer, *British Museum*

Attic white-ground perfume-vase depicting a pair of maenads, *British Museum*

Attic red-figure cup from Vulci, showing a flute-player and dancer, *British Museum*

Attic red-figure amphora showing King Croesus of Lydia preparing to immolate himself on a pyre, *Musée du Louvre, Paris*

Gold ear-ring from Lefkandi in Euboea, *Eretria Museum* (Print: M. R. Popham, British School at Athens)

Back of a silver-gilt mirror from Kelermes, Kuban district, *Hermitage Museum, Leningrad.*

Bronze tripod-cauldron from Altintepe

Hoplite armour from a warrior's grave at Argos, *Argos Museum* (Print: Greek Archaeological Service)

Ionian electrum stater, perhaps from Miletus, showing an ibex, *British Museum*

Silver didrachm from Aegina depicting a turtle (Print: Sale Catalogue)

Silver drachm from Croton displaying a tripod (Print: Sale Catalogue)

Silver tetradrachm from Athens showing Athena and an owl (Print: Sale Catalogue)

Silver didrachm of Athens showing a Gorgon's head (Print: Sale Catalogue)

Silver didrachm of Thebes showing a Boetian shield (Print: Sale Catalogue)

Silver didrachm of Thasos showing a satyr carrying off a nymph (Print: Sale Catalogue)

Silver decadrachm of the Macedonian tribe of the Derrones showing a man driving an ox-cart (Print: Sale Catalogue)

MAPS

INTRODUCTION

The ancient Greeks are so significant that they demand to be studied in their own right, and not merely as forerunners of ourselves. Yet at the same time, different though many of their circumstances and problems inevitably must have been, they *were* our forerunners, the ancestors and sources of our own western civilization – for better or worse.

The numerous statements that were made a century ago, and less than a century ago, to the effect that this was so have stood the tests of the intervening years. Certainly we nowadays have much wider knowledge about other and remoter forerunners, from Sumeria (Mesopotamia) and Ebla (Syria) onwards. But what we learn about them fails to diminish – indeed, curiously, even enhances – the vital role of the Greeks, who were, in any case, far closer to us in date and therefore more directly ancestral. Our modern, additional knowledge about civilizations that were much older and further away from that of the west, is relevant (Appendix 1), but not the whole story; for it is western civilization that we are considering.

The Greek heritage was transmitted through Rome to Byzantium and the Italian Renaissance. But that is not what we are concerned with here. A study of the later phases of ancient Hellenism would be more aptly concerned with such problems, and some of the answers, I hope, emerged from my own volume on the Hellenistic world, *From Alexander to Cleopatra*. But the more one contemplates the Greeks, who have played this enormous part in the forming of our own lives, the more one wants to find out how it all began. According to the traditional definitions, the story is divided into three parts, relating to early, classical and Hellenistic Greece respectively. One has to define periods, certainly, since otherwise history would be hard to write. And there are suitable landmarks: the Persian Wars mark a transition between early and classical Greece, and the Hellenistic epoch can be said to have begun with Alexander the Great. What I want to examine here is the long early period that preceded both of those chronological turning-points.

But let us avoid employing, for any part of this epoch, the term 'archaic' – invented originally for discussion of artistic themes, relating to the years between *c.*720 (or 750) and 480 BC – because it possesses the dictionary significance of 'primitive' and 'antiquated'. No such pejorative epithets are appropriate for the early Greeks, whose doings and sayings added up to one of the most creative periods in world history. The term 'classical', too – relating to the following period – originally referred to art that was 'first-class', of the first rank,[1] with the same implication that what had been done before was only second-rate. But that, in art or other fields, is a wholly untenable view of the Greeks of earlier times. Without in any way belittling the achievements of the 'classical' fifth and fourth centuries, which would be a ludicrously misguided enterprise, what went before is equally marvellous – and all the more so because it developed from such exceedingly small beginnings.

Moreover, there are two special reasons why it is tempting to examine what the early Greeks were doing, making, saying and thinking. These two reasons are, in a sense, contradictory. One of them is the enormously increased attention that has been paid to this half-millennium by scholars during recent years, and especially during the past decade. It seems the right time to try to assess how far these various endeavours have enabled us to move ahead. However, the second reason why the theme presents a challenge is, paradoxically enough, because our evidence regarding the various aspects of this epoch is still quite remarkably inadequate. On the literary side there are terrible gaps; and such information as we possess is more often than not seriously anachronistic and heavily biased in emphasis, selection and assessment (particularly on the part of later Athenian writers, who provide the bulk of what has come down to us). On the archaeological side, certainly, there have been important, indeed sensational, discoveries, including some that are of very recent date. But they, too, for all their distinction, are unbalanced and fragmentary. They brilliantly illuminate minute spaces, while the rest still remains in darkness. To write about the Greeks of these 'pre-classical' periods is therefore a most exacting detective exercise. That I have fallen short of this challenge I realize only too well. I should like to express my profound indebtedness to the experts whose work I have so freely drawn upon, and to add that where I have gone wrong the fault is mine and not theirs.

There is another major difficulty. In endeavouring to reconstruct this story, the scanty and arbitrary survival of information is not by any means the only problem. Another lies in the absence of an obvious central concentration point, such as Rome provides in Roman history.

For the Greeks, by way of contrast, were highly, intensely and deliberately decentralized. Nearly 700 city-states are known to have existed; it would not be surprising if we discovered, eventually, that the real number was twice as large. It was asserted, according to Herodotus, that the Greeks were a single people, united by common blood, customs, language and religion.[2] But they were also very sharply divided among themselves, since every one of these hundreds of city-states was politically independent of every other.

This presents the student of their history with a grave dilemma, especially relating to the earlier period with which this book is concerned. If the immediately subsequent time – the so-called classical age – were instead under consideration, the dilemma would still be there, but it would be a good deal less acute. It would be less acute since, in that later age, the Athenians so completely dominated the picture, first because so much of the evidence comes from them and is about them, and secondly because the extent of their achievements was so overwhelmingly great, that the 'classical' Greeks could be reasonably described, to a large extent, in terms of what was happening at Athens.

Even for the classical period, however, that concentration and centralization can easily be overdone. As far as the earlier epoch is concerned, it would be completely out of place. Two reservations, it is true, are necessary. First, for this earlier period, as later, a huge part of our surviving information already happens to come from, and relate to, the Athenians. And secondly they were already, in this earlier period, doing remarkable things. However, these reservations must be placed in their correct context. For despite the patchiness and pro-Athenian imbalance of the evidence, it remains imperative that we should try as hard as we can to discover what was going on in other parts of the Greek world as well. And Athens, in this earlier period, *was only one of a number of outstanding centres*. It is, of course, both undesirable and impossible to include even the briefest account of what was happening in all the multitudinous city-states (and other Greek organisms, such as tribal groups and markets). But it does seem essential to have a look at at least about fifty of them (and to offer brief notes on a dozen or two more).

And that is what, rather unusually, I shall be endeavouring to do in this book. I can only hope I have selected without going too far wrong. More will be said about Athens than about anywhere else, not only for the two reasons already given – quantity of evidence and sum of achievements – but also because some of what we learn about the place can be extrapolated to enlarge our knowledge of what was going on elsewhere. Even so, Athens will occupy only about one-ninth of the volume.

It will be clear from the foregoing remarks that I am tackling the history of the early Greeks from a geographical viewpoint. This involves a sharp departure from the frequently implied or tacitly accepted view that modern Greece is somehow or other the sole and more or less coterminous heir of ancient Greece. This is, of course, not so, as the Greeks of western Asia Minor, south Italy, Sicily and south Russia, with all their abundant and versatile achievements, actively bear witness.[3] That is why I have preferred 'The Rise of the Greeks' to 'The Rise of Greece' as the title of this study.

On the whole, this geographical organization of the material relating to the early Greeks works well, because each of their separate, sharply divided city-states often pursued its own idiosyncratic political and cultural development. Moreover, the geographical arrangement brings out a very significant point: it shows where the leading personalities of the age came from, or in a few cases, when it seems more important, not where they came from but where they principally worked. No apology is offered for stressing such 'great men' – writers, thinkers and artists, as well as politicians and soldiers – for such individuals played a huge part in the rise of the Greeks. Indeed this emphasis on persons, even if unfashionable, is positively demanded by the acute competitiveness between and within the various city-states, and, in consequence, between the individuals who were their most prominent members. Furthermore, most of these personalities bear strong identifying marks of the places with which they were chiefly associated, marks which would be obliterated if we did not discuss them city by city. True, the geographical principle of arrangement does not work perfectly and has its loose ends;[4] but I still believe it is best. The history of the Greeks, as much as the history of any other people, or perhaps rather more, is indissolubly linked with their geography, and remains incomprehensible if this is not constantly borne in mind. Besides, any alternative principle of organization would seem to operate less effectively.

However, I have also attempted, at the outset, to generalize about as many aspects of the early Greeks as possible, by prefacing my geographical survey with a general account which indicates the principal developments of the epoch theme by theme instead of, as on later pages, state by state. And with the same purpose in mind I shall conclude the book with two comparative chronological tables. The first aims to offer an overall picture of the sequence of events, setting out the principal Greek regions in parallel columns. The second table is intended to serve a further, special task, which I believe to be particularly essential, though it is not always undertaken in such books: namely, the placing of those events and personalities in relation to other, non-Greek civilizations – described in the Appendices – which belonged to the same period and impinged strongly on the Greeks or were influenced by them.

I am very grateful to Linden Lawson and Candida Brazil of Weidenfeld and Nicolson for seeing the volume so efficiently through the press, and to Maria Ellis, Jennifer Oddy and Peter James for providing useful assistance. My wife's help, too, as always, was invaluable.

MICHAEL GRANT, 1987

1 The Ancient Mediterranean

CHAPTER 1

THE EARLY GREEKS

During the third millennium BC there were people in Greece who did not speak Greek, or any language related to it. An echo of their language survived in Greek place-names, for example those including the non-Indo-European suffixes -nth and -ss (-tt in the Attic dialect), such as Corinthos, Parnassos, Lykabettos. But in about 2000–1900 BC – at the beginning of what archaeologists call the middle Helladic or middle Bronze Age – invaders, speaking a version of what later became Greek, came in from the north, and devastated most of the previous habitation centres.[1]

During the centuries that followed, and particularly after c.1600, Greece clearly came under the influence of the 'Minoan' civilization (as it is called today, after the legendary King Minos), which was based on Crete and possessed a strong outpost on another island lying to its north, Thera (Santorini). But the brilliant fluidities of Minoan art were given a stiffer, grander and more hieratic appearance by the culture of the mainland, which took its modern name 'Mycenaean' from its imposing centre Mycenae in the Argolid (north-eastern Peloponnese), although there were other centres too, notably Tiryns in the immediate neighbourhood, and Pylos in the south-west of the same peninsula, and Thebes in Boeotia (central Greece). The northernmost outpost of this civilization, as far as we know at present, was Iolcus in Thessaly.

The princes who ruled at these elaborate fortress–palaces, around which humbler settlements clustered, maintained a luxurious way of life, exemplified by the lavish gold-work found in their tombs and by the syllabic script ('Linear B') which they utilized to keep record of their extensive possessions.[2] The Mycenaeans were not only formidable warriors but enterprising seamen, who travelled and established markets and outposts throughout the eastern Mediterranean, and at a considerable number of harbour-towns on the central and western shores of that sea as well. Whether it is true that these 'Achaeans', as Homer called them, also captured Troy in north-western Asia Minor overlooking the Hellespont (Dardanelles), the theme of the *Iliad* (Chapter 5, section 1), we cannot tell.

From the later part of the thirteenth century, however, this whole civilization somehow became engulfed in the prolonged series of destructive movements of peoples – in many cases closely related to the fall of the Hittite empire (Appendix 1, note 19), which, as we know for example from Egyptian records, gradually convulsed and shattered the whole of the Aegean region and near east. Who these peoples were is often uncertain; they were no doubt extremely mixed, and the whole process seems to have been very complex. At all events, within a couple of generations the whole Mycenaean civilization was destroyed, with the help, probably, of internal feuds and disunities; and the palaces and bureaucracies which had exercised general control seem to have been the first to go.

At this juncture, as pollen-analysis reveals, populations sharply declined, reverting to pastoralism.[3] The art of writing was lost for several centuries to come, the use of stone for construction purposes vanished, and Greece became a country of villages, making an impoverished pottery (Sub-Mycenaean, *c.*1100–1050) which displayed stolid, insensitive shapes and hand-drawn designs of circles and half-circles. The darkness of this 'Dark Age' is not just due to our own comparative ignorance about what was happening, but represents a real and traumatic transformation.[4]

In spite of a variety of doubts and rival theories,[5] it is possible to accept, on the whole, the ancient conviction that one of the principal results of all those centuries of upheaval was the arrival in the Peloponnese of a new wave of Greeks (or at least the heads of royal or noble families and their followers) known as the Dorians, who had come down to the west of Greece from the north by way of the border areas between Thessaly and Epirus.[6] Later legend maintained that they were led by the Heraclids, descendants of the hero Heracles, and that their arrival (in *c.*1120) was a 'return', since Heracles' son Hyllus had allegedly already come to Greece (and died there) at an earlier date,[7] before the Trojan War.

This supposition, however, of an earlier arrival by the Dorians under Hyllus was a fictitious antedating, designed subsequently in order to make their presence look more venerably antique, and to assert a claim to descent from Heracles. The story also served to legitimize the seizure by these Dorians – who were unknown, in this area, to heroic, Homeric legends – of territories that had figured prominently in those legends, identified with the lands of Agamemnon, the grandson of Pelops, from whom the Peloponnese took its name.

Only Euboea and Athens, among major centres, seem to have

successfully resisted the Dorian invasion. On Euboea, the site of Lefkandi (Lelanton) reveals startling lavishness in the very depths of the 'Dark Age' (Chapter 4, section 1). Athens (Chapter 2, section 1) later claimed not only to have held out but to have been the leader of a mass emigration of people originating from other parts of Greece, described as the Ionians (after the mythical hero Ion). In order to escape from the Dorians these refugees moved across the Aegean and settled on the western coast of Asia Minor, and its offshore islands: the region that became known as Ionia. Other migrants to Asia Minor and its islands, from Thessaly and Boeotia, settled in Aeolis to the north of Ionia, and Dorian settlers came further south. In most of these coastal and insular areas of western Asia Minor, there was extensive ethnic admixture with the pre-existing inhabitants, which, added to the blendings that had accompanied the protracted migrations, make it hard to speak of a unitary Greek 'race'.

However, all these people spoke the Greek language. But they spoke it in a variety of different dialects. As far as we can reconstruct these forms of speech from the later evidence available to us, they fell into two major divisions, West Greek (Dorian and North-West Greek, introduced by the newcomers to the Greek mainland after the fall of Mycenae) and pre-Dorian East Greek (Aeolian, Ionian [of which Attic was a sub-dialect] and Arcado-Cypriot [spoken in Arcadia in the central Peloponnese on the island of Cyprus]).[8]

The widely distributed pottery known as 'Protogeometric' (c.1025–900), initiated by Athens and then developed in the Argolid and over a wide area extending from Thessaly to the northern Cyclades, displayed circular designs drawn no longer by hand, like those of the preceding Sub-Mycenaean ware, but by the compass, and painted by a multiple brush with patterns that neatly define the clear-cut shape of the vessel.[9] This Protogeometric pottery transforms the previous Sub-Mycenaean efforts so radically that it must be seen as marking a new start, looking not backward but forward to the artistic triumphs of the future – though the directness of any such continuous debt has been questioned.

The arrival of more settled conditions in the tenth century heralded the epoch of urbanization when towns and cities came into existence. A favourite Greek term for this process was *synoikismos*, or *synoikisis*, uniting under a single capital.[10] But this could happen in various different ways. A group of villages might physically amalgamate to form one township, as was the case, for example, at Sparta and Corinth, creating an urban focus for a previously scattered population. Or the villages could remain where they were and agree to accept one of their number as their centre, so that it became the metropolis; that is what happened in Attica, where the rise of Athens did not extinguish the villages of the territory but subordinated them to the new urban unit. Most Greek cities comprised an acropolis (*polis*) on a high bluff and a township (*astu*) which lay beneath it and came under its control and protection, particularly against pirates, who were an ever present danger.

No less decisive was the emergence of these urban concentrations as the nuclei of politically independent city-states. During the years 850–750 this became the characteristic form of Greek life. There were, it is true, other, alternative forms of organization, notably the *ethnos*, tribe or group of tribes lacking civic institutions, of which the Thessalians provided the most notable example;[11] but in general, as time went on, it was only the more backward Greek communities that maintained this type of structure. On the other hand there were, as we saw in the Introduction, hundreds of Greek city-states, none very large and some exceedingly small.[12] Each of these was called a *polis* (although, confusingly, the same term was employed not only for a city's acropolis but for the city itself as an urban unit). City-states were not new. True, the settlements round the Mycenaean cities (even if a memory of them, or their survivals, influenced the new post-Mycenaean urban groupings, as is doubtful) may not have contained sufficient municipal institutions to merit such a description. But it would be difficult to deny the title to all the cities that had long been in existence within the near east, especially in areas such as Syria and Phoenicia, and particularly at the various times when they evaded great-power control.[13]

However, it is quite certain that the Greeks, while organized in households (*oikoi*), clans (*gene*) and phratries (brotherhoods)[14] – of which more will be said in connection with Athens – invested the concept of the city-state, into which all these units were incorporated, with an entirely new richness and reality. These Greek states included a stretch of the surrounding countryside[15] – not always very productive since, as Herodotus remarked, 'Hellas and poverty are foster-sisters,'[16] but essential to the Greeks, whose emphatic aim was to make their *poleis* self-sufficient, agriculturally and in every other way. Indeed, so self-sufficient did each state set out to be that the whole social, economic, moral, intellectual and artistic life of a citizen (*polites*) revolved around its narrow confines. He identified himself with its life to an extent which must surely have been unprecedented, and which would be found intolerable today.[17]

In particular, his life centred around the city's *agora*, or gathering place (a more accurate rendering than 'market-place'). It was there – as perhaps earlier, in Minoan and Mycenaean times (cf. Drerus,

Chapter 6, section 1) – that the citizens met informally to conduct business or take part in religious processions and athletic displays. They also, no doubt – being Greeks – discussed politics. But originally these gatherings in the *agora*, even if dignified by the name of an assembly, still exercised little political power, because such early assemblies only existed to hear and applaud decisions announced from above – that is to say, announced by the monarchs, who, if tradition is to be believed, originally governed the cities.

For Aristotle maintained that the newly arising city-states had at first been ruled by monarchies, small-scale replicas of the great kingships of the Mycenaean past.[18] In recent years this assumption has met with doubts, increased by the fact that we have no systematic or comprehensive information about any such monarchies. That is true, but the argument *ex absentia* is scarcely valid when we are told so little about any other Dark Age phenomena, and although generalizations are impossible, since every state had a history of its own, the Aristotelian hypothesis does still seem applicable to a fair number of these early communities.

However, as time went on, such monarchs of Dark Age Greece, where they existed, proved unable any longer to maintain autocratic power in the face of competition by their nobles. Such nobles, therefore, in varying stages – for example, if the king proved ineffective in time of war – gradually weakened the royal authority, and in the end substituted rule by themselves, as an aristocratic group, finding it more sensible to share the power with one another than each to fight against the rest for an autocratic kingship that had in any case ceased to be a viable proposition.

Previously the monarch as a single individual, and now the nobles corporately, claimed to govern and judge by divine right, handed down from the gods from whom they proclaimed their descent.[19] In this position, therefore, they were able to assert a monopoly of 'virtue' (*arete*), and thus a monopoly of the power to provide good government (*eunomia*), so that to disobey them was declared to be sinful. These nobles were generally little more than farmers and herders like everyone else, helped by a few artisans and slaves, yet it was they who owned the best land; and they maintained certain aristocratic traditions. They could ride, and owned horses where these were available, so that Aristotle describes some of the first aristocratic regimes as 'constitutions of horsemen (knights)'[20] (cf. below, and note 32). The elaborate network of gift-exchange, guest friendship and hospitality described by Homer presumably reflects customs that would not be too unfamiliar to his eighth-century hearers. The male drinking groups (*symposia*), for whose entertainment some of the best poetry of the age was composed

5

and sung, constituted another cherished aristocratic tradition, of lasting political significance.

In one region, Western (Opuntian) Locris, in central Greece, we have evidence (relating to the fifth century, but no doubt applicable earlier) of 100 noble houses and a citizen assembly restricted to 1,000. We hear of 1,000-strong assemblies, again at a number of other Greek centres as well, notably Cyme in Aeolis and Colophon in Ionia, no doubt including the aristocrats, and perhaps part of the class next beneath them. Sometimes, too, there were assemblies of only 600, or just over 200 (Corinth), or even 180. But in many cases those assemblies still left all real power in the hands of a small group of leaders, 'the council of the great-hearted elders' whom Homer causes Agamemnon to summon in the *Iliad*.[21]

The Geometric period of Greek art and pottery lasted from *c*.900 to *c*.700 (early *c*.900–850, strong 850–800, ripe 800 to before 750, late 750–700), and once again, as in the Protogeometric epoch from which it developed, Athens showed the greatest power of ceramic invention, although there was also basically similar though regionally divergent Geometric pottery elsewhere, notably in Argos, Corinth, Boeotia, Naxos, Paros, Thera and Melos. The style is what its title suggests: a series of regular, repetitive, rectilinear patterns over the entire surface of the vessel, including meanders, zig-zags, swastikas and triangles, formed by brushwork which followed the circling of the potter's wheel and rhythmically emphasized and articulated the contours of the vase. Near-eastern influence (see Appendix 1) is very generalized, rather than providing models or copies; the abstract, tight repetitiveness of Geometric designs may owe a debt to the decoration of eastern metal objects. But this firm, architectonic, intellectually disciplined command over clearly apprehended principles of logical analysis is specifically Greek, like the Protogeometric art before it, but more so.

Small friezes of animals began to appear on these Geometric vases, and then pots of huge dimensions, including especially an extraordinary specimen by the 'Dipylon Master' (*c*.770–760), began to display painted friezes of human scenes. The parts played in this development by near-eastern and late-Mycenaean art are hard to assess, although the former was more influential than the latter (and, in recompense, these Athenian vases were exported as far as Syria and Cyprus). A funeral scene has been identified with the funeral of Patroclus in Homer's *Iliad*, perhaps not very convincingly, since these figures on the vases are highly stylized, schematic, linear and incorporeal. Yet here are the first indications of how the Greeks conceived

6

the human figure, and the first artistic demonstrations, also, that they regarded a concern with man and his works as of primary importance.

Probably the most influential development during the whole of this half-millennium occurred during the eighth century, when Greek lands again became open to the near-eastern influences that have just been mentioned. That openness had likewise existed during Mycenaean times; and in those regions which had not suffered destruction during the break-up of the Mycenaean civilization commercial and cultural contacts with the near east had never been broken during the subsequent Dark Age. But they had only been maintained in a few areas and to a limited extent, and it was not until the eighth century that such links were revived on a very considerable scale.

By this time various channels of communication were involved, including Cyprus and Crete, which, like Euboea and Athens, had escaped the post-Mycenaean destruction. But particularly important points of contact were Al Mina and other market ports (*emporia*) which the Euboeans led the way in establishing on the coast of northern Syria (Chapter 6, section 4). These links with the Syrian trading harbours played an important part in what became a veritable, volcanic eighth-century revolution in Greek affairs, although, as the *Epinomis* by an imitator of Plato pointed out, the Greeks never failed to adapt and alter what they borrowed to suit their own requirements and genius.[22] In the field of art, the most conspicuous result was the 'orientalizing' painting of Corinthian vases (Chapter 3, section 2), on which abstract geometrical ornament was dramatically abandoned in favour of a writhing mass of animals and monsters and other curvilinear designs, owing debts to north Syria, Phoenicia, Assyria and neighbouring near eastern lands (Appendix 1). The new vases circulated far and wide, and rapidly won imitators in other Greek cities.[23]

Moreover, this eighth-century revolution was not restricted to art, but affected every walk of life. It accompanied the maturity of the Greek Iron Age. Iron had been in use from before the turn of the millennium (the 'early Iron Age'),[24] but an enormous development of iron metallurgy between *c*.750 and *c*.650 improved and accelerated the speed and efficiency of life in many fields, and under this more stable mode of existence the population of Greece multiplied to a remarkable extent.[25]

This increased number of inhabitants encouraged a wholesale switch from pasturage to arable farming, and food-production notably intensified. Nevertheless, there was still not enough farm land to go round.[26] There was, it would appear (despite the lack of concrete evidence), serious over-population, prompting, as time went on, demands

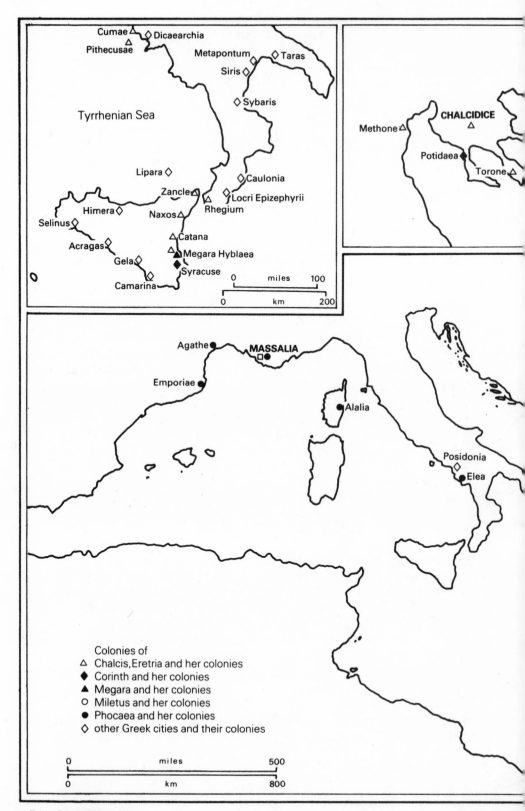

Colonies of
△ Chalcis, Eretria and her colonies
◆ Corinth and her colonies
▲ Megara and her colonies
○ Miletus and her colonies
● Phocaea and her colonies
◇ other Greek cities and their colonies

2 Early Greek Colonization

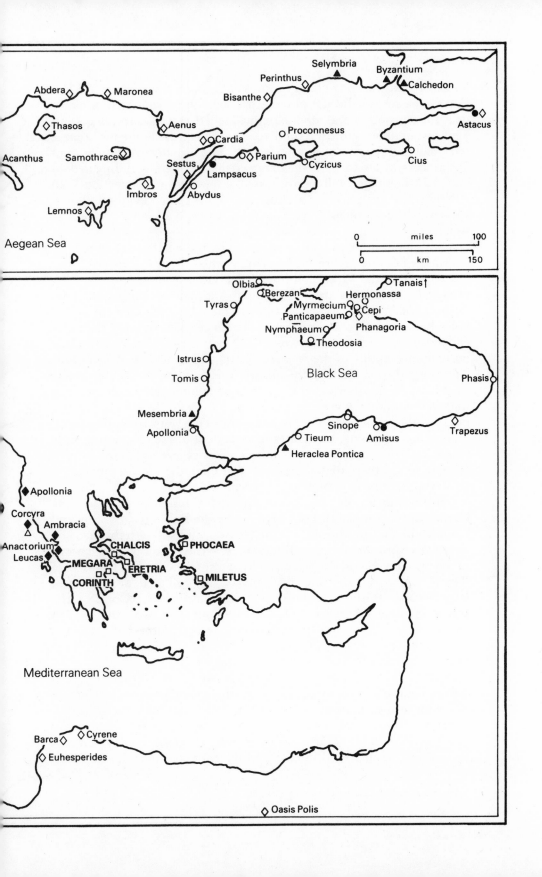

Aegean Sea

Abdera Maronea
Thasos Aenus
Acanthus Samothrace
Sestus
Imbros Lampsacus
Lemnos Abydus

Perinthus Selymbria Byzantium
Bisanthe Calchedon
Cardia Proconnesus Astacus
Parium Cyzicus Cius

0   miles   100
0   km   150

Olbia Tanais†
Berezan Hermonassa
Tyras Myrmecium Cepi
Panticapaeum Phanagoria
Nymphaeum
Istrus Theodosia

Black Sea

Tomis Phasis

Mesembria
Apollonia Sinope Trapezus
Tieum Amisus
Heraclea Pontica

Apollonia
Corcyra
Ambracia
Anactorium CHALCIS PHOCAEA
Leucas
MEGARA ERETRIA
CORINTH MILETUS

Mediterranean Sea

Barca Cyrene
Euhesperides

Oasis Polis

for the 'redistribution of land'. The situation was worsened by the fact that Greek society did not practise primogeniture, so that on a man's death his property was divided equally between all surviving sons. This meant an unremitting subdivision of soil until allotments became too small and poor to support existence. The misery that this continuous process was to cause to the impoverished farmers, resulting in debt and debt-bondage, will be discussed elsewhere in connection with Athens (Chapter 3, section 2), from which most of our evidence comes. However, the problem must have been widespread in other areas as well.

The demographic pressures provoked by these hardships caused an enormous number of Greeks, from many cities, to move overseas. The ensuing territorial expansion impelled Plato to compare his compatriots to 'ants or frogs around a pond'[27] – a pond extending from the farthest coasts of the Black Sea to the Pillars of Hercules (Straits of Gibraltar). The Greek world, after the Mycenaean collapse, had first expanded, as we saw, some two or three centuries earlier, as a result of mass immigrations to the western coasts and islands of Asia Minor. And now, during the eighth century, the number of city-states was doubled. This is known as the 'age of colonization', although the cities that were founded, known to the Greeks as *apoikiai*, 'away homes', did not resemble colonies in any modern sense of the word, since they were, or very soon became, city-states independent of the originating state whose emigrant people their founders (later revered as heroes – note 45) had led to these distant shores. Well might Sophocles later place sea-faring first among human achievements.[28]

Outstanding among the eighth-century 'colonial' foundations were Cumae in south-western Italy founded by the Euboeans, Sybaris and Croton in the south-east of the same peninsula established by Achaeans from the northern Peloponnese – the region became known as 'Great Greece' – and Zancle and Syracuse in Sicily. The founders of Zancle and Syracuse came respectively from Chalcis and Corinth, whose representatives also created a colony at Corcyra (Corfu) in the Ionian (southern Adriatic) Sea. These colonizations were undertaken by private enterprise, but with the approval of the mother-city, with the assistance, very often, of people from other communities, and with the sanction, when obtainable, of the Delphic oracle.

And so, by this means, the old, long-vanished network of Mycenaean communications in the central Mediterranean had been reconstructed, although now in competition with the Phoenician city-states, led by Tyre and Sidon, which themselves established Carthage and many other colonies in the same areas (Appendix 1). Despite this rivalry, in the seventh century the Ionian city of Phocaea continued the exploitation of the western Mediterranean, culminating in the foundation of Massalia.

By that time, however, other city-states had fulfilled a similar role on the eastern seaboards of the same sea, where (among a huge number of settlements from various states) Megara founded Calchedon and Byzantium on the Thracian Bosphorus, and the Black Sea coast was peopled thickly by Miletus, some of whose foundations, notably Olbia, acquired an importance scarcely equalled by any Greek state of the homeland. Moreover, as far afield as north Africa, the Aegean island of Thera colonized Cyrene.

Colonies sent Greece metals (in great demand among aristocratic and oligarchic governments and their members and armies) and raw materials and foodstuffs, importing finished articles from the homeland in exchange. But such commercial enterprises could also be conducted, not necessarily by formally established colonies (city-states), but by trading-posts (*emporia*) lacking colonial status. Pithecusae and Cumae (before its colonization) had been of that character, and in Egypt the pharaohs allowed the *emporion* of Naucratis to possess different quarters reserved for a considerable number of Greek states.

The earliest information about suitable sites for trading-posts or colonies must have come from previous traders (or pirates). A notable extension and reawakening of commercial activity dated from shortly before 850, the time when sea communications were improving. This trading was still on a small scale, as might be expected from the small size of the ships. It was an integral part, however, of the Greek civilization of the time, although goods also circulated from non-commercial motives as well, for example through the gift-exchanges and sanctuary dedications that formed part of the aristocratic way of life. These nobles alone, as the major landowners and directors of tenants and craftsmen, could equip ships and send them to sea (employing warships, which sacrificed cargo-carrying to speed and battle-effectiveness, for trading until the sixth century, when large, sail-driven 'round-ships' or merchantmen were constructed for bulk cargoes). Trading, like colonization, in early Greek times was not initiated by city-states but was a matter of private, not always co-ordinated individual enterprises.

Yet the instinct for productive investment (as opposed to the use of wealth for enjoyment or display) was curiously lacking, by our standards. Socrates (allegedly) and Aristotle were among those who voiced a distaste for profit-making production and for the mechanical occupations that were necessary to keep it in being. Such attitudes contributed to the scarcity of technological advances among the Greeks, and this scarcity was further encouraged by the strong tendency of philosopher–

scientists to prefer theoretical argument to practical, empirical invention – a tendency about which more will be said later on in this chapter.

Certainly, then, there was a tendency to look down on such activities as retail-selling or 'counter-jumping'. Aristotle was professedly expressing a preference for the old-fashioned, aristocratic, agrarian way of life. Yet it is not entirely clear to what extent these nostalgic prejudices mirrored a state of affairs that had ever really existed during the earlier, aristocratic epoch of Greece. On the contrary, as Plutarch observed in connection with Solon, 'the calling of a merchant was actually held in honour in early Greece' (compare Sappho's brother Charaxus, Chapter 5, section 4). And at Corinth (where novel types of ship were invented and constructed [Chapter 3, section 2], forming exceptions to Greek technical stagnation), it is doubtful if such views at any time prevailed, for as Herodotus remarked, 'the Corinthians, *least of all Greeks*, have a prejudice against craftsmen'.[29]

Commercial activities, that is to say, *did* take place, on a limited scale, among all classes in early Greece. And in these operations men from different city-states were obliged to work together. But any collaboration with men from another state must have gone against the grain, for the very essence of relations between the various Greek communities was conflict. The intensive introspectiveness of their existences was habitually accompanied, as we know, by inability to get on with the city-state next door, or indeed, for any length of time, with any other city-state. Consciousness of the problem, displayed by various efforts to prevent or mitigate warfare, and the fact that already before 600 some of these governments began to maintain permanent representatives (*proxenoi*) in each other's capitals scarcely altered the situation. As Plato later chillingly pointed out, the natural state of affairs between one Greek state and another was war.[30]

Local wars were rarely fatal to entire states, because the victorious soldiers could not stay away from their farms for too long. Thus it caused widespread shock, and seemed a grave atrocity, when Croton destroyed Sybaris. Nevertheless, inter-city wars were almost incessant, and were devastatingly wasteful and weakening. It is a curious phenomenon that people as intelligent as the Greeks should have been so bellicose, so incompetent in the conduct of their foreign relations. They fought because they could not secure the resources required to give themselves the self-sufficiency that every city-state was determined to attain; in consequence, the required assets had to be seized, if possible, from another state by force.

This phenomenon was closely connected with another, namely the Greeks' deeply rooted and intense sense of competition and contest (*agon*), expressed in Homer's *Iliad* when Achilles' father Peleus urged him always to try to excel all other men.[31] Within the enclosed circle of city-state life, this widespread competitive ambition among citizens, curbed from extreme excess by a similar desire on the part of everyone else, made for a great deal of valuable activity. Transmitted, however, as it was, into corporate relationships between city-states, it meant that the resulting fragmentation and particularism created, and created permanently, what was little less than a free-for-all between states.

This being the case, each city had to build up its military strength, and the result was what was known as the 'hoplite revolution', in which Argos, Chalcis and Corinth fulfilled leading roles. The hoplites were heavily armed infantry, replacing less effective armies in which 'knights' and horses (though these were rarely procurable in sufficient numbers, except in Italy, Thessaly, Euboea and Cyrene) had played a prominent part.[32] The body-armour of the hoplite comprised a helmet with nose and cheek guards (first seen at Corinth), a breastplate or cuirass (Chalcis) and greaves – all made of bronze,[33] by techniques learned partly from the east and partly from central Europe. The principal protection of these infantry warriors was a heavy, round or elliptical bronze shield (Argos) secured to the left arm, and their weapons were a short, straight iron sword (Chalcis) and a nine-foot-long thrusting spear.

The phalanx in which the hoplites fought is depicted, like their equipment, on vases. It was a close, tight mass of soldiers eight lines deep, who fought by shoving (*othismos*), while every man protected his neighbour. We have moved out of the epoch of individual duels and heroic acts, immortalized by Homer, into an age of corporate, cohesive, disciplined action, on behalf not of one's ego but of the state to which one belongs.

This change had political implications. The new development did not favour the proletariat, since all hoplites had to pay for their own armour, that is to say they had to own sufficient property for this to be possible. But although the nobles may have been the most enthusiastic among the hoplites, such fighters were not all of aristocratic birth; indeed only a small proportion of them could claim such a qualification. Yet it was these men, the defenders of the state – as Aristotle pointed out – who ultimately controlled it and called the tune[34] (claiming, for example, an equal share in whatever booty became available). Thus although the nobility had been responsible for bringing the hoplites into existence, for the defence of their regimes (seeing a political advantage in restricting this warlike role to the relatively prosperous), the very existence of such a soldiery contributed largely to the eventual broadening of those birth-based regimes, and so helped to bring about their downfall.

Meanwhile other phenomena of the time were contributing to the same end. The opening of the Mediterranean world, as we saw, had greatly expanded trade. True, the aristocrats had not been averse to sponsoring or even engaging in trade, but it was inevitable that in due course some men lacking nobility of birth should also gain distinction in this field. Moreover, great areas of Greek life had been changed by the introduction and adaptation of the Phoenician or north Syrian alphabet (probably through north Syrian ports and Chalcis – see Chapter 6, section 4, and Appendix 1),[35] after half a millennium of illiteracy following the disappearance of the Mycenaean 'Linear B' script.

One effect of this new writing was a rapid increase in education.[36] Moreover, although Greek communities, being talkative, still retained their predominantly oral character, the novel alphabetic script was soon seen as a perfect instrument for public, secular values. In particular, people now began to want to view and read their city's laws (*nomoi*) in writing; the days when the kings and nobles had just arbitrarily imposed their 'god-given' rulings (*thesmoi*) from above were past.[37] So men described as law-givers arose in the cities, and even if Lycurgus at Sparta is a myth, Thaletas propounded laws in Crete (where portions of the earliest-known legal code came from Drerus), and his alleged pupil Zaleucus did the same at Locri Epizephyrii in southern Italy, and Charondas at Catana in Sicily and elsewhere. These last two examples are significant, since there was a particular demand for written laws in the new cities of the west, with their more emancipated lives and their clash of customs between men of different homelands: laws were needed to consolidate these heterogeneous citizen bodies. However, similar developments occurred in the homeland as well, notably at Athens, Thebes and Corinth.

These laws seemed harsh to later generations; indeed, by writing them down, the various city authorities presumably intended to restrict liberty and licence, rather than encourage them. Yet the eventual effect was the opposite: the sight of written laws gave the citizens a new idea of their rights and possibilities, and thus led (as some resistant nobles had gloomily forecast) to reforms, or, more often, to unfulfilled hopes of reform. Here, then, was another phenomenon which before long weakened the noblemen's regimes.

The alphabet came just in time to write down the recently completed *Iliad* and *Odyssey*. These epics had been composed orally, and were chanted to the accompaniment of a rudimentary lyre (the *phorminx* or *citharis*) in stately but easily flowing hexameters (six feet of dactyls, long–short–short syllables varied in speed, movement, tone and mood by spondees, consisting of a pair of long feet)[38] by a poet identifiable in the case of both poems, though some would not agree with this, as Homer (Chapter 5, section 1). The awesomely unsurpassable quality of these two works caused them to become the principal educative influences upon all Greeks for all time to come, providing exactly the inspiration they needed for their own endeavours.

The very different epics ascribed to Hesiod and Boeotia in central Greece – the *Theogony* foreshadowing more philosophical discussions of the creation of the universe, and an earlier composition, the *Works and Days* (Chapter 4, section 4) – are generally regarded as slightly later than the Homeric poems, since they depict a later and less heroic form of society. But the criterion is an unsound one, since the authors of such epics were imaginative poets, not contemporary historians, and were, besides, writing in widely separated regions where ways of life and processes of development were by no means identical or parallel.

The (evidently lesser) orally sung forerunners of Homer's and Hesiod's poems are lost. Lost too, are innumerable early examples of other types of poetry, not epic in character, which are referred to in the *Iliad* and *Odyssey*,[39] and which likewise formed an integral part of the performing tradition. This non-epic, dramatic poetry of the Greeks, a blend of words, music[40] and dancing, is loosely described as 'lyrical'.[41] But the term is ambiguous, and the poetical corpus it is employed to describe is better divided into two parts, choral song accompanied by the lyre and other instruments (at which Archilochus of Paros, and Alcman and Stesichorus – resident at Sparta and Himera respectively – excelled), and monody (the verse of Alcaeus and Sappho of Lesbos), in which the poet sang solo and accompanied himself or herself on the lyre (or flute).

Another sort of classification, much favoured by the Greeks, was according to metre. The invention of elegiac poetry was variously ascribed to Archilochus and to Callinus of Ephesus. This elegiac verse consisted of dactylic and spondaic couplets comprising a hexameter and pentameter (five feet), so that more intimate and topical effects than those of the mouth-filling wholly hexameter verse could be achieved. The word 'elegy' was perhaps connected with some eastern word for flute, so that the form of poetry it was employed to describe may at first have been a flute-song. The ancient idea that it originated in lamentations remains dubious. At all events, the metre came to be used for many purposes, including not only flute-songs (*scolia*) sung at aristocratic dinner-parties (*symposia*), but, particularly, amorous and historical themes, and the warlike exhortations of Tyrtaeus and Solon.

The iambic metre (again the term is near-eastern), based not on dactyls and spondees but on iambi (short–long), was especially associated with satire and invective, for which it was employed by Archilochus and Semonides. These apparent expressions of personal feelings, as well as the even more powerful and varied poetical views pronounced in a variety of metres by the monodists, are often thought of as directly reflecting the individual experiences and feelings of their authors, and thus as marking the beginning of a new 'lyric age', following upon and superseding the age of the epic. This interpretation, however, is based on a misunderstanding of the poets' procedure: the *persona* which they present is an imaginative, literary construction – whether original or conventional – and does not necessarily reflect any event in which they personally had been involved. When Alcaeus, therefore, writes that he fled from a battle and dropped his shield, or when Sappho describes the feelings of a lover, one cannot be sure that they are depicting what actually happened to them; what they are concerned to achieve, instead, is the creation and projection of a poetical image, just as the 'narrator' in a modern novel should not be identified, at least wholly, with the novelist himself.

Certainly Greek lyrical poetry has far more analytical and introspective aims than epic: its approach is quite different. But it follows from what has just been said that a 'lyric age', in which writers begin to describe their own feelings and lives, is a suspect conception. Besides, the various forms of 'lyric' poetry which are referred to by Homer must have predated him, so that the idea of an orderly chronological succession from an epic to a lyric period has to be abandoned. Both, or rather all, these types of poetry went back to folksongs extending far behind Homer and Hesiod and Archilochus into the deep mists of time, before an alphabet arrived to rescue such pieces for posterity.

Religion pervades many of these poems at every point, or at least is never forgotten. For it was not just an appendage to Greek existence but an essential and ever-present part of that existence, pervading all its activities. Yet the religion of the Greeks is also disconcertingly difficult to comprehend, although consideration of its various diverse geographical centres one after another in this book may, it is hoped, gradually cast more light on the mystery. It was, of course, a polytheistic religion. It had room for a large number of gods and goddesses, who, despite extensive overlapping, represented different aspects of life, mirroring the multiplicity of the human world, and were attached more or less closely to their own special shrines, although the principal deities were also recognized everywhere. Links with the ancient past were very strong, yet, as so often, we are faced with the paradox that, at the same time, the Greeks made something new out of it all.

Their debt to the past emerges most clearly in connection with the great goddesses, Hera and Demeter and Artemis. All these perceptibly, in their different ways, echo the Earth Mother or Mistress of Animals of earlier civilizations: Hera's epithet 'ox-eyed' (Boopis) and Athena's owl at Athens recall times when animal totems had been worshipped. On the other hand Zeus, the chief of the gods and lord of the sky, was a later importation, brought in during the convulsions that accompanied and followed the fall of Mycenae; and Apollo, the dread shining one, the most Greek of gods despite his apparently un-Greek name and origins, made his appearance at the same time.

The origins of Greek religion remain something of a mystery. They were sometimes attributed, unconvincingly, to Egypt, but Homer and Hesiod were credited, more plausibly, with the remarkable achievement of standardizing and welding together the Olympic gods for Greece. A strong team, too, Homer in particular makes of them, as subsequent Greeks noticed (sometimes, like Xenophanes, with disapproval): a collection of perilously powerful divinities, full of vices and foibles. These failings were on human lines, since one of the most distinctive features of Greek religion, for which Homer again must take a lot of the credit, was its anthropomorphism, uniquely developed among the major religions of the world. These gods and goddesses are human beings writ large, because the Greeks, with their lively dramatic and plastic sense, were so conscious of the potentialities of men and women that they could not imagine the deities in any other shape.

In early times, at least, these divinities, while admired for their beauty and strength, were not consistently thought of as representing ethical concepts or ideals, either in their own behaviour or in their requirements from men and women, except that Zeus, various facets of whose power were described by specific epithets, expected certain basic forms of good behaviour, such as the protection of suppliants and hospitality to strangers. Other kinds of misbehaviour such as *hubris* – self-indulgence at the expense of others (see Chapter 4, section 2) – could on occasion be punished, although the idea that the gods resented over-prosperous mortals does not clearly antedate 500 BC. But these deities could be savagely dangerous if men and women did not acknowledge them (that is what the Greek term *nomizein* means – not 'believe in') and if they were not placated; this was an anxiety-appeasing religion of formal reciprocity, *do ut des*, I give you so that you shall give me.

Now, what they primarily needed was sacrifice, and best of all the blood sacrifice of meat, which satisfied the guilt and exultation of the sacrificers, affirming life by its encounter with death (as well as providing welcome left-overs for food). So the principal centres of early worship were sacrificial altars, not the temples which in due course grew up behind them; altars and temples alike may well have been financed at first not only by communities but by rich individuals.

Great sanctuaries came into existence, for Zeus at Dodona and Olympia and Nemea, for Apollo at Delphi (Pytho) and Delos and Didyma and Claros, for Hera at Argos and Samos and near Croton and Posidonia, for Artemis at Ephesus, for Poseidon at Isthmia beside Corinth. The evidence for the direct continuity of such Greek sanctuaries down from Mycenaean times is conflicting or dubious (and in any case, if and when it existed, a change of deity was usually involved). But such major places of worship entered a decisive phase in the eighth century, influenced civic development and expanded enormously in the 200 years that followed. Some of the centres became famous for oracles; the oracular shrines at Dodona and especially Delphi gained enormous influence.[42]

Around four sanctuaries, too, developed great festivals, the Olympian, Pythian, Isthmian and Nemean Games. These gatherings may perhaps have gone back to Homeric funeral games for the dead heroes, although this interpretation of their origin is disputed. In their mature form they were eloquently praised by Plato for the refreshment and 'wholeness' they bestowed on every participant.[43] Yet their role in the unification, or otherwise, of the Greek world was contradictory. On the one hand their Panhellenic nature did something to counterbalance the particularism of individual city-states. But at the same time the contests which were the essential feature of these regular concourses formed a supreme example of the unrestrained competitiveness which so sharply kept those states apart; and it was the same spirit of competition (*agon*) that stimulated the abundant dedications of works of art to the sanctuaries, especially at Olympia and the Samian Heraeum, by cities and individuals all over the Greek world. These dedicated objects included, from the eighth century onwards, two successive types of huge bronze cauldrons, of Syrian inspiration – prestigious monumentalizations of domestic pots, decorated with ornaments which foreshadowed subsequent sculpture.[44]

Alongside the worship of the Olympian deities was a whole range of other, more popular cults, frequently of a local or territorial character – defining the individuality of each *polis*. Such cults venerated regional or national heroes (*heroes*), notable dead men or women, historical or legendary, generally at their actual or supposed tombs.[45] And there were also ecstatic and underworld ('chthonian', fertility) rituals: represented, for example, by the cult of Dionysus (from Thrace) and the secret Mysteries of Demeter (at Eleusis). Towards the end of the early period cults of a 'chthonian' nature attained importance because of the salvation in the afterlife which mystic initiations into their rituals could excitingly bring – excitements which had been lacking in the shadowy nullity of the afterlife presented, for example, by Homer.[46]

At Eleusis priestly duties were at first the hereditary prerogatives of certain families, but there and elsewhere professional priesthoods did not exist.[47] For, despite the ever present power of Greek religion, there was no Church and no canon of orthodoxy. So much is clear enough from the bewildering variety and contradiction of Greek myths. These, too, were all-pervasive and came from a great diversity of origins and purposes, for which no single comprehensive explanation is acceptable. Appealing to our intelligence, emotions and imagination, they symbolized problems beyond our grasp. They sought to explain natural and social phenomena. They recorded folklore. They justified rituals, or were justified by them. They served many a patriotic purpose, for the glory of this or that city-state or its governing aristocracy.

Or they just told stories. Homer's sort of story, with its vivid but scarcely reverent pictures of divinity, opened the floodgates to later rationalizations. However, regardless of such intellectual developments, most of the myths, even if one could not exactly regard them as historically 'true', remained forever unforgotten, and somehow continued to be taken seriously. The mythology of the Greeks, a living testimonial to their belief that human and human-like behaviour provides a fascinating and central subject for study, is of immeasurable depth and wealth, and remains one of their most extraordinary imaginative creations.

Meanwhile, however, in other respects, the life of the Greeks was continuing to change. This was very noticeable, for example, in the political field. For, before long, except in socially backward regions such as Thessaly, regimes in which rulership was exercised by elite groups, owing their predominance to birth and ancestry alone, were ceasing to exist. This came about by different means at different cities, but in a substantial group of advanced maritime states the aristocracies were brought down by men described by the Greeks as 'tyrants' and here as dictators.

The word *tyrannos*, which is probably of Phoenician origin (related to the Hebrew *seran*), was first used, as far as we know, by the poet Archilochus of Paros, with reference to the non-Greek King Gyges of Lydia (*c.*685–657; see Appendix 1).[48] Gyges was a man who had brought down an existing regime by violence, setting himself up in its place as absolute ruler, and that was what in Greek lands, too, *tyrannos* signified.

For the dictators of Greek city-states had likewise usually done both those things: by forceful methods, each of them had broken through into local politics, and taken supreme control.

Among the most important Greek city-states only Sparta and Aegina escaped dictatorship altogether. It may, however, have been in Ionia that the institution first appeared (under the influence of what had happened in neighbouring Lydia). But our evidence is tenuous, and it is possible that the first dictator instead arose on the mainland. This pioneer may have been a ruler of Argos – the leading city of the Peloponnese during the whole of the earlier period of Greek history. His name was Pheidon. The date of Pheidon has been much disputed; but his accession, often placed too early, is now convincingly attributed to c.675, and no sooner. He does not, however, quite fit in with the usual classification of 'tyrants' or dictators because, according to Aristotle, he was a 'king who became a tyrant', that is to say not an intrusive noble or non-noble upstart, like the others who came later, but a hereditary monarch (basileus) who exceeded his constitutional powers.[49]

More readily classifiable as tyrant–dictators were Cypselus of Corinth, Orthagoras of Sicyon, Polycrates of Samos, Thrasybulus of Miletus, Phalaris of Acragas and Hippocrates of Gela. Each of these men subverted an aristocratic government and replaced it by his own dictatorial rule. Partially or wholly noble themselves, they attracted whatever dissident or disadvantaged aristocratic support they could – and they also sought, with success, to gain the favour of the not wholly aristocratic but fairly prosperous hoplites (already in existence, whether their phalanx tactics were fully developed yet or not), many of whom no doubt felt that under the old aristocratic government their role as their city's military backbone had not gained them the political say that they deserved.

It was characteristic of such dictators to form ambitious foreign contacts and alliances and dynastic marriages, and to develop their fleets – a process that reached its climax under Polycrates – and by such means also to increase their trade. This commercial activity was assisted by the wide extension of coinage – the conversion of pre-monetary lumps of metal into pieces possessing a guaranteed weight and design, first on one side (the other merely incised with a punch-mark) and later on both, first made of electrum (pale gold) and then of silver.[50]

Miletus, under Thrasybulus (c.600) or conceivably just before he gained power, followed soon afterwards by Ephesus, Cyzicus, Mytilene and Phocaea, borrowed the idea and use of coinage from Lydia. It was the Lydians who had brought it into existence, perhaps drawing on partial Assyrian and Mesopotamian precedents and weight systems, to facilitate payments by the royal treasury (such as the financing of mercenary armies and ships and buildings) and payments into the treasury as well (leases, taxes, fines). The Greek cities, when they started making their own coins, used them for similar purposes. Inevitably, too, as was suggested above, the invention was found convenient for exchange and commerce. In this field, it is true, the lack of small denominations was hampering. And there was metrological anarchy; different places coined on their own weight-standards. This caused a complex and disconcerting inter-city situation. Out of sheer necessity, however, two principal standards came to prevail throughout the Greek world, the Aeginetan and the Euboic–Attic (based respectively on Mesopotamian and Syrian metric frameworks). Indeed, efforts were even made to reconcile and relate the two standards, by creating the concept of a *mina* (one-sixtieth of a talent) weighing 425 grams, which constituted 70 Aeginetan and 100 Attic (and 150 Corinthian) drachmas. Nevertheless, innumerable local complications and variations remained, with the obvious result that most coins, at first at least, did not travel very far.

However, this invention of coinage that the Greeks took over from Lydia was of vast and growing importance. And it was clearly the city-state dictators who took an important, early initiative in developing its possibilities, highly conscious of the political and civic prestige conferred by the possession of a mint, and of the opportunity to increase this prestige still further by the employment of talented coin-designers (of whose work more will be said below).

Furthermore, absorbing and exploiting hints from their aristocratic forerunners, the dictators spent lavishly on public buildings and state cults and festivals, thus centralizing artistic patronage in their own hands and diminishing the tradition of old family- and clan-based ceremonials.

To meet these enlarged financial requirements, they introduced taxes on sales and produce of the soil, as well as a series of harbour-dues. These impositions were not, of course, likely to be popular, but Cypselus and Orthagorus, the dictators at Corinth and Sicyon, reputedly broadened their political base by making friendly gestures towards the pre-Dorian elements of the population. It was their deliberate policy, however, to leave the laws intact.

Their sons, Periander and Cleisthenes respectively, proved even more successful than their fathers had been. But thereafter – and the same occurred in other cities – such dictatorships, isolated by their lack of legitimacy, became suspicious, forcibly oppressive and unpopular, thus earning the term 'tyrant' the bad name it had already acquired in the ancient world and which it still possesses. And so these regimes fell, and the age of dictators more or less came to an end, except in Sicily, where they continued to recur time after time because political stability proved unattainable, and in Asia Minor, where local autocracies were later found convenient by their Persian suzerains.

Elsewhere in the Greek world, although the pattern varied greatly from place to place, it was normal for a dictatorship to be succeeded by an oligarchy – that is to say, by a government of the few, whose qualification, however, was no longer birth (though no doubt well-born men, despite the laments of Theognis of Megara that their god-given rights were neglected, found a place) but a sufficiency of wealth, primarily expressed in terms of land but also now, very conveniently, in terms of the recently instituted coinage. Even before the age of the dictators, as we saw, the aristocratic regimes that governed the cities had been obliged to admit elements owing their position to wealth as well as birth. After the dictators had gone, few wholly birth-based aristocratic governments continued to exist, except in retarded areas such as Thessaly and in the very special case of the Spartans, whose regime combined the features of various types of constitutional system, and by maintaining this curious but effective balance managed to take the leadership of almost the entire Peloponnese over from Argos.

In the cities that went through a phase of dictatorship, therefore, the normal sequence can be described (with some over-simplification) as aristocracy: dictatorship: oligarchy. When there was no intervening stage of dictatorship, aristocracy was directly followed by oligarchy. The stated ideal of the latter, as of the former, type of government was *eunomia*, respect for the laws within a harmonious whole in which everyone knew his place. The oligarchic governments presided over citizen bodies of limited numbers which were often equated and identified with the hoplites. Sometimes, like the nobles before them, they met together in an assembly, which still, however, under the guidance of 'the few', did not decide very much; and in other cities assemblies were dispensed with altogether.

Yet this neglect of popular representation was by no means universal, and became less so. It was noted, for example, that in some states popular elements, notably the less aristocratic sections of the hoplites, had joined with oligarchs in abolishing the dictatorships; and the time was to come when in many cities these hoplites would take control from the oligarchies, replacing them by democracies in some form or other, in which the dominant element would be an assembly consisting of a far larger proportion of the male population then hitherto – men who would thus contrive, however briefly, to obtain a measure of access to political power during the course of their lives. Such democratically inclined states proclaimed *isonomia*, equality before the law, in preference to *eunomia*.

Sparta was a democracy of a kind, in the sense that its male population (other than Helots, slaves and dwellers round about) were equals (*homoioi*); and a mid-sixth-century inscription of Chios emphasizing the *damos* (*demos*, people) suggests that something of the sort was under way on the island at that time. But a very real lead was subsequently taken at Athens, where shortly before 500 BC Cleisthenes, building on the reforms of Solon who at the start of the century had released debtors from their crippling burdens, seems to have introduced (as one can discern through later conflicting propaganda) a great many features of the famous Athenian democracy of the future.

The city-states of Sicily, as we have seen, were exceptional, because their endemic internal troubles meant that dictators continued to exist. However, most other cities of the Greek world, while not returning to dictatorships, likewise were, and remained, all too liable to internal political troubles of their own: between oligarchs and democrats, between privileged and unprivileged, between rich and poor. The Greek word is *stasis*, faction, which means anything between legitimate differences of opinion on public affairs to savage inter-party violence – which all too often occurred. It was especially frequent in colonies, where the families of original and later settlers, for example, came into conflict.[51] The classic description of *stasis* is by Thucydides, describing the terrible convulsion at Corcyra in the early 420s.[52] Yet if we had the necessary information, we should surely find the same conditions applying at Corcyra, and elsewhere, a century or two centuries earlier, they are recorded at Megara as well. The city-state was a brilliant idea, and full of brilliant ideas, but it was destined eventually to fail, because of the lethal combination of *stasis* within and constant hostilities with its Greek neighbours without.

The seventh century had witnessed all-important developments in Greek architecture and sculpture alike. The Greeks derived the concept of monumental stone architecture from the Egyptians, whose achievements some of them saw for themselves at Naucratis and elsewhere in Egypt from the later years of the century onwards. But, as usual, they subjected what they found to comprehensive modifications, partly suggested, it would seem, by wooden and Mycenaean prototype dwellings and halls (*megara*), of which sufficient traces were still to be seen.

The earliest temples erected on this relatively large scale were to be seen at Corinth (where the first 'orientalizing' pottery had appeared *c*.720) and upon Corinthian-influenced territory. These buildings belong to what was later known as the Doric Order. Its massive, fluted column-shafts have no bases and rise to capitals which consist of convex, cushion-like mouldings, surmounted by flat rectangular slabs. Above spreads the plain horizontal architrave and above that again the frieze, which comprises triglyphs (panels divided by vertical grooves into three bars) alternating with metopes (square panels, often with sculptural reliefs, set back from the face of the triglyphs). At the crown of the whole edifice rises a sloping cornice, and at either end of the roof is a triangular pediment, enclosed between the cornice above and the frieze beneath, and likewise providing a framework for sculptors.

The Doric Order illustrates the Greeks' sensitivity to rhythm. Its horizontal and vertical lines plant the buildings upon the landscape, leading the eye upwards and giving the impression of a mass that is majestically differentiated from the earth, but does not soar heavenwards and attempt to annul the laws of gravity, like a Gothic cathedral. These clear-cut outlines and sparkling sharp edges, picked out by tinted details, were the outcome of bracing thought; and, as a further result of such mental precision, 'refinements' were introduced, that is to say subtle curves, tilts and bulges, to satisfy optical and aesthetic needs (and to ensure stability and drainage). In all temples from c.600 the entire masonry was stone (to support the heavy roof-tiles); marble was extensively used from the sixth century onwards. The finest Doric temples were masterpieces of taste, proportion, patterned symmetry, serenity, power and repose.

The Ionic Order followed soon afterwards, in and around the coasts of Asia Minor, and most remarkably in the temples of Hera at Samos and Artemis at Ephesus, which far exceeded in size anything of the kind that had ever been seen before. These enormous buildings, displaying forests of columns reminiscent of Egypt, indicate that the city-states (for these great buildings were erected at public, not private, expense) devoted larger funds to the construction of Greek temples than to any other activity, with the exception of war.

Free and uninhibited in style until conventions became established, the Ionic Order was lighter in its proportions than the Doric, and its decorative mouldings displayed greater lavishness. The flutes on the columns were more numerous and more deeply cut, and each column had a base. The Ionic capital,[53] of which the earliest-known versions came from Smyrna and Phocaea, displayed lateral spiral scrolls or volutes – developed, after considerable amendments, from near-eastern and particularly Phoenician designs – and was surmounted by an architrave in three bands, above which extended an 'egg and tongue' moulding, beneath a row of dentils (small projecting tooth-like blocks). Sometimes, too, there was a sculptural frieze, replacing the triglyphs and metopes of the Doric Order.

Such friezes, and the high reliefs that filled temple pediments, represented the outstanding achievements of early Greek sculptors, and illustrate their close relationship to the architects. Nevertheless, large-scale statuary in the round, independent of architecture, also developed simultaneously and rapidly. It replaced, and partially evolved from, the small figurines with wig-like hair, mainly female, known as 'Daedalic', which had proliferated, in various materials, throughout Greek lands, from the first or second quarter of the seventh century onwards; these 'Daedalic' artists had been subject to the influence of Phoenician and Syrian terracotta statuettes, perhaps initially experienced by the Cretans, whose sculptor Daedalus was said to have taught two eminent pupils, Dipoenus and Scyllis, later emigrants to Sicyon.

The principal influence, however, which led to the creation of the new large-sized sculpture may be regarded (though some have contested this) as Egyptian, like the impulse which prompted monumental architecture. These massive statues (found mostly at Athens) seem to have been made first, shortly before 650, at Naxos and Paros in the Cyclades archipelago, where marble was ready at hand, although there was also a longstanding sculptural tradition at Samos, and other centres contributed as well.

The primary theme of this innovative art was the masculine nude (*kouros*), reflecting the predominance of naked males in Greek daily life. Serving as grave-markers or votive dedications or cult-images, these *kouroi* represented the god Apollo or his servants. What their sculptors sought to do was to reproduce the radiant reality of young manhood in permanent, depersonalized guise. Moreover, a steady process of development is discernible throughout the sixth century. For, depersonalized though they were, these images from various parts of the Greek world nevertheless reflected a constant striving towards naturalism and realism, representing, at a distance, those same ideals that would inspire Renaissance and subsequent artists until the age of Picasso. And yet, even during their maximum phase of evolution in c.525–500, such *kouroi* always remain at least a step or two away from total naturalistic portrayal, not so much because their sculptors had failed to master the problems of anatomy – for they had very largely done so, although it was not until the next century that the process was completed – but because they were still seeking, through the male human body, to depict an ideal rather than a photographic reality.

Female statues (*korai*), too, were made extensively at a number of centres. Intended for sanctuaries rather than graves, they represented goddesses or their servants and acolytes – whose images were dedicated, perhaps, when they left the service of the deity on marriage.

Within the established conventions, this female statuary evolved as perceptibly as its male counterpart. But this process assumed a different form. Here the attention which, in the case of the masculine figures, had been devoted to their bodies, was concentrated instead on the elegant lines and rippling folds of the women's drapery – first a plain long woollen dress, inherited from Daedalic art, and then (represented in colours) a woollen robe (*peplos*) worn over a fine white linen tunic (*chiton*). These statues, with their famous 'archaic smiles', display a delicacy which owed much, at Athens and elsewhere, to the influx of artists from Ionia, whose own native cities were threatened and overrun by Persians. But in this, as in other branches of Greek art, what is commonly described as the 'archaic' manner began to be transformed into less thoroughly stylized 'classical' forms by *c*.500.

Meanwhile superb reliefs continued to be made; and, on a smaller scale, the designing of both gems and coins attained extraordinary versatility. Gems remained an exquisite upper-class art, necessarily with a limited production.[54] But coins (see above, and note 50) rapidly became much more numerous; cities showed eagerness to outdo each other in the artistic beauty and distinction of their designs. Sometimes these portrayed a patron deity or hero, such as Aphrodite at Cnidus, Dionysus at Sicilian Naxos, Arethusa at Syracuse, the mythical founder Taras or Phalanthus at Taras, Athena at Athens and Poseidon at Posidonia and Potidaea. Or the sacred figure was represented by his or her emblem, the turtle (sacred to Aphrodite) at Aegina, Pegasus (the winged horse of Bellerophon) at Corinth, and the owl of Athens.

Alternatively the design could be the badge or symbol of a city: often a local product, such as the silphium plant at Cyrene, a ram at Salamis in Cyprus, a barley-ear, a bull, and a dolphin at the south Italian cities of Metapontum and Sybaris and Taras,[55] or grapes and a wine-jar at two islands of the Cyclades, Peparethos and Naxos. Another wine-producing island, Thasos, prefers to depict a sexually excited satyr (servant of Dionysus) carrying off a nymph. Sometimes the city-badge takes the form of a pun, like the seal (*phoke*) at Phocaea, the cock (*hemera*, day) at Himera, and the rose (*rhodos*) at Camirus and Ialysus on the island of Rhodes. Other badges are those of noble families or individuals, seemingly guaranteeing early coinages at Ephesus (note 50), or placed on coins, perhaps, by the state in order to flatter them (Chapter 2, section 4). Miltiades the elder, in the Thracian Chersonese (Gallipoli peninsula), depicts a four-horse chariot, celebrating his victory in the Olympic Games.

Another mighty artistic sixth-century accomplishment, in which, even if Corinth had been the pioneer, Athens later took an unchallenged lead, was the uniquely rich, rapid and varied evolution of painting on pottery. The first part of the century witnessed the climax of the two-colour black-figure style. A design is applied to the reddish buff clay with dark paint, improved to a shining black glaze, and details are marked with incised lines. The decorative patterns that had figured so largely in earlier vase-paintings have been substantially reduced, and the greater part of the vase is devoted to narrative themes, often of a mythological character.

Athenian black-figure pottery circulated far and wide, and an even larger distribution was enjoyed by a new technique which began to appear in about 530. This was the red-figure method, in which black-figure is reversed: for now the decoration is left in the ground colour, and it is the background, instead, which is painted black. Inner markings are made by thin lines no longer incised but drawn and glazed. This style makes greater freedom possible. Like the sculptors, however, these artists did not yet move all the way to the naturalism which increasingly characterized the painting of later epochs. But they became adept in depicting the moment of maximum action; and from the mid-sixth century onwards a number of artists experimented in foreshortening – at first restricted to inanimate objects, because heroic man still seemed best suited to a two-dimensional presentation. Black-figure and early red-figure master-painters alike achieved heights of power and moving beauty of which the medium has never again found itself capable.

While these developments were under way in the fine arts, the Greeks were also creating rational and scientific thought. A number of outstanding thinkers are unsatisfactorily grouped together as the 'Pre-Socratic philosophers'. But they were at the same time both less and more than philosophers, in the sense in which the term is used by anyone today. They were less because they had still not finished emancipating themselves from earlier, mythological conceptions of the universe – though, encouraged no doubt by Homer's cool treatment of the gods, they moved a long way in that direction, apprehending that, in spite of their dependence on these divinities, individual human beings are autonomous creatures whose actions are largely determined by their own wills (the crux that was to enthral the tragic poets of the following century). Nevertheless, their approach was still less than 'philosophical'. Yet these Pre-Socratics were, at the same time, *more* than philosophers, because they concerned themselves with an enormous range of phenomena which today would be associated, not with philosophy, but with one of the sciences.

The first of these men, Thales, Anaximander and Anaximenes of Miletus, wanted to know what the universe and the world came from, and what they were made of. And in the process of this enquiry, conducted orally by Thales and in written prose by his two successors (a revoluntionary step, creating new and more rigorously analytical modes of expressing thought), they took a great step forward towards the creation of logical reasoning – which must therefore be credited to their native Ionia.

Two other Ionians, however, emigrated from Ionia in the face of Persian conquest, and will therefore be considered in this book in relation to the west, where they went to live (Chapter 7, sections 2 and 4). One of them, Xenophanes of Colophon, wrote verse in which he ruthlessly criticized the anthropomorphic picture of the gods presented by Homer and Hesiod. The other, Pythagoras of Samos, was a disconcerting blend of pioneer mathematician, medicine-man and creator of a religious society, which gained control of the city of Croton. He and a further Ionian, Heraclitus of Ephesus (author of a treatise in prose) began to shift the emphasis from the universal macrocosm to the microcosm of the human soul, ascribing the existence and development of both alike to the conflict of opposites – a duality which, in the century that lay ahead, was to be sharply contested by the 'monism' of Parmenides of Elea, who saw reality as a single, indivisible, imperishable unity, so that apparent diversification, according to his paradoxical view, is unreal and non-existent.

Each of these men, competitively claiming, in the Greek fashion, to improve on their predecessors, wanted to relate the particular instance to a general law. Yet, despite the acuteness of their questions and the openness of the arguments, these were mainly advances towards theoretical rather than practical science. The aim of these thinkers was to understand man and nature in theory. Some of them were also keen observers of phenomena – but not many. Greek science was delayed because empirical observation, on the whole, did not come to be considered important.[56]

Nevertheless, the achievement of the sixth-century Greeks, in a wide variety of fields, was stupendous. They were only able to accomplish such a very great deal because they disposed of the leisure to do so. Unemployed leisure, in consequence, was an ideal which they explicitly appreciated, and although Plato's and Aristotle's disdain for physical labour was never wholly typical (it seems doubtful if Solon, for example, shared it), a Greek did often seem somewhat pitiable, to himself and others, if he had not enough to live on without working. For the idea of 'work for work's sake', or of labour as a saleable market commodity, was lacking. That is why leisure, as Aristotle declared, seemed all-important, being 'more desirable and more fully an end than business'.[57]

And if you had to work, he said elsewhere, it was disastrous to work for someone else: 'a free man should not live for the benefit of another'.[58] The idea was not a new one, since in the *Odyssey*, for example, there was no misery (the shade of Achilles declared) equal to that of a poor man (*thes*), who had to sell his services to someone else.[59] Nevertheless, despised though poor, free unskilled workers sometimes were, they predominated numerically over slave labour until after 500.

However, slaves, though few at first or (according to one ancient view) non-existent, were gradually rising in number throughout this early period. All previous states had been slave-owning, in varying degrees, and the same was still the case among the Greeks.[60] Slaves, it is true, were never more than an auxiliary element in Greek economics (the free poor tended to regard them as fellow workers), yet the Greeks would have been badly off without them. They were the property of their masters, like tools (except that they could also inspire fear). They might not be treated decently; they certainly were not in the plague-spot of Attica, the silver mines belonging to Athens at Laurium. But, on the whole, it seemed sensible to look after them, in the same way as it would be foolish to damage one's tools.

Ancient writers, attracted by polar opposites, tended to see a simple, bilateral contrast between free men and slaves. This made them too much inclined to ignore the fact that there were also various other categories of person who did not qualify as citizens – people who lived, and ranked, in between citizens and slaves. At Athens and elsewhere, for example, there were *metoikoi* (*metoeci*, metics, settlers, resident aliens), who took part in most of the activities of the community, playing a very prominent part in industry and commerce, but still did not possess citizen status.

Furthermore, at Sparta, and in various other territories, there was a further category of person bearing the designation of *perioikoi* (*perioeci*), dwellers round about.[61] They lived in their own townships and villages, but served in their city's forces, and again played varying parts in its industrial and commercial activities. But they, likewise, took no part in political life. In Spartan Laconia, too, once again, as in a considerable number of other Greek lands (under a variety of names), there were Helots[62] – often descended, it was said, from the earlier inhabitants – who were not slaves, yet could be roughly described as serfs, and were often suspected, in consequence, of being potentially subversive.

But the numerically largest element lacking political participation in the Greek city-states was provided by their women. It is difficult to generalize about them, first because our only evidence about their position is derived exclusively from male sources, and secondly because – in so far as we do possess information at all – it suggests that their position varied considerably from one Greek centre to another.

In and around the islands off the west coast of Asia Minor there were early signs that women would have a larger role to fulfil than eventually turned out to be the case. Homer's women, apparently reflecting the life of his time (although it is hard to be certain about this – Chapter 5, section 1), are not indeed decision-makers but play a significant background part in what goes on. Subsequently, however, Sappho (born *c*.612) reveals the existence in Lesbos of a female society that enjoyed a remarkable practical and emotional autonomy. But even in the isles a very different attitude had motivated the malevolence of Semonides of Amorgos (who came originally from Samos – Chapter 5, section 1); and on the mainland future patterns had already been foreshadowed by Hesiod's obsessive fear of women, revealed in the myth of Pandora.

Thereafter, although as usual we depend too much on evidence from Athens – where women seem to have enjoyed less freedom than almost anywhere else in Greek lands – certain generalizations, following on from the attitudes of Hesiod, became possible. Sparta and Crete, it is true, present more liberal pictures, and at Cyrene, in the late sixth century, a woman, Pheretime, even became dictator of the city, foreshadowing the queens of Hellenistic times. Yet before that epoch, females, generally, never possessed citizenship in their city-states, never held office and took no overt part in political activities at all. Disallowed charge of their own affairs, they were, as a matter of law, under the care of a male, and they had no legal right to own or dispose of property. Of course, family affection existed, as anywhere (tombstones bear witness to such feelings), and it would be absurd to deny that women were indispensable in all the obvious domestic ways. Moreover Herodotus goes further, when, indirectly but with cumulative emphasis, he stresses their full partnership with men in the establishment and preservation of the social order.

As in so many other respects, however, his approach is unusual. The attitude of Hesiod and Semonides is far more customary. A great amount of the literature of the Greeks echoes their poisonous hatred of women – or rather reflects a deeply anxious fear of them and of what they might be capable of doing. For in this repressively male-dominated society, marked by a voluminous sexual vocabulary and by exaggerated obscenity at festivals, there existed a curious sort of sexual *apartheid*. Despite their obvious indispensability for procreation, women seemed a mysterious, dangerous, polluting, 'other' element, and the Greeks were acutely afraid that they might get out of step, might break out from their appointed and domesticated place.

That is the implication so often behind their emphatic and dramatic appearances in mythology and literature, which seem to present so curious a contrast, very often, to the actual restrictive limits of their participation in Greek life. That is the implication, for example, of the outrageous Amazons, of the comic inversions of sex-roles in Attic comedy, and of the terrifying, doom-laden female villains of tragedy. Euripides' *Bacchants* even takes its name from the Maenads who tore King Pentheus apart – and they are servants of the god Dionysus.

This last role reminds us that religion was the one exception to the absence of women from Greek public activities. They were permitted their own rituals, such as the Thesmophoria, in which they played a leading and exclusive part (with outspoken stress on their role in fertility). For it was recognized that the deities had their wild, savage, untamable side – so sharply opposed to the orderly male culture of 'normal' Greek civilization – and that women seemed well suited to serve this aspect of the divine world, full of disruption and inversion, in which customary rules were in abeyance. After all, that was how Greeks thought of marriage: as the taming of wild, ungovernable, basically irrational womanhood. Thus many a Greek vase shows a man leading his wife off forcibly by the hand into her wedding, which amounted almost to a symbolic death. Once married, moreover, she dwelt in a precarious mediating position between two households, not necessarily trusted by either. For in most Greek city-states a woman had, in law, no standing in any question relating to her marriage, any more than she possessed other legal rights.

An extreme instance of this was provided by a girl who had no brothers. When this disastrous absence of a male heir occurred, the Greeks arranged for her to be married off to her nearest agnatic relative, i.e. relative on her father's side, in a fixed order of precedence, starting with her father's brother, if possible. Such a woman, whose lack of a brother made her responsible for perpetuating the *oikos* into the next generation, was described at Athens as *epikleros*, 'attached to the family property' (*kleros*) – and Solon passed legislation on this subject (Chapter 2, section 3).

The position of the *epikleros* (somewhat modified in Sparta and Crete) merely illustrated the general debarment of women from making decisions about their own matrimonial destinies. True, the community, by such measures, was displaying a keen interest in their role as transmitters of property and thus preservers of continuity, but it did so in such a way as to confirm that they were regarded as incapable of a self-determined act. Male Greek opinion was also insistent on premarital virginity; and with this in mind women were expected to marry young – at about eighteen or nineteen according to literary sources (their bridegrooms being older), though there are reasons to suppose that weddings at sixteen, or even a good deal earlier, were by no means uncommon.

These attitudes promoted a society that was far more markedly homosexual than our own. Once again the city-states varied considerably in their attitudes and regulations concerning such practices. But, as before, it is possible to offer certain generalizations. Within a community in which the women were mostly kept at home and the men spent their days with other men or boys, occupying themselves with politics or athletic exercises or war – or with the male drinking parties (*symposia*) of the aristocratic clubs (*hetaireiai*) – homosexual attitudes were inevitable, and they tended to be more intense, profound and complex than men's relations with women. At cities, indeed, with old-fashioned 'heroic' social structures such as Sparta, Thebes, Elis and Thera, male partnerships were explicitly accorded varying degrees of customary or even legal recognition. And everywhere artists, as we have seen, concentrated strongly on the nude masculine form.

The paintings on innumerable vases bring out another point as well: that pederasty was far more favoured than homosexual relations between contemporaries. A whole philosophy was built up round the former type of relationship, based on the idea that the lover was the educator and military trainer and partner of the beloved, and would do everything to earn his admiration. Plato later made one of his spokesmen, Phaedrus, declare that the most formidable army in the world would consist of pairs of male lovers;[63] and in the fourth century this 'ideal' was actually realized at Elis and in the Sacred Band of Thebes.[64] Official attitudes to the homosexual sex-act itself evidently varied, though disapproval of sodomy is recorded. But the general position was that the younger man or boy, the beloved, must not be seen to derive pleasure from sex, and indeed should stave off his lover's physical attentions, adopting the role of the pursued – rather as, in heterosexual life today, a girl (if, perhaps, slightly old-fashioned) may feel required to put up an initial resistance at least of a token character. According to the unwritten rules of ancient Greek homosexual relationships, the youth could finally grant 'favours', out of gratitude for what had been done for him by his protector, and that obviously meant the sexual act. Of female homosexuality less is heard, and on vase-paintings, too, less is seen, though efforts to deny that Sappho's Lesbian circle shunned its physical practice seem misguided, and such behaviour was spoken of at Sparta and elsewhere.

At the end of the period discussed in this book the entire elaborate political, social, economic, intellectual and artistic structure that the Greeks had established was mortally threatened – by the Persian great power that lay to their east.

The Persian king Cyrus II the Great, after conquering the kingdom of Lydia (546), had, in consequence, taken over from the Lydians their suzerainty over the Greek cities on and off the coasts of Asia Minor. Then Darius I penetrated into Europe and annexed Thrace (c.513–512), within easy reach of Greek lands. Next the Ionian cities, and others, had rebelled against him (499–494) – and two cities lying farther west, Athens and Eretria, sent ships to help them. Herodotus was right to believe that this made the Persian Wars inevitable.[65] Those conflicts are outside the scope of this book which seeks, instead, to portray the Greek world up to the time when they broke out.

CHAPTER 2

ATHENS

1 EARLY ATHENS

Attica is a triangular promontory extending over approximately 1,000 square miles, about the size of Derbyshire or Luxemburg and slightly larger than Rhode Island. It forms the easternmost part of central Greece, separated from Megara (to the west) by Mount Cerata and from Boeotia (to the north) by Mounts Parnes and Cithaeron. The Aegean Sea forms the boundary of Attica to the south-east, the Euripus channel (dividing off Euboea) to the east, and the Saronic Gulf to the south. At this southernmost extremity stands Cape Sunium, which gave Attica its original name of Acte, denoting an arm of land protruding into the sea. Four lines of mountains – from west to east Aegaleos, Hymettus, Pentelicus and Laurium – divide the territory into three plains, the Pedia (containing Athens), the central Mesogeia, and the Thriasian plain (with Eleusis as its chief town – section 2).

The Attic fields were ploughed three times a year to keep their upper layer loose. Yet the territory, in Plato's words, is a 'fleshless skeleton', of which the bones show through in large slabs of bare rock.[1] Only one-quarter of the surface of the territory was cultivated, and its unusually dense population found, as time went on, that it had to import a great deal of grain, although during the hot summers the deep roots of vines and olives could draw on the moisture stored up in the lower soil. Despite the hard struggle, natural produce was listed as one of the assets of Attica. Other assets, when they came to be developed, included the silver (earlier copper) of Laurium, the marble of Mount Pentelicus, and the clay of the River Cephisus; and a permanent strength was the compactness of this relatively large geographical unit within its mountain barriers.

The large population of the region goes back at least to the later Bronze Age, to which numerous sites can be attributed; and rich graves of the fifteenth and fourteenth centuries have come to light in Athens, although they are not of the same grandeur as their counterparts at Mycenae and Thebes. In the *Iliad*'s Catalogue of Achaean (Greek) Ships, which largely reflects a late Bronze Age state of affairs (Chapter 5, section 1), the only Attic centre to rate a mention is Athens; it probably controlled a large part of Attica. The city stands in the south-eastern part of the plain, three miles from the sea.

The Athenians claimed that they were 'autochthonous' (indigenous) inhabitants. Their mythical king Erechtheus was believed to have been the son of Gaia (Earth) herself, and it was said that he had been brought up by Athena (from whom the place took its name), after her successful struggle with Poseidon, whose son Theseus, however, became the city's hero. On the precipitous Athenian citadel-hill known as the Acropolis – some way from the sea, as at Corinth and Argos, so as to be out of the range of pirates – stood an olive-tree supposedly planted by Athena to commemorate the divine confrontation. Its ultimate successor is still shown.

According to tradition, Dorian invaders (Chapter 1 and notes 4–7) launched a concerted invasion of Attica, but failed to capture Athens. It is possible that their presence in western Attica is confirmed by the novel appearance of single cist-graves – shallow tombs dug in the ground and lined and rooted with stone slabs – replacing, in those times of insecurity, the large chamber-burials of the past. As for Athens itself, however, it remains justifiable to conclude that the fortress resisted one or more waves of hostile invaders, who after suffering rebuffs bypassed the city.

Some evidence for that troubled age can be seen in the abandonment of houses on the slopes of the Acropolis, while the citadel itself was evidently strengthened by new fortifications, and by the construction of steep steps designed to provide protected access to a water supply in the event of a siege (*c.*1225). There were stories of refugees from the invasions flocking into the town, notably from Pylos in the Peloponnese, according to the poet Mimnermus, who claimed that they married into the Athenian royal family and that he himself was one of their descendants.[2]

But what was the origin of that royal house, or indeed of the Athenians as a whole? At some stage they began to call themselves 'Ionians'; the name is mentioned in the Homeric poems. But how widely people thus described were distributed on the mainland in the late Bronze Age is disputed, and it is also impossible to determine, with any confidence, where they came from, although they evidently represented a complex ethnic mixture, no doubt intermingled still further by the migratory influx into Attica.

'Athena' and 'Athens' are not Greek names, and Hecataeus was

evidently aware of a strong non-Greek strain, since he indicated that
the city's early inhabitants included an aboriginal people described as
'Pelasgians'[3], which became a convenient portmanteau term for early
and vaguely understood non-Hellenic peoples. Subsequently, however, mythologists concluded that 'Ion' had settled in Athens and had
divided the people into its four tribes (named after his sons).[4]

Athens was also described as 'the eldest land of Ionia'.[5] For, according to a powerful and persistent local tradition, it was the Athenians –
excessively swollen in numbers by all the refugees – who under one or
more princes of their royal house led the 'Ionian migration' to western
Asia Minor and its isles (Chapter 5) in the sixth generation after the
Fall of Troy.

The Athenian contribution may have been somewhat exaggerated in
the telling, notably by Thucydides, who was intent to find historical
precedents for the Athenian League of his own fifth century. Nevertheless the Attic dialect of Attica and the Ionic dialect of the Asian coast
remained similar, and the two regions possessed tribal organization
and festivals (notably the Apaturia) in common. In the main, therefore, despite doubts that have been expressed, we may accept the later
Athenian claim to a very prominent role in the emigrations to Ionia,
extending, it may well be, on certain occasions, to their actual leadership, although the process was evidently much longer and more gradual than tradition recorded, and there must also have been migrants
from other Greek centres as well, not necessarily passing through
Athenian territory.

Meanwhile Athens itself, whose legendary king Codrus was later
believed to have sacrificed his life in the defence of his country, apparently continued to defy the turbulence all around, and remained in
existence, however anxious and precarious, as one of the very few
examples of urban survival in the whole of Greece, now that Mycenae
and Pylos and the other Bronze Age centres had been destroyed; so that
the Athenians carried on their lives in a sort of Mycenaean twilight.

As their lack of prominence in the Homeric poems suggests, however, they did not achieve a very quick or thorough recovery from the
crisis, partly because they had lost many of their best men from emigration, but also, it seems, because Attica was no longer unified. Nevertheless, Athens may have retained control over at least the eastern part of
Attica; and unlike so many other parts of the Greek homeland, this
region was fairly densely settled during the decades before and after
1100, so that by 1000, if not earlier, there were signs of solid progress.
This was the first mainland zone in which iron (probably of near-
eastern origin) appeared, as well as the practice of cremation, which
became common at Athens from c.1050. Anchorages on the sand beach

of Phaleron and within the deep-water inlets of Piraeus and Zea (on either side of the Munichia promontory) enabled the Athenians to maintain sea-borne communications with the islands, including Cyprus.

In keeping with the immunity from invasion that Athens had enjoyed, a measure of continuity with the departed Mycenaean world is visible in its pottery. Vases in the Protogeometric style ($c.1050/1025-900$), slenderer and more carefully finished than the earlier Sub-Mycenaean – due to execution on a faster wheel, with brushes and compasses – were made at a variety of different centres, and did not start among the Athenians. But Athens, once it had mastered the style, seems to have become its principal diffusion and distribution point, before the end of the tenth century; and it was at Athens, to judge from the abundant evidence of cremation burials in the Ceramicus quarter, that Protogeometric pots attained their highest structural and artistic quality.

This might seem to invite the conclusion that the later supremacy of Athenian classical art derived from this early superiority. But such a conclusion is disputed on the grounds that the later classical peak cannot be traced back with any directness or certainty to its very different predecessors. Yet the link may be there all the same. In any case, artistic leadership had, for a time, passed to the Athenians when they were producing Protogeometric vases, and it remained with them after that style had been replaced by the Geometric in their workshops. For unless we are deceived by the greater abundance of its wares (as seems unlikely), the Geometric art of Athens displayed a greater vigour and skill than that of other Greek states. However, it was not long before the local workshops of those other states gradually began to assert themselves. Whether this can be ascribed to a decline of Athenian influence is uncertain, since Attic Middle Geometric pottery ($c.850-770/750$) was exported widely, and went even to Cyprus and Syria. Moreover, at the beginning of that period, the Ceramicus cemetery at Athens had shown a remarkable wealth of Geometric pottery. This may be because the processing (cupellation) of silver at Laurium (revealed by excavations at Thoricus) was bringing an increase of prosperity.

An epoch-making step was taken when the Dipylon Master at Athens ($c.770-750$) invented, or developed, the late Geometric style on huge vases – vessels four or five feet high, standing on graves as their markers, containing holes through which drink-offerings to the dead could be poured.[6] These great pots supplement their abstract geometrical decoration by the inclusion of friezes on which ships and animals and human figures make their appearance. The ships thus depicted (with surprising frequency) reflect the current revived interest in trade-routes. The bands of diminutive animals on these vases display one of the few Geometric ideas borrowed from the near east (Appendix 1), either directly from ivory reliefs or embroidery, or indirectly by way of Attic gold diadems reflecting near-eastern motifs, though the specific forms of the Geometric beasts display a novelty that is Greek.

The groups of human beings on these pots, portrayed according to a process of abstract, linear, distorted stylization – and perhaps inspired, again, by near-eastern models (including basketry) as well as by surviving specimens of late Mycenaean figured art – have been tentatively identified as representing figures and scenes from Homeric poems (Chapter 5, section 1). For example, a funeral scene might be intended to recall the funeral of Patroclus. In this case they may be seen as symbolizing a sort of Greek Renaissance or revival of the heroic past, based on the new diffusion of this epic poetry, and interpreting current events and achievements in the light of that story, upon vessels displaying a proud artistic elephantiasis. Yet although a hexameter couplet on a prize jug of c.730 reflects the innovation of writing, which almost coincided in date with the Homeric poems, their connection with these vase-designs cannot be regarded as proved. Granted that a few specific mythical scenes may have been deliberately selected for portrayal, most of the pictures are general and unattributable. There may, of course, have been other masters on a par with the Dipylon artist, men whose works have disappeared. But as far as we can tell, it was he who became the first Greek painter to consider human figures seriously – the first identifiable personality, one might add, of Greek art, whose work is recognizable by a consistent, rhythmical, obsess-ively corner-filling, narrative craftsmanship that is all his own.

The unusually rich burials which the artists of such late Geometric monster vases chose to adorn reflected massive changes in Attic society. For the unification, or rather reunification, of Attica (commemorated by the annual festival of the Synoikia) may well have been far advanced by c.900, by which time the incorporation of the principal plain (Meso-geia) was complete. The single state thus constituted and consolidated, comprising a unique co-ordination of town and country, not only pos-sessed (for Greece) unusually substantial dimensions but proved exceptionally stable. This was a form of amalgamation (synoecism) which involved not transfers of population but the retention of existing communities under centralized control.

And yet myths and traditions continued to preserve memories of little independent states in Attica, and even after these states had been reduced to the rank of villages, as now occurred, amalgamation by no means meant that they lost all their autonomous initiative; on the contrary, after the early momentum of centralization had somewhat flagged, many Mycenaean villages and domains in the Attic country-side were settled once again, in a process of rural resurgence (c.750–730). Throughout the territory, the number of detailed graves multiplied sixfold during the course of the eighth century, suggesting an unusually large increase in the birthrate, amounting to an annual rate of about 4 per cent. It has also been conjectured, though inevitably proof is lacking, that the population of Attica quadrupled between 800 and 750, and almost doubled again during the half-century that followed.

The people were still organized in a hierarchical series of kinship groups going back to very early epochs, and claiming descent from the settlers who were said to have accompanied the legendary Ion to the region. These groups comprised the *oikos* (family), *genos* (clan), phratry (brotherhood) and tribe – a series of concentric (though sometimes overlapping) fortifications against the outside world. There is a theory that this whole structure and its components were late and artificial. But the Homeric poems already bear witness to some such early tribal organizations, and it can still be regarded as a reasonable hypothesis that the early Attic population was subdivided into these kinship groups, and indeed that after the destructions of c.1200–1000 it was they which replaced the collapsed political system and came to form the dominant pattern of society. Blood relationship was the basic social factor in early Athens – in Athens of the early Iron Age, that is to say, for it cannot be described, with certainty, as a Mycenaean legacy, since such a structure would not have served a very useful purpose in the days of the much more powerful Mycenaean kings.

The most essential of the post-Mycenaean units was the *oikos* or family, the primary institution through which life was largely organized, property held (most family heads being subsistence landowners), and continuity ensured. The *oikos* consisted of a more or less extended household group supplemented, in the more powerful units, by numbers of free and slave dependents. It was the economic and physical expression of the *genos* or clan. This consisted of a group of families (or perhaps in some cases of a single large family, including adult sons and their wives), which claimed descent from a common ancestor (though non-kinsmen were admitted from an early date) and was knit together by shared cults. Whether all Athenians were in early times members of a *genos* is uncertain; perhaps not, because the *gene* were certainly dominated by nobles, and may indeed, at first, have been entirely confined to them. Marriages were arranged by the heads of these *gene*, which, although they originally had no place in Athenian or other Greek law (Homer does not mention them), later became more important than the *oikoi* and decided major issues by their alliances and rivalries.

As for the phratries – each, it appears, containing thirty *gene* – they took shape at an early date (qualifying for mention in the *Iliad*), probably as a military group, the 'blood brotherhood'; an ancient phenomenon (though the term phratry does not happen to be found in surviving Mycenaean 'Linear B' texts). And so in the *oikos* – *genos* – phratry pyramid, which provided the structure of this pre-urban tribal world, the phratries stood at the apex, beneath only the tribe itself. The total numerical strength of a phratry was perhaps comparable to that of a village or city-ward.

Increasingly important from about the eighth century onwards, phratries involved all the main stages of an Athenian's life and acted as the focus of all his activities. Reflecting the fact that each group in the social order from *oikos* and *genos* upwards was also a religious union (and revered its own particular hero, who gave it its name), every phratry held an annual festival (the Apaturia) to worship its protecting deities (Zeus Phratrius and Athena Phratria) and to enrol new members. Nor was it only members of the phratries' constituent *gene*, the *gennetai*, who were enrolled, but the phratries also began to admit, at some stage or other, a considerable number of unrelated, humbler retainers and followers – peasants and craftsmen and questionable, unproven citizens – lacking ancestry in a *genos* (and therefore also lacking good arable land); for, despite various alternative explanations, it is this outer fringe of phratry members which seemed to represent the category described by the Athenian writers as *orgeones*.

There were three phratries in each of the four Athenian tribes, or *phylai* (hence another mysterious term *trittys*, 'third', which appears originally to have been a synonym for phratry, in its territorial aspects, employed for local administrative purposes). The two forms of unit, phratry and tribe, are mentioned together in the *Iliad*.[7] Tribes with the same names (note 4) also existed in the Ionian cities of Asia Minor and correspond with four cult titles of Zeus. The tribes, presided over by their own leaders, were personal associations of kinsfolk, and their earliest known function (reflected by Homer) was military; they are unlikely ever to have been wholly local or geographical entities.

According to tradition, which it seems reasonable to accept, the tribes of Attica and Athens were united under a single king of the Medontid line, descended from Medon, the son of the legendary Codrus. Yet the civic organization of the land was at first rudimentary, comprising little more than a series of political, legal and religious alliances between the tribes, phratries, clans and families that have been described. It was the king's job to hold them together, as far as he could, although despite his prestige, and his formal superiority to the 'kings' of the four tribes, he remained a less impressive figure than his Mycenaean predecessors. Before 700, however, as elsewhere in the Greek world (but not everywhere, as non-urbanized units, *ethne*, still remained), this loose structure had evolved into the more tightly integrated civic system characteristic of a *polis*, although the town of Athens itself did not become more or less urbanized until nearly a centry later, and even then its population was still barely 10,000.

The Athenian Medontid monarchy – we are told, and it seems plausible enough – lost its functions piecemeal to a group of aristocratic officials. What seems to have happened, at an early date, is that a new official, the polemarch (war-chief) was appointed to share power with the king, and then later the king found himself subordinated to an archon (regent) for civil affairs. Subsequently, it was believed (although the precise course of events, as outlined by ancient writers, is of doubtful authenticity), a king named Acastus surrendered his monarchical position altogether, in favour of an archon (later 'first archon') appointed for life[8] (though a separate king–archon for religious business was also retained). The next step occurred in the mid-eighth century, when this lifelong first archon's post was replaced by a ten-year period of office. From some later date (683–682 or 682–681?) a new appointment began to be made every year.

By this time, then, the various functions that would have been formerly united in the single person of the monarch were divided among this functionary (the first archon), and the king–archon, and the polemarch. The first archon and polemarch were appointed by election, and chosen 'on the grounds of birth and wealth'.[9] The first archon, after whom the year was named, held the principal power and was the centre of political life and strife; and the military expert, the polemarch, ranked below the other two, so that the headship of the state was already a civilian affair. After the middle of the seventh century, and perhaps earlier, these three archons were supplemented by six more, the *thesmothetai*, 'layers down of the law', who were needed because of the growth (and litigious character) of the population. From this time onwards, then, there was an annually elected board of nine officials.

They were advised by a council, the Areopagus, which derived great prestige from its alleged creation by the gods. Its members held office for life. They were Eupatridai (noblemen): in some Greek states early councils only admitted heads of families, but whether this was true of the seventh-century Areopagus remains obscure. A further body, the Assembly (*Ecclesia*), comprising all citizens, was still shadowy and largely formal, without much of a share in decision-making.

During this period of political evolution, art, too, continued to develop. In Athenian (Protoattic) vase-painting, the Analatos Painter (*c*.700) was a pioneer and the Nessos Painter came late (*c*.620). Learning from the Corinthian orientalizing and black-figured techniques, these artists created works which rebelled against Geometric discipline and displayed a robust and massive, though sometimes crude, individuality and distinctiveness.

In *c*.632 (or possibly after 621), a prominent Eupatrid named Cylon – the son-in-law of Theagenes, the dictator of Megara – attempted an autocratic *coup d'état* at Athens by attacking the Acropolis. His enterprise failed and he was murdered, probably because the Athenians resented his Megarian support. It is quite likely that Cylon professed some kind of radical tendencies, hoping to draw on current agrarian discontents (further discussed in section 3); but, if so, he was premature, because Athenians, in sufficient numbers, were not yet thinking in radical terms. And in any case his attempted *coup* was not primarily inspired by democratic ideals, but was rather the product of sharp conflicts between the aristocratic heads of different Eupatrid clans. After the collapse of the rising, his followers sought sanctuary, but were killed by the initiative of another leading house, the Alcmaeonids, whose deed earned them expulsion from Attica. The Alcmaeonids were later regarded by their enemies as 'rogue aristocrats', though their bloodthirstiness may have been no more than a fairly characteristic manifestation of the squabbles between noble leaders.

At all events, there had been serious trouble, and, whether Cylon (or the Alcmaeonid clan) was 'radical' or not, it appears that the citizens of Athens, aware that elsewhere in the Greek world laws were being written down (first, apparently, in Crete and then in south Italy and Sicily), had become increasingly unwilling to accept the rulings of Eupatrid *thesmothetai* and judges, based on merely arbitrary, oral decisions as opposed to any written legislation. For in 621–620 a certain Dracon was appointed to codify the Athenian laws. It is not necessary to suppose that he was elected as archon; he may, instead, have received a specific personal appointment as law-giver, like earlier appointments at Locri Epizephyrii and Catana and elsewhere.

Dracon's law-code, not accompanied by a 'constitution' – the belief that he had enacted one was later and anachronistic – has sometimes been interpreted as a Eupatrid attempt to relieve the popular discontents on which Cylon had been hoping to play. Of this we cannot be certain, but the laws of Dracon do seem to have been significantly progressive in at least one respect – that is to say in their definition of homicide, in which they introduced (it would appear from a fifth-century republication)[10] the concept of intention, distinguishing between murder and accidental or justifiable manslaughter. Thus Dracon was beginning to assert the claim of the state to intervene in blood-feuds. These had previously been clan and family affairs, devolving entirely on the kinsmen of the victims, but now, instead, the state was trying to play a leading part, which it did by encouraging the view that such carnage defiled the gods of the community and made the shedder of blood impure in a religious sense.

Dracon's other measures, however, seemed very severe to later generations, which saw them as 'written in blood'. For example, stealing a cabbage was punishable by death. Moreover, his laws of debt differed between the well-born and the base-born – between clansmen (*gennetai*) on the one hand and their hangers-on (*orgeones*) on the other – since the former, if they fell into debt (of which more will be said in section 3) at least were not sold as slaves, the fate which, according to Plutarch, befell the poor.[11] But harsh though these penalties were, even if no harsher than they had been before, the important feature of Dracon's legislation was that it set out the grim position in writing, thus bringing it (though this may not have been what he had in mind) into a glaring floodlight of public attention, in which such archaic arrangements seemed outrageous.

During the period now coming to an end, Athens had somewhat faded from Greek inter-state history. Having at one time been a member of the League of Calauria (Poros, off the eastern Argolid – Chapter 3, note 2), after *c*.730 the city had lost its earlier maritime initiative, owing to the hostility of Argos and the naval control over the Saronic Gulf asserted by the island of Aegina (described at the end of this chapter). The Athenians, unlike so many other cities, sent out no colonies, presumably because the relatively large size of Attica had for a long time staved off land-hunger. But as the worsening debt crisis indicated, this relatively tranquil situation was now coming to an end. Before the end of the seventh century the increased population of Attica, even if not sufficient to drive too many people off the land, meant that new steps had to be taken to feed them, and what this signified in practice was that something had to be done to control the grain-route from the Black Sea and Propontis (Sea of Marmara – Chapter 8, section 2).

And that, therefore, is what the Athenians now undertook. Under the leadership of Phrynon, an Olympian victor, they seized the town of

Sigeum (near Yenişehir) in the Troad (north-western Asia Minor), located beside fertile land in a strategic position upon the south side of the entry to the Hellespont (Dardanelles). Its seizure involved prolonged warfare with Mytilene (Lesbos), whose ruler Pittacus killed Phrynon in a duel. But the conflict was adjudicated in favour of Athens by the dictator of Corinth, Periander, though the Athenians did not establish full control of Sigeum for another half-century.

2 ELEUSIS

Much nearer home, perhaps in $c.675$ – though earlier and later dates have also been advocated – Athens had completed its control of Attica by reducing Eleusis to subjection. The most important centre in the territory after Athens (and later the Piraeus), the place was situated in a land-locked bay east of the small Rharian plain (at the head of its fertile Thriasian counterpart) in a strategic location opposite the island of Salamis (note 15) and at the junction of roads leading from Athens, the south and the north. Dating back to the early Bronze Age, Eleusis had hitherto taken advantage of its naturally strong acropolis to remain independent of Athens, under its own kings, but now it was absorbed, so that the whole of mainland Attica was a single Athenian unit.

Eleusis owed its widespread renown to the locally celebrated Mysteries (initiation rites) in honour of Demeter and her daughter Persephone (Kore, the Maiden). The cult of Demeter, in some form or another, had already been celebrated in the late Bronze (Mycenaean) Age, or at least as early as the eleventh century BC. For that seems to be the date of the remains of a *megaron* (porched house) that was apparently the first shrine of the goddess. It was succeeded by a circular or apsed building, perhaps in $c.800$, the epoch to which numerous female inhumations on the site, probably of priestesses, have been attributed.

The myth told how the goddess, seemingly a fusion between a pre-Hellenic underworld deity and a Mesopotamian corn-goddess, was anguished by the seizure of her daughter Persephone by Hades (Pluto), the god of the lower realm. The rape of Persephone had caused the fertility of the earth to be blasted, rather as the disappearance of the Hittite Telepinus stopped the growth of crops and the birth of animals; and similar stories appear in Mesopotamian and Canaanite mythology (Appendix 1).

During the course of her wanderings in search of her daughter Demeter came to Eleusis. There, the daughters of the monarch of the place, Celeus, found her seated beside a well, and took her into the royal household, where, amid miraculous happenings, she nursed the king's son. Revealing her identity to the Eleusinians, the goddess with-

drew to a temple constructed for her, until Zeus agreed that Persephone might return to the upper world for two-thirds of the year.
Thereupon, Demeter revived the earth's fertility, by sowing the first
seeds of corn in the Rharian plain, and before ascending to Mount
Olympus with her daughter she disclosed to Celeus 'the conduct of her
rites and all her Mysteries'.

As the term 'Mystery' – derived from *muein*, to keep silent – suggests,
the character of these nocturnal, torch-like ceremonies remained
secret, in accordance with the primitive idea that outsiders should not
be allowed to know the true names of a community's deities and how to
enlist their aid. And besides, this was a sort of enlarged family cult to
which, in theory, the head of the family admitted whom he pleased. But
the Mysteries of Demeter cannot have been or remained very secret,
since their later hall had room for 4,000 worshippers, and all men,
women and children of Greek speech, including slaves, were eligible for
initiation, provided only that they were untainted by homicide.

From such fragmentary evidence as has come down to us, it seems
that the rites acted out the rape of Persephone and her mother's arrival
at Eleusis to search for her, and culminated in a ritual in which the
torches employed to illuminate the proceedings were thrown in the
air. There also appears to have been a display and procession of models
of genital organs and statuettes of men and women engaged in sexual
acts,[12] since human love-making was thought to stimulate the fertility
of the crops, and by the same token obscene invectives (believed to have
been the origin of iambic verse) were shouted out.

By *c.*600, a few generations after the takeover of Eleusis by the
Athenians, they had succeeded in elevating its cult to Panhellenic
status. This widespread enthusiasm was owed, above all, to the special
benefits in the afterlife which the Mysteries, embodying successive
stages of initiation, were able to offer: the renewal of the crops pledged
renewal of life after death,[13] very different from the bleak prospects in
the Homeric poems. 'Blessed is he who has seen these things before he
goes beneath the hollow earth,' wrote Pindar,[14] 'for he understands the
end of mortal life, and the beginning [of new life] given of god' –
whereas for non-initiates 'everything there would be bad'. The cult also
made an obvious and irresistible appeal to that submerged half of
Greek society, its women, by accepting the female experiences of Persephone and Demeter as a model and source of this posthumous
salvation.

For such reasons the Athenian state was eager to develop the cult
under its own control, thus canalizing, beneath a guise of
respectability, the ever more widespread but also suspect ideas and
excitements embodied in such uncivic, mystic worships and folk-

traditions, so that they were able to mould the Mysteries, in their historic form, as the finest flower of Greek popular religion. The Festival of Greater Eleusinia was celebrated in the second year of each Olympiad, with lesser celebrations in the other years, and the cult was initially administered by two Athenian lay families, the Eumolpids and Kerykes, of whom the former claimed descent from the Thracian Eumolpus, believed to have been the first celebrant at Eleusis. At about the same time as this elevation of the Eleusinian cult, the grave and gay *Hymn to Demeter* – one of the most dramatically and magically exciting of the misnamed 'Homeric' Hymns – was composed, probably at Athens, to recount the myth of the goddess.

These various developments seem to have been accelerated in the time, and by the instigation, of the Athenian statesman Solon, to whom the construction of a new 'holy of holies' (*anaktoron*) at Eleusis may be attributable; and it is of him that something must now be said.

3 SOLON

We first hear of Solon because Athens, having completed its absorption of mainland Attica by annexing Eleusis, inevitably began to covet adjacent, strategic Salamis as well. For this island lay just off the Eleusinian coast, and was needed by the Athenians to secure the sole use of its harbours and anchorages as terminals for their Black Sea grain-route.[15] But Salamis, though its early history is variously recounted, belonged to Megara (Chapter 3, section 5), which had annexed it from Aegina (note 45), so that Athens (with which the island's piratical population had long maintained links) now embarked on a struggle to seize it from the Megarians. However, any success achieved by this enterprise can only have been temporary at best, since a few years later Solon is found urging his discouraged and demoralized countrymen to launch further attempts to achieve annexation.[16]

Solon is the earliest Greek statesman whose own words we are able to read and hear, written in grave, forceful, dramatic poetry, which seemed suggestive of an oracle.[17] Deeply involved in the public events of his time, he employed his literary gift to explain his political views, perhaps reciting his verses at aristocratic *symposia*, where such matters were likely to come up for discussion. Solon was an intellectual who also happened to be a vivid propagandist. He was apparently of noble origin but of moderate means: probably, as the tradition stated and his travels and economic measures suggest, a merchant – a new breed, a nobleman from a landowning family who had embarked on mercantile activity.

His career, however, is hard to reconstruct; already by the fifth and fourth centuries he had become a mythological figure, anachronistically praised or blamed for the merits or defects of the democracy of those later epochs. Yet the effort to find out what he himself did and thought must be made, and, although our best source (Plutarch) wrote nearly 800 years after his time, extreme scepticism need, nevertheless, not be resorted to. It appears that the agrarian problems of Attica which had been gathering in previous years eventually erupted into a crisis of rivalry between powerful clans. Some of these clans made bold or rash promises to the discontented poor, so that other houses appealed to Solon to save them from total chaos on the land or dictatorial revolution. In consequence, this exceptional combination of thinker, poet and businessman was appointed chief archon (according to ancient tradition) in 594/593 or 592/591 (it has also been strongly suggested that, by the occupancy of some special office or other, his legislative activity may have been centred upon, or extended to, 580/570, though this cannot be proved).

Attica was, indeed, in agricultural and economic trouble, and even probably on the verge of civil war. The basic reasons for this sort of crisis have already been made clear. Landownership was concentrated in the hands of a small minority, while as population increased many farms were subdivided between sons until the allotments had ceased to be viable. All the time the poor were becoming even poorer, trying unsuccessfully to farm the unproductive, marginal, hill-foot land; it was a knife-edge, depressive situation which a few years of bad crops were enough to make altogether intolerable.

The main problem was that these distressed citizens – often men just above the dividing line set by Dracon, at which default led to immediate enslavement – were compelled to borrow grain from their richer neighbours. By doing so, they became *hektemoroi*, 'sixth-part men'. This much disputed term probably implies that their indebtedness had lost them control of their land to their wealthier creditors. Thereupon the latter planted on the plot they had thus acquired markers of wood or stone (*horoi*), as a sign that this land, and the debtor himself who had lost it to them – as well as his whole family – were in the power of his creditors, until his obligation was fulfilled. And even then all was still not well, for the creditors only permitted him to go on farming his recovered soil on the condition that he handed over one-sixth of the produce, thus becoming a 'sixth-part' man. This was a heavy burden, especially when poor ground was concerned, of which even the loss of a tenth part (tithe) would have been severe, and particularly at a time when the new existence of written laws (those of Dracon) had raised over-optimistic expectations, and when many other citizens had become so much better off, owing to their profits from foreign trading.

But Solon used his powers with considerable boldness. All debts for which land or personal freedom was the security were cancelled, and all borrowing on the security of the person was forbidden in future, so that every form of debt-bondage was ruled out. Those deprived of their farms got them back, and Solon recorded his removal of the markers, 'setting free the fields that were enslaved before',[18] while it was ordered that those who had been sold into slavery, wherever they had gone, should be redeemed. He also 'limited the rate of interest'[19] – that is to say, tenants' interest payments to their masters were restricted to an endurable level.

He had achieved a remarkable breakthrough. But he was well aware that he had done so only by means of an effortful and delicate compromise – the work of a shrewd operator, with an eye for manipulation. 'Deploying all his strength', he had 'thrown his stout shield over both parties' – and as a result, he declared, most people had taken offence.[20] The rapacity of rich creditors had been staved off, and they had lost a lot, which clearly cannot have pleased them. Yet it may well be that he had saved them from a much worse fate, since he had resisted the wholesale distribution of land on an egalitarian basis that was the demand of his poorer supporters, as elsewhere in Greece.

For Solon, in so far as our defective evidence enables us to tell, seems to have been by conviction one of the great moderates of history, who wanted to rectify injustice but condemned both extremes – a peculiarly difficult and thankless role, as history still shows every day. But it must be added that his moderation, even if it denied the poor a sweeping land distribution, did eventually promote a kind of social revolution, in which a free peasant majority, formerly victims of oppression, emerged as the basis of Athenian society, equipped with a sense of individual rights; and there is no need to deny that this was Solon's aim. But one eventual result, perhaps, he had not foreseen. The rescue of the *hektemoroi* created a major labour problem for the creditors, which could be met only by the massive importation of slaves from abroad, though this phenomenon did not make itself felt, on a substantial scale, until many years later.

Solon's concern for the ordinary citizen seems to have made itself apparent in other respects as well. He established for the first time the right of any citizen to initiate proceedings at law. Thus a third party could intervene in a lawsuit on behalf of someone wronged, and 'anybody's wrong was everybody's business'. One very important feature of this enactment was that the intervening citizen was able to act independently of his family, or clan; the old kinship links, already dented earlier, were now significantly weakened. They seem to have been weakened in another respect as well, because, reinforcing Dracon's moves to shift murder penalties from the family and clan to the state, Solon now made it impermissible for the family to kill a killer at all; instead it had to institute legal proceedings, of an elaborate nature.

True, things did not move too fast – public authority was still relatively weak. But an important further step towards strengthening its powers had been taken.

Solon was not, however, wholeheartedly concerned to weaken the old links based on families and clans. On the contrary, while admittedly trying to take murder cases out of their hands, he was positively eager to encourage and perpetuate the family in another respect. For certain of his measures, if Plutarch is correct in assigning them to his authorship, showed a determination to protect family property. In particular, he legislated regarding that class of women known at Athens as *epikleroi*. These, as mentioned in Chapter 1, were girls who had no brothers. In consequence, they became 'assignable' (*epidikoi*), that is to say compelled to marry their nearest relative on their father's side, in a fixed order of priority, starting with his brother. This state of affairs shows with great clarity the powerlessness which Athens was determined to inflict on women – especially as rising democratic feelings began to impose the social norms of the majority, which supported such restrictive measures, although women, as elsewhere, possessed a safety-valve owing to their prominence in certain religious rituals.[21] Athenian tragic and comic poets were soon to discuss freely the numerous paradoxes which femininity involved.

Now, Solon did not set himself up as a liberator of women, and probably he shared the general view that they must not be allowed to get out of line. Yet he did, we are told by Plutarch, look very carefully at their family responsibilities. One of his measures appears to have been the introduction of wills, which made it necessary to make regulations regarding the marriages contracted by these *epikleroi*. Men were discouraged from becoming adopted into other families, as they sometimes liked to do, in the hope of claiming a rich *epikleros*. Furthermore, old men were discouraged from seeking such a mate in order to enjoy her wealth without providing an heir. The means Solon was said to have employed to this end were bizarre, for he was said to have laid it down that the husband of an *epikleros* must have sexual intercourse with her not less than three times every month, and that if he was unable to do so she was allowed to go to bed with her next of kin in order to secure children for her own (that is to say her father's) *oikos*.

Solon did not seek to emancipate women, but was adapting current institutions to produce the most advantageous result, namely the survival of families that would otherwise have been extinguished. And, indeed, his measures even show a clear appreciation of the precious indispensability of women – in their capacity as transmitters of property and thus of the social order.

The steps he took to prevent covetous old men from breaking into other families and upsetting marriages may also have been partly devised to prevent inter-house strife that would have disturbed the city's peace. And the same was perhaps his intention in establishing brothels, equipped with prostitutes bought for the purpose. However, it is possible that his attitude to women was somewhat detached, since his poetry reveals pederastic tendencies that seem to go beyond literary convention.[22] Yet, even if so, he (like Dracon, it was said, before him) passed measures to protect boys against sexual assaults. He was also said to have taken an interest in their education, requiring every citizen, by law, to teach his sons letters. And Athens, at about this time, took the lead in relegating military training from first to second place in the scholastic system.

Such domestic measures played a prominent part in a far larger mass, indeed an extraordinary cascade, of Solon's laws, which seemed to have aimed at nothing less than a comprehensive codification. This was his most important and durable achievement, lasting for centuries. Like earlier statesmen elsewhere – first of all in Crete and at Locri Epizephyrii in south Italy – he seems to have seen his task as the reduction of customary laws to writing.[23] But, as elsewhere, this very process (like his debt reform, which was not part of the code) inevitably nudged society in the direction of reform.

To the same end, the institution known as the Heliaea figured prominently in Solon's programme. The term originally meant 'assembly', and now came to dignify the Athenian Assembly (an ancient but previously somewhat shadowy, formal and powerless body), or possibly referred to one section of its membership, sitting in its judicial capacity to hear appeals from individuals against the decisions and verdicts of state officials.[24] This activity was probably, to begin with, limited to matters of death, exile and loss of citizen rights; a wholly unrestricted right of appeal would have represented a democratic ideal which nobody had so far envisaged. Nevertheless, this was a beginning of democratic justice, for a significant principle had been established: that an aggrieved man could appeal directly to his fellow citizens to give him his rights.[25]

Solon drew upon his mercantile experience, by stimulating agriculture. He pressed for the production of olive-oil, probably in pursuit of a general back-to-the-land policy, and in order to give its producers an additional resource against oppression; another motive, too, according to Plutarch, was to swell the export of this oil in order to pay for the foreign grain that Attica increasingly needed. The exportation of all other products of the soil, however, was banned, and this particularly applied to grain, so that it should not be sold to potential enemies,

Aegina and Megara. Solon also fostered trade and manufacture by promoting the training of sons in their fathers' skills.

In addition, he adopted a policy of encouraging metics (*metoikoi*), permanent immigrants whose crafts and skills could now serve an invaluable purpose. This large class of resident aliens (mostly Greek), although unenfranchised – like slaves and women – possessed a recognized status in the Attic community, enjoying the full protection of the law, paying a modest tax, and sharing Athenian citizens' eligibility for military service (voluntary except in time of war). However, metics were debarred from owning land. This meant that instead they specialized in manufactured goods, of which the exportation, added to that of oil, was already helping them to make a mark in the city and its port: hence Solon's interest in exploiting their contribution (he also presented a relatively small proportion of metics with citizenship).

A political economist, in the modern sense of the word, he can scarcely be called, since, in pursuance of the old religious moral code, it was his natural inclination to blame semi-divine personifications such as Greed and Injustice for what had gone wrong with society. Yet his interest, and personal involvement, in trade, despite his noble birth, gave this occupation a cachet, and to doubt whether a rise in commercial and industrial prosperity was one of his intended aims does not seem reasonable: he undoubtedly gave the community a great push in that direction.

Solon also, possibly in a second stage of his activity, introduced changes in the constitution, which, although once again obscured by subsequent retrospective tendentiousness, were evidently of vital importance both for his own time and for the future. In the first place he divided the citizens into four census-classes (*tele*): *pentakosiomedimnoi* (men whose land annually yielded at least 500 bushels of grain, or the equivalent in other produce), *hippeis* (knights, who could provide their own horses for army service), *zeugitai* (roughly 'farmers', probably from *zeugos*, a yoke of oxen; men earning between 200 and 300 bushels), and *thetes* (those who earned less; especially hired labourers).[26] The first category was new; it constituted a small but obviously influential group of partly aristocratic and partly non-aristocratic rich (or relatively rich) men, reflecting and embodying recent increases in wealth. The other groups, in various forms, had all been of older origin, but Solon formalized them as parts of his new civic structure.

Once again he was striking a non-partisan balance between conservatism and progressiveness. His classification was conservative, in so far as it followed the old aristocratic ideal requiring that every one should know his place, in a system of *eunomia*, good order and stable government: there must be no question of violent dictatorial changes, for 'I do not wish to do anything with tyrannical violence.'[27] Yet by setting up wealth (timocracy) instead of birth as the framework of his hierarchy, he created the concept of an impersonal state, as opposed to arbitrary noble leadership, and thus opened up a decisive breach in the supremacy of the Eupatrids – which, aware of the ruthlessness of some of them, he was apparently not sorry to do.

Even the *thetes*, although too poor to provide their own arms and armour and not yet admitted to any office of state, were theoretically entitled to attend and vote in the Assembly and serve in the Heliaea. To what extent, and from what period, they exercised this right in practice remains uncertain. Yet such a move towards incorporating them into the political community seems to have been an Athenian innovation, which other cities, as far as we are aware, remained slow to follow. As for the 'middle-class' *zeugitai*, the way was now open for their participation in government. Admittedly the chief offices of state, the nine archonships (and the life membership of the ancient Areopagus that their tenure entailed) were still available only to the two classes above them (or even, until 487/6, to the highest class only) – once again, be it noted, on the basis of wealth, not birth.

But what proved really significant was that the *zeugitai* seem to have been entitled to serve in an altogether new council, the Boule. This body, consisting of 400 members – 100 from each tribe – was attributed to Solon, at least from the later fifth century BC (and perhaps much earlier as well), and although strenuous efforts have been made, especially in recent years, to dismiss it as a fabrication by later local chronicles (Atthidographers) in order to provide a venerable, fictitious precedent for the subsequent Council of Five Hundred (of Cleisthenes – section 5 below), the attribution of an earlier Council of Four Hundred to Solon may still be regarded as acceptable. Despite the inventive proclivities of later Athenian writers, such a sweeping and wholesale theory could scarcely have been perpetrated and generally accepted if it was totally fraudulent.

Assuming, then, that Solon created a new Council of Four Hundred, what were its functions? It is best to conclude that we do not know, even though it was described as one of the 'two anchors of the state'.[28] But what it evidently did, in general terms, was to serve as a partner to the Areopagus in keeping the city steady; and at the same time it provided a safeguard against oppressive decisions from that aristocratic body, by limiting its day-to-day authority (although the Areopagus retained its checks on incoming and outgoing officials, *dokimasia* and *euthuna*, until *c*.462). In creating his new Council, Solon may well have had the precedent of Sparta in mind.

Whether, like the later Council of Five Hundred, his Council of Four Hundred was already probouleutic (preparing business for the Assembly [Ecclesia]) we cannot tell. But it is quite likely that the Four Hundred were elected by the Assembly, which – although popular sovereignty was not yet a concept present in anyone's mind – had evidently come to be recognized by Solon as a reality to be reckoned with, since he is on record as pronouncing that the *demos* or citizen-body, which was synonymous with the Assembly, was worthy of privi-lege[29] – a genuine political force, so that all his hopeful supporters among the citizenry had reason to feel satisfaction. Once again, Solon had shown himself to be the archetypal man of compromise. Yet, likewise once again, this very act of holding the balance between old and new had given prominence to the new, reaching out towards a future political philosophy within which democratic institutions could grow.

Solon liked bodily comforts, appreciated a beautiful woman or boy, and saw what a good thing it was to possess sons, foreign guest-friends, useful horses and hunting dogs. But he also knew that neither they nor anything else could stave off illness or death, which came upon him painlessly when he was eighty years old. It was his greatest satisfaction that, despite all pressure, he had refused to accept the dictatorship of Athens.[30] He wanted the people to be contented, but did not want to order them, or to tell them how to achieve this condition; they must find out for themselves.

4 PISISTRATUS AND HIS SONS

However, Solon's hope that the Athenians, after receiving his general guidance, would work out their own salvation proved misplaced. He lived long enough to see what was happening instead. Although his law-code and some of his social reforms were destined to survive, his political changes had not succeeded in averting, indeed had provoked, immediate new problems of a damaging nature. That is to say, his removal of the blood criterion, which had hitherto maintained aristo-cratic power, set the battleground for a renewed struggle. For the aristocrats were determined to frustrate his reforms (aimed at creating a broader base), and yet Solon, true to his spirit of compromise, had left intact enough of the old system of families, clans and tribes to ensure subsequent conflicts.

The nobles could still whip up the backing to fight for their weakened but not demolished positions, striving to seek voting support for the candidates they themselves proposed for office. And this backing had to be provided by the middle and poorer classes, who in addition to retaining their old local family, clan and tribal allegiances now enjoyed new civic rights and ambitions in Athens. With their help, therefore, the ancient rivalries of the great Eupatrid houses revived with fresh savagery. The crisis is evident from the archon-lists. For in 590–589 and 586–584 no archons could be appointed: there was *anarchia*.

What had happened was that three main factions, all led by aristocrats, had arisen in the Assembly. These three factions later became known as the Plain (*pedieis*), the Coast (*paralia*) and the Hill (*diakria*). This neat geographical classification, cutting right across earlier divisions, ignored the fluidity and overlaps that in fact existed – and unduly distracted attention from conflicts based purely on personal or family feuds. The three terms, therefore, are best seen as popular concepts or slogans rather than as clear-cut geographical units, although it is true that they did reflect more or less loose connections with regions of Attica, and perhaps took their names from the districts to which the faction leaders belonged.

The Plainsmen were dominated by the old Eupatrid families, which did not like Solon's reforms. The men of the Coast included many craftsmen and traders (*demiourgoi*, *orgeones*), and favoured the moderate Solonian constitution; they were led by members of the Alcmaeonid clan, who associated themselves with Solon's relatively progressive views, after their return from the expulsion which their murder of Cylon's supporters had brought upon them. The Hillsmen, who had probably hived off from the Coast, were for the most part shepherds and agricultural workers employed on large estates, notably in northeastern Attica. Their release by Solon from debt-bound dependence had not fully succeeded in relieving their impoverishment, or in assuaging the radical democratic feelings induced by these hardships.

It must not be thought, however, that the years following Solon's reforms witnessed nothing but political differences and convulsions. For this was also a period of artistic ebullience, during which the sculptors and painters working at Athens began directly to foreshadow the glories of subsequent epochs. Thus the long procession of sculptured young men (*kouroi*), a form of art which had apparently originated from the marble-rich islands of Naxos and Paros in the Cyclades, achieved a memorable development in the subtly designed, powerful and complex structure of the Moschophorus (Calf-Bearer), a youth with a calf on his shoulders, dedicated by (Rh?)ombus the son of (P?)alus to a deity, perhaps Athena (*c.*570/560).

At about the same time the Athenian potter Ergotimus and painter Clitias broke away from the only moderately distinguished Protoattic style of vase-painting by the creation of the François Vase, found at

Clusium (Chiusi) in Etruria and now in the Archaeological Museum at Florence. This lavishly decorated piece, 26 inches high, basically black-figure but with polychrome additions, marks a new epoch – as the potter and painter alike seem to be aware, since they proudly sign their names on their joint creation. Clitias has depicted 270 human and animal figures on this vase, with 121 accompanying inscriptions. He is primarily a miniaturist, concentrating on exquisite detail, so that there is still a certain lack of coherence in the overall composition. Yet this elaborate scheme of figure scenes, drawing extensively on myth, displays an unprecedented, monumental narrative complexity that the Corinthians (first looked to by Athenian vase-painters for their models) had never achieved. The incised metal-working and perhaps textile techniques from the near east upon which Clitias, directly or indirectly, was able to draw, have been rethought to remarkable effect. The François Vase is a manifesto proclaiming the splendid future of Attic ceramics, and at the same time signalling Athens' conquest of markets hitherto dominated by the Corinthians.

Very soon afterwards, this commercial and artistic supersession of Corinth was sealed by the powerful development of the black-figure pottery which that city had inaugurated. The background of these products of Athens was their natural surface of excellent red, buff or orange clay from the local river Cephisus, exploiting particles and glazing processes which provide a brilliant sheen. The superimposed paintings consisted of an equally glossy black pigment of almost indestructible strength, and their sharp, incised outlines conveyed a powerful illusion of organic movement within space. These black-figure vases offered lavish scope to original genius within their chosen field and limitations.

Two black-figure artists are outstanding. One was the 'Amasis Painter', perhaps identical with a potter who signed his vases by that name (in which case we have an unusual example of a potter who himself painted the vases he had made). The Amasis Painter was active from $c.561$ to $c.514$, and during this long period worked on many different scales and a wide variety of subjects, taken from mythology and daily life alike.[31] His work is highly finished, and his lithe figures display a mannered grace, accompanied by touches of vivid, unexpected humour.

Meanwhile, during the third quarter of the same century, the different but equally individual Exekias – who unmistakably signed as painter as well as potter – enriched his figures with delicate engraved details. Exekias specialized in scenes loaded with dramatic tension and emotion (foreshadowing the tension and emotion of literary tragedy), and innovated by depicting not only critical moments of action but the tense pauses that preceded them. His work achieves a psychological depth and sensitivity of feeling that could scarcely have been exceeded in so restricted a compass.

While this Athenian black-figured pottery was establishing itself as the foremost ceramic product of the Greek world, the political background in the city, dominated by the three parties of Plain, Coast and Hill, had taken a turn that would not have been unfamiliar elsewhere but which in Athens was entirely unprecedented – for an autocratic, dictatorial regime ('tyranny') came into being.

This was the work of Pisistratus, who claimed descent from the kings of Pylos and was related on his mother's side to Solon. Archon in 569/568, he gained distinction in a war against the Megarians, which temporarily lost them their port of Nisaea to Athens. Next, he assumed the leadership of the Hill faction, which may indeed have owed its existence to him – or at least its clear definition – and through his agency drew into its ranks a number of lately enfranchised but impoverished city-dwellers and other vociferous or discontented elements. In 561, with the help of a bodyguard granted him by the Assembly, he assumed dictatorial power. Ejected from this position by the Plain and Coast factions, led by Lycurgus (head of the Eteobytad clan) and Megacles (leader of the Alcmaeonids) respectively, he subsequently profited from a quarrel between the two factions to make it up with Megacles, whose daughter he married. But Pisistratus did not consummate the marriage, broke with Megacles and attempted a second *coup d'état* at Athens (555). Again it failed, and again Pisistratus withdrew, in the company of his supporters and his friends.

But this time he put his withdrawal to excellent use, settling in the border-area between Macedonia and Thrace first at a new foundation of his own, Rhaecelus (later Aenea) on the Thermaic Gulf, and then near Mount Pangaeum, whose immense mining wealth in gold and silver thus became available to him. At about the same period, too, Miltiades the elder, an adventurous member of the Philaid clan, occupied the Thracian Chersonese (Gallipoli peninsula), and ruled it autocratically as a pocket principality, encouraging Athenian settlers to join him. He took this action with the support of Pisistratus, who also, during these years of waiting, forged a number of valuable alliances with various other Greek states. Then in 546, with decisive foreign support, as well as help from inside Attica itself, he landed near Marathon, defeated his opponents and established his dictatorship for the third time, retaining the supremacy until he died in 527.

Backed by a mercenary army (including Thessalian cavalry and probably Scythian archers) owed to his connections abroad, Pisistratus was said to have governed the city with moderation, as citizen rather than tyrant, supported by most of the nobility and people. The reason why the nobility, on the whole, accepted him was because he was one of themselves and because he upheld the old tribal structure and ethic. But he insisted on restraining their internal conflicts – indeed this maintenance of public order was the basic *raison d'être* of his regime. In thus taming the Eupatrids and compelling them to fit into the constitutional framework, he permanently restricted their power.

Pisistratus finally established the rule of the Athenians over Salamis (following a Spartan arbitration in their favour, against Megara), and cemented closer relations with other Aegean islands as well. He asserted Athens' claim to be the mother and leader of all Ionian Greeks, instituting an Ionian phase in Attic art, and bringing the point home by taking the festival at Delos into his care.

He also maintained his previous interest in the coastal lands of Thrace and Macedonia, rich not only in metals but in timber, and occupying a strategic location on the grain-route from the Black Sea. Moreover, soon after his final return to Athens, he seized or resumed control of Sigeum across the Hellespont (Dardanelles), handing it over to his son Hegesistratus (Chapter 8, section 2). Having secured, by this means, his lines of communication to the Pangaean mines – the date when the local Laurium mines were sufficiently productive to contribute is uncertain – it seems to have been he himself, though some prefer a slightly earlier chronology, who issued a series of Athenian silver pieces known as *Wappenmünzen* ('coat-of-arms coins') because they display armorial devices or badges. These used to be regarded as autonomous and perhaps competing issues made by the noble families themselves, to celebrate, for example, the election of one of their number to an archonship, but the series was, rather, issued by Pisistratus himself as a gesture of reconciliation with the Eupatrid houses. (Alternative attributions of these types to the badges of his mercenary forces, or to the ten post-Pisistratid tribes, have not won universal acceptance.) Perhaps the appearance of the national symbol of a Gorgon's head on one of the coins symbolizes the transition to a coinage no longer concerned to honour families and clans.

At the same time Pisistratus helped small and medium farmers, who obtained a reasonably secure and independent position. They were supported by the creation of a state loan-fund – a necessary step seeing that Solon had banned loans secured by the body of the debtor – and their position was perhaps safeguarded by the establishment of thirty circuit judges, whose functions superseded the jurisdiction of local aristocracies.

However, Pisistratus' attentions to the farmers and peasants were by no means at the expense of Athens itself, upon whose poorer

57

inhabitants – swelled by landless peasants to whom the urban sector gave greater opportunities – his power partly depended. For he took steps to make the city more prosperous, and started the process by which it outstripped the countryside, despite the improved condition of the farmers who inhabited those rural areas.

The revenues from Pangaeum that enabled Pisistratus to maintain his position were swelled by flourishing Athenian trade (to which a vast expansion of black-figure vases bears witness), by the seizure of lands from the Alcmaeonids who had fled once again, and by the earliest-known direct taxation of citizens. This included a duty on produce, probably amounting to 5 per cent, which was made possible by the increase in agricultural resources, and was employed to augment the farmers' loan-fund; and a progressively increased tax on trade was also introduced.

The dictator was equally determined to unify the state by religious means, through a persistent centralization of cults. At Eleusis (section 2 above), he rebuilt the Hall of Initiation (Telesterion), a meeting-place for worshippers such as was rarely to be found in Greek lands; its roof was held up by twenty-two columns. Aristotle also credited him with the organization of the Greek Panathenaia festival in honour of the goddess Athena, and even if, in fact, its foundation (in a simpler form) antedated his regime, it was under Pisistratus that the festival became a central event in the Athenian calendar, as a rival to the four great international festivals led by Olympia. Staged annually, but with special pomp every fourth year, the Panathenaia appears (at least by the fifth century, and perhaps already in Pisistratid times) to have occupied an eight-day period during the month of July. A new robe was presented to Athena on these occasions, and athletic and musical contests were held in her honour. The victors in the games won amphoras filled with oil from the sacred groves of the goddess, and successful musicians received prizes of money.

All this was part of an aggrandizement of Athena as the protectress of his new, great Athens and of Pisistratus himself who was its ruler. Athena had probably started as a localized divinity of pre-Greek times, who survived as protector of the palace–citadel and patron of some Mycenaean prince, and retained as her symbol the owl which recalled an ancient totemic animal cult and was destined to become the principal design of the Athenian coinage. She was Athena Polias, an agrarian mother goddess, but also Athena Parthenos, the warrior–maiden archetype of the woman who triumphs in a man's world by denying her femininity in favour of bellicose male fierceness. This she also strangely combined with a prudent, practical intelligence and a powerful patronage of the arts of peace.

The second major festival which Pisistratus either instituted or, more probably, took over and to which he gave a splendid place in Athenian cult was the Great or City Dionysia, held in the spring in honour of Dionysus. This deity, whose worship came from Thrace (Appendix 2), possessed a popular appeal, his worship and enjoyment being available to all, including freedmen and slaves. So he enjoyed favour from dictators in pursuance of their search for broad-based supports; and Pisistratus took steps to bring the cult of Dionysus Eleuthereus from the Attic village of Eleutherae (a dependency of Athens in north-western Attica) to his capital, lodging the god's statue in a sanctuary beneath the south-eastern slope of the Acropolis, to the accompaniment of solemn sacrifices and celebrations. But the link with Eleutherae was not forgotten, for it harmonized conveniently with the autocrat's desire to support the peasantry and its cults, and to unite the city and country populations.

Moreover, Pisistratus felt eager to raise cultural standards, and was in a position to afford heavy financial investments to achieve this aim, even if they did not produce a visible or immediate return. One of the results of this policy was the emergence of a novel and distinctive literary genre – tragic drama. For it was now that the presentation of tragic plays became established as a regular feature of the festival of the City Dionysia.

The origins of this type of theatrical show have been endlessly discussed.[32] What emerged was a gradually dramatized improvement upon various kinds of entertainments already existing in different parts of Greece (including, it was believed, Corinth, Sicyon and Megara). A wide range of earlier poetic genres was drawn upon, adapted and incorporated, including choral song (especially the 'dithyramb': see Corinth, Chapter 3, section 2), solo lyrics, elegiac and iambic poetry, mimic dancing celebrating the suffering of Dionysus and other themes, and ancient humorous revelries in which individuals or choruses dressed up as satyrs or in other guises.

In later times three playwrights entered four plays each at the City Dionysia (three tragedies and a satyr play – note 37), but according to tradition it was a certain Thespis who presented what passed as the first tragedy in c.534, winning a prize for its performance. His precise contribution to the dramatic form is uncertain, and much of what was attributed to him may in reality have constituted a gradual, multiple development. But what he may have done, as Aristotle reportedly suggested,[33] was to supplement earlier choral performances – which had already employed mime and impersonation – by a prologue and set speech or speeches (*rhesis*). This was probably not sung, for the most part, but spoken or declaimed (though accompanied by the musical beat of a double flute, the *diaulos*). The actor–conductor–director introduced for this purpose – perhaps the poet himself – was known as the *hypocrites*, 'answerer', or rather 'explainer' or 'interpreter': in declaiming his recitations he could represent a character who had, in earlier entertainments, only been described in narrative verse.[34] The *hypocrites* could also converse with the leader of the chorus,[35] whose part had arisen out of ritual and who continued to dance and sing traditional or newly composed songs (often embodying the narratives mentioned above), but could also fulfil an equivocal role as a corporate character in the play, as would be seen in the hands of the great masters of Athenian tragedy (Aeschylus, Sophocles, Euripides) who emerged in the following century. A second founder of this tragic drama was Phrynichus, who won his first victory in 511/508, and was remembered for the beauty of his lyrics, the many varieties of dance he invented, and his introduction of female characters – though their parts were still acted by men.

The first tragic plays shown at Athens were perhaps performed by actors who came from Eleutherae, or from another sanctuary of Dionysus at Icaria (north-east of Athens, near Marathon). In the city, the obvious traditional location for dances and similar performances was the *agora*.[36] However, tragedies, from the beginning, seemed to have been staged at the location beneath the Acropolis to which Pisistratus had imported the statue of Dionysus, with the front of his temple as the background.

This was a place where the slope could accommodate seated or standing spectators, perhaps on wooden structures. The performance they watched from above took place on a flat, usually circular dancing-floor (*orchestra*), consisting of hard earth, upon which a low wooden platform may have been erected. Behind the orchestra, for the convenience of performers, was a wooden hut or tent (*skene*), which could also serve as a background for the plays.

The origins of Attic comedy are as mixed and as old as those of tragedy, and the appearance of disguised or masked figures on Athenian vases a little before and after 500 (as on seventh and sixth-century pots from Corinth and Sicyon) bears witness to more or less crude forerunners of comic drama. But the developed art, performed first at the City Dionysia and then at another festival of Dionysus, the Lenaea, belongs to the following century (*c.*487, Lenaea 440).[37]

Another art which flourished under the Pisistratids was sculpture, particularly in the hands of those who made the marble maidens, *korai*, of whom so many superb examples have been found on the Acropolis, where they were buried after the Persian Wars. The predominance of

Athens as the site of such finds tends to conceal the fact that the places of origin of many of these *korai*, and the earliest ones at that, lay in the Cyclades (Naxos, Paros), which were linked so closely by Pisistratus to Athens, and indeed it was from those islands that many of the examples found at Athens had come. But Athenian artists, too, had their own invaluable contribution to make, first through a brief period of strong Ionian influence (following the immigration of Ionians fleeing from Persian encroachment after 546) – productive of fine modelling, and an elegant, enigmatic, voluptuous quality – and then by their own more solid, serene contribution, which was specifically Attic.

In spite of the subsequent prejudice against 'tyrants', it was admitted, even by good later democrats, that the rule of Pisistratus could be looked back upon as a Golden Age. He had prudently refrained, as we saw, from disturbing the existing Solonian constitution, or from otherwise encouraging any major social upheaval, and the effective financial policy, which was his creation, had enabled him to stimulate national festivals, build temples and conduct a foreign programme of bold expansion and skilful diplomacy.

By these various means – adding up, for the first time, to a coherent Athenian policy – he had truly forged the unity of Attica and Athens. For their inhabitants, life was no longer just a desperate struggle to survive; on the contrary, the increase in prosperity was widespread. In addition, although dictatorship is not democracy – and Pisistratus, from a back seat, remained very much in charge, exercising control, for example, over elections – his regime had nevertheless, paradoxically, paved the way for the democratic system of the future. For he had restrained and tamed the Eupatrid nobility; and his astute guidance had provided a whole generation, over a wide spectrum of society, with a picture of how a state could be peacefully run.

Pisistratus was succeeded by his sons Hippias and Hipparchus. Their rule, as long as they both lived, was mild. Taxes were reduced, and Eupatrid support was gained by the appointment of the Philaid Miltiades the younger and the Alcmaeonid Cleisthenes to archonships; the former was dispatched to maintain his uncle and namesake's Athenian regime in the Thracian Chersonese (*c*.516). Furthermore, Hipparchus encouraged the arts, and made Homeric recitatives a feature of the Panathenaic Festival. A large statue of Athena in the Acropolis Museum (*c*.525–520), now restored, formed part of a pediment sculpture of the Battle with the Giants (Gigantomachy) – the earliest-known marble pediment – belonging to her Old Temple, of which the renovation was carried out in these years. So Athens was becoming a finer city, although it was not until another half-century had passed that it showed any really impressive signs of wealth or grandeur.

It was also, perhaps, in c.520 (or possibly a decade or two later) that the Athenians inaugurated their famous, long-lived and widely circulating silver coinage bearing the head of Athena and the picture of an owl, and based not on the weight standard of hostile Aegina (section 5), popular on the mainland, but on the 'Attic–Euboic' standard of a drachma weighing about 4.25 grams, adapted from the currency of the Euboean cities.

At about the same time, a new red-figure technique of vase-painting perpetuated and enhanced the supremacy that Athens had gained in this field. Employing the exceptionally fine Ceramicus clay, which contained iron producing a rich red colour, potters now evolved a complex three-stage process of firing that enabled them to improve further on the graceful shapes created by their black-figure forerunners. Moreover, these new painters – if that is what they should be called, for they used hardly any colouring – reversed the procedure of their black-figure forerunners, leaving human and other forms in the natural red surface colour instead of painting them black, and covering the backgrounds with black paint instead. At the same time, the incisions which had outlined the earlier designs were replaced by brush-drawing, in long fluent sweeps. This new method provided greater freedom and flexibility, permitting the faithful depiction of muscular structures and ambitious poses, together with varied and realistic details of features and clothing.

The invention of this red-figure style is ascribed to the Andocides Painter (that is to say, one of the painters who worked for the potter Andocides), who was a pupil of the black-figure painter Exekias and had himself done a good deal of black-figure work, sometimes, indeed, combining the two techniques on a single vase. Less sensitive than Exekias, the Andocides Painter was an artist whose work displays an elegant grace – reflecting, it might seem, the luxury of the court of Hippias and Hipparchus; his figures are drawn on a grand scale, and convey a sense of depth. The court also attracted distinguished writers from other Greek centres, notably Simonides of Iulis on the island of Ceos, who was to achieve his greatest fame after the Persian Wars.[38]

However, the regime of Hippias and Hipparchus ran into difficulties. This was largely because of an economic recession caused by the Persian advance under Darius I. Rhaecelus, occupied by Pisistratus, and the Pangaean mines, over which he had established a considerable measure of control, were both lost. The Athenian brothers' rule became harsher: and in 514 Hipparchus was murdered. His assassins

Harmodius and Aristogeiton, who paid for the deed with their lives, were later honoured by a statuary group sculpted by Antenor, and went down to posterity as the 'tyrant-slayers' who had ended the dictatorship – misleadingly, since they had failed to kill Hippias.

It was instead (although this fact proved unwelcome to their rivals later on) the noble Alcmaeonid house which led the movement that brought him and his regime down. After one of their returned members, Cleisthenes (named after his maternal grandfather the dictator of Sicyon) held the archonship in 525/524, Hippias had expelled the clan (along with others). However, Cleisthenes instigated King Cleomenes I of Sparta – with which the Pisistratids had formed close connections – to drive out the Athenian autocrat (510), which he did, allegedly by enlisting Delphic support.

5 CLEISTHENES

Cleomenes subsequently fell out with Cleisthenes, but the Spartan's attempts to supersede him by a rival aristocratic faction-leader Isagoras (508, c.506), and then to restore Hippias to his dictatorial office (504), proved total failures.

On the second of these occasions the Athenians defeated the armies of two of Sparta's allies, Chalcis and the Boeotian League, on one and the same day, a double victory which greatly increased Athenian self-confidence. Boeotia, which had already fought Athens for Plataea without success in c.519, was not finally defeated, but Chalcis was, and the lands of its nobility were confiscated for 4,000 Athenian settlers, known as *klerouchoi* after the allotments of land (*kleroi*) that they were given. These migrants introduced a new type of colonization by retaining their Athenian citizenship (unlike settlers in normal colonies, who became citizens of their new foundation), so that although geographical distance from the mother city obliged them to create organs of local self-government they remained liable to Athenian military service, acting, when necessary, as a garrison defending the interests of Athens.

In the course, or at the end, of these excitements – perhaps in a series of several stages, from c.506 to c.500 – Cleisthenes, backed by popular support ('adding the *demos* to his faction')[39], was granted or assumed the powers needed to prevent the destruction of his own Alcmaeonid party, which was getting the worst of the internal struggle. Armed with these powers, he asserted his authority and seized the chance to introduce the most famous constitutional reforms in Greek history.

They displayed an extraordinary complex design. Employing Spartan developments as a precedent (Chapter 3, section 3), Cleisthenes superseded the four antique Attic tribes (note 4), which had been dominated by the nobles – and which had excluded many of the new citizens created by Solon and the Pisistratids – in favour of ten new tribes, unlinked with the old tribal past. The four old tribes were allowed to survive for religious purposes, but it was upon their ten newly created successors that the future of Athens depended. For they came to form the basis of all aspects of public life. One such aspect was military service, since each of the ten tribes was required to supply a regiment or squadron to the army, and this soldierly function of the new tribes meant that their cohesive *esprit de corps* developed rapidly. It was encouraged by religious sanctions, since each tribe was named after a mythological hero allegedly buried at Athens – except for two of the heroes, whose burial places were shown at Salamis and Eleusis. A number of foreigners and slaves were admitted into these ten Cleisthenic tribes. Their creation represented a deliberate attempt to break up the old regional, conservative allegiances. For one thing, the new tribes were not units of local government; their headquarters were in the city. And, above all, any reversion to the old regionalization was prevented by means of the ancient institution of the *trittyes* (thirds). These, as we saw earlier (section 1 above), had probably been territorial synonyms and substitutes for the phratry, used for purposes of administration. There had been twelve of them, but Cleisthenes raised the number to thirty. That is to say, there were still three in each tribe. But each of these three *trittyes*, in every tribe, was based on a different region of Attica from the regions to which the other two *trittyes* in the same tribe belonged, so that people were 'mixed up', and opportunities for local loyalty were dissipated.

Moreover, in order to avoid any resuscitation of the old trouble-making factions of the Plain, Coast and Hill, the three regions were novel creations which by no means completely corresponded with the three old areas. The new regions were Town (*astu*, including Athens, Phaleron and Piraeus and part of the adjacent plain), Coast (*paralia*, comprising most of the former territory of the same name, but including additional coastal zones), and the Interior (comprising parts of all the former areas).

Cleisthenes also divided the ten tribes and thirty *trittyes* into demes (*demoi*), about 140 in number, which, for practical purposes, replaced the aristocratic clan and phratry organization. That antique system, it is true, continued to exist for religious purposes and functions, but the deme was now the fundamental subdivision of society. Demes from each of three new regions were included in all the ten tribes. Having originally been villages or city-wards or small towns (section 1 above), these demes varied greatly in size. After the initial registrations, membership was hereditary and did not depend on residence, so that the members of a deme were not concentrated in a single place.

Nevertheless, demes maintained their own list of members and members' property (and kept lists of metics as well), so that they could furnish the state with information required to enforce civic obligations – and were able, also, to exert control over the right to Athenian citizenship: to be an Athenian citizen meant being registered on the official roll of one's paternal deme. The demes also possessed their own land, social life and religious cults, as well as their own assemblies (perhaps rarely convened). Such activities, under the leadership of an annually elected *demarchos*, counterbalanced and therefore weakened the corresponding organs of the old clans and phratries. Granted the passive nature of rustic life, the wealthier and more aristocratic demesmen (and those belonging to demes near Athens) must have retained a considerable measure of authority. And yet this new local autonomy furnished not only the rich, but every Athenian citizen, with the opportunity to gain some understanding of the process of state government – without having to rely upon a local patron or a dictatorial head of government, or upon his faction.

The extension of political activity and authority to the citizenry in general was given expression by Cleisthenes' new Council (later Boule) of Five Hundred members. The tradition ascribing to Solon the creation of a Council of Four Hundred to supplement, and largely supersede, the Areopagus was probably correct (section 3 above). But we hear little of Solon's body, and it was the Council of Cleisthenes which dominated the future. Its 500 members comprised fifty men, over the age of thirty, from each of the ten newly created tribes. Every one of the demes that constituted each tribe was represented on the new Council in proportion to the size of its population; and in this way, the Council served as a bridge between city and countryside, while at the same time staving off the rise or revival of parties and political interest groups, and thus contributing to the creation and development of the Athenian democracy.

The Council met daily except on holidays and unlucky days. Its business was prepared by a committee manned by fifty of its own members (*prytaneis*), each group serving for one-tenth of the year. The group currently in office was on duty every day, under the guidance of one of its number, who also acted as the committee's chairman (*epistates*). Whether this system existed, in its final form, as early as the time of Cleisthenes is not clear, but the multiple duties of the Council must presumably have required some such 'agenda subcommittee' from the outset. For the Council was entrusted with far-reaching and varied deliberative and administrative duties. Moreover, it monopolized the initiative in all law-making, and possessed important judicial functions, notably the right to investigate alleged illegalities. Council members served for a year, and could serve for a second year after an interval.

The method, however, by which, in these early days of the body's existence, they were selected cannot be determined for certain. At first elected and unpaid, from c.450 (or 462) at least they were appointed by demesmen by lot (sortition). Our efforts to discover how early this had been the case are befogged by the determination of later Athenian writers, including Aristotle, to attribute features of the later democracy to excessively early dates.[40] But at least by the time of Cleisthenes the lot was in use, and henceforward the members not only of the judicial Heliaea (if it was a committee of the Assembly and not the Assembly in its entirety) but also of his Council were appointed in this way.

The lot was believed by the Athenians to possess a religious sanction, since it left the decision to the gods. At a subsequent date, this procedure came to be exalted by radicals (but reputedly deplored by Socrates) as a supreme principle of the ultra-democratic system they admired, since it gave everyone an equal chance.[41] And democratic, in this sense, it was, though not democratic in the other sense of allowing merit every opportunity to secure its place: the lot, as critics pointed out, takes no interest in merit.

However, this system, during the subsequent centuries of Athenian democracy, did not work as badly as might have been expected. This was largely because so many ordinary citizens had received a basic political and administrative training in the various local community bodies, so that sortition could not go far wrong. But especially in the early period the method was also subjected to a very important qualification: the lot was taken only from names chosen through a previous process of voting (*prokrisis*) by the demes, so that in fact the candidates eventually chosen by lot had been drawn from a short-list of men selected by a vote, that is to say on the basis of merit. Whether this 'middle way' had been established at Athens by Solon or not (a matter on which Aristotle seems to contradict himself, note 40), it must already have played a part in the arrangements of Cleisthenes.

The Assembly, as well as the new Council, now possessed considerable powers, which had scarcely been the case before. The relative strength of these two bodies, at the time of Cleisthenes and during the decades that followed, is difficult to assess, but the task has to be attempted, because upon the answer to this question depends our estimate of the thoroughgoing character, or otherwise, of the early or incipient Athenian democracy (democracy among male citizens, that is, because women, metics and slaves were excluded).

In favour of the supposition that the Assembly held the upper hand, reference could be made to its right to amend or reject, during its forty meetings each year, the motions placed before it by the Council. Moreover, the Assembly retained in its hands certain essential functions, including the responsibility for declarations of war; and the annual change in the entire membership of the Council deprived it of the corporate feeling that might have prompted a stand against the Assembly's 'sovereign' authority. Besides, the citizen membership of the latter body had become more articulate and more radical, and also, with the growth of the franchise, much larger. When the herald cried out, 'What man has good advice to give the *polis* and wishes to make it known?' he was issuing a genuine invitation to the entire voting body: here was direct (not, as today, representative) democracy in action, inviting political oratory before wide, interested, participatory audiences.

All the same, it was the Council which determined what business should be placed before the Assembly, and in what shape – and it met more frequently than the Assembly (which, moreover, only voted by a show of hands). The Council also replaced the Areopagus (now or a little later) in preparing that business (*probouleusis*); and it subsequently had to see that the Assembly's decrees were carried out, so that the formula 'the Council and People decided' possessed real significance.

A second important limitation of the Assembly's powers was the establishment during these years of a board of ten generals (*strategoi*), one from each of the ten tribal regiments or squadrons, to command Athens' military forces. The *strategoi*, who at first came from noble and wealthy families, were *not* appointed by lot, because of the specialized nature of their duties, but were elected by the Assembly – and they could be re-elected an unlimited number of times.

The polemarch, as of old, still led the state's forces out to battle, and fought in a position of danger. But he and the other archons were no longer as important as they used to be. A sign of this change was the decision that they, too, like the members of the Council, should be appointed by lot, out of a select list of *prokritoi*, chosen by the demes (a system abandoned in the fifth century in favour of two successive lot-takings). Our confused sources make it difficult to determine when the archons came to be appointed in this way; 487/486 is a possible date, but on the whole it is more likely that this, too, was an arrangement made by Cleisthenes. (The date when scrutiny of candidates for archonships, and audit of their performance, were instituted was *c.* 462 [cf. section 3 above]).

Evidently the creation of the *strategoi* constituted a greater limitation upon the Assembly's untrammelled sovereignty than archons, with their diminished powers, were any longer able to impose. But an equally potent restriction upon that body's freedom of action, viewed as a democratic expression of the people's will, came from within its own ranks and from its own character.

For, although anyone could get up and speak in the Assembly, we also learn that anyone speaking foolishly was at once shouted down. That is to say, a fair measure of expert knowledge was needed to address not only the Council but the Assembly as well – and the only people with the time to acquire such knowledge were members of the leisured aristocratic class, so that the upper ranks of society, and the determined self-perpetuating lobbies that they formed, were still the predominant element. However, a man who thus became a leading figure in the Assembly only prevailed by personally exerting and asserting his powers of persuasion before this audience, over and over again. He did not receive automatic, pre-eminent deference because he belonged to this or that faction or class. Indeed, it was Cleisthenes' deliberate intention, we are told, to eclipse such previous factional associations or loyalties (*synetheiai*),[42] fostered by the aristocratic clubs and *symposia* which stood at the centre of an early Greek city's political, social and cultural life (though here he was not entirely successful, since these institutions defied and survived all such attempts to eliminate them).

Cleisthenes was again thinking along similar lines, aiming at the prevention of internal factional warfare, when he introduced the extraordinary institution of ostracism. This was a method of banishing prominent politicians who had become unpopular. Any Athenian who wished such a person out of the way inscribed the man's name on a fragment of pottery (*ostrakon*), and if the total number of votes exceeded 6,000, the man whose name headed the list had to go into exile for ten years. Although no one was ostracized until 487, Aristotle's indication that the procedure had been devised by Cleisthenes can be accepted.[43] But he was not equally right to believe that ostracism was intended as a safeguard against the revival of dictatorship; or at least, if this was so, it was only a secondary aim, or one of the original aims, perhaps, which became overlaid. The main purpose of the process, as the course of events later showed, was to prevent clashes with and between aristocratic opponents. For there were many Pisistratid supporters still at Athens, and indeed for other reasons as well political leadership

68

remained fragile – as Cleisthenes, himself earlier a violent faction-leader, knew only too well. So he concluded that only the temporary removal of one or other of such contestants could enable the state to survive. Certain features of ostracism suggest a conscious recollection of a very ancient religious custom, namely the removal of a community's pollution (*miasma*) by the driving out of a scapegoat. The exile of a tiresome politician would effectively silence him; for Athenian civilization was still mainly oral, and in an oral culture if you remove a man physically he has lost his lines of communication, and can no longer make trouble.

This provision for the removal of factious nobles was yet another of Cleisthenes' moves towards 'giving the people a share in public affairs'.[44] By taking these measures, he did not, it may be supposed, foresee the huge power of the Athenian democracy in the following century. Yet he pointed firmly towards that power by vouchsafing the people, the Assembly, a glimpse of what it would eventually achieve. The contemporary description for the degree of democracy established by Cleisthenes, or existing in his time, was *isonomia*, equality under the law, replacing the aristocratic hierarchic orderliness described as *eunomia*. True, the old framework had not been destroyed, but it had been overlaid by a new one; as elsewhere, the old *thesmos*, 'ordinance' fixed by an authority, was now supplemented and partly replaced by *nomos*, law or custom adopted by a community as a result of its own decision. The *isonomia* of Cleisthenes, though it did not all come into force at once but emerged gradually, was a sophisticated, intricate and experimental array of new political institutions, adding up to the most democratic form of government that had so far been devised by human ingenuity, and establishing the essential features of Athenian society for 200 years.

This last decade of the sixth century also witnessed what many, justifiably enough, regard as the climax of the Athenian red-figure style of vase-painting. New and more wholehearted attempts were made to achieve realism: this was no longer just the decoration of a flat surface but a window on a three-dimensional, foreshortened world, in which, while mythological themes still prevailed, human scenes were increasingly prominent, depicting, for example, the life of aristocratic youth and Dionysiac revelries.

Among several bands of painters, one clearly defined group of outstanding talent, launching the 'classical style' of the future with revolutionary assurance, has been described as the Pioneers. Certain of these artists, notably Euphronius and Euthymides and the Cleophrades Painter, displayed a precision and mastery of line comparable to the

finest achievements in contemporary sculpture. While capable of depicting the plump forms of prostitutes (*hetairai*) in meticulous detail,
Euphronius also employed his versatile mastery of shading and colour
to illustrate the pain of military combat. When he began to lose his
eyesight, it was said that he turned from painting to making pottery
with equal distinction. Euthymides, notable for the sure economy of his
supple linear drawings, exulted in depicting obliquely twisted, statu-
esque human anatomies. But the finest draughtsman of the years
around 500 was a painter who worked with the potter Cleophrades, an
aesthetic individualist remarkable for his strong and fluent outlines
and spacious monumental compositions. Elegant vase painting on a
white instead of a black ground, influenced by east Greek fabrics, had
also been introduced by this time, perhaps by a certain Nicosthenes.

The external politics of the age of Cleisthenes were overshadowed by
the encroaching might of Persia. When Darius I had invaded Thrace
and marched over the Danube in *c.*513/512, it is possible, or even likely,
that he already had in mind the eventual conquest of all mainland
Greece. Athenian opinion on the attitude which ought to be shown to
the Persians was divided. When King Cleomenes I of Sparta twice
attempted to install their protégé Isagoras at Athens the Athenians
sought an alliance with Darius – but then veered away, and repudiated
the terms offered them by the Persian satrap of Sardis. The
Alcmaeonids, led by Cleisthenes, had probably been behind the initial
attempt to enlist Persian support, and its failure may have weakened or
destroyed his position, though after his death, which perhaps occurred
in *c.*500, he was duly granted a state tomb.

6 ATHENS AND AEGINA

After Athens, in 506, had defeated the Chalcidian and Boeotian armies
on one and the same day, the Boeotians, as we saw in the last section,
were still not finally crushed, and in addition Athens had now become a
rival and determined enemy of its neighbour on the other flank, Aegina.

This mountainous, volcanic and somewhat unapproachable island
lay in the Saronic Gulf, midway between Attica and the Peloponnese,
thus occupying a position which, despite its small size of only thirty-
two square miles, had guaranteed its importance in Mediterranean
commerce from the earliest periods. Dorian invaders of Aegina in
*c.*1100 BC, who subjugated an earlier Thessalian settlement (of which
traces have come to light on the slopes of Mount Elia) had been joined
in *c.*950–900 by further immigrants, perhaps from Epidaurus,

(Chapter 3, note 2), which was believed to have maintained control over the island for a time.

However, like Epidaurus, Aegina became a member of the Amphictyony (League) of Calauria (on the island of Poros), an early confederacy comprising the principal maritime city-states on the Saronic and Argive Gulfs as well as Orchomenus in Boeotia. It is possible, however, that for a time Pheidon of Argos (Chapter 3, section 1) controlled the island (although the report that he employed it as a mint was erroneous). Thereafter, however, Aegina avoided the phase of dictatorial government that occurred at other cities, and developed a stable oligarchic, mercantile regime. Under this administration, the Aeginetans not only developed a profitable transit, pedlar trade, but became, in the seventh century, a Greek sea-power of the first order.[45]

From c.595/590, or perhaps a little later, they began to issue silver coins with the design of a turtle, the earliest of all coinages in or near the mainland. It circulated widely for centuries to come, establishing one of the two principal monetary weight-standards of the Greeks (the other being the Euboic–Attic), based on a drachma of about 6 grams (and ultimately reflecting a Syrian metrical structure of a *mina* comprising 50 shekels [staters]). This Aeginetan standard was adopted throughout the Peloponnese, in much of central Greece and in many islands. Aegina also developed the oldest system of weights and measures known to the Greek world.

There was a large Aeginetan temple of Apollo (of which only fragments remain), and on the adjoining Cape Colonna a somewhat later and smaller but famous shrine of Aphaea (a pre-Greek goddess, assimilated to Athena). Columns of this building survive, as well as sinewy pediment sculptures in at least two styles (now in the Munich and Athens museums) perhaps datable to c.520–500 – unless the second master is a decade or two later. These sculptural groups, indebted both to Peloponnesian solidity and to Attic–Ionic grace, bring scenes of the Trojan War to life, and point to the future possibilities of free-standing statuary. Indeed the Aeginetans had already asserted their primacy in bronze sculpture as well, of which Onatas was a renowned practitioner: he and Callon and Glaucias were said to have excelled in the representation of the nude male body.

There was often rivalry between Aegina and Samos, notably at the trading station of Naucratis in Egypt – where Aegina was the only city-state from old Greece to possess representation. But above all it was Athens which inevitably schemed to break the naval and commercial success of the uncomfortably close Aeginetans. Solon had already passed laws designed to restrict their trading,[46] which caused the islanders to ally themselves first with the Spartans (though it is uncertain if Aegina actually became a member of the Peloponnesian League) and then with the Boeotian League. But after the League, together with Chalcis, had been defeated by the Athenians in 506, they almost inevitably became locked in prolonged life-and-death conflict with Aegina, the 'Heraldless War'. Between the oligarchy which controlled Aegina and the more democratically inclined Athenians there was no common ground. Pindar was later to praise Aegina's *eunomia*, rule by the rich. Early in the fifth century, Herodotus records, they massacred 700 members of the *demos*, that is to say advocates of a broader form of government.[47]

This hostile attitude of the Aeginetan ruling class meant that when the Athenians looked likely to come into conflict with Persia they could, at first, expect no help at all from the still unbroken power of Aegina, which, on the contrary, might easily, and perhaps rightly, be suspected of favouring the Persians, in the hope that their unfriendly Athenian neighbours would be destroyed. After the Athenians had displayed their enmity to Persia by sending twenty ships to help the Ionian revolt (499–498), it was with Aegina in mind that they soon went into reverse and withdrew their force precipitately from Asia Minor, for fear of what the island city would do in its absence.

The election of Hipparchus (evidently a member of the family of Pisistratus, whose son and joint successor had borne the same name) as Athenian archon in 496 shows that a pro-Persian faction still had some power in the city. On the other hand, there was widespread distress among the Athenians when the Ionian rebellion's failure was accompanied by the sack of Miletus (494); and in the following year (or somewhat later) the tragic dramatist Phrynichus, who wrote a play on the subject, was fined for recalling the misfortunes of his city's Milesian friends.

Meanwhile the Persians, for their part, had by no means forgotten the hostile intervention of the Athenians in the revolt, and were determined to take their revenge; so the scene was now set for the Persian Wars. With these on the near horizon, the far-sighted young Themistocles, during his archonship of 493 or in another subsequent office, began the development of Piraeus as a fortified port. His reasons for taking this decisive step were no doubt mixed. The Persian peril was one of them; and trade was another. But an additional motive was fear of the Aeginetans, and the desire to be able to resist them, especially if they attempted a stab in the back when the Persian threat materialized – a fear that was not finally eliminated until the Athenians captured the island more than two decades after the Persian Wars had come to an end.[48]

CHAPTER 3

THE PELOPONNESE

1 ARGOS

The Peloponnese is the extensive and largely mountainous peninsula of southern Greece, separated from the rest of the mainland by the isthmus of Corinth. The Greeks interpreted its name as *Pelopos nesos*, the island of the mythological Pelops, grandson of Zeus, whose family the Pelopidae (to which Agamemnon belonged) were believed to have been kings of Mycenae or Argos.

The principal divisions of the Peloponnese were the Argolid, Achaea, Elis, Arcadia, Laconia and Messenia. The triangular Argolid lay in the north-eastern region of the peninsula, flanked on the north-east and south-west by mountains and on the south by the sea. The city of Argos stood near the ruins of the Bronze Age palace–fortresses of Mycenae and Tiryns – dimly reflected in the Mycenaean kingdom of Agamemnon in Homer's *Iliad*, where the whole region is described as Argos, which was understood to mean 'the plain' – the central plain that formed the nucleus of the Argolid.

The city of Argos, based on two citadels upon the Aspis and Larissa hills, was situated in the southern region of this plain. Occupied since prehistoric times, the place played a significant part in the Bronze Age, as recent excavations have emphasized. This importance was echoed in the stories surrounding the monarch Adrastus, who, according to mythology, was the son of King Talaus and, after being driven out to Sicyon and then returning to Argos, became the leader of the Seven against Thebes and subsequently led the second attack on the same city, conducted by the Epigoni (Afterborn, sons of the chiefs who fell in the first war); both expeditions formed the theme of many sagas. Adrastus' grandson was Diomedes, who in Homer's *Iliad* ruled Argos as a dependant of Agamemnon of Mycenae before playing a leading part in the Trojan War and then setting out on western wanderings.

After the fall of Mycenae and Tiryns, Argos was believed to have

AEGEAN SEA

IONIAN SEA

ISTHMUS OF CORINTH

GULF OF CORINTH

Saronic Gulf

R. Asopus
Megara
Pegae
Mt.Sciron
Nisaea
Nauplia
Lechaeum
Pitsa
Sicyon Isthmia
Cenchreae
Helice
Corinth
Nemea
Calauria
Epidaurus
Tenea
Prosymna
Hermione
Troezen
Halieis
Phlius
Ornea
Mycenae
Tiryns Sepeia
Mantinea
Argos
Hysiae
Thyrea
Tegea
Prasiae
Mt.Parnon
Therapne
Mt. Taygetus
Sparta
Amyclae
Limnae
Olympia
Pisa
Pylos
R. Alpheus
R.Helisson
R. Eurotas
C.Malea
Cythera
C.Taenarum

Rhium

MEGARID
CORINTH
ARGOLID
THYREATIS
LACONIA
ACHAEA
ARCADIA
PISATIS
ELIS
TRIPHYLIA
MESSENIA
PELOPONNESE

0   miles   50
0   km   80

3 The Peloponnese and the Isthmus of Corinth

come under the control of the legendary Temenus and his son Cissus, reputedly descendants of the most renowned of all Greek heroes Heracles, the son of Zeus and Alcmene, doer of valorous deeds for humankind, averter of evil and trusty helper.[1] The Dorians liked to describe their immigration as the 'Return' of the Heraclids (Chapter 1 and note 7; suggesting that they were following in the path of Heracles' son Hyllus, and were therefore descended from the hero himself); and this was a particularly popular fiction at Argos, which cherished the tradition that Heracles' birthplace was Tiryns nearby.

As a matter of archaeological and historical fact, the site of Argos shared in a widespread disruption of the Argolid in c.1200 BC; the Dorian invasion can be attributed to c.1075/1050. In this latter period a group of scattered hamlets amalgamated to form an urban centre beneath the Larissa citadel, and this, in due course, replaced vanished Mycenae as the principal city of the Argolid; it was as well placed as its predecessor to control the plain, and its water supply was better. Begun on a modest scale, the settlement developed slowly over the next 300 years. By the ninth century a small community had put down stable roots, and by 700 it had been transformed into a larger town, incorporating additional Dorians from the smaller towns of the region. Almost half the known Dark Age burials of the Argive plain (now known to be much more numerous than was previously thought) are at Argos itself.

The early character and development of the town are known to us only in the vaguest terms, because the local histories of Socrates and Deinias (both probably of the Hellenistic period) have not survived. It is clear, however, that Argos became the earliest centre of Dorian power, not only in the Argolid, but in the entire Peloponnese. Its earlier population was subordinated but not enslaved, becoming *perioeci*, dwellers around (cf. Chapter 1, and note 61), who were sometimes known as Orneates, perhaps because the village of Ornea was the first locality in the region that the Dorians brought under their control; and these *perioeci* were also called *gymnetes* or *gymnesioi*, light-armed troops. Some Dorians from Argos subsequently moved on to occupy Epidaurus upon the Saronic Gulf.[2]

The great schools of Mycenaean art had come to an end with the destruction of their Bronze Age centres, but unpretentious Sub-Mycenaean pottery was subsequently manufactured at the surviving hamlets, later giving way, apparently with some abruptness, to the handsomer Protogeometric style, which Argos (before Corinth or Thebes) learned from the Athenians. Subsequently, the Argives developed their own school of Geometric pottery, second only to Athens, evolving, soon after 800, an independent style characterized by a range of rustic panels and figure scenes (some of the first to be seen in Greece).

But early Argos was particularly prominent in metal-work. Before the tenth century was over it already possessed its own silver refinery, undertaking the cupellation of the metal, and Herodotus described the hammered and cast bronze griffin heads projecting from the rims of early cauldrons as 'Argolic',[3] indicating that this was the principal centre, or at least one of the principal centres, of their manufacture. Such cauldrons were often cult-utensils, of which the employment at Argos was carefully regulated by law: and they were frequently dedicated in the Argive Heraeum.

The city owed much of its renown, from a very early date, to the proximity of this Heraeum, the famous sanctuary of the goddess Hera. There had been Neolithic and Bronze Age forerunners of the shrine at Prosymna nearby, and Hera had been a local fertility deity, an 'earth-mother' whose epithet 'ox-eyed' (Boopis) recalls an epoch of animal worship. Then, later, she was brought together with Zeus as his consort in a typical 'divine marriage' of Bronze Age and Indo-European deities (the name of the local hero Heracles means 'Hera's glory').

The most ancient Heraeum stood on the highest of a series of terraces built on the hillside as it rises from the Argive plain, and was one of the first temples in Greece to be peripteral (surrounded by columns). An epoch-making structure both in dimensions and in character, it possessed a terracotta-tiled roof instead of the customary timber and thatch, and may also have been the earliest shrine to display stone columns, though at first only the bases of the columns were made of stone, with wooden columns above. This original Heraeum may have dated from the eighth century; the date of a terracotta model of a building found on the site, perhaps representing the temple, is not quite certain, but the model was probably made before 700 (like others found at Piraeum [Perachora] near Corinth [section 2]). And the uppermost terrace of the temple itself likewise seems to belong to a similar date. Its dimensions indicate the power and wealth that Argos must already have possessed in order to embark on such an operation.

This being so, the sanctuary, which possessed such importance that Hellanicus and Thucydides later employed its list of priestesses as a chronological framework for Greek history in general, can be reasonably included among the achievements of Argos' outstanding king and personage, Pheidon.

As early as the time of Temenus' grandson, it was believed, Argive monarchs had been reduced to the status of mere figureheads. But if so, this process underwent a reversal when the throne came to be occupied by Pheidon. Owing to the divergent myths and legends encrusting his career, ancient writers differed as to whether he was the sixth, seventh or tenth in descent from Temenus, a difference that would locate him at a wide range of contradictory dates extending between 900 and 700/650 BC. Modern writers, however, have mostly narrowed this disagreement down to a choice between the early eighth and early seventh centuries. The later of these two attributions suits most aspects of his known activities better, and if, as seems reasonable, we may amend an allusion by Pausanias to the king's interference at Olympia from the 'VIIIth' Olympiad (748) to the 'XXVIIIth' (668),[4] it is this seventh-century date that can be accepted.[5]

Pheidon seems to have been a hereditary monarch who exceeded his constitutional position by assuming autocratic powers, or, as Aristotle put it, he was 'a king who became a tyrant'.[6] By occupying this role of tyrant–dictator, it was he (unless he had unknown Ionian predecessors) who launched a phase of Greek, and especially north Peloponnesian, history which was characterized by such dictatorships. To speak of his 'Argive empire' would probably be an exaggeration; but his achievements seem to have been remarkable, and it was generally recognized that, under his rule, Argos enjoyed greater power and prosperity than ever before or since.

Proclaiming the recovery of 'the domain of Temenus', he first completed the reunification of the Argive plain, and occupied the island of Aegina (Chapter 2, section 6), at this time the most important trading centre in the vicinity (thus initiating the belief, denied by numismatists, that he 'invented coinage' at the Aeginetan mint). Then, if we adopt the chronology accepted here, it was he who may have led his people to a decisive victory over the Spartans at Hysiae (c.669), perhaps involving the repulse of a Spartan invasion. This success enabled the Argives to extend their influence into the western regions of the Peloponnese, where Pheidon apparently took over the management of the Olympic Games from Elis and restored it to Pisa (section 6 below). It may also have been at this time that Argives colonized Curium in Cyprus.

Although the evidence is uncertain, Pheidon's successes were probably due to his pioneer possession of the hoplite (heavy infantry) troops of which the existence in many Greek city-states revolutionized their early history (Chapter 1). The hoplite double-gripped shield was known as 'Argive' or 'Argolic' because the Argives were said to have invented it[7] – an assertion which, even if incorrect, suggests that they at first enjoyed a near monopoly of its manufacture – and a warrior's splendid grave of c.725–700 excavated at Argos contained well-developed hoplite armour, notably a bell-shaped breastplate and corslet and a heavy helmet of Assyrian type.

The hoplites' armour was a complex heritage, but Argos evidently played a pre-eminent part. Moreover, although at the time of the Argive burial phalanx tactics had not, it would seem, been substantially developed, Argos is likely to have played a leading part in its subsequent evolution, as in the earlier creation of hoplite arms. Pheidon, according to this supposition, reigned at a formative and decisive moment in the process; and under his leadership the Argive troops at Hysiae may have provided one of the earliest successful examples of this long-lasting form of Greek warfare. Such a development, certainly, would provide the explanation of Pheidon's triumphs that seems to be required. It may well be, also, that the new phalanx under his control, perfected upon the broad Argive plain to which its tactical methods were suited, was the partly or mainly middle-class force that enabled him to maintain his authority over the Argive nobles. With victories such as Hysiae in mind, a poet in the Palatine Anthology pays a tribute to the outstanding excellence of the warriors of Argos.[8]

Although, as we saw, it would not be true to say that Pheidon struck the first Greek coins at Aegina, it is likely enough (as was also reported) that he dedicated to Hera of Argos the spits (*obeliskoi*) which had hitherto served as a medium of exchange and precursor of coinage: fragmentary spits have been unearthed in association with the late-eighth-century Argive panoply of armour, as well as in the Heraeum itself. Moreover, we learn of seventh-century dedications of a fistful (*drachma*) of such spits to Hera – the wealth of this late Geometric period being expressed, in the Peloponnese, in terms of iron.

The political power of Argos, however, does not appear to have survived Pheidon for any appreciable length of time; perhaps it was checked by the rise of Corinth (whose dictatorship was said to have been inspired and prompted by Pheidon). Nor did the Argive autocratic government survive Pheidon for long; at about the end of the century the kingship was defunct, and was replaced by the rule of an aristocratic or oligarchic junta.

During the period that followed, Argos established an artistic ascendancy exemplified by two huge stone figures of early sixth-century date at Delphi, identified by name as the Argive heroes Cleobis and Biton; the figures are signed by their compatriot Polymedes(?).[9] Politically, however, the government was less successful, proving incapable of uniting the Argolid, much less the entire Peloponnese. In particular, the dictator Cleisthenes of Sicyon (*c.*600–570) took

steps against Argos' claims to regional supremacy, erasing all venera-
tion of its hero Adrastus; and the elevation of the Nemean Games, at
which Adrastus was especially honoured, seems to have been Argos'
retaliatory gesture.

For those Games, held at the believed scene of Heracles' First
Labour (the killing of the Nemean Lion), were under the control of the
small town of Cleonae, which lay on the northern border of the Argolid
and was under Argive domination. The local festival had existed earlier, and indeed its antique origin was attributed to Adrastus himself
(or to Heracles); but at first the contests had merely been of local
significance. Now, in 573, they were elevated to Panhellenic status,
thus becoming the fourth and last of the great Games – an Argive act
intended as a counter-measure to the hostile behaviour of Sicyon.
Henceforward, the Nemean Games took place in alternate years, with
crowns of wild celery as their prizes.

The main problem of the Argives was their endemic bad relationship
with Sparta, a deep-rooted rivalry which (despite arguments to the
contrary) has been traced back as far as the eighth century, and, in a
more serious form, to the seventh. In the years following 560, when
Argos, according to Pausanias, had inspired the Spartans' alarm by
expelling the population of the coastal town of Nauplia,[10] they
launched a declared policy of protecting other Peloponnesian states
against such encroachments, and invaded the Argolid in c.546.

The extraordinary Battle of the Champions then took place, at
Thyrea in the disputed east-coast territory of Thyreatis. According to a
formula devised by the authorities of the Argive Heraeum, 300 Argives
fought against 300 Spartans (an economical military formula of which
sufficient use, perhaps, has not been made in modern times). Two
Argive warriors and one Spartan survived, and both sides claimed the
victory, so that a subsequent general engagement could not after all be
avoided. After heavy losses on both sides, the Spartans were the
winners, and the Argives cut their hair short in mourning, for their
claims to Peloponnesian supremacy had been frustrated.

But not for ever, or in every field, since a bronze-worker, Ageladas
(c.520/512), achieved renown; a flute-player, Sacadas, was the most
famous performer of the century; and, according to one theory, songs in
honour of the sufferings of Adrastus were among the forerunners of
Attic tragedy. The political influence of Argos, too, began to revive,
encouraged by the failure of Sparta's interventions at Athens in the last
decade of the sixth century. In c.494, however, the Spartan king
Cleomenes I landed an army on the coast of the Argolid near Tiryns,
and in the ensuing battle at Sepeia 6,000 Argive soldiers were slain.

The Argives, in desperation, mobilized their *perioeci* and other non-citizens. But their defeat, even graver than the setback at Thyrea, had virtually eliminated them for a generation, and they were never a major power again.

2 CORINTH

Corinth stood beside the isthmus at the north-eastern extremity of the Peloponnese, controlling its communications with the rest of mainland Greece. On the west side of the isthmus lay the Gulf of Corinth (leading to the Ionian and Adriatic Seas), and to its east the Saronic Gulf, an indentation of the Aegean.

The ancient urban centre was on the slopes of Acrocorinth, an impregnable acropolis situated six miles west of the isthmus, two miles inland from the harbour-town of Lechaeum on the Gulf of Corinth, and eight miles from Cenchreae, a second port on the Saronic Gulf.

The site of Acrocorinth, dominating a small but fertile and populous coastal plain, was inhabited from the Neolithic epoch, but during the later Bronze Age seems to have been eclipsed by Korakou on the coast, which may be the 'wealthy Corinth' of Homer's *Iliad*,[11] dependent on the kings of Mycenae. Equated with the otherwise unknown city of Ephyra, Corinth was related in Greek myth to Sisyphus, the folklore master-thief, condemned for ever to roll a stone up a hill, from which it always rolled down again; and another mythical hero of the place was Bellerophon (rider of the winged horse Pegasus), whose links with southern Asia Minor reflect trading relations with that region. As the Mycenaean civilization gradually collapsed, Dorians migrated into the area in about the eleventh century BC and conquered Corinth, under the leadership, according to tradition, of Aletes, whose descendants then successively occupied the Corinthian throne.

During the eighth century, perhaps in its early years, Corinth was urbanized by the amalgamation of eight adjacent villages, followed by the early coalescence of many other settlements, too – on either side of the isthmus – whose inhabitants welcomed this protection from the piracy endemic in the region. Non-Dorians in the area were reduced to a serf-like subordination under the name of 'Wearers of Dogskin Caps'.

Rapidly developing the export of their Geometric pottery, the Corinthians established a settlement on the Ionian (Adriatic) island of Ithaca (*c.*800), and colonies (believed to have been approximately simultaneous in *c.*733) at Corcyra (Corfu, further north where that sea is almost at its narrowest), and Syracuse (Siracusa) in eastern Sicily. These foundations, undertaken with the approval of Delphi, were the nuclei of the Corinthians' extensive colonial network, with which they maintained an unusually close connection.[12]

At the period which witnessed the establishment of these two colonies, or a little earlier, they also annexed the northern part of their own isthmus (the southern section of the Megarid), in order to safeguard their maritime traffic. In this area, at Piraeum (Perachora), have been found the remains of a building of eighth-century date which throws light on the most ancient history of Greek architecture and Corinth's evidently very early role in its development. This was an apsidal structure, which evidently possessed painted rubble (wattle and daub) walls, a thatched roof, a gable and a porch. To judge from early dedications, it was, or was associated with, a sanctuary of Hera Akraia and Hera Limenia, whose precinct has been identified a hundred yards away. A terracotta model of a simply designed shrine, now dated to c.725–720 (and therefore approximately contemporary with a counterpart from the Argive Heraeum, section 1 above), has been discovered in the buildings, and restored (with some conjectural elements).

The sixth Corinthian king of Aletes' dynasty bore the name of Bacchis, and his descendants were the Bacchiad line. After five members of this house, however, had supposedly reigned, the Bacchiad clan as a whole, comprising intermarrying families who all – perhaps with questionable authenticity – claimed descent from the royal family, abolished the monarchy, traditionally in c.747, and established their own aristocratic government. Under this regime, membership of the citizen Assembly was restricted to no more than 200 members of their own clan, under the direction of a council of eighty (with a steering committee of eight) and a yearly president. Strabo stressed the thoroughness with which, first as kings and then as an aristocratic junta, these Bacchiads, 'a rich and numerous and illustrious family ... maintained their domination for nearly two hundred years, and without disturbance reaped the fruits of their trading'.[13] The Bacchiad aristocracy employed Corinthian lawyers from its own ranks, Pheidon (not the Argive) and Philolaus, to define and justify its own privileged position (Philolaus legislated on the size of families, in order to preserve them).

The epic poet Eumelus, the leading Peloponnesian bard of his time (c.725 or the following century), himself belonged to the same Bacchiad clan and apparently wrote a 'history' of its earlier kingship, founded on a novel use of archival and legal material which was no doubt doctored to magnify the interests of his house. He also wrote a Prosodion (Processional Song) for a Messenian choir sent to Delos. In addition, Eumelus showed a precocious interest in the Black Sea region, which although colonized by Miletus interested the Corinthians as well.

For they, under Bacchiad guidance, were intent on making the most of their geographical position. With this in mind, they constructed a fleet, exploited their colonies as far as these allowed them to, developed – as Strabo observed – their commercial activities (entrusted for the most part to resident or visiting aliens), and derived the most abundant profits of all from the exaction of transit tolls on freight across their isthmus, thus amassing wealth, by Greek standards, on a legendary scale.

'The Corinthians', according to Herodotus, 'least of all have a prejudice against craftsmen' (Chapter 1, note 29). They produced ivory, bronze and perhaps stone statuettes, and excelled in the modelling of moulded figurines. Line-drawing, too, Pliny the elder reports,[14] was invented by a Corinthian named Cleanthes – unless an Egyptian, or Greek in Egypt, named as Philocles deserved the credit, or a man from the ancient city of Sicyon, eleven miles north-west of Corinth – and 'some say painting was discovered at Sicyon, others at Corinth'. This is a tradition which evidence seems to support, as far as the Corinthians are concerned, for they took a decisive lead in producing and exporting a remarkable, long-unchallenged series of pottery styles, known successively as Protocorinthian and Corinthian, which were initiated in the later eighth century, reached their zenith early in the sixth, and continued to hold the field until c.550. The clear, whitish clay of Corinth, burned pale green or buff, was coated with a shiny pigment, which provided a lustre varying from black to bright orange, painted with silhouette designs (sometimes displaying long-disused techniques of incision), and decorated with a swinging, swirling riot of curvilinear patterns.

These vases formed a characteristic feature of the orientalizing movement diffused through Greece by the revival of communications with centres on the Syrian coast (Chapter 6, section 4), where Corinthian pots, as excavations confirm, dominated the scene from the first quarter of the seventh century. Syrian pottery, however, was not imitated by these Corinthian artists, since they did not find it interesting. But they eclectically derived many motifs, with original amendments, from the details of bronzes and sculptures and ivories and no doubt textiles (although these have not survived) from near- and middle-eastern regions of which the products came to the Syrian coastlands. The Corinthians favoured the depiction of animals – goats, deer, dogs, birds and lions (in Syrian and then the showier Assyrian guise), as well as sphinxes and griffins and monsters representing the untamed

demonic powers encompassing mankind. For a long time they preferred this sort of subject-matter to the human scenes that were
being cautiously introduced at Athens and elsewhere.

Some of the finest Protocorinthian pots, which evolved rapidly in
the early and middle years of the seventh century, are tiny scent and
oil bottles (*aryballoi*), adorned with disciplined designs displaying a
neat and refined miniature delicacy. Then followed a phase during
which a Protocorinthian masterpiece, the Macmillan Painter's Chigi
Vase (*olpe*) of *c*.640 (in the Villa Giulia Museum at Rome), illustrated the greater possibilities of large-scale compositions,
unprecedentedly employing four colours, and depicting, now,
human beings, boldly combined in close-knit groups.

The simpler, 'black-figure' colouring, in which black designs were
painted upon a background left in the clay's natural colour, had also
by this time been invented at Corinth (though it later became much
more famous at Athens). The years round 625–620 witnessed the
development of the 'Ripe' Corinthian style;[15] its massive success
inspired cruder and flashier techniques, although the drawing of
human figures improved.

One wine-jar (*oinochoe*) of the later seventh century, an Etruscan
piece from Tragliatella imitating a lost Corinthian original, shows
two of the most explicit heterosexual love scenes in Greek art, and
abstractions of female genitals had appeared on Corinthian *aryballoi*.
Such designs were in keeping with the Corinthians' lasting reputation for sexual indulgence and laxity. This ill-fame was largely
based on their cult of Aphrodite (identified with the Syrian Astarte-
Ashtoreth), who bore the name Urania, as in Cyprus, and was
served, as in Asia Minor, by temple-harlots, whose activities were
believed to contribute to the fertility of the natural world. The international reputation of Corinthian prostitutes remained unequalled.[16]

Shortly before 600 Corinth reached its commercial climax,
flooding the western world with its products and re-exporting Egyptian terracottas, scarabs and amulets in exchange for Sicilian wheat
and Etruscan metals. Corinthian wares also penetrated into the interior of the Balkan peninsula, and reached the Greek cities of Asia
Minor, although Miletus, for example, made its own rival products.
Moreover, Corinth's own colony, Corcyra (apparently under a
government of democratic intentions, since an inscription of *c*.600
mentions *damos*, the people, four times in five hexameter lines),
became another, and often hostile, competitor, heavily defeating the
mother-city in a naval battle at Sybota (*c*.664 or later), which, to
Thucydides, signalized the beginning of Greek naval warfare. However, it was not until the commercial lead passed to the Athenians,

in c.550/540, that Corinth's drive to produce, and export, its own pottery flagged.

Its first, pioneer, temple of Apollo (later replaced), excelling all its known predecessors elsewhere both in length and in breadth, seems to date from c.700 or a little later, and a shrine of Poseidon at Isthmia (Krias Vrysi), on the territory annexed from Megara, goes back approximately to the same time; scraps of painted plaster show that it was adorned with large figures of animals. These two temples show what seems to be a quite sudden, novel appearance both of monumental buildings and of the Doric architectural style, representing Corinth's most important and original single contribution to Greek artistic civilization.[17]

Not long after these developments the city came under the control of a family and dynasty of dictators – the earliest of such 'tyrants' known from a reasonable amount of historical evidence (in addition to an even larger than usual incrustation of legends). The founder of this house, Cypselus, removed the Bacchiad aristocracy from power and ruled in its place. He himself was a fringe member of the same clan, for, although his father Eetion was an outsider of pre-Dorian stock, his mother Labda (who was lame) belonged to the Bacchiad house. Cypselus may have held the presidency of the oligarchic Assembly, justifying his subsequent usurpation accordingly; while at the same time he quoted the precedent, and seems to have enlisted the support, of Pheidon of Argos. In addition, he offered rich dedications to win goodwill at Olympia and Delphi, where his Corinthian treasury was the oldest and wealthiest of such buildings, enriched by the munificence of Lydia (Appendix 1).

Ruling Corinth for some three decades, from c.658/657 to c.628 (despite modern reattributions to dates thirty or forty years later), Cypselus killed a number of Bacchiad leaders and expelled other members of the clan, distributing their lands (in fulfilment of a slogan popular in a number of Greek cities) among his supporters, who included not only a surviving section of the aristocracy but many of the poor. This increased landownership meant an equivalent rise in the number of citizens, and either Cypselus or his son (unless this was the work of the subsequent oligarchy) organized them in a novel, anti-aristocratic distribution among eight territorial tribes, cutting across the hereditary 'brotherhood' units or phratries. At about the same time, the city's laws were rescued from their earlier, arbitrary Bacchiad interpretations, and made public in a codified and probably revised form. Cypselus used the word *dikaiosei*, claiming to have 'put Corinth to rights' or 'given it justice' or 'formulated a set of rules'.

Some called him bloodthirsty, but later writers described him as mild. He found it possible to dispense with a bodyguard, but is likely to have been backed by an efficient, heavy-armed hoplite army, on the lines already and recently, it would appear, established by Pheidon of Argos (section 1 above, and note 7). Whether hoplite support was actually available early enough to help Cypselus win the throne is doubtful, but at all events it helped to keep him there: a hoplite phalanx is shown vigorously going into battle upon the Chigi Vase of c.640, and excavations have uncovered an early, rudimentary example of a 'Corinthian' helmet, part of the hoplite's equipment. Cypselus probably succeeded Pheidon of Argos as one of the prime employers and exploiters of the hoplite phalanx, and this, largely manned by the rising commercial and agricultural middle class, must have formed one of the principal pillars of his regime.

The surviving Bacchiads, who had fled from Cypselus' rule in Corinth, took refuge at Corcyra, but they found themselves hemmed in by an extension of Corinth's control over the Gulf of Ambracia (Arta). That was brought about by the settlement of dependent Corinthian colonies, under the leadership of three of the king's sons, at Ambracia and Anactorium and on the island of Leucas, and further north at Epidamnus (Dyrrhachium, Durrës) in Illyrian territory.[18] This western expansion was the most lasting and valuable political legacy of the dictators of Corinth; and, in the economic field, it enabled Corinthian pottery to find its way, in large quantities, to Greek south Italy and Sicily.

Under Cypselus' son Periander (c.628–586, according to the preferred 'higher' chronology), this export traffic continued to increase, and the city reached the zenith of its prosperity. He laid a drag-way (diolkos) across the isthmus in order to enable ships to be hauled from one sea to the other (thus enlarging his revenue from tolls), and his fleets, based on the harbours of Cenchreae and Lechaeum, sailed the two seas at will.

Corinth invented at least one, and very possibly all three, of the principal successive forms of Greek warship, the penteconter, bireme and trireme. It remains disputed to what extent these innovative Corinthian naval designers, who must be credited with some of the few qualitative technological advantages attributable to the Greeks, belonged to the age of the dictators or to the preceding or subsequent periods; but their creations, at one stage or another, must have played a considerable part in building up the strength and power of Cypselus and Periander. Traders from Syria and Phoenicia helped to provide the expertise that enabled the constructors of Corinthian vessels to get to work. They were also able to draw on the experience of earlier, ninth-century, Greek shipbuilding known to us from paintings on pots.

At all events, confronted with the need to create duplicate navies on both seas, the Corinthians established their maritime supremacy for centuries. Before 700, versions of the penteconter began to appear on their vases, and during the following century this type of warship became predominant. They were fast-moving ships strengthened at the prow by a pointed, single-pronged, tapering ram (*embolos*), sheathed in bronze. The penteconter accommodated twenty-four rowers, in two lines, and two steering oars at the stern. This was a menacing instrument of war, but it was too long and slender, and therefore perilously unseaworthy, as well as hard to manoeuvre.

The eighth-century biremes incorporated a new and revolutionary idea. Their twenty-four oarsmen sat in two rows of benches, *one above the other*, twelve along the gunwale and twelve along the lower thwarts (rowing through ports in the hull), so that the length of the ship was not increased, indeed was actually diminished, while speed was improved. Reliefs of the Assyrian monarch Sennacherib (705–681) show that his Phoenician(?) sailors were already operating such vessels, which were more compact, sturdier and more seaworthy than the penteconter, and presented a smaller target to enemy rams. That, probably, was the eastern source from which Corinth derived the idea.[19] The four ships which, as we learn from Thucydides,[20] the Corinthian shipwright Ameinocles constructed for the Samians were probably biremes. It is disputed, however, whether he visited Samos while Corinth was still ruled by an aristocratic government, in *c.*704, or fifty years later, when the dictator Cypselus had taken over.

The trireme that followed was explicitly described by Thucydides as a Corinthian invention.[21] His suggestion, however, that this too was pre-Cypselid, though it finds some support, has been queried, since no other evidence for this type of craft comes from a date earlier than the third quarter of the sixth century – though it is possible to reconcile the two dates by combining the theory of seventh-century invention with a late-sixth-century date for the general use of such ships. The trireme developed directly from the bireme but had room for twenty-seven oarsmen at each of two levels, plus the superimposition of a third row of thirty-one rowers on either side, seated three on a bench, with each rower pulling an individual oar (not two or three to an oar) and working it through a laterally projecting outrigger (*parexeresia*). Equipped with a bronze-covered ram that terminated in three prongs instead of one, each trireme was furnished with a light deck for the stationing of marines, who could number fourteen spearsmen and four archers. Twenty-five petty officers and five officers made up the full complement.

Sacrificing weight to mobility, the trireme improved on all its forerunners in speed, ramming force and manoeuvrability in the sheltered waters which were habitually chosen for sea battles. It was equally employable as ship of the line, or troop and horse transport, or convoy or dispatch vessel; and it proved ideal for amphibious operations because it was so light and easy to draw up on shore.

Yet the trireme did not, all the same, entirely displace earlier types of vessel, because its operation required expert skill and training which were difficult for city-states less rich than Corinth (and later Athens) to afford. Moreover, it lacked space – mainsails were left ashore before a battle – and could only carry a few days' rations on board; indeed, these ships were beached every night to enable their crews to eat and sleep. Besides, despite all that oarage and canvas could do, their low gunwales were vulnerable to bad weather and the open sea. Nevertheless, the development of the trireme in Corinthian shipyards created a decisive element in naval warfare for very many years to come.

Periander, who no doubt benefited from these discoveries, earned inclusion in the ranks of the Seven Sages. His court, at which the arts fulfilled a significant role, attracted the most famous poet and composer of the age, the almost legendary Arion, summoned from his home at Methymna on the island of Lesbos. Legends clustered round Arion's personality; Herodotus declared that he was the first man to write, name and sing dithyrambs.[22]

These were poems in honour of, though not necessarily about, the god Dionysus, whose cult Periander fostered because of its popular appeal. Originally crude and unorganized vintage songs, they evidently achieved artistic form and literary status in the hands of Arion, who converted them into swiftly moving, exciting hymns, sung and danced by a chorus of fifty boys wearing elaborate satyr-like costumes and impersonating their parts with mimetic gestures. In keeping with the belief, held by some, that Athenian tragedy (Chapter 1, section 4), went back to Peloponnesian rather than Attic origins, Arion's achievement caused him to be regarded as one of the forerunners or even founders of the dramatic art – which is likewise foreshadowed by the appearance of masked and padded dancers (associated with Dionysiac demons) on early sixth-century Corinthian vases, where they are seen performing scenes of a dramatic character.

Corcyra was brought to order by Periander's power – and reduced to the status of a dependency of Corinth – while new Corinthian colonies were founded at Apollonia (c.600), higher up the same coast in Illyrian territory (Chapter 8, section 1, and note 3), and at Potidaea, strategically located on the Aegean coast of Macedonia. Alliances were established with a number of Greek and other states, mainly those in the hands of dictators (notably Miletus, under the control of Thrasybulus), though republican Athens, too, was one of his allies.

Periander was a passionate man, who earned for the term 'tyrant' (dictator) the opprobrious and bloodthirsty significance it has borne ever since. This is because the upper classes of Corinth remembered that he had oppressed them more determinedly than his father, as well as killing his own wife and banishing his own son to Corcyra – of which the authorities, however, incurred his threatening displeasure, according to Herodotus, because they put the young man to death.[23] Periander's other sons also predeceased him, and he was succeeded by his nephew Psammetichus (named after Periander's Egyptian ally, King Psammetichus II), who was assassinated three years later, in c.581. And so Corinth's dictatorship came to an end. To celebrate its termination, the bones of dead Cypselids were cast out beyond the frontiers of Corinthian territory, and houses belonging to them were razed to the ground.

Their regime was succeeded, as so often happened when dictatorships fell, by an oligarchic government. At Corinth this lasted impressively for nearly 200 years, since the bulk of the citizens, deriving their revenues from landed estates (and augmenting them by trade), were content to preserve the traditional conservatism of a Dorian state with its preference for hierarchic good order. Although little is known about the character of this administration, it seems to have combined a narrow constitutional base (represented by a small, powerful board of officials, the *probouloi*, and a council limited to eighty members) with a more liberal property qualification for citizens (members of the Assembly) than had existed under the old Bacchiad aristocracy, because the new regime needed this extension to attract middle-class hoplites, who had supported the dictatorship. It was perhaps at this stage (c.581) that the Isthmian Games were established by the leading families, to celebrate the return of republican government.

The Games were held in honour of Poseidon, beside his seventh-century sanctuary at Isthmia. In c.560/540 the reconstruction of another major shrine of the same period, the temple of Apollo at Corinth itself, confirmed the leadership of that city, and of the north-eastern Peloponnese in general, in the evolution of Doric architecture. The new building had six columns at either end and fifteen on either side (seven remain), and displayed a new external colonnade and cult-image. Limestone (*poros*, covered by stucco painted red and black) was at first employed in place of wood in the outer parts of the building, and the roof was covered by yellow and black terracotta tiles. They were regarded as a Corinthian invention, and a shrine generally believed to have been a little earlier, the temple of Artemis at Corcyra, is likely to have been designed and executed by Corinthians. It possessed a sculptural pediment, recalling a widespread belief that Corinth was the original home of Greek sculpture, a claim supported by the lead its artists had earlier taken in the production of figurines in various media.

In spite of this apparent Corinthian architectural activity at Corcyra, it was during this same period that their revived oligarchy was obliged to relinquish definitively its control over the island, which became independent and hostile. Another Corinthian colony, Ambracia, followed the Corcyraean lead by likewise striking out on its own as an independent state, under a democratic government. With their other colonies, however, the Corinthians remained friendly, and this was particularly notable in the west, where they dispatched artists and craftsmen as far afield as Etruria (notably those accompanying Demaratus to Tarquinii in the early seventh century – Appendix 3).

Corinth also issued silver coins which were known as 'colts' or 'foals' (*poloi*) because of their representation of Bellerophon's winged horse Pegasus. This series was inaugurated in c.570, only about a quarter of a century after the earliest coinage in the mainland area, that of Aegina (Chapter 2, section 6); but the Corinthian standard differed markedly from Aegina's, being based on a much lighter drachma of only three grams (adapted, it would seem, from a version of the 'Euboic' standard). Corinth's geographical position ensured that the 'colts', like their Aeginetan and Attic–Euboic counterparts, played an important part in Mediterranean commerce. In a sense, it seems paradoxical that this coinage was instituted in c.575, since it was a mere quarter of a century later, or less, that the pottery of Corinth was losing its western monopoly to Athenian wares, a phenomenon which reflected the comparative eclipse of its trade. Nevertheless, since Athens did not yet possess the necessary shipping on its own account – as late as the 490s it had to borrow twenty ships from Corinth (against Aegina) – the Corinthians may have earned revenue by supplying the Athenians with ships for the transportation of their pottery and other goods.

Meanwhile, in its foreign policy, the Corinthian oligarchy was cautious. It confronted the growing power of the Spartans in the Peloponnese by forming a conciliatory alliance with them (c.525) against Argos. But in 506 the leaders of Corinth's army parted company with an expeditionary force led by Cleomenes I of Sparta when they realized he intended to intervene in order to restore the dictator Hippias at Athens, which, they felt, was too risky or undesirable an enterprise; and shortly afterwards they persuaded Sparta's other allies to withhold their support from any such action. However, what the Corinthian oligarchs let it be understood that they were doing was to 'mediate' between Cleomenes and Athens. This was their speciality, since in 519 they had mediated between Athens and Thebes, and in 491 they likewise acted as arbitrators between Syracuse and Gela.

Although they fought well in the subsequent Persian Wars, they had in fact entered upon a period of decline. But it was a gradual decline, from a glorious past – 'thou hast seen glory in all her beauty, all her forms,' declared Walter Savage Landor – and it was not until the second century BC that Antipater of Sidon could write: 'O Corinth, Dorian Corinth, where is thy beauty now?'[24]

3 SPARTA

Laconia, of which Sparta (Lacedaemon) was the capital, comprised the south-eastern region of the Peloponnese, bounded on the west by Messenia, on the north by Arcadia, and on the south and east by the Aegean Sea. The territory contains two longitudinal, protective mountain chains, Taygetus to the west and Parnon to the east, terminating respectively, at either extremity of the Laconian Gulf, in Capes Taenarum (Matapan) and Malea (beside the island of Cythera, now Kithira). The two ranges are separated by a forty-mile-long valley and plain, which contained the Eurotas (one of the few rivers in Greece to flow all the year round) and its tributaries, and formed the nucleus of a larger, more fertile and more nearly self-sufficient piece of land than any other Greek community possessed, containing abundant natural products, among which barley was the staple crop.

During the latter half of the second millennium BC, Laconia was a prosperous Bronze Age Mycenaean state, of which the mythological presentations in Homeric epic (Chapter 5, section 1) display Menelaus as the monarch; the abduction of his wife Helen, daughter of Zeus and Leda, by Paris the son of Priam, king of Troy, was declared to have been the cause of the Trojan War. Prehistoric remains at Sparta, however, beside the northern end of the Eurotas plain, are sparse, although, three miles to the south, there was a settlement at Amyclae – the location of a late-Mycenaean shrine of Hyacinthus, subsequently known as the beloved of Apollo – and another habitation centre existed at Therapne, two miles to the south-east, where the dwellings adjoined a shrine dedicated to a nature goddess and her keepers.

The Dorian invasions of Laconia were traditionally attributed to Eurysthenes and Procles, described as Heraclids (descendants of Heracles – see Chapter 1) and the sons of Aristodemus the brother of Temenus, founder of Argos; the new occupants were said to have received Sparta from Zeus himself, as his gift (hence the local worship of Zeus Tropaeus). Archaeology confirms that the Mycenaean civilization in the area seems to have crumbled gradually in c.1200–1100 – owing to wars or pestilences or famines or a combination of all three. And then, during the tenth century, amid prolonged shifts of population, a second wave of invaders or immigrants (unless, as an alternative theory propounds, they were a depressed native population that rose against its masters) settled in four or five villages round what later became the Spartan acropolis, as well as in certain other parts of Laconia which, although by that time thinly populated, still for a period remained independent of Sparta.

The earliest Laconian Protogeometric pottery (c.1000–950), of which specimens have been found at the lowest level of the shrine of Orthia (later assimilated to Artemis) at the village of Limnae, has been thought to mark the beginning of settled conditions, under Dorian occupation. Protogeometric shards at Amyclae, however, found at the holy place which was now dedicated to the Spartans' tribal god Apollo, display peculiar features that reflect a measure of continuity from the Bronze Age (even though the names of the deities had been changed), corresponding to a tradition that the place remained relatively undisturbed by the Dorian invasions.

At Therapne, on the other hand, there is at present no evidence for direct continuity. But there are remains of a sanctuary on three platforms, the Menelaion, from c.725: here the old Mycenaean nature goddess was resuscitated in the form of Helen, while the helpers of the goddess reappeared in the guise of her divine brothers the Dioscuri (Castor and Polydeuces [Pollux]) and her husband Menelaus. At about the same epoch, the altar of Artemis Orthia, hitherto made of earth, was replaced by a simple stone temple within a walled precinct, in which many statuettes and reliefs and ivory carvings (before and after 700) have been found.

By this time – indeed, it would seem, already from the ninth century onwards – the group of local settlements in the area had united to become the town of Sparta, 'not synoecized (coalesced)', as Thucydides observes, 'but settled according to villages' – and remarkably lacking, he points out, in the usual architectural features of a Greek city.[25] Nevertheless, Sparta, at the meeting-point of main routes to the world beyond, profited not only from the products of the surrounding plain but also – as a versatile smith's quarter confirms – from the possession of iron mines, which were a rarity in Greece and may have been worked from antique times.

These natural advantages ensured that, despite the underdeveloped appearance of the town itself, Spartan communal institutions evolved rapidly, so this can be regarded as the first *polis* of the classical type on the Greek mainland. However, its institutions were also peculiar. The early history of the Spartan city-state is an obscure and disputed subject, owing to the propagandist efforts of many later writers concerned to praise or dispraise its governmental and social system. Yet certain details are preserved by the poet Tyrtaeus (see below). And they are echoed, with a slightly different emphasis, by a document known as the Great Rhetra (later thought to be a Delphic oracle), which was supplemented and amended by a more conservative 'Rider', and subsequently described by Plutarch.[26] Too much importance, however, must not be ascribed to the Rhetra, since, as recent research indicates, it may not be of early- or middle-seventh-century date after all, but an invention of the fourth century BC.

All the same, the principal features of the Spartan constitution are clear. There were two jointly reigning kings, who belonged to the Agiad and Eurypontid families. Both these lines claimed descent from Heracles; and indeed, although that takes us back to legend and myth, the origin of the monarchy must have been very ancient, even if, as is probable, it did not assume the actual form in which we know it before *c.*650–600 BC. The powers of the two hereditary kings were primarily military; they provided a check upon one another[27] – that was a stabilizing factor – and were usually, though not always, obliged to compromise with the other forces in Sparta's political life.

Those forces included annually appointed ephors ('overseers'), eventually five in number, who were elected from citizens aged between thirty and sixty, held office for a single year, and enjoyed far-reaching executive, administrative and judicial powers. Indeed, the ephors' powers enabled them to supervise most of the daily life of the Spartan citizenry, and at the same time to limit the powers of the Council of Elders (*gerousia*). This latter body, allegedly founded with Delphic sanction, consisted of thirty elected members aged sixty or more.

They prepared the business of the Assembly (*apella*) beforehand. All Spartiates (free-born Spartan citizens) over thirty years of age were members of this Assembly. They were the 9,000 *homoioi*, Equals or Like Ones – equal in law and in theory, and each possessing his own allotment (*kleros*) of land. These Spartiate citizens or Equals comprised, and were synonymous with, the hoplite army, developed out of the old warrior bands. The five companies in which this hoplite force was organized (*lochoi*) were the military expression of the five Spartan tribes (*obai*), which replaced the old three Dorian tribes, the Hylleis, Dymaneis and Pamphyloi (retained for religious purposes only). This new Spartan army was better trained, more effective in its phalanx formation and more admired and feared, than any of its counterparts elsewhere in the Greek world, and seemed to justify the claim that the Spartans, improving on Argive models, were the true developers of the hoplite machine.[28]

The relative powers of the Spartan Council of Elders and Assembly have been extensively discussed and disputed (like those of their Athenian counterparts); they must, obviously, have varied from one epoch to another. On the one hand the authority of the Council's venerable members made it a safeguard against rash enterprises, and its preparation of the Assembly's business gave it a chance to influence the way things went. Yet the decisions of the Assembly, in the last resort, were binding, and it was its members, the Equals, who provided the infantry that made Sparta the dominant power for many miles around. So there was at most times, between these bodies, a delicately balanced equilibrium, which contributed to Sparta's strength.

This Spartan administration was described by some people, according to Aristotle, as a 'mixed system' combining monarchy, oligarchy and democracy.[29] But it was the extent to which the last-named of those three elements made its appearance that was especially notable. For the description of all Spartiates as Equals was not merely a euphemism. Inevitably, they were not equal in land-wealth, or in personal distinction. Yet they were, quite early on, equal in law and in status, as could not yet be said of any other Greek city. Here was a citizen body whose every member possessed legal rights (and obligations) overriding the personal authority of any single individual or group.[30] Thus in respect of basic equalities Sparta was the first authentic, thoroughgoing democracy among the Greeks or anywhere in the world, *as far as its citizens were concerned.*

Like all other Greek city-states, however, it only provided citizen status to a limited range of the population. And indeed at Sparta, as in a number of other communities elsewhere, it was not only women and slaves who were excluded. For there were also groups that consisted neither of citizens nor of slaves, but ranked intermediately between the two. These included the numerous *perioeci*, 'dwellers round about', who had kept their own towns, but renounced all independence. They engaged, however, in commerce, industry and navigation, as Spartiates did not. And in due course they also came to serve in the hoplite phalanx, though even this did not entitle them to become Equals. Furthermore, alongside, and beneath, the *perioeci* were the Helots, who (once again as in certain other states [Chapter 1, note 61]) led a serf-like existence, collectively owned by the Spartan community and paying (to individual Spartiates) a tribute equal to one-half of their crop, in return for an understanding that they would not be sold away from their homes. It has been suggested, although this is not entirely certain, that both categories, *perioeci* and Helots, were at least in part of pre-Dorian origin.

Although the stages by which such a complicated system evolved cannot (despite abundant attempts) be reconstructed, the process was clearly stimulated and accelerated by military events. These were concerned with Laconia's western neighbour Messenia, which after an important Bronze Age existence (led by Pylos) had been occupied by the Dorians, supposedly led by Cresphontes – an uncle of Sparta's legendary founders – but had remained independent of the Spartans. In the First Messenian War (*c.*740/730–720/710), however, Sparta partially achieved the conquest of the country – and grouped the Messenians together with the other Helots who lived in subjection to its rule.

This great increase in land wealth committed Sparta to a largely agricultural future. However, there was also some foreign trade and emigration, and one very rare example of colonial enterprise can be noted, since in 706, according to tradition, Taras (Tarentum, Taranto) in south-eastern Italy was founded by Spartans. The founders of the settlement, people said, were the 'Partheniai', products of liaisons between Spartan women – conducted while their husbands had been away at the war – and *perioeci* or Helots, although the story may be a fiction (perhaps explaining some geographical name), and the settlers may, in reality, have been dissidents (discontented by Messenian land distribution) whom the homeland wanted to get rid of, however little it could afford the loss of able-bodied men. In *c.*669 this shortage of manpower became prominent after the Spartans had received a severe setback at the hands of an Argive army at Hysiae. But the Second Messenian War, probably fomented by Argos (*c.*650–620?) – in which the Messenian resistance leader Aristomenes became traditionally known as Sparta's arch-enemy – was successfully crushed by Spartan victories which completed the conquest of the south-western Peloponnese. It was probably in response to this desperate crisis that the hoplite army, swelled by *perioeci*, assumed its unequalled dimensions and quality.

Nevertheless, far from meriting the reputation for uncultured militarism that they subsequently acquired, the early Spartans, from *c.*700–550, not only imported a wide range of luxury products but themselves excelled in a number of arts. Bronze-work, ivory carvings, terracotta reliefs and pottery were among these achievements. Moreover, the city was also the principal centre of Greek choral poetry and music, which attained its maximum development in Dorian lands, and was represented by at least two major seventh-century schools at Sparta.

The leader of one such school, the elegiac poet Tyrtaeus – who is likely to have been a Spartan citizen, although his renown prompted other cities to make subsequent counterclaims – wrote marching songs in epic language, modified by Doric elements, in order to rally the Spartiates, who were clearly in serious disarray at the time, against the rebel Messenians in the Second War. He was said to have held the office of general, and, as stated above, it is to him that we owe a skeleton description of the Spartan constitution, allegedly in the form of a Delphic oracle. His works were subsequently collected under the title of *Eunomia* (Law and Order), one of the catchwords of the epoch. In place of the *Iliad*'s ideal of the individual knightly champion, these poems praise the beginnings of the hoplite phalanx that guaranteed this *eunomia* and its civic ethic, fighting shoulder-to-shoulder collectively, as a team. After enumerating a list of personal advantages – royal blood, fine appearance, athletic ability, eloquent speech – the poet concludes that the supreme guarantee of manly virtue is courage in the face of the enemy.

Alcman, too, probably lived during the later years of the seventh century (though a later date has received some support), and seems to reflect the luxury, prosperity and relaxation conferred upon at least part of the Spartan population by the outcome of the Second Messenian War. He may have originated from Lydia or Ionia. But Sparta was where he worked, and it later claimed to be his birthplace. He was believed to have been a slave, granted freedom because of his cleverness – which was learned, frivolous and eccentric.

Alcman, like Tyrtaeus, played a major pioneer role in the creation of choral lyric. The most substantial of his surviving fragments comprises a hundred verses from a *Song of Maidens* (Partheneion), a glorification of the religious initiatory experiences of young women, sung and danced by ten of them to a goddess before dawn, at one of the great Spartan festivals. The atmosphere is that of a happy social occasion, and Alcman's loosely constructed verses seem to echo the conversation of the maidens who were the singers. He wrote love poems as well, about 'girls who cast glances that are more melting than sleep or death'; and indeed he acquired a reputation as the founder of erotic poetry. But the beauty of nature, too, fascinated him, so that his observation of the tranquil countryside was magical and moving – and unusual for centuries to come. Alcman felt sadness about old age: because he could no longer take part in the dance and was not like a kingfisher, which, when it becomes old, is carried over the waves by its mate.

Terpander of Antissa on Lesbos likewise worked at Sparta in the mid-seventh century. The fragments ascribed to him do not look very authentic, but he was said to have written 'nomes' (*nomoi*), in which he set his own and Homer's verses to music. They were to be sung as vocal solos accompanied by the lyre, which was a more elaborate instrument (*cithara*) than the *citharis* or *phorminx* which had first been employed for Homeric recitations. Another poet, Thaletas, who was also believed to have been a pioneer law-giver, migrated from Sparta to Gortyna in Crete; and during the sixth century Stesichorus of Himera and Theognis of Megara resided at the same city.

The temple of Artemis Orthia was rebuilt in *c.*570. Sparta's potters and painters produced wares of excellent quality, borrowing from Corinthian styles, but also displaying originality – for instance in a cup of *c.*600 decorated by black and purple fish, and in a design that showed King Arcesilaus II of Cyrene presiding over the loading of a ship with wool. Theodorus of Samos and Bathycles of Magnesia on the Maeander were among the leading Greek sculptors working at Sparta, and excellent bronze-work was still to be seen. (For the possibility that the Vix Crater [bronze mixing bowl] was Spartan, see below, Chapter 7, note 75.)

However, by the time of these achievements the *agoge*, the complex of austere, communal and totalitarian socio-military institutions for which Sparta became so famous, had already come into force and begun to exert its full effects. The system was associated with the name of the law-giver Lycurgus – said to have been a pupil of Thaletas – although, as was recognized in antiquity, he may have been a product of myth; as 'legislator' he received the cult-worship accorded to 'heroes' (many of whom were originally divine figures), and the Delphic oracle was said not to have known whether he was originally man or god.

The dates of the gradual introduction of the Spartan *agoge* have been much disputed; but the period around *c.*700/600 enjoys favour. Many of its features, as described by Xenophon and Plutarch, are of a primitive character, and display analogies with the customs of warrior tribes in other parts of the world. In particular, however, these institutions could be paralleled among other Greeks, the Cretans, from whom they were often believed to have been derived. But not all ancient authorities accepted this,[31] and the resemblances are, in fact, only due to a common primitive origin. The nucleus of the system, therefore, probably existed at Sparta since the earliest Dorian epoch. However, the discipline was presumably tightened, and enforced on all Spartiates, during or after the emergencies of the Second Messenian War. For these crises imposed a heavy strain on the political and social structure, necessitating, for example, a repressive intelligence system, involving the notorious secret police, the *krypteia*. This police network became an integral part of the *agoge*, since Helots may have outnumbered citizens by six to one – and were feared as potential rebels.

Every Spartan infant was examined shortly after birth by the 'elders of the tribesmen', who rejected weak or deformed babies and ordered them to be thrown over a cliff. By way of contrast to the emphasis on the family (*oikos*) found at Athens and elsewhere, those who passed the infancy test at Sparta were taken away from their families at the age of seven or eight, and enrolled as members of a 'herd' (like herds of horses or cattle, requiring domestication) under the control of a senior Spartiate. At thirteen they passed into another series of herds, and for the next fourteen years (characterized by year-groups with curious archaic names) they worked their way through state-controlled, state-oriented training curricula of an increasingly brutalizing nature.

Sinister details of these programmes are recorded. In no other city were boys so completely deprived of their homes and relatives. They were enrolled in a squad (*bua*) – part of a troop (*ila*) – commanded by an *eiren*, a youth serving as a prefect under a camp commandant (*paidonomos*); and later, at the age of twenty, they themselves reached the status of *eiren*, devoting their days to military service but not yet in possession of full citizenship. It was at this stage, perhaps, that they became eligible for one of the famous or notorious Spartan messes or dining-clubs (*pheiditia, sussitia*) – on which the entire social and military organization of the state came to depend. Each mess was about fifteen strong, and a single blackball was enough to veto or postpone election. For the wretched food that was provided (including a sort of haggis), each member was debited with a mess-bill, and failure to pay this – or, for that matter, to complete the training schedule – resulted in demotion from the Spartiate ranks to the status of Inferior, which involved a loss of political rights.

At the age of thirty they were admitted to the Assembly, but their lives continued to centre round the mess. These taciturn ('Laconic'), unquestioning and ruthless young men did no work, except training, athletics and fighting. They lived and fought with their mess-mates, and the grim, one-track, cohesive system, 'like an army camp', in which they were submerged – aiming at the single end of the national interest and survival – made them, for a long time, far the best soldiers in Greece.

Inevitably, however, the system produced a special brand of homo-sexuality. As elsewhere, there was a recognized relationship between the lover (*erastes*) and the younger loved one (*eromenos*). But in Sparta the role of the lover was almost official, for he was held accountable for the performance and behaviour of his loved one[32] – a system which Xenophon described as 'the perfect form of education'.[33] However, he rather surprisingly adds that any carnal relationship between the two was illegal. This was evidently the story spread from Sparta,[34] probably in an attempt to provide moral justification for the city's strange customs, but no such law is likely to have been respected in practice, though homosexual pairing among Spartans was not so exclusive as it became, for example, at Thebes.

Despite the prevailing homosexual ethos, a Spartan was expected to marry at about the age of twenty (late for Greece); bachelors were ridiculed, and suffered legal disabilities. But the barrack-room life of these citizens meant that their women were left a great deal to themselves, and in consequence enjoyed a freedom not experienced at other cities. They suffered, it is true, from vetoes on jewellery, cosmetics, scent and coloured clothes. The nature of the marriage ceremony, too, was startling. For the custom was for a Spartan bride to have her hair cut, and put on masculine clothes, whereupon she was carried off by force and laid on a hard bed in a room where she was left alone. Then in came the bridegroom, who had sexual intercourse with her briefly, before returning to the men's quarters.[35] Thereafter, the pair were only allowed to see each other in stealthy secrecy, often until the first child was born.

However, apart from such aberrations – indicative of a society more at home with all-male relationships – the Spartans treated their women unusually well, since with the state constantly at war their biological role as bearers of Sparta's all-important children was seen to deserve as much respect as that of the father. So they, like the men, were permitted and encouraged to undergo physical training – perhaps in the nude, or perhaps not – and they engaged also in musical activities, but were spared the domestic chores and weaving and woolwork customary elsewhere among the Greeks. Athenians considered this freedom shameless, and criticized the costume worn by these ladies, the *peplos*, with slit skirts which showed substantial portions of their thighs.

Spartan women also enjoyed unusually ample property rights, remained free for a long time to marry late and whom they liked, enjoyed exemption after marriage from the crippling laws restricting the rights of wives, managed their absent husbands' affairs, spoke up freely, and were believed to engage in husband-sharing and to take on other lovers as well (including young men, when their husbands were old, and Helots when their husbands were away fighting, according to the foundation-story of Taras). Such adultery is not unlikely, owing to the continuous and urgent need to maintain and increase the Spartan birthrate.

But if women, apart from the sinister marriage ritual, appear to have gained from Sparta's disciplinary system, in other respects it suffocated development. In particular, the city's archaic, self-sufficient institutions kept it lagging behind the rest of Greece in economic and financial development. Thus primitive iron spits, employed – as at Argos and other Greek cities – to provide rudimentary units of account before the introduction of coinage, continued to hold the field at Sparta (until as late as the fourth century).[36] The iron was mined on the southern spurs of Mounts Taygetus and Parnon, and silver money was prohibited – owing to its corrupting effects – so that trade had to be carried on by barter. And eventually (not immediately) this persistence in archaism, together with the narrow attitudes implanted by the social and educational system, caused a decline not only in material refinement but in the literary and visual arts as well (though first-class bronze-work still continued even after 500).

The sixth century, which witnessed major developments in Sparta's rigorous *agoge*, was also the time of forward steps in its international relations. Many of these happenings can be attributed to Chilon – later regarded as one of the Seven Sages – who was the most famous of all ephors and may, indeed, have done much to shape or reshape that office to equal and rival the dual kingship.

In their frontier wars the Spartans were generally successful.[37] But Tegea in Arcadia defeated them (*c*.590/580), so during a truce they turned their attention to propaganda instead, secretly digging up from Tegean soil, and removing, the bones of a very large man, whom they proclaimed to have been the legendary Orestes, son of Agamemnon – and master in his day, it was said, of the entire Peloponnese. Thereafter, claiming to lead and favour not only Dorians but also non-Dorians (typified by the 'Achaean' Orestes), the Spartans turned the tables on Tegea. Instead of seizing its territory, however, they astutely formed a defensive alliance. This marked the inauguration of a new policy (praised by the Delphic oracle), of which the declared aims were the liberation of other city-states from autocratic dictators ('tyrants') and, in particular, protection against Argos, which had for so long been the leading power of the Peloponnese and was still a dangerous competitor.

This line of propaganda proved successful, and by the middle of the century, after taking the precaution of befriending King Croesus of Lydia (Appendix 1), Sparta had created a powerful military and federal coalition. It is known today as the 'Peloponnesian League'. Since, however, the League was administered by the Spartan Assembly and a Congress of Allied States, the ancients accurately described it as 'the

Lacedaemonians (Spartans) and their allies'.[38] The widely praised Spartan attacks on dictators in other cities, of whom quite a number – even allowing for patriotic exaggeration – were overthrown by the initiative of Sparta and its League, resulted in the installation of a network of friendly oligarchies. Relying on these partisans, the Spartans were ready, in 546, to invade the Argolid, and after an inconclusive Battle of the Champions at Thyrea (300 on either side; cf. section 1 above), the general hoplite engagement that followed resulted in a victory for the Spartans. This success secured their frontiers for a generation, led to the annexation of border districts and the island of Cythera, and gained Sparta recognition as the leading power of Greece, far beyond what the size of its population warranted.

This forward policy was adventurously pursued by Sparta's forceful, ingenious but violently undiplomatic King Cleomenes I (c.519–490) of the Agiad line. Claiming like Chilon to be 'not a Dorian but an Achaean', Cleomenes sought to extend Spartan suzerainty even beyond the Peloponnese and the Corinthian isthmus, and in pursuance of this policy he expelled the dictator Hippias from Athens (510). But his three subsequent attempts to set up a pro-Spartan regime there – including a concerted effort with Chalcis and Boeotia (507–506), proved unsuccessful, owing to the obstructive tactics of his fellow monarch Demaratus, abetted by the Corinthians. Next, Argos attempted recovery and revenge. However, a complete Spartan victory at Sepeia near Tiryns (c.494) confirmed the relative positions of the two states for evermore. So the net result of Cleomenes' dramatic deeds, despite all the vicissitudes of his career, was the strengthening of Sparta.

Yet his failure to produce male heirs put him in a weak position, and in 490/88 he came to an unhappy end. First, his attempt to punish Aegina (Chapter 2, section 6) for 'Medism' or pro-Persian sympathy – the first time, incidentally, that he showed any appreciation of the Persian danger – was once again thwarted by Demaratus. Then Cleomenes persuaded (or, as it was said, bribed) the Delphic oracle to declare Demaratus illegitimate, had him deposed, and went with the new king Leotychidas to arrest the Aeginetan leaders. But the enterprise went wrong, and Cleomenes had to escape his personal enemies at home by fleeing to Arcadia, where he raised a force against his own city. Recalled to Sparta, he was put under arrest by his own family, and stabbed himself to death.

Although these events happened just outside the chronological boundaries of the present book, they are relevant, as well, to the earlier parts of Cleomenes' reign, because, according to Herodotus, it was a widely held belief that he suffered from madness.[39] The historian is admittedly unfair to the king (relying too much on the views of his older half-brothers, who resented him as an intruder), and the Spartan opinion that he went off his head because Scythian envoys taught him to drink wine unmixed with water need not necessarily be true. But acceptance of the view that he was mentally unstable would help to explain some of the oscillations of his reign. Yet his talents were exceptional; and they had brought him more power than any Spartan monarch had ever possessed before.

4 SICYON

Sicyon ('town of the cucumbers'), about eleven miles north-west of Corinth, stood on a spacious high tongue of land near the foot of two broad plateaux, at the meeting-point of the two deep gorges of the Rivers Asopus and Helisson. One of these plateaux constituted the city's acropolis. Inhabited during the late Bronze Age, Sicyon appeared in the *Iliad* as a dependency of Agamemnon of Mycenae.[40] According to another myth it was the place of refuge of Adrastus when he was driven out of Argos; he was said to have joined his mother's father Polybus there, and married Polybus' daughter, and succeeded him as king, before returning to Argos.[41] The Sicyonians maintained a cult of Adrastus.

After the collapse of the Mycenaean civilization their town was refounded, it was said, by Phalces the son of Temenus, ruler of Dorian Argos, to which it at first remained subordinate. In addition to the usual three Dorian tribes, the Hylleis, Dymaneis and Pamphyloi, the place possessed a serf class (resembling the Spartan helots), known as 'Club-Carriers' (*Korynephoroi*) or 'Weavers of Sheepskin Cloaks' (*Katonakophoroi*),[42] comprising the descendants of the earlier population. The first habitation centre of the Dorian city is not yet excavated, and the ancient harbour has disappeared.

Sicyon possessed substantial and well-watered dependent territory, renowned for its fruit and vegetables. Its antique royal house was superseded at some stage by an oligarchy, and in c.655 (as at Corinth, a suggested lower chronology seems unacceptable) this in turn was replaced by a dictatorship, which thereafter ruled for a century – a longer period than any other known dictatorial regime elsewhere. The founder of this dynasty, Orthagoras, seized control after his appointment as general and following the successful conduct of a frontier war. According to Aristotle, he gained a reputation for mild and almost constitutional government,[43] the antithesis of what the term 'tyrant' subsequently came to mean. Under his rule, his brother Myron I won the chariot-race at Olympia in 648 and dedicated a treasury there in the names of 'Myron and the people of Sicyon'. Myron II, Orthagoras' son and successor, was murdered by his brother Isodamus.

The most famous of the dictators of Sicyon, however, was Myron II's nephew, the warlike but versatile Cleisthenes (c.600–570). In the First Sacred War (c.595–583), arising out of a dispute between the Delphic authorities and Cirrha, he played a leading part in Cirrha's destruction, thereby gaining a predominant role at Delphi itself. He won victories in the chariot-races of its Pythian Games, as well as those at Olympia, and in 576 (?) invited suitors from all parts of Greece to compete for the hand of his daughter Agariste. The occasion displayed a splendour reminiscent of Homeric traditions of political gift-exchange and guest-friendship, and the widespread and impressive origins of the competitors for Agariste's hand represented a tribute to Cleisthenes' international connections and prestige. The fact that several of them came from north-western Greece and south Italy suggests that Sicyon, although it planted no colonies itself, was aiming, with some temporary success, to obtain a share of Corinth's western trade. Agariste, however, was awarded to Megacles of Athens, later head of the Alcmaeonid clan (and their son was the Athenian statesman Cleisthenes – Chapter 2, section 5).

Cleisthenes of Sicyon was said to have invented the offensive new names, or nicknames, of Piggites, Assites and Swinites for the three traditional Dorian tribes in his city.[44] But this story is doubtful. True, his early favour to moderate and liberal (Dorian) aristocrats and plutocrats did not last. Yet, being, as was claimed and admitted, a 'law-abiding' ruler like Orthagoras before him, he can scarcely have wanted to offend the entire dominant body of Sicyon's Dorian-descended citizens. The report sounds like a later travesty by hostile lampoons. What Cleisthenes may, in fact, have done was to give the three traditional tribes a new set of names, of a by no means uncomplimentary character but intended to supersede the traditional Dorian designations; and it might also have been at this time that a fourth tribe, the Aegialeis (men of the coast), was created, perhaps to incorporate some of the non-Dorian Helot-like serfs whose ancestors the original immigrants had subjugated.

The point of these moves was that Cleisthenes regarded Argos as his enemy. Prompted by this hatred, he expelled from Sicyon the cult of the Argive hero Adrastus, who was supposed to have taken refuge in that city, importing instead the worship of another hero, Melanippus, a Theban who according to legend had been Adrastus' deadliest foe.

With the same intention of demoting Argos, Cleisthenes transferred the principal religious entertainment of Sicyon, the performance of 'tragic choruses', to the worship of the popular deity Dionysus, for this meant depriving the expelled Argive cult of Adrastus of these shows.[45] Certain literary authorities, asserting a Peloponnesian origin for Greek tragic drama, with its strong Dionysiac associations, attributed these beginnings to the Corinthians (section 2 above). But a strong claim was also made for Sicyon,[46] where reciters of poems (the epics of Homer) are known to have existed in the early sixth century, and where also – though the same was true at Corinth – locally fabricated vases show various kinds of crude dramatic displays. Subsequent writers mentioned a 'tragic poet' Epigenes of Sicyon (supposedly rebuked for polluting the cult of Dionysus by the introduction of themes that were not related to his story).[47] What can probably be credited to Sicyon is an important, or even a decisive, part in elevating choruses to an artistic level.

The Sicyonians were also pioneers in the art of sculpture, although our evidence is once again based on much later literary information. For Pliny the elder and Pausanias report a tradition that Dipoenus and Scyllis, the sons or pupils of the Cretan sculptor Daedalus, moved to the mainland and founded a school at Sicyon (c.580–577?), a city 'which was for long the motherland of all such industries'.[48] Employing many Peloponnesians (later eminent) as their apprentices, these two men were claimed to have been the first to make their names in the art of marble sculpture. Their work may be reflected by the Sicyonian treasury at Delphi, where the figures on the metope reliefs, despite rigid stances and almost foldless draperies, display satisfyingly bold paratactic compositions.

When Cleisthenes asked the Delphic oracle to bless the suppression of Adrastus, he was said to have received the disagreeable reply that Adrastus had been the king of Sicyon and Cleisthenes was a mere thrower of stones. If this was truly the way in which the authorities at Delphi responded, displaying such ingratitude for the autocrat's rich gifts, then either they were finding his control of their communications across the Gulf of Corinth distasteful, or they saw that the days of dictators were already numbered – at Epidaurus and Corinth, for example, their regimes had already ended. And this soon happened at Sicyon as well, for in 555 its ruler Aeschines was deposed by Spartan intervention, and all members of Cleisthenes' family suffered expulsion from the city. To the accompaniment of Delphi's pious denunciation of tyranny, an oligarchic regime was established in the autocrat's place.

In the political field republican Sicyon could not achieve much, since the proximity of Corinth and its citadel, Acrocorinth, was excessive and overpowering.

In the realm of art, however, the picture continued to be different. Fragmentary wooden panels (small easel-pictures) of *c*.530, found in a cave at Pitsa nearby, recall the Greek theory that the 'discovery' of painting should be attributed to Corinth or Sicyon, and that line-drawing was first accomplished by a man from one or the other of those states.[49] Any such 'invention' must of course have been far earlier, but the Pitsa panels are nevertheless notable. What they depict is a sacrificial scene and procession of votaries, with women conversing. Delicately drawn and harmoniously designed, they depict a wider range of colours – red, brown, blue, black, white – than can be seen on painted pottery. And so they cast an isolated, fitful ray of light on the recorded but vanished role of Sicyon in the development of this art. Or should the panels be regarded as a Corinthian rather than a Sicyonian achievement? For although found on the territory of Sicyon, they were dedicated to the nymphs by a Corinthian, and bear an inscription in the Corinthian alphabet.

However, in another field at least, Sicyon was unmistakably in a position to rival Corinth. This was bronze-work, in which the Sicyonian achievement culminated, towards the end of the sixth century, in the masterpieces of Canachus, famous for his statue of Apollo Philesius at Didyma in western Asia Minor.

5 MEGARA

Megara lay in the narrow but fertile White Plain, the only lowland segment of the Megarid; this territory formed the northern section of the Isthmus of Corinth (and was therefore not strictly part of the Peloponnese, though it is most conveniently described here). The Megarians possessed a harbour (Pegae) to the west, on the Gulf of Corinth, and another (Nisaea), more accessible and convenient, to the east, on the Saronic Gulf of the Aegean Sea.

The place, which had already existed in the Bronze Age, is one of the few in Greece to bear a Greek name, Megara, 'Big Houses'. According to mythical tradition, it owed its walls to the hero Alcathous (helped by Apollo), and belonged subsequently (although this was Athenian propaganda) to Athens: it was in the pass leading through Mount Geraneia, linking the one city to the other, that the Athenian hero Theseus was said to have killed a brigand, at a place near Sciron, so that the region was called the Scironian Rocks.

The Dorian immigrants to Megara, probably arriving by way of Argos and divided into their usual three tribes, reduced the previous inhabitants to serfdom and settled down in three villages (or groups of villages) – hence the continuing plural form of the place-name Megara – which were said to have fought against one another, though with unusually chivalrous courtesy. In c.750, however, these villages coalesced, as far as political organization was concerned, into a city.[50] The three old Dorian tribes at some stage were replaced by five, corresponding, perhaps, to a new topographical configuration, or conceivably introducing certain pre-Dorian elements. These new tribes appointed five generals (at first dividing their duties with the king, who subsequently disappeared), and created administrative officials (demiourgoi). Each tribe provided a military contingent to the army, which helped to make Megara one of the leading states of early Greece.

In particular, benefiting from its geographical situation on the Isthmus, it soon provided a trading link between Greece and the west and east – like its neighbour Corinth. The Megarians developed a woollen industry, famous for its cloaks. But, above all, because of impatience with the smallness of their territory, which did not exceed 180 square miles, they fulfilled a pre-eminent, pioneer role in Greek colonization. And it is for this activity above all that Megara deserves to figure among the noteworthy Greek communities of the epoch.

Thus very soon after the earliest Greek settlements in Sicily the Megarians colonized Megara Hyblaea on the island's east coast. The traditional date was 728, during a period, it has been suggested, when Megara was a vassal of Corinth, to which, if this chronology is correct, it no doubt owed this initiative (undertaken so close to Corinth's own recently founded colony at Syracuse); Megara, with a population never exceeding 40,000, could scarcely have managed such enterprises without outside help. According to Thucydides,[51] the Megarian immigrants to Sicily first made two or even three successive false starts, on sites that had to be abandoned. Finally they were given coastal land by a native Sicel king, Hyblon, after whom they called their new colony Megara Hyblaea. The locality was defenceless, and could only have been settled with local co-operation. However, it possessed a water supply, beaches that could serve as small harbours, and a coastal plain four miles deep and nine miles long. Excavations have demonstrated that a city-plan was established at Megara Hyblaea from the outset, although it did not yet possess the orthogonal (rectangular) regularity associated later with the name of Hippodamus of Miletus. A good deal of the pottery found on the site was of local manufacture, but much was also imported, bearing witness to a moderately prosperous situation.

Subsequently, however, the Megarians of the homeland shifted their colonizing activity, with much more sensational and influential results, from the west to the north-east. The switch was probably due to deteriorating relations with Corinth. Its army in c.740 had probably advanced into the Megarid and seized its southern sector, including

Piraeum (Perachora). The Megarians, supported perhaps by Argos and Aegina, regained some border territory in c.720, under the leadership of Orsippus (victor, and the first naked runner in the Olympic Games), but by 700 Corinth had re-established itself in the area. To Megara, which depended so much on sheep-raising and woollen manufactures, the loss of this territory was a very serious blow. Besides, Corinth was now threatening their exclusion from their Western markets as well.

In consequence (this time perhaps with the encouragement of Miletus) Megara turned its attention to the Thracian Bosphorus, a rich fishing region – in which tunny could be trapped as it migrated from the Black Sea to the Mediterranean – and the strategic channel through which Black Sea grain had to pass on its way to Greece. The first of these colonies seems to have been Calchedon (Kadıköy) in Bithynia, on the southern shore of the Bosphorus, of which the traditional foundation date was 685. Then, only a few years later – at a date variously assigned to 668, 659 and 657 – another group of Megarians, their numbers no doubt swollen by companions from other cities, settled on the magnificent site of Byzantium on the opposite European shore. Before founding Byzantium, Megarians had settled at Selymbria farther to the west, and another town, Astacus, was probably established by the Megarian colony Calchedon. As a result of these settlements, although the history of their relations with the mother-city cannot be reconstructed, the rulers of the little state of Megara in Greece came to regard the Bosphorus, and the eastern end of the Propontis (sea of Marmara), as their special preserve, so they tried to prevent the Samians from establishing a rival colony at Perinthus, although in this they were unsuccessful (602). (For these colonizations, see also Chapter 8, section 2.)

Meanwhile, during the latter half of the seventh century (c.640–620?), quarrels among Megara's aristocratic leaders offered a classic opening for a would-be dictator: and this proved to be Theagenes. In preparation for his *coup*, he was said to have first gained the confidence of the poor by 'slaughtering the cattle of the rich, when they were out grazing beside the river'.[52] The probability is, however, that he was not a great lover of the people or of democracy but a 'god-descended' Dorian aristocrat who used this method to make himself popular – though no doubt, if there is any truth in the story at all, the cattle of his political opponents were selectively singled out for destruction, since a wholesale massacre would have been ruinous to the whole community.

Thus Theagenes joined the group of dictators in whom this northeastern region of the Peloponnese specialized. He endeared himself to his people by building a fountain house and a tunnelled water-conduit, and married his daughter to an influential Athenian nobleman, Cylon, who attempted with the help of a Megarian force to establish himself as his fellow dictator at Athens. This attempted imitation failed, but nevertheless the Megarians, taking advantage of Athenian internal strife, seized Salamis from Aegina (from Athens, it was said later) to compensate for the loss of resources and trade they had recently been suffering at Corinth's hands.

Later, however, Theagenes was expelled by oligarchs – men whose power was based on making and exporting woollen goods, rather than on the birth qualifications of the old aristocracy. But then the oligarchs in their turn were overthrown by a wider group including members of the poorer classes. Plutarch's description of this administration as an 'unbridled democracy' is anachronistic. Nevertheless, it showed radical tendencies. For what happened – once again according to Plutarch, and here comparison with the later crisis encountered by Solon at Athens gives his account plausibility – was that a new Megarian law obliged creditors to return to debtors the interest the latter had paid them. This requirement, unsurprisingly, must have proved unacceptable to the richer classes, for the 'democratizing' government proved shortlived, and an oligarchy returned to power. This whole series of rapid, convulsive changes seemed to ancient writers a classic early example of *stasis*, the warfare between rich and poor (and between one aristocratic group and another) which was to play such a dominant part in subsequent Greek history.[53]

Light is thrown upon this period of internal strife by 1,400 verses ascribed to Theognis of Megara (who may later have become a citizen of Megara Hyblaea). The collection, evidently, includes the work of later writers as well. However, many elegiac lines still remain attributable to Theognis himself, composed in the more widely known Ionic dialect rather than in his native Doric; they were intended to be sung at dinners of the noblemen's clubs (*hetaireiai*), accompanied by the flute.

A master of graceful versification and bold and vivid metaphor, Theognis emerges as an extreme conservative, who truculently supports the claims of aristocratic blood and breeding. In addition to deploring the upstart lower classes – whose temporary admission to a share of power he witnessed with horror – the poet equally dislikes the new rich and the nasty values of their new colonial world. With these social targets in mind, he spells out the characteristic Greek code according to which the worst of all sins is *hubris*, greed for the possessions of others, which stood at the opposite pole from moderation. It had already destroyed many great cities, of which Megara, it seemed to him, was likely to be the next.

Theognis is also a determined pederast – offering the most substantial concentration of homosexual poetry before the Hellenistic age – and writes unpleasantly about women, although he admits that there is no more satisfactory fortune than to have a good wife. He regrets, however, that while men take the trouble to secure suitable mates for their cattle, they themselves have now become accustomed to contracting marriages in which the merits of good blood are ignored.

Both Megara and its colony Megara Hyblaea, according to Aristotle, claimed to have 'invented' Greek comedy. The claim of Megara Hyblaea is said to have been based 'on the grounds that the poet Epicharmus was of their country'.[54] This would seem to suggest that the Sicilian Megarians regarded that eminent pioneer comic dramatist as a native of their own city rather than of Syracuse, as is more generally and plausibly supposed (Chapter 7, section 3). As for the mother-city of Megara, Athenian comic poets refer to its comedies, describing them as obscene. They appear to have depicted stock figures, including, for example, a cook and his assistant; and after the downfall of the Megarian dictatorship, the 'inventor' of the genre, Susarion, was said to have felt able to present performances, imbued with a political tone, in which Dionysiac satyrs played a principal part.[55] Thus a kind of comic drama existed at Megara before its appearance at Athens. True, it need not necessarily be supposed that there was a strong Doric element in later Attic comedy, but the clowns of Megara probably exercised some influence, and an Athenian type of comic mask, the *maison*, was derived, according to one view, from a Megarian actor of that name.[56]

After losing their port of Nisaea to Athens in 569/568 (perhaps not for the first time, and not permanently), the Megarians' long-drawn-out struggle over the island of Salamis again resulted in defeat, some decades later, after a Spartan arbitration had gone against them. But in compensation they extended their power in the north-east, by sending ships through the Thracian Bosphorus (with the help of their settlements in the area, and with Boeotian assistance as well); and they founded the colony of Heraclea Pontica in Bithynia, on the southern coast of the Black Sea (c.560–558). Overlooking a natural harbour, the first of any consequence reached after traversing the Bosphorus, Heraclea lay in the tribal territory of the Mariandyni, whom the colonists subjugated as Helot–serfs, subsequently maintaining themselves from the profits of a fertile hinterland and sea-fisheries. The government of

Heraclea Pontica, which exhibited democratic inclinations, soon extended its control eastwards along the coast, and established colonies of its own on the western, European Black Sea littoral and in the Tauric Chersonese (Crimea).[57]

At home, however, Megara had by now lost its position as one of the leading powers in Greece, and shortly before 500 it became one of the members of the Peloponnesian League, under Spartan domination.

6 OLYMPIA

Olympia was situated in Pisa (Pisatis), a territory bordering upon Elis in the north-western Peloponnese.[58] It lay at the foot of the low hill of Cronus, the father of Zeus, where the Rivers Alpheus and Cladeus meet before they break out into the fertile plain leading to the Ionian Sea, seven and a half miles away. Archaeological evidence records the continuous habitation of Olympia from c.2800 to c.1100 BC.

Subsequently, after the Dorians arrived, it became the scene of the most important athletic festival in the world. According to the Odes of Pindar, which glorified the victors, the Olympic Games were established by the arch-hero Heracles himself,[59] and this was the version handed down at Elis. But local tradition at Olympia itself preferred to attribute the festival's foundation to the mythical Pelops (from whom the Peloponnese acquired its name), after he had slain Oenomaus, king of Pisa, taking the dead man's daughter Hippodamia as his wife. Mound-graves which were believed to be those of Pelops and Hippodamia went back to a period before 1000 BC, and cults of Cronus and Gaia (Earth, whose oracle was said to have given Olympia its earliest renown) and her daughter or synonym Themis (Right) and Eileithyia (goddess of childbirth) may be earlier still.

The worship of Zeus of Mount Olympus – Olympian Zeus, from whom the place took its name – within his Altis precinct, a rectangle measuring 650 by 500 feet, was introduced by the Dorians, perhaps in more or less direct continuity with one of the earlier cults. The site has yielded tenth-century finds of terracotta and bronze statuettes of the god, with raised arms reminiscent of Mycenaean deities. The cult of Zeus was served by the Iamids, a family of seers.

A local athletic competition was being held at Olympia by c.900 at the latest, under Dorian auspices. The Games, in their more developed form, seem to date from the eighth century. They were believed to have been inaugurated in 776, the earliest date in Greek history regarded as historical rather than legendary, although the method by which this precise estimate was reached (by Hippias of Elis, in the later fifth century) was unscientific. Lists of early victors in the Games name athletes who came mostly from the western Peloponnese and especially Messenia, but subsequently Olympia's maritime accessibility to the west drew many successful competitors from Greek Sicily and south Italy.

The Altis has yielded numerous finds of early dedicated artefacts, notably bronze cauldrons of eighth-century date and north Syrian inspiration. At first building on the site had been minimal; even Zeus' altar was just an ever renewed mound of ashes piled up after sacrifices. The most ancient architectural remains are those of a reconstructed temple of Hera of c.600. The first monumental shrine, perhaps, on the mainland of Greece, it was made, initially, of mud brick walls on dressed stone bases, and its roof stood on wooden columns. The temple contained statues of Zeus and Hera herself, whose head has been discovered.

This building seems to have been constructed under the auspices of the Pisatans, who may have secured control of the Games in the seventh century, as a result of intervention by King Pheidon of Argos. If so, however – and the whole matter is obscured by later recriminations – they lost this role in c.572, after a prolonged struggle (rather than at the outset in 776, as was believed by Strabo)[60] to the larger community of Elis, which was in the process of asserting its control over Pisatis.

The Games were now reorganized on a Panhellenic basis. This was a tribute to their widespread popularity, which was probably stimulated, rather than discouraged, by the inability of Elis – because of its political insignificance – to raise difficult and embarrassing claims and issues. The enhanced status of the Games was demonstrated by the presence at Olympia (as at Delphi) of a succession of finely decorated treasuries established by various Sicilian, south Italian and other Greek cities to house their offerings, since these – including extensive arms and armour, the booty of wars – had become too numerous and abundant to find room in the local temples.

The Olympic Games were one of the four major athletic festivals of Greece, the others being the Pythian (at Delphi), Isthmian (near Corinth) and Nemean (under the control of Cleonae, a dependency of Argos). The Games at Olympia, although they exceptionally found no room for music and poetry, were recognized as the greatest of the four, and gained their Panhellenic status and reputation 200 years before any of the others.

They were held, for more than a millennium to come, every fourth year in August and September, between the grain harvest and the garnering of the grapes and olives. Three heralds dispatched from Elis declared a Sacred Truce for the duration of the festivals, and no war between Greek city-states ever prevented them from being held. If states engaged in hostilities failed to lay down their arms for the duration of the truce, a heavy fine was inflicted, its size calculated according to the numbers of troops involved.

In their eventual form these competitions continued for five days. The first day was preparatory, dedicated to sacrifices and prayers to the gods. The second witnessed the chariot-race – the sport of kings, and the favourite spectacle – followed by the horse-race, as well as the Five Events (*pentathlon*); and on the third day (which was always timed to precede the full moon) there was a procession to the altar of Zeus. This was followed by three junior contests between boys. The fourth day brought the three men's running events, and the wrestling, all-in wrestling (*pankration*) and boxing. The fifth and last day was dedicated to final celebrations, including thank-offerings and a banquet for the victorious competitors.

Despite much discomfort, perhaps as many as 40,000 or 50,000 people, from all over the Greek world, attended the Olympic Games. These concourses did something to counterbalance the separatist fragmentation of the Greek city-states. Yet the influence of the festivals, great though it was, never proved enough to achieve this reconciliation effectively, and in any case the entries were not made, as now, by states, but by individuals (who had to be free-born Greeks). However, although the only prizes were wreaths woven from a sacred olive tree in the precinct of Zeus, the winner of an Olympic event was often rewarded, after he returned to his own city, and honoured for the rest of his life.

When the Games were revived in modern times, it was hoped that they would be conducted in an amateur spirit: for this was supposed to have characterized the original festivals. But any such interpretation of the ancient contests was illusory, for they were engaged upon with such intensive concentration that an advanced degree of professionalism inevitably arose. It was not for nothing that *athlon* meant, not play, but struggle, suffering and pain.

A remarkable by-product of the Games, however, was the encouragement they gave to artistic endeavours. A great deal of the finest early metal-work was made for dedication at Olympia. Moreover, these occasions subsequently provided a major encouragement to Greek sculpture, so largely based on the human body which such contests glorified – the male body, because women were excluded from participation, though additional running races, outside the main schedule, were eventually introduced for their benefit, in honour of Hera.

4 Central and Northern Green with inset of Attica

CHAPTER 4

CENTRAL AND NORTHERN GREECE

1 EUBOEA: LEFKANDI, CHALCIS, ERETRIA

Euboea (Evvia) is the largest island, after Crete, of the Aegean archipelago, between 4 and 30 miles wide and 106 miles long. It was only separated from Boeotia and Attica by the narrow stretch of water known as the Euboean Sea, which reached its minimum breadth in the Euripus channel – at one point less than 100 yards wide – much frequented by coasting vessels so as to avoid the rocks and currents of the eastern Euboean coast looking out over the open Aegean. The inhabitants of the western part of Euboea during the Bronze Age, the Abantes (supposedly men of Thracian origin from Aba in Phocis), receive a mention in the *Iliad*'s Catalogue of Achaean Ships. In the far north and south of the island, the early populations were described as northern tribesmen of a different origin, known as Ellopes and Dryopes respectively.

The historic Euboean cities were Chalcis, Eretria, Histiaea, Geraestus and Carystus. The most important of them were Chalcis and Eretria, situated not far apart on the south-west coast. This sector, forming part of the territory of the Abantes, came under the influence of neighbouring Boeotia during the late Bronze (Mycenaean) Age. Then followed the immigration of a branch of the Ionian Greek people, at about the time, apparently, when their kinsmen moved into the Cyclades and Ionia. Thereafter the two principal Euboean cities played an independent, pre-eminent part in the re-emergence of Greece that was to follow.

Chalcis, which dominated the narrowest section of the Euripus, maintained certain Minoan religious traditions, and was believed, perhaps fictitiously, to have been colonized by Cothus the Athenian after the Trojan War. Eretria lay to the south-east, where the waters widen out from the Euripus. The site of a Bronze Age habitation centre, it had formerly, according to Strabo, borne the name of Melaneis; after the Trojan War it was said to have been settled by Aielus from Athens, taking its name from a market-place in that city. But Strabo also recalls, probably with greater cogency, the existence of an earlier local place-name Arotria (as well as an alternative derivation from Eretrieus of Macistus in Triphylia, a region of the Peloponnese).[1]

Early Chalcis and Eretria set the combative tone of later Greek history by permanently disputing the ownership of the Lelantine Plain, named after the Lelanton (now Kalamontari) stream or torrent. The medicinal waters of the Lelanton which lay between them were adjoined by mines exceptionally yielding both copper and iron. It is here that remarkable discoveries have now been made, beside the modern village of Lefkandi, which may have been known as Lelanton in ancient times; but Lefkandi could also be identifiable with 'Old Eretria', referred to by Strabo,[2] unless, alternatively, it was a dependency of that place.

Occupying a broad peninsula with a good anchorage, and well situated to control the Lelantine Plain, Lefkandi had been flourishing as a Mycenaean (late Bronze Age) settlement in c.1150. But what remains, in the present state of our knowledge, exceptional is the degree to which the place prospered after the Mycenaean collapse, during the ensuing transitional period (from c.1075) which we describe as the 'Dark Age' – though in Euboea (as in parts of Crete and Cyprus) there was no apparent recession to justify such a title. For the people of this settlement at Lefkandi, although extremely few in number (just how few is a matter of dispute), were evidently among the very first in Greece to acquire luxury goods from the near east, and especially from northern Syria and Phoenicia.

Thus finds in cremation-graves – notably at Toumba, a small hill overlooking the Lelantine Plain to the north, and facing the sea to the west – include a faience (bluish glass) necklace of mid-eleventh-century date, glass beads and blue grit (a component of glass), vases and a plaque and Egyptian ring of similar material, and a set of bronze wheels that were possibly of Cypriot origin. Additional contents include Athenian Protogeometric pottery (c.950–900), as well as pots of a native Euboean Protogeometric style, while a 14-inch-high terracotta centaur displays surprisingly early figure-work.

Excavations at Lefkandi have also revealed the remains of an apsed building, probably of tenth-century date. Its form and character show a sophisticated precocity unparalleled, as far as we know, in contemporary Greece. Made of mud-brick upon a stone foundation, with an interior facing of plaster and surrounding verandahs which were colonnaded with wooden posts, the structure displays unexpectedly large dimensions, 149 feet long and 36 wide. To judge by the presence of pits for storage jars, it seems to have been a secular residence, though it also points the way to the monumental temples of the future.

This building turns out to have been overlaid by two lavishly furnished graves. One of them is the tomb (possibly a *heroon*, or hero's shrine) of a warrior who, to judge by his grandeur, must have belonged to a royal or formerly royal line. His bones and ashes were found lodged in an amphora; they were wrapped in strips of cloth, of which, most unusually, portions have survived. The second grave proved to contain the cremated remains of a woman. She was wearing gilt hair-rolls, large dress pins, and a brassière fronted by large discs. A sacrificial knife lay by her head – perhaps indicating that she met her death as a human sacrifice. The skeletons of three or four horses were discovered beside her. An adjoining foundry, dating from *c.*900, shows that it was not felt sufficient to import near-eastern metal-work, but that the techniques by which this was made were also copied locally. Lefkandi became even richer, as gold and other luxuries continued to arrive from the east in increasing quantities. But cremation burials abruptly ceased in *c.*865, although life continued, on a much diminished scale, until *c.*700.

If, as has been suggested, Lefkandi was the 'Old Eretria' mentioned by Strabo, the termination of these burials may have been caused by the evacuation of the site – and perhaps of other villages as well – in order to bring about the physical and political unification of 'New Eretria; but there are chronological problems involved in this view. At all events, the revived Eretria was a town of impressive size, six miles east of Lefkandi, rich in gold and bronze, yielding pottery datable to *c.*875–825, and containing a temple of Apollo Daphnephoros (*c.*750) and a hero's shrine. The unification and urbanization of Chalcis, transformed from five formerly separate villages into a city famous for its metal-work, seems to have dated from the same period. Hesiod won the prize of a tripod at a poetical contest accompanying the funeral of Amphidamas of Chalcis (section 4 below).

The political relationship of Lefkandi with Chalcis and Eretria cannot be reconstructed, but it must have been close. What is certain is that Euboea profited from its strategic location by taking the lead in resuming the overseas commercial activities suspended at the termination of the Mycenaean epoch. While even earlier eastern contacts have been noted at Lefkandi, Chalcis became a major manufacturing city, and its ruling aristocracy, like that of Eretria – forming a constitution of knights succeeding to monarchic rule, according to Aristotle[3] – did not disdain to engage, or employ men to engage, in such operations themselves.

A large part in recapturing these contacts was played by at least three ports in northern Syria, Al Mina, Posidium and Paltus (Chapter 6, section 4). Gold and silver, and various objects that the Greeks used as models for their 'orientalizing' art, came to the Euboeans and other homeland Greeks from these centres (and perhaps from trading quarters in Phoenician cities as well). Then some of these imports, in turn, were passed on by the Euboeans to their markets (*emporia*) at Pithecusae and Cumae in south Italy (Chapter 7, section 1), where they were traded with the Etruscans (Appendix 3). Moreover, even after the rival claims of other centres (Chapter 1, note 35) have been considered, there is a strong case for supposing that the Phoenician alphabet (Appendix 1), adapted to invent the Greek script, made its first appearance at Chalcis by way of these north Syrian ports. One of the very earliest alphabetic inscriptions has been found at the Euboean *emporion* of Pithecusae.

Meanwhile Chalcis – no doubt with the assistance of emigrants from other cities – had also played a dominant part in the foundation of Rhegium (before c.720), which may have been the earliest Greek colony in the far south of Italy, deriving importance from its strategic location on the Sicilian Strait (Straits of Messina), which must have reminded the settlers of the Euripus at home. Moreover, as early, it was said, as c.734, men from Chalcis had also established the first Greek colony in Sicily at Naxos, to which Leontini (founded by the same man, Theocles) and Catana were added soon afterwards, the principal motive of these Sicilian settlements being the acquisition of agricultural land.

Thus Chalcis had played a predominant part in the rediscovery of the western world. In addition, it collaborated with Eretria to colonize the three-pronged promontory named Chalcidice on the Macedonian coast (Chapter 8, section 2). Here Chalcis – where the aristocratic government left many citizens without arable land at home – planted more than thirty settlements (once again with the aid of others) on Sithone and parts of Acte, while Pallene and the Thermaic Gulf received Eretrian colonists. All these new foundations developed legends which quoted the Delphic oracle as playing a part in their establishment. They had access to good grain-growing country, and could also exploit their hinterlands to become sources of supply for the slave-trade.

However, shortly before 700, the two Euboean mother-cities of these colonies became locked in a violent and prolonged dispute regarding the ownership of the rich Lelantine Plain that lay between them – the earliest Greek war that has a good claim to be regarded as historical.

The possible outcome was a matter of acute interest to various Greek states. For not only were the two combatant cities' interests overseas at stake, but Chalcis controlled the vital Euripus channel between Euboea and the mainland, and Eretria dominated a number of Aegean islands, notably Andros, Ceos and Tenos. Both sides, therefore, were able to muster a number of allies. For example Samos, Thessaly and Corinth (despite colonial rivalry) seem to have sided with Chalcis, while Miletus and probably Megara supported the cause of the Eretrians.

An oracle reputedly awarded Chalcis supremacy among all Greeks in regard to the quality of its fighting men[4] during this period of aristocratic warfare which preceded the age of the hoplite phalanx – although, as the city's name 'bronze-town' suggests, it may have significantly improved the breastplate which later played such a part in hoplite armament. Its cavalry, too, was impressive enough to earn its landowning aristocracy the name of Hippobotae, 'Horse-Breeders'. At Eretria, likewise, the ruling class were known as Hippeis, 'Horsemen', and it is recorded that the city could mobilize 600 of these, as well as 60 chariots and 3,000 infantry.

One engagement in this Lelantine War, we are told, resulted in a major victory for Chalcis, with the help of Thessalian cavalry augmenting the excellent local force. It is not clear, however, that this success proved decisive, for although Eretria, as a result of the war, apparently fell from its role as a leading city-state – losing Andros, for example, which planted its own colonies in Chalcidice (c.655) – Chalcis, too, was henceforward eclipsed as a major commercial power by its former ally Corinth. Probably both Euboean cities were at least temporarily ruined or eclipsed by the prolonged hostilities (which also apparently resulted in the final destruction of Lefkandi). Yet, although further disputes over the Lelantine Plain continued to recur, Chalcis was still able to persist with its northern colonizing programme; and Eretria built impressive fortifications, produced a series of colossal high-stemmed vases (c.700–650), and possessed a goldsmith's shop which has yielded a rich hoard.

Some time before 600, a dictator Tynnondas imposed himself upon the Euboeans, or upon some of them – his name is Boeotian and suggests the domination of the island, for a time, by the Boeotian League – while other dictators, Antileon and Phoxus, are recorded as having established control over Chalcis. Our source for their rule is Aristotle, who adds that the removal of these autocrats was followed by 'oligarchic' and 'democratic' governments respectively, although it may be supposed that, in fact, the Horse-Breeders eventually resumed their pre-eminence without a great deal of change. Eretria, too, experienced

the rule of a dictator, Diagoras, who forcibly replaced the former aristocratic government before or after 550 (perhaps it was he who allowed the
Athenian Pisistratus to use the city as a launching-pad for his successful
coup). But a shipping law of *c.*525 (?) gives the title of Eretria's principal
official as *archos*, presumably the head of an oligarchic government.[5]

Early in the latter half of the sixth century, Chalcis inaugurated a
silver coinage. Its obverse type was the eagle and serpent of Zeus
Olympios, and the reverse displayed the city-emblem of a wheel. A
'Euboic copper talent' had already been a unit of reckoning in very
early times; and the new currency launched the 'Euboic standard'
which, in heavy and light form, and in half a dozen local versions
(including Attic and Corinthian), competed with the Aeginetan standard as the principal unit of Mediterranean commerce. While the
Aeginetan standard prevailed in the Aegean area, its 'Attic–Euboic'
counterpart prevailed in Chalcidice, Cyrenaica and the west. Both
standards were ultimately based on a Syrian metrological system
based on fifty shekels (staters) to one *mina*.

As Athens increasingly came to the fore, and its pro-Euboean Pisistratid faction was driven out, it became predictable that the leading
Euboean city, Chalcis, should be anxious about possible encroachments from that city. Consequently when Cleomenes I of Sparta organized a coalition to attack Athens in 507/506, he was joined in a
three-sided assault by Chalcis and the Boeotian League, which
commemorated their alliance by placing a wheel, the emblem of
Chalcis, on its coins. Both the Chalcidian and Boeotian armies, however, were defeated upon their own territories by the Athenians on one
and the same day. They lost numerous prisoners, who had to be
ransomed, and Athens annexed part of the territory of the Chalcidians,
breaking the supremacy of their oligarchs and settling 4,000 of its own
men of military age as smallholders (cleruchs) who retained Athenian
citizenship and served as a garrison.

In later times, at least, the men of Chalcis (at home and in their
colonies) enjoyed a special reputation for pederasty, for which
'Chalcidize' became a synonym. Athenaeus described them as
remarkably keen on the practice, and Plutarch cited from Aristotle a
popular song to the same effect. The tradition was even given a
mythological backing, for according to one version Ganymede, beloved
of Zeus, had himself come from Chalcis and was snatched up by the
god in the neighbourhood.[6]

As for Eretria, when the Ionians launched their revolt against Persian
rule (499), its aid, together with that of Athens, was sought by the
Milesian Aristagoras, and the Eretrians, who owed a debt of gratitude

to Miletus, joined the Athenians in responding by the dispatch of five triremes. The smallness of this number may be due to the dispatch of a second Eretrian expedition to Cyprus, where it defeated a Cypriot fleet in Persian employment. This hostility to Persia was to cost the Eretrians, at the hands of Darius I (490), the destruction of their city and the deportation of its inhabitants.

2 DELPHI

Delphi (Pytho) was in the central Greek territory of Phocis.[7] Its site is spectacular, situated on the steep lower slopes of Mount Parnassus, beneath the two towering Shining Cliffs (Phaedriades) and overlooking the Gulf of Corinth, which lies six miles away to the south, 2,000 feet below. Inhabited from the later Bronze Age (at first at Lycoria, near the Corycian Cave), the place was believed by the Greeks to be the central point of the whole earth, because Zeus had released two eagles, one from the east and one from the west, commanding them to fly towards the centre, and it was at Delphi that they met.

The place derived its holiness and renown from Apollo, a god of Anatolian origin who, after absorbing northern elements, had been imported there by Dorian invaders or immigrants. However, a different set of divinities and monsters had presided over the site in the past. The *Homeric Hymn to Apollo*, a seventh-century composition incorporating earlier traditions, half about Delphi and half about Delos, tells the story. The gods worshipped in the two places may originally have been separate, but the *Hymn* unites them, recounting how when the god came from Delos to his new holy place at Delphi beneath snowy Parnassus, he found there, and slew, the fabulous, murderous she-snake Typhaon or Typhon (identified with a Delphic monster Python), guardian of the sacred spring Cassotis. 'Whoever encountered the she-dragon,' the Hymn continued,

> the day of doom would sweep him away, until the Lord Apollo, who deals death from afar, launched a powerful arrow against her. She fell, torn by bitter pain, and lay drawing great gulps of breath and rolling her body about. A dreadful and indescribable noise burst forth as she writhed this way and that amid the wood: and so she gave up her life, breathing it out in blood.[8]

But the same Hymn goes on to tell another tale about the god's arrival at Delphi. According to this version, while he was pondering who should serve him and offer sacrifice to him there, he assumed the form of a dolphin and passed from the peak of a wave on to a ship from the Cretan city of Cnossus, which was thereupon miraculously diverted from Pylos, the port for which it had been bound, in order to come to land instead at

Cirrha (Xeropigadi), beside the fertile plain named after Crisa, a formerly Mycenaean town of which Cirrha had been the port, as it next became the port of Delphi.

'Then, like a noon-star,' continued the Hymn, 'the lord, far-working Apollo, leapt from the vessel: flashes of fire flew from him thick, their brightness reaching to heaven.'[9] He ordered the ship's crew to become his servants, and to worship him as Apollo of the Dolphin, Delphinios; and so they did. This, it was believed, was how the name of Delphi originated, though an alternative explanation ascribed its origin to a mythical founder Delphus, son of Poseidon and Melaine; an altogether different, Cretan derivation of the word is more likely than either of these etymologies.

The Hymn presents Apollo both as menacing archer and as peaceful god of the lyre. He was glamorous and formidable, what every young Greek would like to have been: lustful (although at the same time the god of ritual purity and healing), both remorseless and merciful in the *Iliad*, and most powerful of all gods next to his father Zeus himself, whose will he pronounced through his oracles.

Nevertheless, deity of the immigrant Dorians though he was, the pre-Dorian, Cretan, Minoan origin of his shrine at Delphi, suggested by the Hymn, appears to be authentic. True, direct and unbroken continuity going back from his cult to the earlier worship has not so far proved stratigraphically demonstrable. However, Minoan objects have been found on the site, traces of a Mycenaean settlement have come to light beneath Apollo's subsequent temple, and more than 200 Mycenaean terracotta statuettes, representing female figures and mostly dating from the twelfth century BC, have been discovered under a later sanctuary of Athena Pronaia: inviting the conjecture that she succeeded a goddess of the later Bronze Age there. Moreover, the dragon in the story belonged to the earth, Gaia, the Bronze Age earth-mother, while the fact that it was always a woman, never a man, who in Greek times continued to act as the mouthpiece of the Delphic oracle may be another survival of the older religion.

For Apollo pronounced his oracles through a priestess, the Pythia. First she drank the waters of Cassotis fountain and underwent purification at the Castalian spring, welling forth from the Phaedriades. Next she sat at Apollo's holy place beside the rim of a chasm, from which rose a vapour, and this she inhaled, submitting herself to its intoxicant influence.

No such chasm is traceable today, and it has been conjectured that the alleged abyss was merely a hole in the temple pavement, leading down to a piece of soil that had been sacred since remoter times. In consequence, there are doubts whether any vapour can ever have risen out of the ground, and the suggestion has been made that the Pythia, instead, drugged herself on potassium cyanide, derived from chewing laurel leaves. Alternatively, there have been suspicions that the whole phenomenon was 'fixed'. But allowance must instead be made for the likelihood of mediumistic, ecstatic emotional suggestion and trance, such as have been noted in various other cultures.

At all events a male functionary or seer transmitted to the Pythia the questions put to her by those who wished to consult the oracle, and she in response uttered a sequence of words, not necessarily comprehensible or coherent, which attendant priests then proceeded to interpret and reword in hexameter verse.[10] Already known to the *Iliad*,[11] these oracles were well on the way to acquiring Panhellenic fame in the seventh century, if not before. They also played a prominent part in the wave of overseas Greek colonizations (which so often set out westwards from the adjoining Corinthian Gulf). That is to say, the leaders of these colonial enterprises told the oracle where they proposed to go, and asked for its approval, the granting of which proved a substantial religious and psychological asset to the emigrants.

It is very difficult, however, to discern the character of these oracular utterances, and to assess, for example, the real extent of their influence on colonial activities. This is because, although some of the surviving texts that record these oracles look genuine, many others are forgeries – concocted either by cities seeking oracular support for expeditions they wanted to undertake or had undertaken, or by the Delphic authorities themselves trying to amend and erase past policies that they would like people to forget. For these reasons, and because of the rumour-inspiring sanctity of the place, a large number of these alleged Apolline pronouncements became the subject of anecdotes, which usually look more or less fictitious. For they were composed, in many cases, to show how cryptic and ambiguous the oracles were, as indeed they were expected to be – turning the questioner back on himself and beguiling him. Nevertheless, the point of these stories usually was that events later proved the oracular predictions, when interpreted correctly, to have been accurate.

In fact, as far as can be made out, these declarations were cautious, leaving room for adaptability to later circumstances – and they seem to have been based on reliable and widespread sources of information. Sometimes, it is true, they went wrong. For example, the Delphic authorities' belief that Croesus, king of Lydia (563–546), could defeat Cyrus II the Great of Persia proved mistaken, and they only extricated themselves from this error by an acrobatic retrospective gloss (for another mistake, in connection with the Persian Wars, see below). But usually the oracles showed good political sense, as Aeschylus was at pains to point out in his tragic trilogy the *Oresteia*.

Delphi also became famous for the somewhat popular and non-aristocratic moralizing tone that the mouthpieces of Apollo's cult increasingly adopted, displayed by the injunctions 'Know Thyself' and 'Nothing too much' inscribed on his temple. It was later believed that by such pieces of counsel Delphi had already been promoting the moral principles of law and order and sweetness and light (since Apollo was Phoebus, god of the sun) as early as the sixth century. But 'Know Thyself' originally meant 'know thyself as a human being, and follow the god' – know your limitations; and it was only under the influence of later philosophic thinking (such as Heraclitus' 'I have searched myself') that the injunction first seemed to refer to a human being's self-knowledge, and came to mean 'examine your conscience'. As for 'Nothing too much', the moderation (*sophrosyne*) that was to rank as a cardinal ideal of the Greeks (because they found it so particularly difficult to pursue) was once again attributed to Apollo's influence. The saying had always meant 'do not overdo things' (do not behave with self-centred neglect of the rights and wishes of others [*hubris*] – or even, later, do not be too successful). The reason why things must not be overdone was because stepping out of line would incur the divine wrath (*nemesis*) – a way of thinking which would be passed on to the ensuing epoch, as a principal theme of Attic tragedy.

After a swift rise during the eighth century, the holiness of Delphi gained renown throughout the Greek world. There were two main sacred zones upon the site, the Sanctuary of Athena Pronaia in the area known as Marmaria east of the Castalian spring, and the Sanctuary of Pythian Apollo himself to the west of the spring. The seventh- or early-eighth-century temple of Athena Pronaia, as we saw, was built over extensive Mycenaean deposits. Adjacent was a sixth-century shrine with two rooms or chapels dedicated to Athena and Artemis. As for the Sanctuary of Apollo, to which the Sacred Way wound up from the road below, the temple, according to the *Hymn of Apollo*, was the work of the architects Trophonius and Agamedes of Lebadeia in Boeotia, who 'laid a footing of stone'.[12] They are legendary figures – Trophonius was also revered as an oracular hero, and according to some accounts he and his colleague were the sons of Zeus or Apollo – but a temple which might merit such a description can scarcely have preceded the seventh century. It stood within a precinct, upon a platform of local conglomerate rock.

From a very early date the cult of Apollo included a festival held every eighth year, the precursor of the Pythian Games (see below), comprising a musical competition which featured a hymn to the god sung to the accompaniment of the lyre. Dionysus, too, was worshipped in association with Apollo – who was believed to leave Delphi for three months of the year, when Dionysus took his place – though it would appear that the Delphic priests modified and toned down the ecstatic features that had characterized the Dionysiac cult when it arrived, early in the Iron Age, from Thrace (see Appendix 2).

A centre which had by now become as important as Delphi could not escape involvement in the politics of the surrounding Greek states. The rise of its priests as colonial counsellors can be related, in part, to the Lelantine War between Chalcis and Eretria in Euboea (c.700), since those of the early surviving Delphic oracles that appear to be genuine are concerned with the colonial foundations of Chalcis and its ally Corinth and their friends, but not with those of cities that took the other side. Indeed, it seems to have been through this Corinthian connection that Delphi first became firmly established, during the course of the seventh century. For when the dictators of Corinth, Cypselus and Periander, offered particularly rich dedications to Delphic Apollo, they were showing their appreciation of the oracle's helpful support of their western colonies.

But Delphi, originally under Phocian control, later entered upon a new phase of its political history when it became the principal centre of the regional Amphictyony ('dwellers around'). This was a league, primarily concerned with religious ritual but occasionally capable of acting together for a political purpose, which, in its earliest-known form, comprised twelve tribes of northern Greece, including the Thessalians (who in the sixth century exercised a pre-eminent influence), the Phocians (who had lost this dominant position to them) and the Boeotians. The original centre of the Amphictyony had been a sanctuary of Demeter at Anthela near Thermopylae (the 'hot gates') or Pylae (the gates), the pass between Thessaly and central Greece – scene of the historic Spartan stand against the Persians (480) – which the Amphictyonic Council was eager to control, to ensure the free passage of its members.

A dispute between Delphi and its harbour-town of Cirrha, over the right to levy tolls on pilgrims making their way to the oracle, caused the Delphic authorities (with the god's blessing, they claimed) to excommunicate Cirrha, which was sentenced to destruction. The Amphictyony, requested to carry out the sentence, responded with gusto, and its commander-in-chief, the Thessalian Eurylochus, led the federal forces in the First Sacred War that followed (c.595–583). Athens (reputedly prompted by Solon) and Sicyon came in on their side. The Amphictyonic troops won a crushing victory over the Cirrhans, whose surviving population was enslaved, and their territory dedicated to Apollo.

It was apparently at this juncture that the Amphictyonic Council moved its principal headquarters from Anthela to Delphi, which was not only holy but, for all its apparent remoteness, enjoyed a central location between the various interested states. The Council now declared it an independent city, and proceeded almost at once to reorganize its musical festival.

These new Pythian Games, now open to all Greeks in a more evident sense than had ever been the case before, were first held in 582/581 (or possibly 586–585), under the presidency of the victorious Eurylochus, whose new role re-emphasized the strong, though temporary, predominance of the Thessalians. Thereafter the Games were held every four years instead of every eight years as hitherto, in the third year of each Olympiad; and, as in the case of Olympia, the Amphictyony proclaimed and sought to enforce a truce between quarrelling states for their duration.

Musical contests – instrumental, singing and recitations in verse and prose – continued to take the first place, but athletic and equestrian competitions modelled on those of Olympia were added. The stadium for the foot-races lay close beneath Mount Parnassus, and a hippodrome was built for the chariot-races in the Crisaean plain. The prizes were garlands of bay-leaves taken from the valley of Tempe.

These Pythian Games, which ranked second only to their Olympic counterparts in Panhellenic importance, enhanced still further the renown of Apollo's oracle, which earned Delphi the title of the 'navel of the world'. His temple precinct contained a mass of gold and silver and ivory and bronze and marble works of art; Herodotus lists the splendid gifts of the Lydian King Croesus (Appendix 1), who modelled himself on similar generosity displayed by his predecessors Gyges and Alyattes (and was rewarded, as we saw, by Delphic support against Persia). The Sacred Way, leading up to the precinct, was also lined by artistic works, commemorating the military victories of one Greek (or Etruscan) state or another against its enemies, Greek or barbarian; while other dedications celebrated athletic or musical triumphs in the Games.

Many of these objects were lodged in, or formed part of, the treasuries, which the various Greek states established, as at Olympia, to house their offerings. A precedent was set by Corinth, to house Lydia's gifts. These buildings were adorned with reliefs, notably the metopes of the treasury of Sicyon (c.560) and the friezes of the treasury of Siphnos (c.525?) which are landmarks in the history of Greek sculpture. The Athenian treasury (c.500?) was the first Doric building to be constructed entirely of marble (for the earlier Ionic Artemisium, see Chapter 5, section 3).

In 548, however, the temple of Apollo and the edifices round about, including the Sicyonian treasury, were destroyed by fire. Then, during the final decade of the same century, a great new temple was erected. It was during these years, too, that the precinct was enlarged to its present size. It was enclosed by a trapezoidal wall (subsequently repaired several times), in which every angle and curve of each polygonal stone is fitted tightly to the next, as a precaution against earthquakes.

This task of reconstruction was made possible by an influx of funds from all over the Greek world, and even from non-Greek states such as Egypt. But the most munificent help of all came from members of the Alcmaeonid clan, who were at that time living at Delphi, in exile from the Pisistratid autocracy at their native Athens. Indeed, it was they who took over the entire contract for the rebuilding, and even improved on the agreement by endowing the new temple with a façade of Parian marble. This earned them Delphic support against the Pisistratids, whom the oracle now commanded the Spartans to expel from Athens.

It was believed, however, according to Herodotus, that direct bribery of the priestess had been needed to secure this result.[13] Whether true or not, this allegation demonstrated that the agents of the oracle were now, or were thought to be, corruptible. Thus in c.490 King Cleomenes I was said to have bribed the priestess to declare his fellow monarch Demaratus illegitimate. The scandalous report came out (causing Cleomenes' death), and the oracle, already discredited by its unwise encouragement of Croesus, opted henceforward for caution. It was this caution that prompted it to advise the Greeks not to stand up to Persia (whose destruction of Miletus Delphi had prophesied correctly).[14] But this proved a serious miscalculation. Indeed, the oracle never recovered its political power again. Yet its religious power over individuals remained potent, and states preparing to go to war still felt it advisable to offer the Delphians that tithe of the booty which guaranteed divine support for their military operations.

3 LARISSA AND THE THESSALIANS

The lofty Pindus mountain range, an extension of the Dinaric Alps, extends downwards through northern Greece, separating its western and eastern regions. To the west lay Epirus; the eastern section consisted principally of Thessaly, bounded by the towering peaks of Mount Olympus to the north (forming a boundary with Macedonia) and

Mount Othrys to the south. Thessaly comprised two extensive plains (originally believed to have formed a lake or lakes), which were fertilized by the River Peneus and its tributaries, and surrounded by mountains. Because of this spacious plainland, renowned for its deep rich soil, Thessaly excelled all other Greek lands in the quantity of its fine horses, large cattle and grain.

A widespread Neolithic culture was followed by the arrival, after c.2500, of people speaking a form of Greek. These newcomers (together with others who settled in Macedonia and Epirus) were the first Greek-speaking peoples to arrive in the Balkans. It was consequently in Thessaly, according to mythology, that Hellen (after whom the Greeks were named Hellenes)[15] begat the founders of all the three reputed branches of the Greek race, Dorus, Xuthus (the father of Ion) and Aeolus. Hellen was believed to have been the son or brother of Deucalion (the Greek Noah), and Thessaly was reputedly known as Pyrrhaea, after Deucalion's wife Pyrrha.

Part of the territory gradually became involved in the culture of the late Bronze (Mycenaean) Age, of which the material evidence is centred upon Iolcus, north of the Gulf of Pagasae (at the foot of the Magnesian peninsula). Iolcus was also traditionally the royal town of Aeson and his son Jason, whose Black Sea expedition (mythically reflecting the explorations of the time) was the theme of one of the oldest Greek sagas, the story of the Argonauts (Chapter 8, section 3). Another series of stories, relating to Achilles and his followers the Myrmidons, was closely associated with Phthia, west of the Gulf.

In c.1140 waves of a people speaking a north-western (Aeolic) Greek dialect, the Thessali, migrated eastwards from Epirus into the land which took its future name, legend recounted, from their leader Thessalus, described as the son of Jason and Medea, or, according to another version, believed to be the son of Haemon and grandson of Zeus. The Catalogue of Achaean Ships in the *Iliad* does not name the 'Thessalians' or their chief towns – with the exception of Iolcus and Pherae, another centre not far from the Gulf[16] – but knows of a network of nine little principalities and a number of unsettled tribes.

During the eighth and seventh centuries, however, the Thessali moved down from the higher ground into the fertile lowlands, and swept away these princedoms (if they still existed), replacing them by the four historic territorial cantons of Thessaliotis, Histiaeotis, Pelasgiotis and Phthiotis. Each canton commanded the allegiance of the populations on its fringes, who ranked as *perioeci*, dwellers round about, as at Sparta, or were subjugated and reduced to the status of Penestae – a serf-like role, resembling that of the Spartan Helots, which they sought to escape, according to Aristotle, by repeated risings.[17]

The chief township of Pelasgiotis, which despite rivalry from Pharsalus in Phthiotis subsequently became the most important centre in all Thessaly, was Larissa, dominating a large and productive plain from its citadel located on a mound, and protected by the River Peneus.

Inhabited from prehistoric times, Larissa was rich in myths, many of which were concerned with the nymph of the same name, who was said to have fallen into the Peneus while playing a game of ball. The wealthy noble house which provided the place with its rulers, the Aleuadae,[18] traced its origin back to Thessalus himself, through his descendant Aleuas the Red, a golden-haired cowherd with whom a she-dragon was said to have fallen in love.

The Thessalian cavalry – the best in Greece, providing the natural basis for an oligarchic system – was already a dominant force among the Greeks in the Lelantine War between the Euboean cities of Chalcis and Eretria (c.700), when these horsemen won a battle for the Chalcidians. During the latter part of the seventh century, or perhaps somewhat later, an Aleuad ruler of Larissa asserted his position as elected military leader (*tagos*), often for life, of a Thessalian League which, after earlier and more localized beginnings, covered the whole of the territory. Its member regions, grouped together in a very loose political union, sent delegates to attend religious festivals at the sanctuary of Athena Itonia near Pharsalus. As time went on, each Thessalian land allotment, or estate, was required to contribute a quota of forty cavalry and eighty infantry to the federal army.

The Thessalians were one of the twelve peoples forming the Amphictyonic Council which controlled the Sanctuary of Apollo at Delphi, and when the First Sacred War broke out owing to a dispute between Delphi and Cirrha (section 2 above), it was the Aleuad Eurylochus, in alliance with Cleisthenes of Sicyon, who took the initiative, assumed command of the Amphictyonic forces, and obliterated Cirrha from the map (591). Eurylochus presided at the Pythian Games which were subsequently established – and under Aleuad leadership the Thessalians, in the years that followed, for a time exercised a dominant influence in the Amphictyony; and indeed, among the city-states and tribal units north of the Corinthian Isthmus, they held an unchallenged military supremacy, reinforced by the installation of local dictators.

Their troops, which had led the Amphictyonic army during the First Sacred War, may already have been the federal force to which reference was made above, and there are certain indications of federal activity in the 560s and 540s. However, the earliest firm evidence for a joint council or assembly dates from 511, when 'by common decision', according to Herodotus, the Thessalians sent an expedition to help the

Athenian tyrant Hippias against his enemies.[19] Meanwhile their country was attracting some of the leading poets of the time. Anacreon of Teos went there in c.514, and associated with King Echecratidas and Queen Dyseris of Pharsalus. At about the same time Simonides of Ceos was the guest of the Scopad dynasty of Crannon (the second town of Pelasgiotis). Simonides paid his hosts compliments, but remarked that the Thessalians were the only people he had never cheated, because they were too stupid.[20]

They were certainly politically backward, since the towns created by the local dynasties, although in some cases fairly substantial, lacked the institutions and amenities of city-states; and although there was some sort of federal organization, it cannot have been elaborately developed, since the Thessalians retained all the elements of their old cantonal structure. This meant that the regional, rival dynasties failed to achieve any real coherence or collaborative union. True, the Aleuads, who issued coinage from the beginning of the fifth century, were impressive – Pindar's earliest-known poem (498) was written for one of their young protégés – but they did not enjoy enough authority to hold the country together. Their cavalry was still good, but, in an age of increasingly expert infantry warfare, their foot-soldiers proved no match for the hoplites of other Greek states.

For these reasons the supremacy of the Thessalians in northern Greece did not outlast the sixth century. Thereafter, outclassed by Thebes (which had heavily defeated them near Thespiae in c.540) and eclipsed as a potential Panhellenic force by Sparta, they occupied an undistinguished role, which was by no means redeemed by their alliance with Persia in 492 (probably against the wishes of Echecratidas of Pharsalus), and by their subsequent failure to resist the invading army of Darius. Thereafter, during the century that followed, Thessaly played little further part.

4 THEBES AND THE BOEOTIAN LEAGUE (HESIOD)

Boeotia bordered on Euboea to the east (across the strait), while to the south-east it marched with Attica, and to the south reached as far as the Gulf of Corinth – it was Plutarch's 'dancing-floor of war',[21] a strategic passageway between the two principal regions of the Greek mainland. The relatively fertile core of Boeotian territory consisted of flat lands controlled by Thebes and by its eternally cramping, though eventually eclipsed, rival Orchomenus, the principal city of the Cephisus valley; these plains produced fine grain and olives, and bred horses. The Catalogue of Achaean Ships in the *Iliad* exceptionally lists no less than thirty-one contingents from Boeotia[22] (and may have been originally composed in that territory).

This prehistoric importance of the country was confirmed by an abundance of myths. A large collection of these centred upon Orchomenus; we are told how its people drained Lake Copais, and imposed tribute even on the Thebans, and how its buildings were constructed by the legendary Trophonius and Agamedes of Lebadeia, architects of Apollo's temple at Delphi (section 2 above; *cf.* also below, note 35). Nevertheless, the surviving mythological corpus relating to Orchomenus is negligible in comparison with the array of sagas centred upon Thebes.

Following upon occupation by a people known as the Ectenians, who were ruled by a monarch named Ogyges, Thebes was allegedly founded either by Zeus' son Amphion or by Cadmus – perhaps a product of Minoan Cretan legend – who came from Tyre in Phoenicia (the Theban temple of Demeter Thesmophorus was said to have been his palace) and sowed serpents' or dragons' teeth producing a harvest of armed warriors. These Spartoi ('sown men'), tradition maintained, became the ancestors of the Theban aristocracy. Thebes also claimed Heracles as its own, in competition with Argos and Tiryns. In addition, the place enshrined the multiple, powerful sagas of the House of Oedipus, told in an epic poem (now lost) known as the *Oedipodia*, ascribed to Cinaethon of Sparta; and the expedition of the *Seven Against Thebes* and their sons led by Adrastus of Argos was the subject of other lost epics by unknown authors (not Homer as was often asserted), the *Thebais* and the *Epigoni*.

Thebes lay at the southern extremity of its plainland. Its acropolis, the Cadmeia, stood on an elongated plateau, half a mile long and a quarter of a mile wide, descending to the rocky gorges of the Rivers Dirce and Ismenus and overlooking the town. During the Minoan and Mycenaean Bronze Age, the Cadmeia was a royal palace-fortress, rivalling Mycenae itself (excavations have now suggested) in impressiveness. It owed its wealth to local agriculture and to its location on the land-routes linking central Greece with the Gulf of Corinth and Attica.

This Theban stronghold, however, as archaeological evidence (confirming the *Epigoni*) indicates, was sacked, burned and abandoned in c.1270 BC. The Homeric Catalogue of Achaean Ships, despite all its emphasis on Boeotia, does not mention Thebes, but only Hypothebae, 'the place below Thebes'. It was during this disturbed period, culminating sixty years after the Fall of Troy, that the Boeotians were said to have arrived in the territory, coming from Arne in Thessaly.[23]

They seem to have constituted a complex cultural (and no doubt racial) mixture, accentuated, after they arrived in their new homeland, by intermarriage with its earlier population. As a result of these blends the Boeotian speech in some areas showed affinities with the Arcadian (pre-Dorian) dialect, although it was more closely associated with Thessalian and Aeolic, while also including certain west Greek (Dorian?) elements.

After this Boeotian immigration, Thebes gradually recovered – the apsidal plan of its temple of Apollo Ismenius may be of early-ninth-century date[24] – and became a city-state, though not strong enough to reduce the other townships of the territory to subjection. By the eighth century there were still a dozen or more independent units, including Orchomenus, Coronea, Haliartus, Acraephia, Plataea, Tanagra, Oropus and Thespiae.

The last-named town, near the eastern foot of Mount Helicon, was the principal centre of southern Boeotia. Among its possessions were two harbours on the Corinthian Gulf, Creusa and Siphae, as well as the valley of the Muses on Mount Helicon and the small township or village of Ascra, probably near the modern Panaghia on the Heliconian slope of Askra Pyrgos. Founded, according to tradition, by Oeochus (the son of Poseidon and Ascra) and by Aloeus' sons the giants Otus and Ephialtes (who piled Pelion on Ossa, and inaugurated sacrifices to the Muses on Helicon), this little place outshone all other Boeotian localities in fame, because it was where, according to his own testimony, the poet Hesiod was born.

Hesiod probably composed his poems, the *Works and Days* and the *Theogony*, some years before 700 BC.[25] It was often discussed whether they reached their historic shapes at an earlier or later date than Homer's *Iliad* and *Odyssey*. The Homeric epics have generally been allowed chronological precedence, but mainly on the grounds that the forms of society that they describe seem earlier than those depicted in the Hesiodic works. This, however, is an unsound criterion, since, apart from powerful differences between Hesiod's Boeotia and Homer's Ionia, the social institutions indicated in the *Iliad* and *Odyssey* may be intended to mirror a state of affairs which had long since vanished by the time these poems were created or completed – and was, in any case, in many respects, more imaginary than real (Chapter 5, section 1). Which of these pairs of poems, therefore, the Homeric or the Hesiodic, preceded the other in date remains uncertain.

Hesiod states that his father, a merchant of Cyme in Aeolis (north-western Asia Minor), was compelled by poverty to migrate to Ascra, where his son was born and worked on rough hill land as a farmer, describing the place (not quite fairly) as 'a hole of a village ... bad in winter, tiresome in summer, and good at no season'.[26] On his father's death the division of the property between himself and his brother Perses (the sort of factor that elsewhere prompted emigration and colonization) became the cause of prolonged disputes between the two men. Hesiod tells of his participation in a poetical contest in Chalcis (Euboea), at the funeral of Amphidamas, when he won a prize with a hymn.[27] There are several versions of his death, one of which records that he was killed at Oenoe in Ozolian Locris.[28] His tomb was displayed at Orchomenus.[29]

His poems display his role as the founder and principal exponent of the second, non-Homeric, major epic tradition, which originated not from Ionia but from the Greek mainland. His hexameters, however – since epic language was related to the genre rather than to the region of its author's origin – employ a mixed dialect which, on the whole, resembles the idiom of Homer, though it also contains certain Boeotian elements. Living in an epoch when Greek writing had only recently made its appearance, it would seem that, while employing an oral style, Hesiod (like Homer) either wrote his poems down himself or, more probably, dictated them to scribes – thus pointing both backwards and forwards in time. Despite stylistic crudities, his verses rise, on occasion, to imposing solemnity and force, and include vivid descriptions, reflecting the poet's distinctive personality, which has been hailed as the first in western literature: the first man who speaks to us about himself in his own words.

The *Works and Days* begins with an invocation to the Muses to sing the praises of Zeus, and continue with a conciliatory plea to his brother Perses, suggesting that, although emulation is good, strife is evil. It is the will of Zeus, or the gods, that human beings have to find it difficult to earn a livelihood. Man's fall was brought about by the curiosity of the first woman, Pandora. She was the daughter of Prometheus, who had made mortals the gift of fire; and it was in order to punish them for receiving this gift that Zeus brought Pandora into existence, a deceitful imitation of a goddess, her evil interior concealed beneath a seductive outward guise. 'Into her heart the god Hermes set lies, and wheedling words of falsehood, and a treacherous nature ... a plague to men who eat bread.'[30] And so she opened the jar in which all evils were stored – that is a metaphor for carnal intercourse; but the metaphor is changed in what follows, when we are told that only Hope remained, caught under the lid.

Hesiod was here adapting ancient vituperative, superstitious, folktale themes about women, derived indirectly from Egypt. Such stories emphasized the social and personal perils and pitfalls created by the female sex – which is crafty, and productive of aches and pains and discontents, yet indispensable. By his stress on this theme Hesiod played a prominent part in establishing and perpetuating the anti-feminist emotion that persisted so enduringly in Greek psychology and history. A wife is a drone who wastes man's substance, not only sexually but economically (since a slave could have performed the essential tasks just as efficiently), and makes no other valid contribution. Thus her insinuation into the human scene represents the whole ambiguous nature of man's existence, which the gods govern by means of duplicity, mixing goods and evils together. Like the Book of Job in the Old Testament, the story of Pandora deals with the classical problem of evil, attempting to explain why we have to suffer so much hardship in a world controlled by a supposedly benevolent Zeus. But here there is a different, distinctive explanation: for everything is blamed on women.

The poem goes on to enumerate the five ages of humanity: Gold, Silver, Bronze, the Age of Heroes (a Greek insertion in an otherwise eastern list), and the Heroic Age, which is unpleasant and will grow steadily worse. Might has become Right: a hawk said to a nightingale when it was caught, 'What are you lamenting about? One far stronger than you now holds you fast.'[31] But, even though this brutal doctrine seems to prevail here and now, men should try to behave decently, because heaven eventually sends prosperity to the righteous, but ruins the wicked. Zeus watches everything, with his own eyes and through his chosen representatives as well. One of these envoys is Justice (Dike), who takes note whenever she is wronged and reports the offence to Zeus; for he, although birds and animals may destroy and eat each other, has made just behaviour the peculiar attribute of human beings.

Next, the *Works and Days* turns to the practical details of the farmer's year. The poet records its stages, and offers precepts on family affairs, the right age for marriage, questions of money, and good manners. In offering these injunctions, the poem displays affinities to the traditional near-eastern genres of Wisdom Texts and agricultural almanacs. In Greek literature, however, no precedent can be identified. Although Hesiod makes use, at times, of national myths, in order to express the divine presence that seemed palpably active around him, he innovates by seeking his *main* subject outside the mythological field. He also summons his audience not to Homeric glory but to a Gospel of Labour infused by sobriety, honesty and thrift. For Hesiod belonged to a world where life was harsh and extortionate and redolent, he felt, of a degeneration of the human spirit. He deplores the miseries of his age, in which 'bribes were devoured and crooked judgements delivered'[32] by petty autocratic figures who were already in decline, during this transitional period when the historical city-state had not yet fully emerged. Hesiod watched this process from the ambivalent viewpoint of an independent, slave-owning farmer, a much-enduring conservative who hated what things had come to, and wanted to register an individualist's surly and cantankerous protest against the unfairness of public authority.

The *Theogony*, apart from a renewed attack on women, is a very different sort of composition. Like Homer, and numerous other poets of subsequent ages, Hesiod again inaugurates the work with an invocation to the Muses. Such passages personify the illuminating warmth which at times enters a poet and fills his being. But Hesiod's invocation is framed in exceptionally personal and heartfelt terms. It also contains what can be described as the earliest literary manifesto that has come down to us. Hesiod declares that poetry contains factual in addition to artistic, fictitious material, and that it is his duty to convey such facts in a truthful manner.[33] His own attempt to do so earned him the pioneer place in every list of writers of didactic (instructive) poetry, which was regarded, in ancient times, as a branch of epic, but a branch that dealt with matters other than war.

In order to convey its factual – and improving – message the *Theogony* reverts to a mythological form. It sets out to explain the divine creation and organization of the universe and the world. The poem ranks as a very early attempt to pull a mass of mythological material together, combining it into a picture which, although still pre-scientific, is already, by virtue of its comprehensive aim, halfway between the variegated incoherence of the ancient myths and the rational approaches of the future. Here is a pioneer lay poet taking upon himself the priestly task of recounting mythology – with a novel purpose. A new stage in the intellectual development of the Greeks has been reached, and the beginnings of Greek cosmological philosophy can be seen not far ahead (Chapter 5, section 2).

Yet the mass of different myths and folktales and genealogies that are mobilized for this task are in many or most cases ancient. In particular, the whole Creation story itself, telling how one supreme god (Cronus) was supplanted by another (Zeus), bears a relation to the *Epic of Kumarbi* and *Song of Ullikummi*, of Hurrian origin, which had passed to the Hittites and were current among the states of north Syria where Hittite traditions were perpetuated – and to a lesser extent the influence of the Babylonian *Enuma Elish* is also to be seen (Appendix 1). By what direct or indirect means such influences reached the poet we cannot say.

Hesiod concentrates largely upon the supremacy that Zeus has won for himself by force, and upon the massive powers of destruction by which he obliterated the rebellions of one giant insurgent after another. (Milton's *Paradise Lost* incorporates many details from the *Theogony*.) This is a progression towards Olympian fulfilment in which the guiding principle of the universe is the order imposed by Zeus, so that despite all the incidental ferocities and obstacles, justice (*dike*) can and will eventually prevail. In a deliberate mutiny against the conventional values of epic, *dike* has replaced *time* (honour) as the central virtue of the community.

Both are abstract political concepts, but Hesiod's emphasis on justice reflects the dawn of a new stage of civic consciousness that would bear fruit, before long, in the work of law-givers in numerous cities.

The second major achievement of the early Boeotians was in the political field: namely their outstanding role in the development of federal institutions, a role only grudgingly recognized by hostile later, and especially Athenian, writers.

In Boeotia, there were many factors operating against progress towards federalism, for upon its territory the usual Greek tendency to fragmentation was accentuated by especially longstanding rivalries between cities that were uncomfortably close neighbours.

Militating against this situation, on the other hand, was the need for Boeotian inter-city co-operation against Thessaly and Athens, and to this end an equable share-out of the region's agricultural resources made sense. In due course, therefore, representatives of the cities began to meet regularly for the religious festival of the Pamboeotia at the sanctuary of Athena Itonia at Coronea. Admittedly, our positive evidence for its celebration does not antedate 300 BC, but the ceremonies are likely to go back several centuries earlier.

This is all the more probable because, as early as *c*.550, the evolution of a political league is specifically demonstrated by a federal coinage.[34] For from that time onwards the coins of a number of Boeotian cities display a common type, namely the famous shield characteristic of the region, round or oval in shape, with semicircular openings at either side. The earliest of these coins bear the initials of Tanagra and Haliartus, while a further issue of similar date, bearing no letters at all, comes from Thebes. A second series of mintages, from about the end of the century, add initials of the names of Thebes and other Boeotian towns. Orchomenus, proud of a rich background of its own,[35] coined with separate designs, which indicated that it did not belong to the League (and the same city even celebrated a military victory over one of the

League's members, Coronea).[36] Orchomenus' abstention is under-
standable, since the lack of any indication of a local place-name on the
earliest federal issues of Thebes, already referred to, had hinted
strongly that the confederacy was an unequal one, for by this omission
the Thebans were intending to suggest their own supremacy.

Thebes was governed by a narrow aristocracy, which ruled arbitrarily (though an early 'law-giver', Philolaus, who came there from
Corinth, must have done something to institute a legal regularity).[37] To
what extent, and at what epoch, qualifications of birth gave way to
those of wealth, we cannot tell, though wealth in due course began to
count for a lot, based especially on breeding and selling the pigs for
which the territory was famous.

This Theban oligarchy's relations with the Pisistratids of Athens (as
with their predecessors) were friendly,[38] until the outbreak of a dispute
in c.519 affecting the small state of Plataea, between Mount Cithaeron
and the River Asopus, near Boeotia's border with Attica. Pressed by
Thebes to join the Boeotian League, Plataea appealed to the Spartans;
but they advised the leaders of the little town to turn to Athens for help
instead. The Athenian government responded to their call, and war
between Thebes and Athens promptly followed (which is what Sparta
had hoped for). The Athenians were victorious, and gave Plataea
additional land, at Boeotian expense. But the incident had earned
Athens the hostility of the Thebans, who joined Sparta and Chalcis
against them, with equal lack of success, in 507–506.

Although one would not realize it from reading Hesiod – and indeed in
rural areas many things looked different – social life among the
Boeotians came to be dominated by homosexuality to an extent
unusual even among the Greeks. For it appears from Xenophon and
Plato that for lovers to have carnal relations with their male loved ones
was not just glossed over in Boeotia, as in most other territories, but
came to be considered positively praiseworthy: Plato, as was indicated
in the introduction, pronounced that this was the case in Elis as well,
and 'wherever men are inarticulate'.[39]

As for inarticulateness, however, the land that produced Hesiod
cannot have been as culturally backward and boorish as its Athenian
enemies liked to suggest. Moreover, in addition to Hesiod, the *Homeric
Hymn to Hermes*, of the later sixth century, likewise probably came from
Boeotia; and the legend that Thebes' traditional founder Amphion
could charm even stones with his lyre, the gift of the Muses, reflects a
strong musical tradition. The reeds of Lake Copais provided the
Boeotians with *auloi* (which were like clarinets or oboes), and a famous
school of performers on the instrument emerged, as well as teachers

and innovators. Sculpture, too, was not ignored in Boeotia. The shrine of Apollo Ptoios, the Ptoion twelve miles north of Thebes, was famous for its archaic *kouroi* and *korai*, and some of the bronze-work of the territory also showed merit.

CHAPTER 5

THE EASTERN AND CENTRAL AEGEAN

1 IONIA: CHIOS (HOMER), SAMOS

Before the end of the second millennium BC the west coast of Asia Minor and the adjacent islands were occupied by migrants from Greece: Ionians in the central sector, Aeolians to their north, and Dorians to the south.

The territory of Ionia, believed by Herodotus to possess the best climate in the world,[1] included large islands adjacent to the shore and fertile mainland valleys beside the lower courses of three rivers, the Hermus (Gediz), the Cayster (Küçük Menderes) and the Maeander (Büyük Menderes). Ionia was settled by emigrants from the Greek mainland. They had apparently fled from the Dorians and other invaders at various times from c.1100 BC onwards.

The tradition that the legendary Ion, son of Xuthus (or of Apollo) and Creusa, led a single movement of colonization – settling for a time, on the way, in Athens, where the four Ionian tribes (Chapter 2, note 4) were said to have been named after his four sons – was probably a later patriotic Athenian exaggeration of what was, in fact, a mixed and protracted process.[2] True, Athens is likely to have played a prominent part in the settlement of Ionia. But that presumption must be placed in a wider context, since the Ionians were a major branch of the Greek people who in early times dwelt in many different Hellenic lands. Their dialect, however, is a form of speech first known to us in the historic Asian Ionia, from the Homeric poems composed in that area.

By the late eighth century twelve Ionian city-states had emerged: the islands of Chios and Samos, and upon the mainland, from south to north, Miletus, Myus, Priene, Ephesus, Colophon, Lebedus, Teos, Erythrae, Clazomenae and Phocaea. These twelve states banded themselves into a religious league, the Panionion, with its sanctuary of Poseidon Heliconius upon a spur of Mount Mycale, taking the place of his earlier shrine at Melia (Kale Tepe above Güzel Çamlı), a settlement which the Ionians, though rarely capable of concerted action,

5 The Eastern and Central Aegean

demolished because of its inhabitants' resistance to absorption. In due course, the kings who ruled at least some of the Ionian states were replaced by aristocratic republics. Later, these fell successively under the rule of Lydia and Persia, which tended, after thus gaining control, to establish dictatorial local governments.

The two large Ionian islands off the coast of Asia Minor, Chios and Samos, both played a major part in the history of the early Greeks, which would have been quite different without them.

Thirty miles long (from north to south) and between eight and fifteen miles across, Chios lay five miles off the principal coastal promontory of mainland Ionia. The early inhabitants of the island were said to have included Lydians and Carians (Appendix 1, and note 17 of this chapter). In about 1000 BC, however, Chios was settled by Ionians from Attica (together, perhaps, with some Abantes from Euboea). These immigrants established their principal centre in a rich and beautiful plain on the east coast of the island beneath what is still the town of Chios.

The remains of archaic houses have been excavated, and traces of another ancient settlement on the southern shore, Emporio (over a Mycenaean site), including a wall and a large aristocratic house with wooden posts supported on stone bases, date from the eighth and seventh centuries BC. The local dialect was Ionic with an admixture of Aeolic. In early days Chios was ruled by kings, of whom one, Hippoclus, was killed in a drunken riot at a wedding, which led to a war against the mainland Ionian city of Erythrae. Subsequently the Chian monarchy gave way to aristocratic government.

A number of cities in the eastern Aegean area claimed to be the birthplace of Homer, to whom the *Iliad* and *Odyssey* were ascribed, and internal evidence from the poems – especially their vivid, varied similes – indicates that this coastal area was the region of their origin (that the two works were the work of the same poet, which is sometimes denied, will be affirmed below).

The most convincing claims to Homer's birthplace were those of Chios and Smyrna, and despite the contradictory and fragmentary nature of our sources – especially the so-called *Lives of Homer*, which aimed at suitability rather than truth – it seems probable that, although he may have been born at Smyrna, he lived and worked on Chios. There (according to Ephorus) he lived for a time at the northern village of Bolissus (Volissos),[3] later the dwelling-place of the guild of the Homeridae, devoted to reciting his poetry, who claimed to have originated from his descendants. In the seventh century the poet

Semonides (see below on Samos) ascribes a passage of the *Iliad* to 'the man of Chios',[4] and at about the same time the Pythian (Delphic) section of the *Hymn to Apollo* (known as 'Homeric', but not by Homer) speaks of him as a supreme poet who 'dwelt in rocky Chios' and was blind.[5] Singing was regarded as a suitable occupation for men who could not see – Alcinous' minstrel Demodocus in the *Odyssey* was blind, and Apollo deprived his prophets of their sight – but the condition could also be metaphorical, since bards, whose lofty status Homer is at pains to emphasize, seemed withdrawn into themselves, fastening their gaze on inward things that escaped the vision of others.[6]

The poems seem to have reached their final, or nearly final, form in *c.*750/700 BC – more than 200 years, that is to say, after the arrival of the Ionians upon the island of Chios, and half a millennium later than the supposed events that their poet purported to describe. Whether these works preceded or followed the very different *Works and Days* and *Theogony* of Hesiod (Chapter 4, section 4) remains uncertain. Shorter lays by earlier anonymous or at least unknown poets, which were evidently combined and amended by Homer to form parts of the *Iliad* and *Odyssey*, may already, before his time, have been amalgamated into longer units, pointing the way towards the two complete epics that subsequently emerged during the vast period that extended between the alleged date of the Trojan War and the time of eventual compilation and composition. But on the whole it seems more likely that the amalgamation of these shorter works into the majestic, complex structure of the two great epics should be regarded as the specific achievement of Homer.

During the intervening centuries, the bards who gave performances had been illiterate, but the vanished songs that they sang had been orally transmitted from one generation to another. They no doubt included numerous recurrent formulas which served as mnemonic guides and landmarks to help the impromptu singers; and such formulas – epithets, phrases and word groups ('rosy-fingered dawn', 'wine-dark sea'), in addition to whole set themes and action sequences – continued to abound in the *Iliad* and *Odyssey*. Indeed, their 28,000 lines include 25,000 of these repetitive formulaic units.

Exhaustive efforts, with the aid of every archaeological technique, to date the objects, institutions, customs and rituals described in Homer's poems have produced mixed results, leading, above all, to the conclusion that he was not concerned to reproduce the features and values of any actual society which existed, or had existed, at any specific date. For, whereas his verses include certain allusions, of a more or less garbled character, to the Mycenaean way of life that had come to an end so long ago – notably, in large parts of the *Iliad*'s Catalogue of

Achaean Ships[7] – there are other, more numerous (though far from systematic) references to the poet's own eighth-century surroundings. On the other hand, a number of further elements derive neither from recollections of the long-past Mycenaean age nor from phenomena existent in the poet's own time, but from a wide variety of chronological points during the half-millennium intervening between those two epochs. Other episodes evidently reflect no historic period at all, and are timeless.

Homer was apparently assisted towards his supreme achievement by a stroke of fortune: for his lifetime seems to have coincided with the reintroduction of writing into the Greek world (Chapter 1, note 35). In this situation the poet, providentially personifying the impact of a literate upon an illiterate culture, may have utilized this new technique in person, and committed his verses to writing (or, more probably, dictated them to others who could write) – an opportunity which helped him, beyond measure, to create coherent, monumental poetic structures far beyond the reach of his oral predecessors.

Nevertheless, it was the antique oral tradition of which he himself was still the heir, and he no doubt composed his poetry for (and perhaps partly while) reciting or chanting aloud, accompanying his words with a simple form of lyre (*citharis, phorminx*). These performances may have taken place at noblemen's feasts or at a major festival, such as the Pan-Ionian meetings on Mount Mycale. On such an occasion, one of the two epics could have been recited in about fifteen two-hour sessions, that is to say during the course of three or four days.

The poems that these audiences were privileged to hear were miracles of clarity, directness and speed, and contain some of the most exciting and moving passages ever composed, as well as many delicate touches of sophisticated humour. The rich traditional language of these dactylic hexameters (Chapter 1, note 38) can rise to every mood and occasion. Philologically speaking, it was a blend of dialect forms in which Ionic predominates, but Aeolic and Arcado-Cypriot elements are also to be found.

After centuries of controversy, it can still be argued (even if this is perhaps now a minority view) that the *Iliad* and *Odyssey* were the work of one poet, namely Homer. Certainly, the *Odyssey* reflects a way of life different from, and later than, the way of life delineated in the *Iliad*. Nevertheless, that presents no serious obstacle to the traditional attribution of both works to a single poet (the differences are no greater than those separating *The Tempest* from *King Lear*). Perhaps the *Iliad* was written when Homer was young, and the *Odyssey* when he was older. But that, once again, is not an inevitable deduction, since the fact that he was telling of things that purported to have happened in two different decades (both remote from himself in time – and both, also, largely products of his own imagination) need not mean that the two poems must likewise belong to widely separated decades of his own life, although arguments based on language, ideas and structure have been put forward to suggest that this may have been the case.

At all events, the *Iliad* and *Odyssey*, tragedy and adventure story, complement one another in a number of subtle ways; and the contrasts between them can best be explained neither by different authorship, nor even necessarily, as has just been observed, by composition during earlier and later periods of their single poet's life, but by different layers in a multiple tradition which that poet had inherited.

The *Iliad* narrates events that supposedly took place at some distance to the north of the poet's own home-country, in the neighbourhood of Ilium (Troy) on the Asian mainland, overlooking the Hellespont (Dardanelles). The poem describes a brief and late stage in the siege of Troy by the combined armies of numerous states of the Achaeans (as Homer calls these pre-Dorian peoples of the Greek homeland), commanded by Agamemnon, king of Mycenae. In association with his brother Menelaus of Sparta, he had prompted the leaders of other Achaean states to join this naval expedition against the Trojan monarch Priam because Paris, one of Priam's sons, had abducted Menelaus' wife, the beautiful Helen.

For nine years the Greek troops have been encamped beside their fleet outside the walls of Troy. But they have not, so far, been able to capture the city, although they have seized and plundered a number of neighbouring towns, mainly under the leadership of Achilles, prince of the Myrmidons of Thessaly, the most formidable and unruly of Agamemnon's allies. The loot from one of these townships provokes a quarrel between Achilles and his commander-in-chief. The dispute concerns Chryseis, a girl whom the Achaeans have made captive. She has been allocated to Agamemnon as his prize, but he is reluctantly compelled to return her to her father Chryses, in order to propitiate the anger of Apollo, of whom Chryses is the priest at Chryse and Cilla and on the island of Tenedos. Agamemnon seeks compensation by taking possession, instead, of a girl named Briseis, who was one of the prizes of Achilles, whereupon Achilles furiously withdraws from the battle against the Trojans, taking his Myrmidon followers with him. This is the wrath which forms the first word of the poem, and it is a wrath, as Homer pronounced, which enveloped countless other Achaeans in disaster.

A truce between the two armies, designed to enable Menelaus and Paris to settle their dispute by single combat, comes to nothing, and the war is resumed. Lacking the aid of Achilles, however, the Achaeans find themselves hard-pressed, but Achilles still refuses to help, despite an offer of handsome amends from Agamemnon. A rampart the Achaean soldiers are forced to construct around their ships and living quarters is stormed by Priam's son Hector. At this juncture Achilles relents to the extent of allowing his beloved older friend and associate Patroclus (with whom Homer, unlike later writers, does not imply that he had a homosexual relationship)[8] to lead the Myrmidons to the rescue of their endangered compatriots. Patroclus is successful, but he dashes too far ahead, and meets his death at the hands of Hector beneath the city walls.

Thereupon, convulsed by grief and fury, Achilles himself finally enters the fray once again, throws the fleeing Trojans back into their city, slays Hector and savagely ill-treats his corpse, thus carrying his anger beyond the bounds of humanity. However, the dead man's father, Priam, in his sorrow, is prompted by Zeus to visit Achilles in his camp at night, in order to appeal for the return of his son's body. Achilles concedes his request, and the poem ends with Hector's funeral, amid an uneasy truce.

Excavations confirm that the small but advantageously located fortress of later Bronze Age Troy ('Troy VIIA') was destroyed in c.1250/1200. Its destroyers *may* have been products of the Mycenaean culture from the Greek mainland – speaking a form of Greek – though this cannot be confirmed. But the Mycenaean civilization itself (together with the form of writing that it practised) collapsed not long afterwards, and it was not, as we saw, until five hundred years later that the *Iliad* and *Odyssey* assumed approximately their present shape.

Nevertheless, this great distance of time did nothing to frustrate Homer's unparalleled descriptive talent. With lively yet disengaged comprehension, each personage is depicted as a distinct individual. The most arresting is Achilles, who possesses in extreme degree all the virtues and faults of a Homeric hero, and most completely embodies the heroic code of honour. A hero, as reconstructed by Homer – not from history but from his own nostalgic imagination, fuelled by revived current interest in what might have happened in that remote past – dedicated his entire existence, with all the aid that his birth and wealth and physical prowess could afford him, to an unceasing, violently competitive, vengeful struggle to win applause, together with the material goods which were its standard of measurement, by excelling among his peers, especially in battle, which was his principal occupation (though oratory also ranked high).

Yet the *Iliad*, at times, seems to debate rather than lay down such principles of heroic conduct. This lust and zest for fighting, which at its zenith seemed to elevate the heroes to a pinnacle not too far short of the gods, is overshadowed by pathos: for they still have no way of escaping the mortal, fatal destiny that awaits them.

This destiny is identified with (or occasionally overrides) those very gods themselves, who, as Herodotus pointed out, were given their names, domains and human appearances by Homer and Hesiod.[9] Amoral, unedifying, they squabble sordidly as they divide their support between the two warring sides in the Trojan War, and strike out viciously in sporadic, frightening, often unpredictable interventions. That is partly why a sense of the fragility of all human endeavour pervades the *Iliad*. The gods never die, but death pounces, in the end, upon men and heroes on earth, becoming the ultimate test of merit, the final and most searching ordeal and fulfilment. Achilles knows he has not long to live: and when, at the deeply moving end of the poem, he meets old Priam, whose son Hector he has slain, the exultant din of war has faded into misery and compassion.

Hector, although he made military mistakes and was inferior to Achilles, had been a noble hero (and a noble enemy of the Greeks), in whom warlike and elegiac elements are blended together. Agamemnon and Menelaus are flawed. There are authentic women in the *Iliad*. The last meeting of Andromache with her doomed husband Hector is poignant. As for Helen (transformed from a moon-goddess into the most seductive of human beings), she was responsible for everything, since it was only because of her that the war had ever taken place.

The *Odyssey* tells of Odysseus' return to his home on the island of Ithaca from the Trojan War. His mythical wanderings lasted for ten years, but the action narrated concerns only the last six weeks of this time. At the outset of the poem, he has come to the island of the goddess Calypso, who compels him to stay there as her lover for nearly eight years, in spite of his longing to get back to Ithaca. There, in the meantime, his son Telemachus has grown up, and his home is filled with uninvited guests, the suitors of his wife Penelope. Eating and drinking at the expense of their absent host, they continually urge her to marry again and eventually insist that she must now choose one or another of themselves.

Odysseus owes his troubles to the enmity of Poseidon, for in the course of his travels he had blinded the god's son, the Cyclops Polyphemus. While Poseidon is away, however, the other gods and goddesses are convinced by the hero's staunch patron, Athena, that they should show him pity and render him assistance. She directs Telemachus to visit Pylos (the kingdom of Nestor) and Sparta (to which Menelaus and Helen had by now returned home) in order to seek information about his father's whereabouts. Meanwhile, Zeus commands Calypso to release her captive. He constructs a raft and sets out, but Poseidon creates a storm, and his ship is wrecked. Eventually, after terrible experiences, he is cast up on the coast of Scheria, inhabited by a well-conducted people, the Phaeacians. On reaching the shore he encounters the princess Nausicaa, and she leads him to the palace of her father, the king of the Phaeacians, Alcinous.

During a banquet in Odysseus' honour, the hero describes his travels and adventures since leaving captured Troy. He tells of his perilous encounters with Lotus-Eaters, Polyphemus, the wind-god Aeolus, the cannibal Laestrygones, the witch Circe, the phantoms of the dead (at the end of the earth, or in the underworld of King Minos?), the Sirens, monstrous Scylla and the whirlpool Charybdis. And Odysseus describes, too, how his men had eaten the cattle of the sun-god Helios, paying for this sacrilege by a storm which destroyed them, so that only he himself had survived to make his way to the island of Calypso, and thence later to come ashore on Scheria.

Soon afterwards, despite continuing divine wrath, the Phaeacians arrange his transportation to Ithaca, where, unheroically disguised as a grimy beggar, he discovers how Penelope's suitors have been behaving in his absence. Guided by Athena, Telemachus gets back to the island from Sparta, and so Odysseus and his son, reunited, plan the destruction of their unwelcome guests. In Odysseus' palace, there is no recognition of the returned hero except from his dog (which thereupon closes its eyes in death) and his nurse Eurycleia. Penelope, once again pressed by the suitors to remarry one of their number, proposes an archery contest, allegedly to enable her to make her choice, but no one except Odysseus can string his own mighty bow. He himself, however, contrives to get hold of the weapon, and lets fly a volley of arrows to massacre the suitors. Then Penelope identifies her long-lost husband, and Odysseus rules his island kingdom once again.

Although tacked on to traditions of the Trojan War in order to justify its epic form, the *Odyssey* is founded on a standard folktale: the story of the man who is away for so long that he is believed to be dead, and yet eventually, after fantastic adventures, returns home and rejoins his faithful wife. Dozens of other wondrous ancient stories, often displaying near-eastern analogies (Appendix 1), are transformed and incorporated into the fabric of this most exciting of poems.

The *Odyssey* resembles the *Iliad* in its commendation of physical courage, and a savage pleasure in bloodshed is by no means lacking. However, there has been a shift (if the *Odyssey* is the later of the two poems) from the doom-fraught heights of passionate heroism towards quieter virtues such as endurance and self-control and patience, while love of comrades and of honour now seems to take second place to love of home and wife – the other type of woman, who menaces male society, being rejected in the person of Circe. In a picture that oscillates between kingship and the aristocratic regimes which sometimes or often, it would seem, succeeded monarchical systems, our attention is engaged by the social and family lives of the noble landowners, living on their estates. And stress is placed on good breeding, courtliness and hospitable guest-friendship, with its elaborate web of gifts and counter-gifts. Nor are humbler folk, such as beggars and suppliants, ignored; more distinctive than the dim soldier-assemblymen of the *Iliad*, they are individually protected by a Zeus who is concerned, to this extent, with morality.

But before the poet comes to the more static second half of the *Odyssey*, in which such themes predominate, the hero is tossed upon many seas, and thrown up on strange lands which, as Eratosthenes pointed out as early as the second century BC,[10] defy identification. Yet, unidentifiable though they are and are intended to be, the wonderful accounts of these places reflect, in a general sense, the bold journeys actually accomplished during the age of migrations, which preceded and prepared the way for the feats of the Greek colonizers.

This archetypal wanderer, the formidable, unconquerably strong and enduring Odysseus, cleverer and more resourceful, too, than any other Homeric hero – not so much 'cunning' as capable of analysing any situation and forming rational decisions accordingly – is the permanent exemplar of the complete man who has struggled against all the hazards of life and has vanquished them, one after another – thus finding out many things, and discovering himself. For all Odysseus' sturdy independence, however, a novel note in Greek thinking (and religion) is struck by the exclusive, protective companionship, admiring and often humorous, that is lavished upon him by the goddess Athena.

The magical Circe, too, is vividly delineated, and so is amorous Calypso, the pair whose sexual domination over Odysseus for a time shockingly reversed, in the Greek view, the natural process. But fully developed personalities are for the first time accorded to females who are human beings and not witches, notably Nausicaa and, above all, the complex, ingenious and resolutely chaste Penelope. Women, it is true, are often still not much more than masculine chattels, dependent on their husbands' prowess. Yet they play a major part in the social system, since they are able to link powerful families in alliance, evoking rich presents.

Moreover, watching and enduring on the sidelines, they possess minds and characters of their own, interpreting the significances and consequences of masculine actions. Less of a sexual chauvinist than almost any other male writer of antiquity, Homer gives his women some freedom. Agamemnon and Odysseus had departed leaving their wives in charge of their kingdoms; and the subsequent infidelity of Agamemnon's wife Clytemnestra – which was to become the theme of Aeschylus' *Oresteia* – posed a crucial threat to the male-dominated social system.

Once composed, the *Iliad* and *Odyssey* in due course became the property of a guild or clan of reciters, practitioners of the most skilled Ionian craft of the age. These, as we saw earlier, were the Homeridae – prototypes and models of those professional reciters of poetry the rhapsodes, named after the *rhabdos* (baton) which they held in their hands instead of singing to the lyre. Possibly, in origin, singers of Homer's own circle, the Homeridae claimed to be his descendants, and belonged to the island of Chios. But they and the rhapsodes after them also travelled (they were among the first Greeks to make a habit of doing so),[11] so that knowledge of the *Iliad* and *Odyssey* spread rapidly.

And indeed, throughout the entire subsequent millennium of ancient history, these two poems, perhaps slightly modified under the Pisistratid dictators of Athens – and then divided into twelve books each in the third century BC – supplied the Greeks with their greatest civilizing influence, and formed the foundation of their literary, artistic, moral, social, educational and political attitudes. For a long time, no histories of early times seemed at all necessary, since the *Iliad* and *Odyssey* fulfilled every requirement. They attracted universal esteem and reverence, too, as sources of general and practical wisdom, as arguments for heroic yet human nobility and dignity, as incentives to vigorous (often bellicose) manly action, and as mines of endless quotations and commentaries: the common property of all Greeks everywhere, a counterblast to the centrifugal fragmentation of Greek parochialism.

Chios issued electrum (pale gold) in *c*.600 and later more ample silver coinage, employing a sphinx, with a peculiarly curled wing, as its civic emblem, a fitting symbol of the city's reputation for a prudent, subtle financial dealing and self-interest.

It was here that a metal-worker named Glaucus, perhaps early in the sixth century, was the first Greek, men said, to discover how to weld or solder iron plates and rods together, instead of the more primitive process of nailing or riveting. Moreover, the island was also the centre of flourishing schools of stone-cutters, notable especially for their female figures (*korai*), of which fine examples date from the second half of the sixth century. Chios is sometimes even credited with the invention of this type of art; its sculptors were recognized as specialists in the detailed depiction of the Ionian white linen tunic (*chiton*) which played such a part in the decorative patterns of these *korai*. Some Chian marble-carvers were working for the Athenians, whose Pisistratid rulers maintained close links with the island.

Among these artists, recorded on an inscription from the Acropolis,[12] was the well-known Archermus, whose grandfather Melas, according to Pliny the elder, had founded a whole family sculptural industry (before the Sicyon school was established), extending over four generations and employng white marble from Paros. Archermus was said to have been the first sculptor to show Nike winged,[13] and statues depicting this theme have been tentatively ascribed to his hand. Chios also produced, throughout the sixth century, a series of vases, which used, wrongly, to be attributed to Naucratis in Egypt where many were found, but were, in fact, made by Chians, confirming the important part that they played at this remote market town. The Chian 'chalice style' of *c*.580–570 is notable for an elegant absence of filling ornament, and eye-catching later examples display naturalistic polychrome decoration.

The island was rich in grain, figs and gum-mastic, but became famous for its widely exported wine – regarded as the best Greek lands could provide – and this was also the speciality of its colony Maronea (before *c*.650) on the coast of Thrace. The Thracian chieftains in the hinterland of the colony supplied the Chians with slaves, and others were imported in large numbers from Asia Minor, Illyria, Scythia and the Black Sea region. Favoured by its central geographical position, Chios (before Delos) became the principal receiving station for the slave-trade; its citizens were said to have been the first after the Thessalians and Spartans to use such barbarian slaves, and the first to obtain them not as prisoners of war but by payment (thus incurring, it was asserted, divine punishment). This industry, gradually developing during the sixth century and fuelling economic expansion, became the principal occupation of the Chians, whose large number of slaves was still noted in the following century.[14]

The presence of these numerous slaves was linked with a self-conscious respect for the rights of free citizens, allied, however, with firm government.[15] The Chians were thus concerned with constitutional progress, as becomes clear from an inscription of *c*.575–550, recording legal enactments relating to the administration of justice.[16] The narrow aristocracy, whose Council of three hundred (steered by a Committee of fifteen) was previously in control of the government, had evidently been overthrown and replaced by a system which, to judge from repeated references to the 'laws' (or ordinances) of the *damos* (*demos*, people), possessed democratic elements, including a voting assembly, comparable to, or even in advance of, those of Solon, who had introduced his reforms at Athens a generation earlier. The citizens of Chios seem to have been entitled to appeal to a council, presumably coexisting with the ancient tribal Council that had hitherto been dominant. This new body, comprising fifty members from each of the civic tribes, was convened monthly to conduct important business, including the hearing of appeals. As for the executive, its traditional state officials, still known anachronistically as 'kings' (*basileis*), were counterbalanced by a new set of people's magistrates (*damarchoi*). In accordance with its general concern for the welfare of its citizenry, the island also possessed an unusually early educational system, because we are told that in *c*.494 the roof of a school caved in and buried 119 children.

Incorporated into the Persian empire by Cyrus II the Great, after his obliteration of Lydia in 546, Chios subsequently joined the Milesians (with whom they had a longstanding friendship) in the Ionian revolt, contributing 100 triremes, out of a rebel total of 353, to fight in the battle of Lade (495). Half of this squadron was destroyed in the disastrous engagement, and, although some of the survivors fled back to their island, many others were murdered at Ephesus, whereupon their Chian homes were overrun and devastated by the Persians.

Samos is a mountainous island measuring twenty-seven by fourteen miles, less than two miles from Cape Mycale at the southern extremity of Ionia.

According to a tradition preserved by Strabo, the earliest population was related to the inhabitants of Caria, in south-western Asia Minor.[17] After Neolithic and Bronze Age occupation, Ionian Greek immigrants, seeking to escape the Dorian invaders of the Greek mainland, arrived from Epidaurus in the Argolid. Led by Procles, to whom they later traced back the origins of their kingship, they seem to have reached the island before 1000 BC. They had the usual four Ionian tribes (Chapter 2, note 4), plus two more that were probably composed of native Carians (note 17), indicating that the immigrants came to terms with that people very soon after they had landed on Samos. The principal settlement of the newcomers (now Pithagoria), located beside a circular 'frying-pan' of a harbour on the south side of the island, subsequently became one of the twelve cities of Ionia. Its inhabitants spoke a dialect peculiar to themselves.

While aristocratic landlords (*geomoroi*) superseded the monarchic regime, Samos derived prosperity from its fertile soil, reflected in a number of complimentary names and epithets applied to the island. But above all it benefited from its position as the maritime terminal of the only relatively safe all-weather Aegean crossing. This advantage enabled the Samians to intercept the trade of their permanent rival Miletus, and provided them with access to the commercial land-routes traversing Asia Minor, where they gained control of a strip of coastal territory. It was reputedly in 704 (but perhaps, rather, in c.654) that Ameinocles of Corinth constructed warships, apparently biremes, for their benefit (Chapter 3, section 2). In the seventh century, they helped Sparta in the Second Messenian War, importing more Laconian pottery (especially after 600) than any other Greek state, and acting as the transit-point to which near-eastern luxuries were brought in exchange.

In c.640/638 a merchant-vessel under the command of Colaeus of Samos started to make its way to Egypt (one of the countries from which the Samians received goods, notably bronzes), and got as far as the Libyan island of Platea. But from there it was driven by storms for an enormous distance, through and beyond the Pillars of Heracles (Straits of Gibraltar) as far as Tartessus, a non-Greek state round the mouth of the River Baetis (Guadalquivir) on the Atlantic coast of Spain. Tartessus supplied the main outlet for the rich silver mines of that region, and provided a link with the copper mines of the same country and with the tin supplied from south-west Britain (the Cassiterides in Cornwall – note 51 below) and probably from north-west Spain as well.[18] Greek ceramics had made their appearance around the mouth of the Baetis at least as early as the eighth century, and shortly before Colaeus' journey, in 648, dedications of what was said to be 'Tartessian bronze' had already been offered at Olympia.[19] But the connection was no doubt strengthened by the visit of Colaeus, who, according to Herodotus, returned home with an enormously profitable cargo, setting up a bronze cauldron from the proceeds in the Samian temple of Hera[20] (see below; they were also notable for their dedications at Olympia). Colaeus' success excited the covetousness of other Greek business and adventurers, for whose benefit he had, by the accident of his journey, accelerated an already existent process of opening up the far west.

Nor did the Samians for long remain content with merchant forays; they were also eager to establish (and, unusually, maintain control of) colonies for themselves, even before the main Ionian wave of such foundations got under way. Thus, at some point in the seventh century, they sent settlers to Minoa on the island of Amorgos, a neighbour of Naxos and Paros in the central Cyclades.

The leader of these emigrants was believed to have been Semonides (though some ascribe him to a later date), an iambic and elegiac poet

who had inherited the poetic tradition from his fellow Samian Creo-
phylus (a friend and pupil, and reputedly son-in-law, of Homer).[21]
Semonides has left us a 118-line-long fragment of his *Iambus on
Women*, the most extensive surviving example of early iambic satire.
With literary skill, but in a spirit of querulous invective, Semonides
points the way, even more decisively than Hesiod (Chapter 4,
section 4), to the anti-feminism that characterized subsequent Greek
literature. This he does by comparing different sorts of women with
various types of animals – weasel women, pig women, horse
women – in a coarsely unchivalrous vein reminiscent of the mutual
sex-vituperation familiar from the folktales of peasants of many
races. Other iambic and elegiac fragments of Semonides dwell on
the general illusions and futilities of human hopes. He was also said
to have written an *Archaeology of the Samians*, two books of elegiac
verse on the history of Samos.

Other colonists were sent from that island to Perinthus (*c*.602) and
then to Bisanthe in Thrace and to the island of Samothrace (later sixth
century) off the Thracian coast, to Celenderis and Nagidus in Cilicia
(Appendices, note 2), and to Dicaearchia (later Puteoli) in south-
western Italy (Campania). In *c*.525 mercenaries from Samos were also
settled at Oasis Polis (the Great Oasis, now Al Bawaiti, in the western
desert of Egypt), and Samian businessmen joined with other Greeks in
the establishment of Naucratis on the coast of that country, founding a
sanctuary which stood next to the temple of Apollo erected by their
Milesian enemies.

The Samian temple at Naucratis was dedicated to Hera, the goddess
whose Heraeum at her reputed birthplace four miles west of the city of
Samos, beside the mouth of the River Imbrasus (formerly Parthenius),
was renowned throughout the Greek world.

Upon this marshy site at the end of a long shelving beach – a location
determined, no doubt, by some long-forgotten ancient tradition –
eight (?) successive strata of prehistoric cult-centres (from *c*.2500 BC)
have been distinguished. Their focus was an altar; and in Iron Age
times a stone altar that could be of tenth-century date – although this
exceptionally early attribution has been queried by some scholars –
was followed by no less than seven more during the next 200 or 300
years. In the course of this sequence, soon after 700, when a
branch of the River Imbrasus had flooded the area, a temple was
erected, the earliest Hecatompedon, i.e. 100 (Samian) feet long (its
breadth was 20 feet). The epoch-making size of the edifice required
the innovation of internal wooden posts to support its pitched wooden
roof; and, exceptionally, the building was surrounded by a narrow

colonnade of slender columns on rectangular stone bases, forerunner of later free-standing porticos (*stoai*).

However, when this shrine, in its turn, was destroyed by a second and even graver flood in *c*.660, a still larger Heraeum came into being, the earliest, as far as we know, to display a double row of columns across the front. At this epoch many Egyptian and other eastern bronzes were dedicated in the sanctuary, and Samian bronze-workers, too, seem already to have been active in this field. The monumental bronze cauldrons which figured prominently in these dedications are especially notable; some of the griffins which formed their handles employed the technique of hollow-casting, learned from contact with Egypt. A remarkable wooden group of Zeus and Hera of *c*.625/600 (now disintegrated) also comes from Samos. Another important local art of the time was the working of exquisite statuettes in ivory, a material probably obtained from Syria. A figure of a kneeling youth is particularly well known.

But Samos also produced pioneer full-scale marble sculpture, notably an image of a woman dedicated by Cheramyes to Hera in *c*.575/570. This supernaturally tall statue owes its cylindrical form, ultimately, to Mesopotamian models. But it also owes a more direct debt to the miniature Samian ivories mentioned above; and yet, like the island's other statues of the same epoch, it successfully starts to exploit the potential strength and subtlety of the larger dimension, for instance in the hang of the clinging robes, and in their relation to the body beneath. Such preoccupations are characteristic of East Greece, where there was greater concern for surface patterns than for the structural problems which interested mainland sculptors. Moreover the marble masons who made the Cheramyes *kore*, like other Samians who designed *kouroi* for tombs and sanctuaries during the first decades of the sixth century, differ from other artists engaged in the same occupation at Naxos in the central Aegean (section 5 below), by dispensing with the angular severity the Naxians favoured. However, a *kore* at Athens, of slightly later date, displays the two schools in active collaboration, combining a Naxian face with Samian drapery.

The life of the Samian Heraeum of *c*.660, which had so strongly stimulated the earlier stages of this art, proved a brief one, for almost exactly a century after its construction yet another temple replaced it, measuring 290 by 150 feet, and approached by a monumental Sacred Way, lined by statues. This enormously opulent shrine, the earliest, as far as we are aware, to join together the lateral spirals (volutes) of an Ionic column-capital – the successful survivor of several different formulas – was believed to have been the work of the architects Rhoecus and Theodorus, reputedly his son (in conflict with an earlier chronology that was proposed; the younger man was said to have made a signet ring for Polycrates [see below], i.e. after c.540).[22] Constructed of *poros* (limestone), the new building was surrounded no longer by a single colonnade, but by a double one. The discovery of a stratum of broken roof tiles shows that at least part of the interior was covered over, and the forest of internal columns supporting this roof caused the temple to be known as 'the labyrinth'.

Rhoecus and Theodorus were also credited with the extension of sculptural hollow-casting to large-size figures, which enabled metalworkers to produce statuary on the same life-size scale as stone-carvers, thus revolutionizing the art of sculpture. For in this art the prestige of bronze – in which figures could be portrayed with free arms – stood higher than marble. It was during the sixth century (c.570–540), under Rhoecus and Theodorus, that the designing of bronze *kouroi* and *korai* enabled the Samian school of sculpture to achieve its most distinguished work. A passage in Diodorus Siculus has been thought to suggest that Theodorus learned the canon of human proportions from the Egyptians, though the interpretation has been questioned.[23] Fine marble statues and ivory figurines and reliefs also continued to be made on Samos, and of these we know a little more, because they have not totally vanished, like the bronzes.

It was also at about this period that a Samian poet named Asius wrote about the vivid colourful gatherings at the Heraeum, as they looked during these great days of the island's prosperity, when the young men of its rich landowning class were famous for their fashionable clothes.[24]

After a period of autocratic rule by a dictator Demoteles, in c.600 (or a little later) the island's aristocracy, in which, by that time, wealth no doubt competed with birth as a qualification, briefly resumed its dominant role. In c.540, however, this regime was overthrown by Polycrates, though he may have inherited a dictatorial *coup* undertaken by an immediate predecessor, perhaps his father. At all events, Polycrates gained power with the help of two of his brothers. Very soon, however, by killing one of them (Pantagnotus) and banishing the other (Syloson) he obtained the dictatorship for himself alone. Thereafter he became an exceptionally powerful monarch, credited with incomparable magnificence.

Polycrates borrowed mercenary soldiers from a fellow autocrat, Lygdamis of Naxos, and recruited a Samian force of 1,000 archers. He also mobilized a fleet including 100 penteconters and 40 triremes (a Corinthian form of vessel, as we have seen, which he developed significantly, and indeed may have been the first to employ on a substantial scale). Utilizing this navy, he launched aggressive and, according to his critics, piratical raids on an unprecedented scale, in an attempt to supersede the power of Miletus – now under Persian control – which was obliged, like Mytilene, to undergo a heavy battering at Polycrates' hands. As Herodotus pointed out, he was the first Greek to understand the importance of sea power,[25] and so he converted Samos into the most effective Greek naval state of his day. He realized that, if suitably employed, his fleet could even enable him to stand up to the forces of major near-eastern land-powers. And so, by this means, he was able for a time to hold the balance between his massive Persian and Egyptian neighbours.

Thus Amasis of Egypt (like his neighbours at Greek Cyrene) was glad to make an alliance with him. But the pharaoh subsequently renounced his friendship, and shortly after the accession of the next Egyptian monarch, Psammetichus III (525), Polycrates sent a force (composed of local dissidents whom he wanted out of the way) to help the Persian king Cambyses to conquer Egypt. Having done so, however, they returned to attack Polycrates himself, but without success, although supported by Corinthian and Spartan contingents. Polycrates allegedly bribed the Spartans to go away by giving them false coins, made of lead with a gilt covering. Whether that detail is true or not, the conflict seems to have put an end to Samos' trading link with Sparta.

However, Polycrates was also looking in other directions. In c.525 he annexed Siphnos, taking over its rich silver mines, and he occupied another island, Rheneia beside Delos, and dedicated it to Delian Apollo, as part of a scheme to control the Delian festival, thereby asserting his claim to the leadership of the Ionian Greeks.

Polycrates also paid attention to the agricultural basis of Samian economy, by importing Milesian sheep and other animals to improve the local stock. His fortified palace stood upon the acropolis (the prehistoric Astypalaea) overlooking the city. The palace no longer exists, though a seated statue of Polycrates' grandfather (?) Aiaces has been unearthed at the principal point of ascent. A wall of the same period enclosed the city and port, of which the ancient mole, 440 yards in length and 38 in breadth, is still the foundation of the modern pier.

The Samians excelled in the practical applications of scientific and technological progress, for which Greeks were not generally conspicuous. They were able, for example, to convey a water supply from a spring to the harbour by way of a tunnel 1,140 yards long. Although perhaps initiated earlier, this masterpiece of ancient engineering and survey was designed and carried out, in its final form, by Eupalinus of Megara, working for Polycrates – whose initiatives in this field were still hailed as the greatest in Greece a century later. Moreover, when the Heraeum of Rhoecus and Theodorus was destroyed by fire, perhaps in c.530 (or 520?), it seems to have been Polycrates (perhaps once again enlisting the help of Rhoecus) who planned and began its reconstruction on a grandiose, megalomaniac scale – so grandiose that, over the course of many centuries, the work was never brought to completion. This new Heraeum boasted dimensions even larger than those of the Artemisium at Ephesus, measuring 357 yards in length and 57 feet in breadth. Standing on an elevated platform, it displayed double external colonnades of twenty-four columns, while the interior was divided into three aisles by further rows of columns. This was only one of the many adornments which Polycrates showered upon Samos, annexing the resources of many cities. He also established a brothel, based on those at Sardis in Lydia.

His cultural ambitions suffered a setback when the most eminent (and eccentric) of all Samian thinkers, Pythagoras, left the island in c.531, perhaps as a refugee from the dictatorship, in order to live at Croton in southern Italy (Chapter 7, section 2). Conversely, however, Polycrates was able to attract to his court a pair of eminent poets from elsewhere, Anacreon of Teos in Ionia and Ibycus of Rhegium in south Italy. Anacreon was summoned from Abdera in Thrace, which he had founded on behalf of the Teans, to become the music-teacher of Polycrates' son. A new kind of lyric poet, not geographically rooted but a travelling professional (cf. Introduction, note 4), he also, at the same time, represented the end of an epoch, being the last important composer and performer of solo song.

Anacreon left three groups of poems, lyric, elegiac and iambic, represented only by fragments today. With light and slightly detached urbanity, sharpened by provocative imagery and twists of perspective, he conjures up in these poems scenes which present a wide range of subject matter – not without a degree of elevation, when this was needed – but above all reflect an elegant, bittersweet world of bisexual amours. Indeed, Anacreon's talent for such themes gained him a unique reputation as the poet of love, wine and song, so that his verses continued to be imitated by other Anacreontica for more than three centuries after his death. His output also influenced both the metrical form and subject-matter of later Athenian tragedy.

Ibycus, whose work seems to have been largely choral in character – representing a continuance of the heroic narrative tradition established by Stesichorus of Himera (Chapter 7, section 4) – rejected the opportunity to become dictator of his own city, Rhegium, and went into exile instead, moving to Samos. One of his scintillating poems paid compliments to a young man named Polycrates who was probably the son of the Samian ruler. This piece, an early example of the genre of the *encomium* (a laudatory ode, generally addressed to a conqueror), has been interpreted as a metaphorical farewell to Ibycus' own earlier narrative material in favour of the erotic subjects fashionable among the Samians, who no doubt admired the style – more mannered than that of Anacreon, but also more immediate, luxuriant and passionate – in which he wrote about such topics. His other themes included birds and flowers and the approach of old age.

It was Polycrates' belief that Oroetes, the Persian satrap at Sardis, would help him to establish a naval empire, and when Oroetes let it be known, perhaps mendaciously, that he himself was plotting against his own king Cambyses (*c.*522) Polycrates allowed himself to be lured over to the satrap's court. But once there he was taken prisoner and mutilated and murdered, and his body exhibited on a cross—a foretaste of what the suzerainty of the Persians might mean to Greeks of whom they did not, or had ceased to, approve.

Then followed, at Samos, the brief dictatorial regime of Maeandrius, who had held office as Polycrates' treasurer and deputy. Maeandrius was the first attested ruler to proclaim 'equality of rights' (*isonomia*), later a widespread democratic slogan; and he instituted a cult of Zeus Eleutherius, the liberator, to celebrate the removal of Polycrates. In pursuance of the same enlightened attitudes, he invited the Samians to audit the accounts he had drawn up as controller of his predecessor's finances. However, those citizens who unwisely fell in with this suggestion found themselves arrested by Maeandrius' brother and put to death. Alarmed by such eccentricities, the Persian satrap, in 517, set up the exiled Syloson, Polycrates' brother, in place of Maeandrius, who thereupon left the island and withdrew to Sparta, leaving his mercenary army behind to attack the Persians. The result was a massacre of the population, for which Syloson was blamed by the Samians.

On Persian orders, the island was repeopled with enfranchised slaves. A Samian engineer Mandrocles bridged the Thracian Bosphorus for Darius I of Persia (*c.*513). However, some fourteen years later Samos joined the Ionian revolt against the Persians. But at the battle of Lade (495) most of its ships deserted the rebel cause, and fled.

2 IONIA: MILETUS

Miletus was the southernmost of the mainland cities of Ionia, lying close to its border with Caria (note 17). This 'jewel of Ionia', as Herodotus called the place,[26] was situated in ancient times at the mouth of the fertile valley of the River Maeander, but is now five miles from the sea. According to legend, the place was founded by the Trojan War hero Sarpedon from Milatus (Mallia) in Crete (or from Lycia, on the south coast of Asia Minor). This tradition receives some support from the unearthing of successive strata of Bronze Age habitation, which seems to have reached its climax during the final phases of the Mycenaean epoch, followed by the destruction of the town's walls in c.1200 BC.

Miletus is the only place on the Ionian coast mentioned in the Homeric poems, in which the population are Carians.[27] According to later Greek writers, they lost the town, in the sixth generation after the Fall of Troy, to Ionian settlers under Neleus, the son of King Codrus of Athens. The arrival of these Ionians at Miletus, probably before 1050, is confirmed by archaeological evidence. The settlers retained the four usual Ionian tribes, but added two more, probably consisting of elements from the Carian population, for these remained, as a tradition that the Ionian immigrants took brides from among them corroborated. Nevertheless, the settlers also took a keen interest in their own heroic roots, under the leadership of their Neleidy monarch, which claimed descent from Homeric heroes and gods. And so, no doubt, they looked with favour on Arctinus, an early Milesian poet of the Epic Cycle, who wrote nostalgically on the sack of Troy and other themes. In due course, however, the Neleid kings were superseded by an aristocratic junta.

Miletus is generally regarded as the earliest Ionian foundation. The original Greek town extended northwards from the lofty Kalabaktepe to the Lion Harbour – one of its four natural harbours – centring round a temple of Athena, beside which a low oval altar of eighth-century date (the oldest so far known in Asia Minor) has been uncovered. But the Milesians also looked inland, extending their territory twenty or thirty miles up the Maeander valley, to the point where hill country began. In these adjoining lowlands the ruling nobility enriched themselves by producing thoroughbred Milesian sheep which, sheared with the assistance of Phrygian and Lydian slaves, provided the finest wool in the Greek world, and was exported far and wide, notably to Sybaris in southern Italy.

However, this Milesian territory, limited by its mountainous boundary, and restricted and endangered by the appearance of the Cimmerians and the rise of the Lydian state (Appendix 1), became a source of internal social strife, because its concentration in the hands of only a few landowners angered those members of the rising mercantile class who did not possess land of their own. The outcome of this problem was an outstanding phenomenon in the history of Miletus, namely the dominant part the city played in the foundation of Greek colonies in distant lands.

The region upon which its adventurous seamen and businessmen concentrated, with contributions from other states (since additional settlers and investments must have been needed), were those adjoining the Propontis (Sea of Marmara) and Black Sea, in order to acquire the unlimited supplies of grain that lay beyond, in southern Russia, as well as to catch the tunny-fish moving down into the Mediterranean every year. For these enterprises the two north-east passages, the Hellespont (Dardanelles) and the Thracian Bosphorus, had to be traversed. From a nautical point of view, these were perilous operations. But Milesian sailors soon found out that helpful south-westerly breezes, and favourable eddies among the currents, could be picked up along the shores, and that even in summer, when northerly winds instead prevailed, a ship could pass through on the night breeze that blew up the two straits; and then when the time came to return, the northerly winds brought it safely back home again.

In these areas, the Hellespont, Propontis and Black Sea, the Milesians founded a number of colonies, estimated at a total variously reckoned at thirty and a hundred, and perhaps not too far from the latter total, once foundations by satellites of Miletus are included in the list.[28] For a considerable period, that is to say, the Black Sea and its approaches became virtually a preserve of the Milesians. At Black Sea centres such as Olbia, for example, it was probably a series of goldsmiths sent from Miletus who provided the Scythians with their lavish gold-work (Appendix 2).

In addition, despite perpetual rivalry with Samos, the Milesians fulfilled a major role in the Greek penetration of Egypt, sending thirty ships, in the reign of Psammetichus I (c.664–610), to found the Fort of the Milesians (c.650, at some site, not yet located, beside the Bolbinitic mouth of the Nile) and then moving upstream, helping to defeat a pretender Inarus, and playing a leading part in the establishment of the Greek marketing centre of Naucratis (Chapter 7, section 4), where they built a temple of Apollo.

The initiative for many of these developments may have come from landless citizens of Miletus, eager to emigrate. However, the dominant members of the city's landowning establishment did not intend to be left out. On the contrary, conducting the government through a council known as the Aeinautai ('Perpetual Sailors'),[29] they sought to extract for themselves the maximum profit from the city's overseas ventures. Nevertheless, in the process, they also managed to gain a reputation for the steady, austere honesty of their commercial transactions, although internal strife between these leaders and the less privileged elements remained endemic, and burst into violence all too frequently.

Miletus also controlled the sanctuary of Apollo at Didyma or Branchidae, on a plateau ten miles south of the city. This was under the direction (at first political, but later limited to religious affairs) of the priestly clan of the Branchidae, who claimed descent from Branchus, a Carian youth loved by Apollo. In prehistoric times, it was recorded, the oracle had been situated at a spring sacred to a local goddess. The subsequent shrine of Apollo, in which pottery of seventh-century date has come to light, enjoyed great and widespread renown.

This holy place was one of the principal assets of Thrasybulus, who established an autocratic regime at Miletus in c.600, developing the profession of dictator into a fine art. He made friends with Periander, his fellow despot at Corinth (whom he was said to have advised, meta-phorically, to 'chop down the tallest ears of corn', though according to another version it was he who received the advice from Periander).[30]

Moreover, another of Thrasybulus' allies was King Necho II of Egypt, who offered a dedication at Didyma. However, the Milesian dictator had to defend his city, over a long period, against another eastern state, that of the Lydians. The founder of their kingdom, Gyges, had already attacked Miletus, but had also helped, paradoxically, to build up its fortunes by overthrowing its rival Colophon, hitherto the strongest Ionian power.[31] Subsequent kings of Lydia, Ardys and Sadyattes, displayed equally aggressive intentions towards Miletus; and now Thrasybulus was obliged to undergo twelve successive annual destructions of his harvests while the next Lydian monarch, Alyattes, assaulted his walls. However, the Milesians were rich and strong enough to survive, and in the end successfully made peace with the Lydian ruler, inaugurating a period of tranquil relations.

At this time Miletus could convincingly claim to be an outstanding city and power. It also, probably, introduced coinage to Greek lands, since electrum (pale gold) pieces attributable to the city, which show the device of a lion with backward-turning head, may well be the earliest of all Greek coins, dating from the time of Thrasybulus and modelled on the earliest issues that had ever been made, the series inaugurated by the Lydians a very short time previously at their capital Sardis (Appendix 1). The Milesian weight-standard appears to have been based on the old 'Euboic' copper talent which the Ionians and Aeolians had brought across during their migrations; 3,600 of the new silver shekels (*sigloi*) made up one talent.

Social dissensions, however, seem to have brought Thrasybulus down, whereupon the city was convulsed, for the space of two gener-ations, by a recurrence of the old internal strife. It was led – apart from two dictatorial revivals under Thoas and Damasenor – by two oppos-ing extremist political associations, the Perpetual Sailors or Faction of

Wealth (Ploutis) and the Barefists or Labour (Cheiromachia). Arbitration by the Parians enforced a compromise in favour of a moderate oligarchic government, but this proved unable to avoid virtual subjection to the Lydian king Croesus (560–546). However, Miletus still maintained a privileged position under the suzerainty of that monarch, who dedicated offerings at Didyma, and indeed may well have assisted in the reconstruction of its temple. This amicable relationship meant that Miletus, flourishing as never before, was unique in avoiding hostile Lydian harassment. Nevertheless, it refused to establish a formal alliance with Croesus, reputedly on the advice of its eminent citizen Thales.

This was the man who came to be regarded as the first of the Pre-Socratic philosophers; and he was also traditionally hailed as the founder of physical science. In consequence, he earned inclusion among the Seven Sages. But he seems to have left no writings, and apart from extensive anecdotal material little is known about what he did or said. He was believed to have been a Phoenician by descent, a tradition which might, perhaps, signify only that his ancestors came from Thebes in Boeotia, allegedly ruled in the Bronze Age by the dynasty of Cadmus the Phoenician (early settlers in Ionia were believed to have included 'Cadmeans'). The name of Thales' father, Examyes, however, is Carian. No doubt the family's ancestry was mixed; but he reputedly belonged to an aristocratic Greek clan, the Thelidae.

It was stated that Thales' anticipation of a bumper olive crop led him to corner Milesian oil-presses and make a substantial fortune. In the political field, too, he supposedly displayed unusual wisdom, by urging the city-states of Ionia to unite and create a federal capital and central council at Teos. But this advice was not taken, so that the Ionian city-states, in the end, failed to collaborate sufficiently to safeguard their independence.

The tradition of a visit by Thales to Egypt, even if inauthentic, was by no means implausible, because that was a land in which various scientific studies were stimulated by the annual fertilizing silt of the Nile – and the Milesians, as we have seen, possessed an important stake at Naucratis. A number of stories seek to display Thales' interest in Egyptian conditions. But the supposition that he was the first to bring the study of geometry from that country to Greece is merely an unjustified deduction from his role as the earliest-known Greek geometrician, though assertions that he developed axiomatic geometry are anachronistic, since his concern rather lay with elementary mensuration (he was said to have measured the heights of the pyramids from their shadows).

His practical knowledge of astronomy earned the admiration of his younger contemporary Xenophanes, though the claim that Thales predicted the year of a solar eclipse (585) cannot be regarded as likely, and even if he did so it was merely a fortunate conjecture, probably based on Babylonian records at Sardis. His interest in astronomy, like his preoccupation with geometry, was prompted by utilitarian needs, particularly by the desire to provide aids for navigation. He was also stated to have discovered the variable lengths of the seasons.

As regards Thales' cosmogony (theory of the origins of the universe), it seems reasonable to accept the view, propounded by Aristotle, that he believed that the world had evolved from – and was destined to return to – water,[32] which is therefore the material of which all material objects consist, for he had noticed that water is everywhere and enters into everything.[33] Despite the apparently arbitrary nature of this proposition, and its debts to unscientific near-eastern beliefs that the earth floats on the seas (doctrines held in Babylonia, for example, or perhaps an authentic Egyptian source is detectable here), the simplicity of Thales' insistence on a single unifying principle in the physical world, despite all appearances to the contrary, marked a major departure from elaborately complex earlier Greek cosmogonies, such as that of Hesiod (Chapter 4, section 4), and established a new and fruitful epoch in Greek thought.

Generalized concepts are the last concepts to appear in the evolution of a language, but Thales was able to envisage them, ask questions about them, and seek rational answers to the questions he had asked. That is to say, for all his special practical motivations, he was capable of aiming at the pursuit of knowledge for its own sake, by means of abstract reasoning combined with the use of the eye and mind. Moreover, his assertion that, the basic substance of water being eternal and divine, 'all things are full of gods'[34] was not so theological and unscientific as it sounded, since it broke new ground by implicitly denying that any distinction between natural and supernatural could be legitimately envisaged. According to this line of thought, if carried a little further, a non-mythological, impersonal interpretation of the universe began to enter the realms of possibility; its essentially unitary character made it practicable to assume, for the first time, that the sum of things was a *cosmos*, an orderly system governed by discoverable laws.

Anaximander was born at Miletus in about 610 and died not long after 546. He may therefore have been almost a contemporary of Thales, though tradition, perhaps correctly, regarded the latter as his teacher. Anaximander's apparent participation in the Milesian foundation of

Apollonia Pontica, on the Black Sea, reflects his typical Ionian participation in political life. But he was also conscious of being a sage, and
wore splendid clothes to proclaim the fact.

Like Thales, Anaximander sought to identify the basic material of all
things in the universe. The conclusion he reached was that this *arche* – a
term not perhaps employed by Thales, meaning not only elementary
constituent but origin as well – can best be described as the *apeiron*,
Boundless or spatially Indefinite (rather than infinite). This was the
Unfathomable Deep of ancient near-eastern speculation (like the
Beginningless Lights that formed the abode of the Iranian god Ahu-
ramazda). Yet by speaking in these terms, despite their eastern echoes,
Anaximander was in fact carrying Thales' attempt at logical explanation a step further. His Boundless was the product of pure reasoning –
as opposed to mere observation, since it was obviously unobservable.
He envisaged this Boundless as surrounding and governing the universe, and believed it to have preceded all other forms of existence. For
it was eternal and unaging – or you could, borrowing the terminology
of Thales, call it divine, coterminous with the gods, although this was a
way of expressing the concept that many later Greeks, owing to the
generally anti-theological drift of Anaximander's views, regarded, in
his mouth, as atheistic.

Evidently, then, Anaximander rejected Thales' belief that the fundamental substance was water (or any other such identifiable material). Yet it was out of water, he agreed, that the earth had originally
come. This hypothesis enabled him to bring in the results of observation after all and forge an attempt at theoretical biology, maintaining,
by an unprecedented evolutionary interpretation, that the higher forms
had developed from lower forerunners, so that human beings, at first a
kind of fish in the water, had shed their scales on dry land so as to adjust
their way of life to this new earthy medium.

The numberless worlds comprising the universe, Anaximander went
on to maintain, are constructed out of pairs of contrasting, conflicting
opposites, such as dry and wet, or hot and cold. These polarized
products of the unlimited primordial matter, he said, 'pay due
compensation to one another'.[35] Such an assertion envisaged time
as a sort of judge, assessing the mutual compensations of the various
components of the universe. Here, then, was a shift away from the
ancient conception of an anarchic and capricious universe towards the
idea that it is, instead, governed by a systematic law. Gods or no gods,
this was a cosmogony detached from theogony.

Anaximander developed the conception that the sun and moon,
composed of fire and enveloped in vapour, pass beneath the earth,
rotating in circles. The sun, he asserted, is an opening in the vapour,

about the size of the earth – another conclusion ahead of its time, since for a century to come the sun was still supposed to be far smaller. Anaximander was also believed to have constructed a model made of wheels which moved at different speeds, indicating the routes followed by the stars and planets. Whether he made such a model, however, is uncertain; more probably he measured these movements by another instrument of his own invention, the sundial or gnomon. He was also the first man to attempt to draw a world map. His map took the form of a diagram which showed the surface of the earth as a disc standing upon a column in the centre of the universe, freely suspended in space.

This was an advance on Thales' conception of a flat earth resting on water, and indeed it has been suggested that Anaximander, rather than Thales, ought to be regarded as the world's first true philosopher. Moreover, his work *About Nature* (*c*.550, or a little earlier, now only surviving in fragments) seems to have been the earliest philosophical essay ever written in prose. This marked an emancipation from the non-scientific conventions associated with Ionian and Hesiodic epic poetry. Applying itself to the novel demands of analysis and categorization, Anaximander's treatise must have been a pioneer effort embodying elements of scientific enquiry and insight which, at the time, were extraordinarily bold and provocative.

According to later tradition, which cannot be verified, Anaximenes was Anaximander's student. At all events he was a somewhat younger man, born not long after 600 and dying in 528/525. He, too, wrote a philosophical treatise in prose, of which, once again, only fragments have come down to us.

At first sight his astronomical system strikes a more reactionary note than his older contemporary's, since he reverts to an antique Babylonian view that the sun and moon, at night, circulate round the disc of the earth, upon which the sky presses down. He also abandons Anaximander's concept of an undefinable universal constituent in favour of Thales' belief that this was a definable material substance. But he discards Thales' supposition that it was water, preferring air (*aer*) instead. It is to define this invisible atmosphere, breathed by the universe, that he chooses to revive and reserve Anaximander's term Boundless or Indefinite.

It has been pointed out, against those who dismiss Anaximenes as retrograde, that had he said 'dissociated hydrogen gas', instead of just 'air', he would not be far from views that are held today. But the strength and originality of Anaximenes' conception best emerges when we note that he has postulated a substance whose capacity for self-transformation can be experimentally apprehended, for instance when its temperature and humidity modify. Understanding this, he pronounced that all changes 'are condensation or rarefaction':[36] the former creates wind, cloud, water, earth and stone, and the latter produces fire. This hypothesis dealt mythological concepts of the cosmos a new and significant blow, since, based on an observable means of change, it offered a rational, physical interpretation of how things are related to the fundamental substance, and showed that alterations in the nature of the universe and the world can be explained without recourse to the supernatural – though, once again, being infinite and immeasurable, you can call air a god or the god if you like, a doctrine which shocked Cicero but appealed to St Augustine.

According to later Greek writers – and it seems reasonable to believe them – Anaximenes envisaged even the human soul or *pneuma* (which is now mentioned for the first time, apart from a probably anachronistic quotation from Thales) as a component of this same air. Such a view was facilitated by an ancient identification of air with breath. In the light, however, of Anaximenes' concept of air as the basis of all things, his theory of the soul created a significant bond between the macrocosm of the world and universe and the microcosm of the individual human being. Indeed, the microcosm may even have come before the macrocosm in his own processes of thought, since he seems to have equated the human soul with air *before* moving on to the conclusion that air is the basic material of the universe.

Here is a correspondence with a doctrine found in the Upanishads, those ancient Indian prose and verse treatises enquiring into the nature of the divine principle and the meaning of salvation. For a comparable Upanishadic doctrine propounds a universal wind or breath which is the life-soul of the world and at the same time of each individual self. That this Indian belief should have become known, directly or indirectly, to Anaximenes need not cause too much surprise, because Upanishad thought corresponded, at many points, with the beliefs of the Indo-European-speaking Persians, whose influence on Anaximenes' immediate forerunner Anaximander has already been mentioned. At about the same time a Milesian poet, Phocylides, continuing and developing the didactic, proverbial style of Hesiod, once again took up this interest in the soul by stressing that human virtue is *moral* virtue – a landmark on the way to the Greek moral philosophy of Plato and innumerable others.

Thus in Miletus, for the first time in history, the human being, as a thinking and feeling personality, began to hold the centre of the stage. But that was only one of a whole host of sciences which this emergence of soaring intellect, sweeping speculation and ebullient criticism helped to launch. True, despite claims that Thales, Anaximander and

Anaximenes were the founders of these sciences, the time for their inauguration had not yet quite arrived; for they were, in many ways, curious rather than scientific, and, despite personal observations, were obliged to base their dogmatic and sometimes naïve conclusions on insufficient evidence. Yet the advances registered by their novel mode of thinking, by their determination to discover what the world originates from, and what it is made of, were decisive. True, their continued citation of gods and the divine shows that a theological mode of expression could not yet be abandoned. Yet the terms were now depersonalized and employed in a partially metaphorical sense – indicating eternity, infinity, ubiquity. These Milesians insisted on the application of rationally comprehensible, unbreachably regular, human criteria to the universal facts of physical existence – and such an endeavour, made possible by the spread of literacy, has been described, perhaps without exaggeration, as the Greeks' greatest single claim to fame.

The leap forward was owed partly to Miletus' outward-looking contacts with eastern civilizations. The mercantile prosperity and self-confidence inspired by these contacts endowed Milesians with the time and leisure to propound and publicly to discuss adventurous conceptions, deducing a regular law and order in the cosmos from the similar principles and institutions which had made their city such a resounding success.

Towards the end of the sixth century, or a little later, new aspects of this broader way of thinking were opened up by another Milesian, Hecataeus. He was born before 525; it is not known when he died. A generation or two younger than Anaximenes, he employed, surviving fragments show, a similar Ionian prose medium, which he handled with elegance and power.

One of the two works that can be attributed to him was variously known as the *Histories* (*historiai*, enquiries) or *Genealogy* or *Heroology* (study of heroes). It devoted a new sort of critical attention to the myths and legends whose stranglehold over interpretations of the physical world and universe Thales, Anaximander and Anaximenes had already been at pains to dispel. Hecataeus was endeavouring to trace the roots of leading Milesian families (including his own), which claimed divine or heroic ancestries, right back to the mythical epoch, and in this process he displayed a curious blend of gullible acquiescence and reasoned criticism. The former quality, displayed in an uphill attempt to rationalize myths into a kind of pseudo-history – not rejecting them, but seeking to employ them as the basis of a chronological system – should scarcely evoke surprise, since no alternative lay to hand, seeing that historiography, in Greece, had not been invented. Yet

Hecataeus' firm determination, all the same, to emancipate himself from the mythographers' iron grip over the past was displayed by his introductory assertion: 'What I write here is the account that I believe to be true. For the stories told by the Greeks are many, and in my opinion ridiculous.'[37]

This brave attempt, despite a doomed methodology, was apparently unprecedented, or nearly so. And so Hecataeus became one of the very first of the *logographoi*: tellers of tales who, making use of family trees, described places and regional customs – set in context by the addition of some background material – and thus pointed the way to annalistic recording and to what writers of history in more general and generally recognized senses of the term, led by Herodotus (a severe critic of Hecataeus) would achieve later on.[38] And it was predictable enough that such protohistorians should at first be Ionians, seeing that history was the offspring of Homeric, Ionian epic.

Moreover, Hecataeus was not only a forerunner of historiography but a pioneer geographer as well. This he had already indicated, before his *Genealogy*, in a *Journey Round the World*, of which 300 fragments survive and which can be ascribed (despite doubts in ancient and modern times alike) to his authorship. The work comprised itineraries and notes, surveying the lands and peoples first of Europe and then of Asia (including Africa) which were to be encountered on a journey round the shores of the Mediterranean and Black Seas, with descriptive extensions inland as far as Scythia and India. Carrying further Anaximander's interest in such far-flung themes, he adapted and improved his predecessor's map (though still dividing the world into diagrammatic segments), and with the assistance of his own travels added numerous comments on local institutions and customs and fauna and flora – not for navigational purposes, but in order to provide information. Although later authorities found Hecataeus credulous, he seems to have been the first writer to attempt a record of the topography and traditions of cities throughout the Greek world, thus initiating the analysis of human societies on a systematic basis.

Following the overthrow of Croesus by Cyrus II of Persia (546), Miletus came under the control of the Persians, whose satrap Harpagus treated the city with favour, subject to the re-establishment of a local dictatorship; and after the suppression of its old rival Samos by the Persians in 517, its citizens became even more prosperous. Their leader or 'tyrant' Histiaeus (like other Ionian autocrats) made himself useful to the Persians during their Scythian campaign (c.513–512), so that he was subsequently presented with the fortress of Myrcinus which stood on the coast-road of western Thrace, near the mouth of the Strymon, and controlled the mines of the hinterland.

However, Darius became suspicious of Histiaeus' loyalty, and summoned him to Susa. There, while held in honourable detention, he plotted the Ionian revolt. His fellow conspirator was his son-in-law Aristagoras, who had succeeded him at Miletus but was now involved in difficulties. These were partly caused by the loss of the Milesian wool-trade with Sybaris, which had been destroyed in 510. But Aristagoras had also, more recently, lost favour with his Persian suzerains, through sponsoring an expedition to Naxos which proved unsuccessful. At this juncture, in order to distance himself from Persia, he resigned from the dictatorship of Miletus, installing a system of more or less democratic government (*isonomia*) in his place. This was a bid to gain popular support, and having made the gesture he crossed over to the Greek mainland to enlist help for the rebellion which he and Histiaeus now planned to launch. The response was not very enthusiastic. Sparta declined to assist at all; Athens sent twenty ships, 'the beginning of troubles', said Herodotus, 'for Greeks and foreigners';[39] and Eretria sent five.

On its arrival off the coast of Asia Minor, the joint force went ashore, moved inland and delivered a surprise attack on the Persian provincial capital at Sardis. Whereupon, although the Athenians withdrew, the uprising spread. Herodotus' impression that the entire revolt should be blamed on the selfish ambitions of the two Milesian leaders was not the whole truth. Its main causes were rather Ionian economic decline, discontent with the local dictators and conscription requirements imposed by Persia. At all events, the Ionians, displaying a Greek failure to achieve sufficient unity, suffered a series of setbacks, and Aristagoras was killed, fighting the Thracians near Myrcinus. During the final phase of operations the Persian fleet, recruited from Phoenicia, Cyprus and Egypt, concentrated its strength against Miletus, and in the battle of Lade (495), off its coast, won a resounding victory, helped by the flight of the ships contributed to the rebellion by Samos, the traditional enemy of the Milesians. In the following year Miletus itself fell to the Persians; the city was sacked amid enormous casualties followed by deportations, and the temple at Didyma was burned to the ground.

This epoch-making destruction of a major Greek centre marked the permanent eclipse of Ionian political power. It also caused deep distress at Athens, where the tragic dramatist Phrynichus was fined for producing a play on such a painful subject as the *Fall of Miletus*. But what mattered most for the immediate future was the massive provocation which the Athenian and Eretrian part in the revolt had offered to Darius. The Persian Wars were evidently not far off.

3 IONIA: EPHESUS, SMYRNA, PHOCAEA

Surrounded by the orchards of Ionia, and commanding the extensive Colophonian plain (note 30), the city of Ephesus stood, in ancient times, upon the south side of the narrow estuary of the river Cayster. Due to the absence of tides to scour out its estuary silt has now driven the coastline much farther to the west, a process that had already started by the end of the second millennium BC.

During the late Bronze Age Ephesus had been the capital of a small pre-Greek, Carian state (note 17) that veered between autonomy and subjection to the Hittites (Appendix 1). According to Greek tradition, the city's founders were Amazons (Chapter 8, section 3), but its population also claimed descent from Ionian colonists led by the Athenian King Codrus' son Androclus, who was said to have expelled the Carian and Lelegian inhabitants. The earliest Ephesian kings may have exercised a quasi-feudal superiority over the monarchs of other Ionian cities – which possibly suggested to Homer his picture of the similar relationship of Agamemnon of Mycenae to the various other Greek princes. The citizens of Ephesus were at first grouped into the usual four Ionian tribes (Chapter 2, note 4), but these were subsequently supplemented by two others, into which non-Ionian Greek settlers, whose ancestors had followed the original settlers, were probably admitted.

The fortified settlement founded by the Ionians (including a shrine of Apollo) stood on the slopes of Mount Pion (Panayirdağ) 1,200 yards west of the world-famous Artemisium. This succeeded a shrine of the Anatolian mother-goddess and Cretan Lady of Wild Things (situated on the sea until this began to recede).

The memory of that ancient deity was perpetuated in the Greek cult of Artemis, whose concern had originally been with uncultivated lands and wild beasts. And so her cult-statue at Ephesus continued to display reliefs of animals. Yet this curious, stiff, archaizing figure, studded with twenty-four egg-shaped protuberances – later interpreted, probably wrongly, as breasts – is very different from the prancing huntress of later times, and remains oriental in appearance. Ephesus always persisted in blending its Greek (Ionian) characteristics with near-eastern traditions.

Excavations have revealed relatively early Greek structures on the site. The first consisted of an altar, which, to judge from gold and ivory objects found not far away (and now in the Istanbul museum), was constructed in c.700 BC, or very little later.

The monarchy which first ruled at Ephesus gave way, in due course – as sometimes, if not regularly, occurred elsewhere – to an aristocratic regime, led by a clan or group of clans of royal descent known as the Basilidae, enriched by the imposition of a transit freight charge (*naulon*). The first electrum (pale gold) coins of the city, some of which bear the city-emblem of a bee, seem to belong to that regime, and to date from the seventh century (for a disputed specimen, see Chapter 1, note 50).

The Ephesians scored a military success against an inland Greek town, Magnesia beside Sipylus in Lydia.[40] In c.675–650, however, the non-Greek Cimmerians, having emigrated from south Russia and overthrown the last king of Phrygia (Appendix 1), came down to the coast and devastated the early shrine of Artemis at Ephesus. It was against this menace that the city's poet Callinus, pioneering the elegiac metre (perhaps borrowed from the Phrygians) and adopting the warlike, admonitory tones of Tyrtaeus of Sparta, sought to raise his countrymen to action. The one long fragment surviving from his works summons men reclining at a banquet to take up arms and protect their country, and declares that a courageous fighter deserves comparison with a hero.

In c.600 (?) the aristocracy of the Basilidae was overthrown by one of their own number, Pythagoras, who set himself up as dictator. Ivory statuettes of this period have been found, representing the continuation of an earlier Ephesian tradition and displaying an original East Greek style which still embodies Asiatic influences. It was also apparently Pythagoras who reconstructed the temple of Artemis, surrounding it by a precinct wall. Nevertheless, because he plundered the rich – thus gaining popular support – he was accused of infringing upon sacred as well as secular laws. The Delphic oracle refrained from supporting him, and he fell.

Then, in c.560–550, work began (and continued for many decades) on yet another Artemisium, a huge building this time, which was believed to be the first monumental edifice ever made entirely of marble – except for the ceiling and roof beams, which were of cedarwood (for rival pioneer constructions, see Syracuse, Chapter 7, section 3, and Corcyra, Chapter 8, section 1). The new Artemisium rivalled or excelled the Samian Heraeum as the largest of all Greek buildings, and ranked as one of the Seven Wonders of the World. It was designed and built by Chersiphron and his son Metagenes, from Cnossus in Crete. But Theodorus of Samos was also called in, so that he could advise on the site near the Sacred Harbour, which was swampy (but could not be abandoned owing to local ritual traditions), since his problem at the Samian Heraeum had been similar.

The statue of Artemis stood beneath a columned canopy in the centre of the shrine. The edifice was long and narrow and probably roofless, and, although various features remain disputable, its interior apparently displayed a forest of colonnades, reminiscent of Egyptian and other near-eastern temples. The exterior seems to have been surrounded by a double row of slender fluted Ionic columns, supplemented by a third across the front, behind which the entrance porch (*pronaos*) contained two further parallel rows of four columns, leading into the main sanctuary. The façade, surmounted by huge, painted, Ionic capitals, supported a marble architrave, bridging an unprecedented span.

The lowest drums of the frontal colonnades were presented by Croesus, king of Lydia, with which Ephesus had for some time maintained friendly relations (playing correspondingly little part in Greek political affairs). This reorientation of the city's foreign policy was in keeping with an internal reorganization which likewise took place during this period of dictatorial rule. The principal change meant the substitution of the old tribal system by an entirely new arrangement. Henceforward, instead of the previous six tribes (the four traditional Ionian tribes, plus two for other Greeks), there were to be five. One of them, the 'Ephesians', contained all the members of the former six tribes, who from now on only counted as six 'thousands' (*chiliastyes*) within this single tribe. The other five new tribes were made up of Greeks of various origins, together with elements incorporated from the native populations of Asia Minor.

Presumably these included Lydians. For a new dictator presiding over Ephesus, named Melas, had married a daughter of King Alyattes of Lydia, and conversely Croesus, too, married the daughter of an Ephesian autocrat. There were Lydian priestesses in the Artemisium, and Croesus' generosity to the temple recalled that the shrine had lent him large sums of money (or conveyed the hope that this would happen). Nevertheless, he brought heavy political pressure to bear on Melas' son and successor Pindarus, who saved Ephesus from complete subjugation to Lydia only by accepting the king's demand that he himself should resign from his dictatorship and retire into private life.

After the Lydian kingdom had been overthrown by the Persians, Darius I (521–486) constructed a Royal Road from his capital Susa which reached the Aegean coast at Ephesus, thus not only greatly widening Greek concepts of geography but enabling the Ephesian merchants to receive consignments of eastern products, especially slaves, for conveyance to other points of the Greek world.

During these years two further dictators of Ephesus are heard of, Athenagoras and Comas, who ruled as clients of Darius I. Their regime was responsible for the banishment of the Ephesian poet Hipponax, who was later credited with the invention of the scazon or 'limping' iambic metre – so called because after five iambic feet (short–long) it terminated not with an iambus but with a spondee (long–long). This trenchant metre was considered peculiarly suitable for satire and parody, and the prickly Hipponax, to judge from surviving fragments, devoted much space to colourful, abusive grumblings about his poverty at his place of exile, another Ionian city, Clazomenae. These complaints were authentically autobiographical, it would seem, rather than merely the expression of conventional literary themes. Hipponax also attacked the Chian sculptor Bupalus, over a woman, rather than (as later stories told) because Bupalus had caricatured him in a statue.

It was likewise under the suzerainty of Darius that the outstanding Ephesian philosopher, Heraclitus, carried out his most important work – he knew the Persian king, it was said, but rejected an invitation to his court. A treatise incorporating Heraclitus' philosophical doctrines was deposited in the temple of Artemis, after they had been gathered together, not by himself – for he never wrote his oral pronouncements down – but presumably by a pupil. The work was later known by the customary designation *On Nature*.

Heraclitus had probably been born shortly after 550, and was active at the end of the century. His father, Blason, belonged to the formerly royal clan of the Basilidae (which still retained religious powers, notably priesthoods of Artemis), but Heraclitus renounced his hereditary privileges in favour of a brother. Critical and lonely by nature, he kept aloof from other men, despising them as sleepers – like sated cattle – and protesting that they disliked anyone of exceptional ability. With his fellow philosophers, too, he felt equally at odds: instead of sharing opinions with them, 'I have searched out *my own self*.'[41]

However, he resembled his earlier fellow Ionian Anaximander of Miletus (section 2 above) in envisaging the transformations of the universe as an unceasing series of changes and exchanges, conflicts and tensions ('as in the bow or lyre-string') between opposites ('war is the father of all things'). In consequence he was later credited with the saying *panta rhei*, all things are in a state of flux: 'You cannot step into the same river twice,'[42] an attitude emphatically opposed by other philosophers, most notably his younger contemporary Parmenides of Elea, who maintained that reality is unchanging (Chapter 7, note 59).

Nevertheless, Heraclitus also conceded the existence of an overriding, all-encompassing unity, in which the apparently contradictory opposites are all linked one to the other, in a single, regular, cohesive system of balanced, harmonious measure and just order. He described this controlling unity as the Word (*Logos*), by which he signified the transcendental principle of the universe that brings into being, and governs, every natural event. The Logos may also be called God – 'one thing, the only truly wise, who does not and does consent to be called by the name of Zeus'.[43] The Milesian thinkers had likewise spoken of the divine powers in this symbolic sense, but Heraclitus identified them even more wholeheartedly with the impersonal, universal process.

This principle of the Logos, unifying all opposites, takes the form of an eternal fire which fills the sky and becomes the sea and the earth, though sea and earth finally revert to fire, so that the unity always persists. At this point Heraclitus advances beyond his Milesian predecessors, Thales and Anaximenes, who had postulated one single fundamental material, water and air respectively, since he sees fire not only as something from which other things are made, and not only, even, as the energy of the universe and resolution of all its tensions, the 'measure of change', but as synonymous with the Logos itself.

Heraclitus also endows this primal force with Reason, and consequently ascribes the best wisdom to those human beings closest to the divine fire, because, he curiously asserts, of their 'dry souls'. For he was deeply concerned with the human soul – like Anaximenes before him, and Plato and so many others after him – and its relation to the world-soul. Like Anaximenes once again, he derived this interest from the Persians and, indirectly, from the Indian Upanishads. 'All human laws', he declared in consequence, 'are fed by the one divine law', that is to say by the unifying Logos that governs the universe. And his further deduction was socially progressive: 'the people must fight for the law as for a city rampart'.[44]

But the foremost challenge of Heraclitus to men and women is that they must comprehend this universal order, and must discover how they themselves, as individuals, can live in harmony with its operation. The soul of each one of us, he maintains, being our intellectual principle, should achieve this not by learning anything (or not at first) but by arousing itself from the inert sluggishness of our mental processes. This inertia, resulting in a total non-recognition of the truth, had even been shared, he somewhat harshly indicates, by such towering figures as Hesiod, Pythagoras, Hecataeus and Xenophanes: they had learned about many things, which had failed, however, to bring them real understanding.[45]

Heraclitus himself believed that, by searching out his own self, he could at least set clues, for others to follow up. Yet his clues are far from easy or self-explanatory. The abrupt, peremptory, riddling, pungent paradoxicality of his surviving aphorisms, full of latent and condensed meanings, indicate all too thoroughly why he earned the nickname of the Obscure (*skoteinos*), and why, as a result, he was widely misunderstood by successive Greek philosophers – though all this controversial darkness fails to conceal the fact that he was one of the most original of them all, and still of an interest today that is much more than merely antiquarian or historic.

Ephesus was not eager to join the Ionian revolt against the Persians, but when the rebel troops landed at Coressus near the city some Ephesians proved willing to show them the way inland, so that they could attack Sardis (498).

After this attack had taken place, however, and the rebels had then withdrawn to the coast, their Persian pursuers routed them near Ephesus, and following the disastrous sea-battle off Lade (495) the survivors of the Chian crews were massacred by the Ephesians, who ostensibly mistook them for brigands but in reality were not sorry to be able to ingratiate themselves with the victorious Persians, whom they had never much disliked.

Smyrna was situated at the head of the gulf named after it, into which the River Hermus debouched. The original town, Old Smyrna, stood on a rocky peninsula (Haci Mutso) beside the north-eastern shore of the gulf. This settlement existed since Neolithic times, but its founders, according to contradictory Greek legends, included non-Greek Leleges (note 17), Amazons (Chapter 8, section 3), and King Tantalus of Phrygia (Appendix 1).

In 1050/950 BC (as finds of pottery reveal), the site was occupied by Greek immigrants: first Aeolians (for the most part from Lesbos – section 4 below), living in oval thatched houses, and then, still not later than the tenth century, Ionians (exiles from Colophon across the peninsula to the south – note 31), who moved into Old Smyrna and took much of the place over. It was later believed that these Ionian settlers expelled the pre-Greek inhabitants, but that may be an anachronistic view concealing an early period during which, in fact, Greeks and others lived together.

Excavations have indicated that a substantial mud-brick fortification wall surrounded Old Smyrna in c.850, by which unusually and unexpectedly early date, therefore, some type of community life and organization must already have come into existence. In the eighth century the place appears to have contained, beneath the acropolis (Kadifekale), between 400 and 500 dwellings (the earliest regular

Greek town-houses known to us), capable of accommodating, perhaps, about 2,000 inhabitants with another 1,000 living in a suburb outside the walls.

According to a strong local tradition, Homer was a native of Smyrna; Strabo mentions a Homereion. The claim was disputed by a number of cities, including especially Chios (section 1 above). But although he lived on Chios he may well have been born at Smyrna.[46]

Another poet whose family lived in the city (though he was also claimed by the island of Astypalaea) was Mimnermus (note 31), reputedly a descendant of the exiled Colophonians who had first made Smyrna into an Ionian instead of an Aeolian city. He was said to have flourished during the years 632–629 BC, but a date early in the following century is more probable, since he allegedly engaged in political correspondence with the Athenian Solon (archon in 594/593 or 592/591). A flute-player by profession, Mimnermus wrote elegies – collected together in two books – of which the surviving fragments contain sensitive, well-rounded images that achieve an imaginative impact. One of these books was later named after the flute-girl Nanno (a non-Greek name); it appears to have been of some length, suggesting that Mimnermus may have been an early practitioner of narrative elegy. But his work also contained a good deal of mythology and legend, especially in relation to Colophon and Smyrna, for the settlement of which by his Ionian forebears he is a primary witness.

However the poet, although he admires military prowess, is mainly preoccupied with pleasure, and in particular he dwells on the carefree joys of shining youth in contrast with the disabilities of old age. This theme prompts him to melancholy reflections on the brevity of our life-span, including a prayer for painless death at the age of sixty, a sentiment which was said to have earned him a rebuke from Solon.

In the course of the seventh century, perhaps after its temporary capture by King Gyges of Lydia (c.685–657),[47] Old Smyrna was rebuilt according to a novel plan. Parallel streets, flanked by regularly constructed houses, provide a unique example of an urban layout of this period, and indicate that a rectangular grid-iron design – traditionally associated with the fifth-century Milesian Hippodamus – was already in use, superseding the old irregular plan of the earlier town. Remains of a large temple of Athena of c.610 have also been uncovered, containing experimental examples of artistic decoration; and the earliest stone columns to have survived in Greek lands are its drums of soft white porous tufa. The first known bell-shaped volute capitals come from Smyrna (or Phocaea), and rare electrum coinages attributed to the reconstructed city show the open-jawed head of a lion, emblem of the mother-goddess Cybele inherited from the pre-Greek inhabitants.

Smyrna profited from its export traffic in agricultural produce from the interior of Asia Minor. During the early years of the sixth century, however, it was again captured by the Lydians, this time under the command of King Alyattes, after he had erected a siege-mound which enabled him to overcome the city's defences. The severe devastation he inflicted was repeated in c.545 by the Persians, who in the aftermath of their obliteration of the Lydian kingdom destroyed the temple of Athena and extensive other portions of Old Smyrna as well. Thereupon, according to Strabo, the local survivors retreated to villages,[48] although some remained on the ravaged site, where the damage may have been gradually repaired.

Phocaea, named after *phoke*, a seal (because of the shape of adjoining islands), was another coastal city of western Asia Minor. The bay which it bordered lay near the western extremity of a headland flanked by two harbours, Naustathmus and Lampster, one on either side of the town. A small stream, the Smardus, debouched into the bay, but Phocaea also dominated the valley of the larger River Hermus, which commanded a major route into the interior. It was the northernmost of the Ionian foundations, and indeed, at the time of the original Greek immigrations, had belonged (like Smyrna) to Aeolis rather than to Ionia – whose league it joined relatively late – since it was the Aeolian city of Cyme which had originally ceded the land to Phocaea's first Ionian settlers. The latter were traditionally believed to have been Phocians from near Parnassus, brought from Attica under the leadership of two Athenians, Philogenes and Damon.

However, the arable soil which thus became available to the immigrants proved insufficient for their needs. Instead, therefore, stimulated by their topographical situation at the end of a promontory, they exploited the advantages presented by their harbours, and became outstanding among all the Greeks for their enterprising seamanship. As coastal terminal of the Hermus trunk road, Phocaea provided an outlet for the commercially active kingdom of Lydia in the interior. With a view, also, to extending their trade in another direction, its mariners founded a colony at Lampsacus, strategically situated beside the northern entrance to the Hellespont (Dardanelles). First they ingratiated themselves with the native (Mysian) king of the region, by helping him against his enemies, and then they seized his town (c.654).[49] Moreover, in association with Miletus, the Phocaeans established a colony at Amisus (Samsun), far away on the south coast of the Black Sea (traditionally in c.564).

In addition they took part in the activities of Naucratis in Egypt, where Phocaea was one of the twelve Greek cities which shared the temple of Apollo known as the Hellenium, dating from the time of the pharaoh Amasis (c.569–525). By this time, too, the Phocaeans, in their own native city, had built a temple of Athena, made of fine white porous stone. They had also initiated what was to be an abundant and widely circulating electrum coinage (accompanied by issues of silver that were initially smaller), depicting the city emblem of a seal, and launching a long and varied series of miniature artistic designs. They were also famous for their dyeing industry.

But their most extraordinary accomplishment lay in the distant west. 'The first of the Greeks', according to Herodotus, 'to make long voyages',[50] it was the Phocaeans who pioneered the remotest and most perilous routes. It was they, for example, who followed up the first Samian contacts with the kingdom of Tartessus around the mouth of the River Baetis (Guadalquivir) in south-western Spain (c.640 – section 1 above), sailing not in merchant ships but in fifty-oared warships (so that cargo-carrying was sacrificed to speed and fighting capacity). The friendly relations that they thus established with the long-lived king of Tartessus, Arganthonius, secured the Phocaean adventurers a large share of the bronze, tin and silver in which the Spanish hinterland abounded.

Pliny the elder also adds a record of a certain Midacritus, who is likely to have been a Phocaean. 'Midacritus', he observed, 'was the first to import "white lead" [that is to say tin] from the "Tin Island" (Cassiteris),'[51] by which he meant, however, not the Scilly Islands but Cornwall ('the Stannaries'). Tin was immensely important to the ancient world, since it was an essential constituent of bronze. It existed in various near-eastern countries as well as in Greece itself, but not in sufficient quantities to make supplies from the west unnecessary. Pliny's words might merely mean that Midacritus sailed to Tartessus in order to pick up a cargo of tin which the Tartessians had acquired from Cornwall. But more probably he himself, by way of Tartessus, adventurously fetched the tin from Britain. On the assumption that Midacritus' expedition was in the mid-sixth century or a little earlier, he and his compatriots were choosing a good time for such enterprises, since their potential rivals the Phoenicians were preoccupied with the encroachment of Persia (Appendix 1).

The Phocaeans also created the historic city of Massalia (Marseille) on the Mediterranean coast of Gaul, at the eastern fringe of the Rhône delta (c.600). They were said to have been ordered by an oracle to take a priestess of Ephesian Artemis to the new colony. Very soon afterwards, Phocaea and Massalia between them planted a settlement on the north-east coast of Spain. This was Emporiae (Ampurias), of which the name, signifying trading port and market, indicates the nature and purpose of the new foundation.

The route from the Aegean to Massalia and Emporiae led up beside the western shore of Italy, and in c.565 the Phocaeans founded a colony at Alalia (Aleria) on the east coast of Corsica, close to the mines of mainland Etruria (Appendix 3). Not long afterwards, in 546, Phocaea itself was attacked and devastated by the Persians, who destroyed its temple of Athena, whereupon large numbers of refugees, under the leadership of Creontides, set sail for the west and joined their compatriots at Alalia. That is to say Phocaea, alone among Greek states, responded to Persian menaces and invasions by a massive, corporate refusal to stay at home, though an important sculptor from the city (?), Telephanes, did consent to remain, and worked for the Persian kings Darius I and Xerxes I.

In order to provide a livelihood for the greatly increased population that these two waves of immigrants had created, the Alalians employed methods which provoked the rulers of Caere, the leading maritime city of the Etruscans, to turn against them, in association with the Carthaginians, who likewise felt that their interests in Corsica (and Sardinia) were threatened by these Greek settlers. The result, in c.540–535, was the historic naval 'battle of Alalia' (though it may not have been fought in Alalian waters). The Phocaeans, against a fleet twice their size, were nominally victorious, but suffered such heavy losses that most of the survivors felt that they had to leave Corsica (even though, it would now seem, the Greek evacuation of the island was not complete). The Phocaeans who thus set sail from Alalia first took refuge at Rhegium (Reggio di Calabria), but subsequently moved on to Elea or Hyele (Castellamare di Brucia) in south-western Italy, where their new colony soon prospered, and, through the agency of Parmenides (Chapter 7, note 59), achieved a philosophical eminence to which Phocaea itself had never aspired.

Some of the Phocaean refugees from the Persians eventually returned to their native city in Asia Minor, and its temple of Athena was rebuilt. Phocaea joined the Ionian revolt (499–494). True, its citizens were only able to send three ships to join the rebel forces, but such was their renown for seamanship that in the supreme crisis, before the battle of Lade (495), the Ionian captains placed themselves under the command of a Phocaean, Dionysius. He trained the marines and sailors in ramming manoeuvres, but after a week of drilling in the heat of the sun they became reluctant to obey further orders. At this juncture the

Persians attacked, and won a decisive victory. As for Dionysius, he captured three enemy ships, but soon fled into Phoenician waters. There he sank a number of merchant vessels, but before long departed from eastern Mediterranean waters altogether, and made his way to Sicily.

4 AEOLIS: MYTILENE

Lesbos is the largest of the Greek islands off the western (Aegean) coast of Asia Minor, south-west of the Gulf of Adramyttium (Edremid). The island, of which the northern part consists of volcanic rock, is rich in hot springs. A Bronze Age settlement at Thermi, on its eastern shore, possessed a close link with Troy on the Asian mainland; while Pyrrha and Kourtir (on the Gulf of Pyrrhaeus Euripus to the south) and Old Methymna (to the north) provide extensive traces of Mycenaean settlements. Homer, mentioning the island a number of times, implies the existence of a central town, but it has not yet been identified.

There were said to have been Thracians at one time on Lesbos; a lyre alleged to have belonged to the mythical Thracian singer Orpheus (Appendix 2) was later to be seen in Apollo's temple. But from about 1130 BC the population came to be dominated by Greek (Aeolian) immigrants, from Boeotia and Thessaly. From Lesbos they spread slowly (because of resistance from the native Mysians)[52] over north-western Asia Minor and its islands (c.1130 to after 1000), all the way from the entrance to the Hellespont (Dardanelles) right down to the mouth of the River Hermus; and in consequence this region became known as Aeolis. Intermarrying extensively with the Mysians – in the hope of overcoming their opposition – the settlers founded a number of mainland cities, of which eleven in the southern sector became grouped together in a League of religious origins. The confederates may have assembled at the temple of Apollo at Gryneum, but were led by the most important of the Greek settlements which was Cyme.[53]

Those other Aeolians who had colonized Lesbos claimed to trace their ancestry back to a mythical figure who gave the island its name, the grandson of the wind-god Aeolus. Fertile soil and favourable climate stimulated the development of a group of five Lesbian cities (Pentapolis) comprising Mytilene (to the south-east), Methymna (settled also from Erythrae, Phocis and Scyros), Eresus (to the south-west, well known for its wheat), Antissa (north-west), and the formerly Mycenaean township of Pyrrha. The hereditary princely families in these towns maintained, on a small scale, an old-fashioned grandeur echoing Mycenaean times.

Far the strongest of the Lesbian city-states was Mytilene, though it never completely dominated the others. Situated, at first, on an islet (which subsequently, through silt and sedimentation, became part of Lesbos), the town later expanded on to its historical site upon the main island. This new location possessed a fine double harbour, which gave shelter from the northerly winds and enabled the city to take advantage of its position on the inshore sea-route. Moreover, Mytilene had a share in the trading port set up by a consortium of Greek states at Naucratis in Egypt.

The Mytileneans were governed by the house of the Penthilidae, claiming descent from a son of Orestes (the son of Agamemnon) named Penthilus, who had allegedly founded the city as a refugee from the Dorian conquerors of the Peloponnese (a dubious tradition, since, as we saw, the immigrants to Lesbos seem instead to have come from farther north). There were at first, it appears, local Penthilid monarchs, and then the clan formed an aristocratic government. Its overthrow, not later than 650, was followed by a period of violence and intrigue, during which, however, the members of the former ruling house still remained active.

A dictator named Melanchrus was slain by a combination of leading families including, or directed by, a man bearing the Thracian name of Pittacus. Subsequently he commanded his countrymen in a prolonged struggle against Athens for the strategic centre Sigeum on the Hellespont, gaining a reputation by his killing of the Athenian leader Phrynon. Meanwhile, at Mytilene itself, three factions had emerged, an alliance of aristocrats, a second party led by the dissident noble house of the Cleanactidae, and a more broadly based group under Myrsilus (apparently an Asian name).

But Myrsilus died, whereupon Pittacus (who had been his supporter, praising his well-stocked, brightly gleaming armour), was awarded, perhaps in c.590, a ten-year appointment as *aesymnetes* (arbitrator or umpire), which gave him dictatorial power in the form later defined as an 'elective tyranny'. After banishing the first, aristocratic faction, he treated his other opponents with restraint, publishing and revising the laws in a spirit of moderate reform reminiscent (perhaps deliberately) of his Athenian contemporary Solon, and thus earning a place among the Seven Sages of Greece. Once his ten-year term of office was over, he resigned, living on for another decade in honoured retirement and leaving Mytilene in a condition of prosperous freedom and peace.

However, he had bitterly alienated the lyric poet Alcaeus, born to a long-established Mytilenean family in c.620 (?). A little earlier, another

Lesbian singer, Terpander of Antissa (who later went to work in Sparta), seems to have introduced the seven-stringed lyre to Greece (from Lydia);[54] some of his countrymen employed instruments equipped with as many as twenty strings, which could play both very high and very low notes. It was in the Aeolian region, and especially in Lesbos, that monodic (solo) song, 'lyric' in the narrower sense of subjective and personal poetry, evolved.

Alcaeus was one of the outstanding practitioners of this art. While he was still a boy, his brothers had helped to strike down Melanchrus. Later, he fought at Pittacus' side at Sigeum. But he and his friends had to withdraw to Pyrrha in order to escape from the hostile Myrsilus, whose death, he declared, was an occasion 'to make merry and drink deep'.[55]

However, what followed did not perpetuate his satisfaction, for when Pittacus assumed control in Myrsilus' place, his former fellow fighter Alcaeus reviled the new 'arbitrator' as a vulgar, boastful, arrogant, envious, splay-footed, big-bellied, drunken, upstart rapist and murderer, declaring that the state which had appointed him was spineless and doomed. Not surprisingly, then, Alcaeus was one of the group whom Pittacus subsequently sent into exile; he retreated to Egypt, perhaps visiting Thrace and Boeotia and Lydia as well. The later tradition that Pittacus, before his abdication, pardoned the poet is of doubtful reliability, but at all events he appears to have returned home before his death, of which the date cannot be determined.

Alcaeus was an extrovert of unforgiving animosity, who personified the rowdy, power-hungry aristocracy to which he belonged. It is not possible to interpret all that he records as historical fact: for example, his assertion that on one occasion he ran away from battle, throwing his shield to the ground,[56] is a piece of poetic convention, echoing Archilochus of Paros (see next section). Nevertheless, Alcaeus remains our most important witness to the course of events at Lesbos in the sixth century. He went to banquets, and much of his poetry was intended for recitation at the feasting clubs (hetaireiai) which played such a large part in aristocratic life (enjoying, at Mytilene, excellent wine). He also composed poems about the Trojan War, and hymns in honour of Dionysus and the Muses and a number of other deities, in addition, Horace tells us, to writing a piece in praise of a beautiful boy named Lycus,[57] which was believed to be the earliest literary expression of male homosexual love. This was by no means, however, the only manifestation of Alcaeus' keen eye for beauty, which relates to a wide variety of experiences. He could communicate uncomplicated emotions, utilizing an impressively wide range of lyric metres for the purpose, including the four-lined stanza named Alcaic after him.

Sappho, the daughter of Scamandronymus and Cleis, was almost Alcaeus' contemporary, and like him was born on Lesbos; perhaps Eresus
was her home-town. After a childhood visit to Sicily (where her family
was living in exile during political troubles at home), she returned to
her native island, and made her home at Mytilene. One of her three
brothers, Larichus, poured the wine at Council dinner parties, and
another, Charaxus, was a merchant (this was evidently an occupation
open to Lesbian aristocrats) who took a cargo of wine to Naucratis in
Egypt, where he had a costly affair with a local woman, Doricha.
Sappho, who disapproved of the liaison, married Cercolas, a wealthy
man from Andros. Their daughter, called Cleis after her grandmother,
was admired for her beauty by Sappho (who herself, it was said, was
short and sallow); she advises the girl how to do her hair, and discusses
her desire for a colourful Lydian hat. The story that Sappho hurled
herself to her death from a promontory on the island of Leucas is
probably a myth.

Her favourite poetic medium was the individual love-song in various
metres (including the four-line stanza that was given her name), accompanied by the lyre. These poems, or the portions that survive of
them, show that without shame or guilt, and with more than a trace of
detached, ironic self-criticism, she possessed a unique talent for con-
veying burning emotion; and she communicates an extraordinarily
direct sense of intimacy. Nevertheless, these sentiments and attitudes
are not quite what they seem.

As the employment of numerous formulaic terms suggests, she is not
documenting her own life. Lyric pieces of this kind (as those of Alcaeus
hinted) are not necessarily autobiographical, but create situations
through which a poet can display his or her feelings and standpoints. It
is in this spirit that Sappho composed the renowned twenty-eight lines
of her 'Prayer to Aphrodite', her only work to survive as a whole. When
she appeals so passionately to the goddess to relieve the pain of unsatis-
fied yearning, the grim counterpart of the splendours and joys of love,
we have no means of deciding if her words mirror a personal experience. But whether that is so or not, her unerringly chosen language and
crisp imagery are infused with a delicate sensuousness and appreciation of nature, and breathe an atmosphere of exotic magic and
incantation.

Such was the oblique fashion in which she chose to express the loves
and losses of her small, intense world. It seems to have consisted of a
group of unmarried women (inimical to other, similar, named associations) whom she led and educated and addressed.[58] The group
appears to have been, in some sense, a religious fellowship (*thiasos*), but
evidently spent much of its time in other occupations, notably the

composition and recitation of poetry, and the contemplation of love. These women enjoyed a social freedom which deliberately set out to differentiate itself from the lives and attitudes of their menfolk – stressing mutuality and individualism rather than domination and subjection and war, and even engaging, we are told by Alcaeus, in beauty competitions.[59] It was an existence free of the hindrances that so markedly limited the lives of other women, at least at Athens, and evidently elsewhere in many other Greek centres as well.

The modern significance of the term 'Lesbian' is derived from the amorous way in which Sappho addressed her female companions. Indeed, her words leave no doubt of her intense feelings for her own sex, which presumably – despite indignant denials in modern times – extended to physical relationships, such as also existed among men; and phrases in her own poetry, even if not entirely explicit, suggest that this was so.[60] But Sappho was also heterosexual enough to get married, and she composed wedding songs, *epithalamia*, for performance by a chorus. Her influence on later Greek poets was powerful. Their allusions to women of Lesbos usually denoted intense eroticism, in relation to other women and to men.

After the peaceful interlude introduced by Pittacus, the Mytileneans first suffered reverses at the hands of Pisistratus of Athens, who finally dislodged them from Sigeum, and were then defeated by Polycrates of Samos, who while at war with the Milesians captured an expedition sent to their assistance by Mytilene – subsequently employing the prisoners to dig a ditch outside his own city-wall.

A Mytilenean, Coes, helped Darius I of Persia in his Scythian expedition (c.513–512), and was rewarded by elevation to the dictatorship of his city. His fellow citizens, however, cannot have been contented with his policy, for they stoned him to death in 500/499, at the outset of the Ionian revolt.

While Aeolis formed the northern third of the Greek settlements on and beside the Aegean coast of Asia Minor, and Ionia was in the middle, the southernmost sector (comprising the coastlands and islands of Caria) was occupied by Dorians. None of their colonies had yet attained sufficient importance to receive detailed attention here. But a brief word should nevertheless be said about them.

They formed a confederation of six communities, Cnidus, Halicarnassus, three cities on Rhodes, and Cos. Cnidus, on the mainland, was settled by Spartans in the earliest years of the first millennium BC, first upon a broad, sheltered bay on the southern coast of the long Cnidian Chersonese (Reşadiye peninsula) and later at the same peninsula's western extremity. The Cnidians exported wine, onions, medicinal oils and reeds for pens and colonized Black Corcyra (Korčula) on the Adriatic coast, and the Lipara (Aeolian) islands north of Sicily. Halicarnassus, on the north coast of the Ceramic Gulf, was founded by colonists from Troezen in the Argolid in *c*.900, but was subsequently expelled from the Dorian League, and by the fifth century was Ionian rather than Dorian.

The offshore island of Rhodes, measuring fifty by twenty-two miles, did not yet form a single, united city-state. Instead it comprised, throughout this period, three small and separate city-states, Ialysus, Camirus and Lindus (which did not coalesce to form the single state of Rhodes until 408). After long Bronze Age (Mycenaean) prehistories (which evoked the story of a foundation by Tlepolemus shortly before the Trojan War), these towns had been established in *c*.900 by the Dorians from across the Aegean. Lindus, acting for all three of them, planted colonies in *c*.688 at Gela in Sicily (with Cretans) and Phaselis in Lycia (southern Asia Minor). In the sixth century the Lindians were ruled by Cleobulus, one of the Seven Sages, under whom the island gained or maintained a central position on north–south and east–west trade routes, and formed friendly relations with King Amasis of Egypt. The best-known seventh- and sixth-century East Greek vases have been attributed to another of the Rhodian cities, Camirus. Subsequently the island came under the control of Battus III of Cyrene and then of the Persians.

The Dorian occupants of Cos, who may have come from Epidaurus, superimposed themselves on an earlier Thessalian settlement.

5 THE CYCLADES: NAXOS, PAROS, DELOS

The Cyclades are a large archipelago in the middle of the Aegean Sea, between the Greek mainland and Asia Minor. They take their name from *kuklos*, circle, because they seemed to form a circle round the holy island of Delos. During the early and middle Bronze Ages (third and second millennia BC) these islands enjoyed a distinctive civilization, and from the seventeenth century several of them received settlers from Minoan Crete. From 1400 they belonged to the cultural sphere of the Mycenaean mainland, and after the decline and fall of Mycenae were occupied by immigrants from continental Greece (*c*.1000), speaking for the most part the Ionian dialect (though southern islands, notably volcanic Thera and Melos – well known for its obsidian or black glass – were colonized by Dorians from Laconia).

The largest and most fertile of the Cyclades was Naxos. In prehistoric times the island possessed an extensive population, and became a production centre of small 'Cycladic' statuary, carved out of local grey or white marble, and smoothed and finished by emery, which was likewise to be found on the island and was known as 'Naxian stone'. The early inhabitants were believed to have migrated from Caria and Thrace; then came Cretans.

A prominent centre in the Mycenaean age, when it served as a staging point for eastward maritime traffic, Naxos originated numerous Greek myths. As its additional name of Dionysia suggested, and its famous wine production (celebrated on local coinage) confirmed, it was one of a number of places which competed with Thrace as a claimant to the birthplace of the god Dionysus (see Appendix 2), who, according to tradition, found Ariadne (abandoned by Theseus) on the island, and made her his bride. Another story recounted that the twin giants Otus and Ephialtes, believed to have piled Mount Ossa on Olympus, and Pelion on Ossa, died on Naxos, where they were commemorated by a cult.

Following the arrival of Ionian settlers – mainly, it was said, from Athens, under Archetimus and Teuclus – the new Naxians, in association with men from other Cycladic islands, joined the Euboean city of Chalcis in creating the earliest colony in Sicily, which was called Naxos after them (c.734). Its founder later went off to establish Leontini and Catana as well. At home, too, the mother-island of Naxos took part in the colonization of the central Aegean, joining Samians and Milesians (?), for example, in the settlement of another island of the Cyclades, Amorgos. During the Lelantine War between Chalcis and Eretria (c.700), the Naxians were once again associated with Chalcis, since the Eretrians had challenged their regional supremacy by seizing control of the islands of Andros, Ceos and Tenos.

As in pre-Greek times, the Naxians played a pioneer part in the evolution of sculpture. In c.650, large-scale statues began to be made of the local marble, and although, as in most matters, neighbouring Paros was a competitor (and Delian and Cretan and Corinthian priorities have also, at various times, been claimed), the first important school of Greek marble-carving may well have been upon Naxos.

One of its oldest products is a female statue dedicated to Artemis on Delos, at that time subject to the Naxians, by one of their women named Nicandre (c.650). The wig-like hair of the figure, described as 'Daedalic' after a Cretan sculptor (Chapter 6, section 1) is of eastern appearance, but its disciplined lines are novel and Greek. Seventh-century lions at Delos, too, are of marble from Naxos – perhaps dedicated by its rival noble families – and a sphinx at Delphi, of early-sixth-century date, displays the same origin. Naxian male and female statues, *kouroi* and *korai*, made their way to Athens, and played a large part in developing the marble sculpture of that city. A *kore* of *c*.560–550, of Athenian provenance, reflects the style of Naxos in its long features, but the technique of Samos in its drapery.

The Naxians exported not only their art and artists but unworked marble as well. The industry developed rapidly, supplying the mainland cities at a time when their own productions were achieving no more than local distribution. The Cyclades also took the lead, from about the middle of the seventh century, in the production of engraved seal-stones, inspired not so much by the east as by Bronze Age pieces that were found and copied, and once again the Naxians may well have provided the principal Greek workshop (though finds have suggested that, another island, Melos, has a claim). Naxos also played a part in the early development of Greek architecture, sharing in the creation of the Ionic capital; and a local architect, Byzes, was believed to have invented marble roof-tiles.[61]

The island was governed by nobles and then by oligarchs, until disputes about their increasing wealth – they were known as 'the fat ones' – incited one of their number, Lygdamis, who had gained office as general, to establish himself as dictator, with the help of another autocrat, Pisistratus of Athens (*c*.545). Lygdamis' rivals were systematically driven out; but in *c*.525/524 (or 517/514?) he was expelled, with the assistance of a Spartan army, and an oligarchic regime resumed control. The dictatorship established by Polycrates at Samos had temporarily eclipsed the Naxians, but his overthrow in *c*.522, and subsequent political convulsions in his city, enabled them to achieve new levels of strength and prosperity (including an abundance of slaves) during the last decades of the sixth century. The forces they were able to raise from their own and other islands amounted to 8,000 hoplite infantry and included a fleet, by means of which they became a minor power.

In consequence, Naxos attracted the covetous ambitions both of the Persians and of the Milesians, and after a local *coup* which placed it in the hands of a democratically inclined regime (*c*.500), the ruler of Miletus, Aristagoras, backed by the Persians, returned a positive response to an appeal from Naxian aristocratic refugees. The joint fleet of the Milesians, Persians and exiles, however, failed to take the island by surprise, and after a four-month siege the expedition withdrew. It was this failure that discredited Aristagoras among the Persians, against whom, as a result, he launched the Ionian revolt. Naxos, penalized for participating actively in the rebellion, was destroyed by the Persians in 490.

Paros, orientated towards Ionia, was second in size, among the Cyclades, to its traditional, more westernized enemy Naxos, which lay four miles to its east. Like Naxos, however, it was able to employ a local marble (white in colour, from Mount Marpessa), thus becoming a second centre of island sculpture in the third and second millennia BC. Although the harbour of Paros admitted only small ships, and was entered with difficulty, myths recorded its colonization by the Cretan king Minos and his sons, who were allegedly expelled by Heracles. Tales of settlement by Arcadians and then by Ionians were recorded, under the leadership of two men from Athens, Clytius and Melas. The Parians appear on the historical scene in the Lelantine War between Chalcis and Eretria in Euboea (c.700 – Chapter 4, section 1), during the course of which they allied themselves with Eretria, since Naxos had taken the opposing side.

Together with Erythrae in Ionia, Paros had founded Parium in north-western Asia Minor a decade or so previously, but the principal testimony to its central role in northern Aegean trade was its colonization in c.650, with the sanction of a Delphic oracle, of the offshore island of Thasos (Chapter 8, section 2), which facilitated the exploration of the gold and silver mines round Mount Pangaeum on the adjoining Thracian mainland. For a generation the relationship between Thasos and Paros remained very close.

The poet Archilochus, of Parian birth, was the illegitimate son of Telesicles, the founder of the colony on Thasos, his mother being a slave who may have come from that island. Archilochus himself, deeply involved in local political struggles, took part in the later stages of that island's settlement. A seafarer and mercenary soldier, he had adopted these careers because a Parian named Lycambes refused to let him marry his daughter Neobule, a rejection which incurred ferocious attacks in the thwarted lover's verses. Settling as a landowner on Thasos ('a land not lovely, not desirable, not loved'), Archilochus died in one of the recurrent battles between Parian colonists and Naxians.

As a poet, he developed a brand of satire in iambics (short syllables followed by long, said to have been developed at Eleusis – Chapter 2, note 12), which earned him the epithet of scorpion-tongued. A recently discovered papyrus has provided thirty-five lines of his 'Cologne' Epode, describing sexual seduction in precise detail, conveyed by well-controlled imagery. The trochaic (long–short) metre is also employed. But Archilochus was the master of an astonishing variety of other metrical forms as well – betokening a long-lost, varied history of earlier songs, coexisting with the better-known epics. Elegiac epigrams were among his works, and victory-songs for the Olympic Games, as well as 'dithyrambs', choral songs to Dionysus (inspired, in Aristotle's view, by wine) which were possible precursors of Greek tragedy (Chapter 2, section 4; Chapter 3, section 2). Other themes found in his verses include his own poetic talent, the various chips on his shoulder, the menace of war, and an eclipse of the sun.

Archilochus probably sang some of his poems at *symposia*, post-prandial dinner parties for the clubs (*hetaireiai*) of wealthy citizens. However, he may also have been the first-known poet to have used writing as an aid to the composition of his works and a guarantee of their preservation (it seems less likely that Homer and Hesiod, personally, did the same). He seems to emerge as the earliest Greek writer who speaks to us of his own feelings: individual, un-Homeric, anti-heroic – here is a man who records that he dropped his own shield when running away from battle. True, Alcaeus was later to say that he himself had done the same, which warns us, once again, that when a poet records incidents purporting to belong to his own life they are not necessarily historical facts, but may instead reflect an inventive, non-autobiographical element of thematic convention.

Nevertheless, the roles that Archilochus thus chooses to assume for his audience permit him to indulge in a whole series of frank self-exposures – boisterous, exhibitionist, robust, oscillating between excitement and melancholy, harshness and sensitivity, the joys of love and its bitter pains, immersion in pleasure and a fatalistic awareness that the unexpected is just round the corner. The invective is tough, but it is mingled with reverence for the gods – not unmixed with fear.

Despite all the popular or literary debts to earlier genres that can be detected or conjectured, Archilochus' reputation as one of the greatest of all poetical innovators and poets[62] – exemplified by the continued posthumous public recitations of his poems along with those of Homer and Hesiod – was justified over a wide field. The Greeks would not have regarded it as strictly accurate to call Archilochus a 'lyrical' writer, since the metres in which he habitually wrote did not fall, according to formal rules of classification, into this category. Yet lyrical, in a more general sense, he was – and indeed the first poet who can be so described. Moreover, he had enabled this type of poetry, at its very outset, to reach supreme heights: crisp, sharp, subtle, dramatic and above all varied. For he himself was a versatile man, 'the servant of the Lord God of War who knew full well the lovely gift of the Muses'.[63] He was honoured by a sixth-century *heroon* (hero's shrine), which was restored 300 years later. A biographical inscription connected with the cult is preserved.[64]

Paros also possesses remains of temples of Asclepius, Apollo,

Artemis, and Zeus Kynthios and Athena Kynthia (two deities likewise honoured at neighbouring Delos); and the eastern end of a second sanctuary of Athena has also come to light, in addition to several shrines on a hill to the east of the city. The principal temple, however, dedicated to Demeter Thesmophoros, has so far yielded no trace.

In the seventh century Paros produced its own vases (formerly labelled as 'Siphnian' and 'Melian'), and quarried and exported much marble for the use of sculptors in other Greek lands. Parian marble was especially favoured because, although coarser than other varieties, it was malleable, and possessed a creamy white or pale smoky translucent surface, brightened by sparkling crystals. Thus, together with its rival Naxos, the island led the transition from limestone in c.650–600 which marked the creation of large-scale statuary. Its *kouroi*, notably a figure *kouros* sculpted by a certain Ariston (c.540), and its *korai* are distinctive, varying between quiet pathos and a more exuberant manner which testify jointly to the existence of an individual Parian school.

Legal and constitutional experts from Paros acquired a remarkable reputation as arbitrators. In 655 they were called upon to adjudicate between Chalcis and Andros, although their state had opposed the Chalcidians in the Lelantine War. And then again, in the second half of the sixth century, Parian arbitrators were summoned to Miletus to reconcile its internal factions. Shortly afterwards, the island seems to have become subject to the widespread suzerainty of Lygdamis, the Naxian dictator. But when Naxos was destroyed by the Persians in 490, Paros succeeded to its place as the principal political centre of the Cyclades; it had taken the precaution of sending a trireme to assist the invaders' fleet.

Measuring only about three miles in length and between a mile and a mile and a half in breadth, Delos – to the north of Naxos and Paros – is an infertile island, made of granite and yellow sand and short of water, but it was regarded as the hub and origin of the Cyclades. Its loftiest point is the rocky and holy Mount Cynthus, rising to a height of 350 feet. The remains of stone huts on the mountain (as in the plain below) bear witness to pre-Greek habitation centres and worships dating back to the third millennium BC. According to Thucydides, these settlers had been Carians,[65] who were driven out, however – according to tradition – by King Minos of Crete. Mycenaean pottery is found more abundantly on Delos than elsewhere in the archipelago, and Mycenaean buildings lay beneath the temples of later times. The principal deity of the island in the late Bronze Age seems to have been Artemis (section 3 above).

Before the end of the second millennium, Ionian colonists arrived from the Greek mainland, inheriting the sacred grotto on Mount Cynthus, and by the time of the *Odyssey* Delos was already famous as the birthplace of Apollo and Artemis ('twins', though their cults were apparently separate in origin). One of the many myths commemorating this double event told how the island had drifted through the Aegean until it was moored by Zeus, so that the wandering Titaness Leto could give birth to the two deities.

The story was told by the *Hymn to Apollo*, an early literary work divided into two parts – evidently by different authors – relating to Delos (lines 1–178) and Delphi (lines 179–546; cf. Chapter 4, section 2). The Delian section of the hymn is self-ascribed to a blind poet of Chios, and was often credited in ancient times to Homer. But its author was not the man who composed either the *Iliad* or the *Odyssey*, and his piece appears to have taken shape later than the Homeric epics, in the middle of the seventh century. However, the work was also sometimes attributed to Cynaethus of Chios, who worked shortly before 500 (and was reputedly the first poet to recite Homer at Syracuse).[66]

This section of the *Hymn* was designed to show how such an unproductive little island could have become a major cult centre. Several versions of the birth of Apollo existed. But according to the *Hymn* Leto, after labour pains lasting for nine days and nine nights, gave birth to the god 'leaning against Cynthus' mountain' (she was also described as grasping a sacred palm tree). No other island, we are told, dared accommodate the birth of so terrible a god, and even Delos was afraid, until reassured by Leto's promise that Apollo would make his temple there. She already appears with Apollo and Artemis on bronze statuettes of early seventh-century date (from Drerus in Crete). The *Hymn* also tells how Delos became the seat of a great festival to which the Ionian states, including Athens, sent a delegation every year to celebrate the birthday of Apollo – and these verses themselves may well have been entered for a poetic competition at the festival.

'Your heart, Phoebus (Apollo),' the author declares,

takes most delight in Delos, where the long-robed Ionians gather with their children and their honoured wives; and they commemorate and delight you with boxing and dancing and song whenever they hold their competitions. A man who came across the Ionians gathered together would say they were a deathless and unageing people; for he would see how graceful they all are, and he would delight his heart in watching the men and the well-girdled women and the fast ships and their many possessions.

Moreover there is this great marvel whose glory will never die: the Delian maidens, the servants of the Far-shooter. For, after praising Apollo, and then Leto and Artemis the archer, they sing a song about the men and women of old, and enchant the tribes of men; and they know how to imitate the tongues of all peoples, and their rattling music.

The cosmopolitan Ionians, then, brought their women to the Delian festival, unlike the Dorians at Olympia.

A small square building on a virgin site halfway up Mount Cynthus may be a very early shrine (though this has been disputed),[67] but the principal sacred area (*hieron*) lay below on the flat ground, beside the sea. Within this dedicated zone, the most ancient worship appears to have centred on the temple of Artemis (the principal deity, as we saw, of the Bronze Age), where a treasure of gold, ivory and bronze, dating both from Mycenaean and from Geometric times, was buried during the rebuilding of the edifice in *c.*700, superimposed upon a long, narrow Mycenaean structure, which probably possessed some religious purpose. There was also an adjacent precinct of Leto, containing a temple which dates in its surviving form to the mid-sixth century.

Nearby was the sanctuary of Apollo. It is uncertain what building, if any, served as the centre of his worship in the early part of the first millennium, since the limestone remains of the earliest of the three temples in the sacred zone seem contemporary with the extant remains of the adjoining shrine of Leto. As time went on, however, Apollo's holy place came to excel all others in the Greek world in splendour, with the aim of exalting, above all other Hellenic peoples, the Ionians, for whom Delos served as the centre of an Amphictyony, or religious league. An epigram, characteristic of Greek thinking, was later inscribed on the temple's Propylaea: 'Most noble is that which is most just, and best is health: but most pleasant it is to win what we desire.'

Callimachus (*c.*310/305–240), in his *Hymn to Apollo*, imagines the epiphany of Apollo, visiting his temple: always beautiful and always young, his unshorn locks shedding dews of healing wherever he goes. To the west of the shrine the base of his renowned, nine-foot-high seventh-century statue still remains *in situ*, and parts of its torso and of one of its thighs lie nearby, where robbers were forced to abandon them. A row of nine lions of equally early date, of which four survive, guarded a processional avenue leading from the shrine to a Sacred Lake, which, ancient writers record, formed a prominent feature of the island's scenery, but has now been drained. The Sacred Harbour close to the sanctuaries was equipped with the earliest-known artificial port-works in the Greek world, including a mole of eighth-century date, jutting out 300 feet from the shore.

Although Delos itself could stake a claim to one of the pioneer schools of marble sculpture (and its bronze-work was also notable),[68] Apollo's statue, made by Tectaeus and Angelion, was dedicated by the Naxians, and the lions were made of marble from their island, which seems to have exercised political control over Delos during the seventh century BC and the first half of the sixth, enriching the smaller, sanctified island from funds Lygdamis of Naxos had confiscated from his own subjects. Then, however, the Delians passed under the influence of Pisistratus of Athens, who, obeying the instructions of an oracle, 'purified' the sanctuary (by digging up corpses and moving them out),[69] with the intention of asserting his control (in place of the Naxians) over the Ionian League and the Cyclades.

Subsequently Polycrates of Samos, too, extended his rival patronage to Delos, inaugurating a new festival and dedicating the neighbouring island of Rheneia to Delian Apollo. But after the fall of Pisistratus and Polycrates, Delos seems to have passed once more under Naxian control.

6 Cyrenaica and Crete

CHAPTER 6

THE SOUTH AND EAST

1 CRETE: CNOSSUS, GORTYNA, DRERUS

Crete, lying south-east of the Greek mainland, and south-west of Asia Minor, is a large island – 152 miles long, and varying in breadth from seven and a half to thirty-five miles. Its soil grew little grain, but boasted a surplus of wine, oil and timber. And although isolated and windy, and deficient in good harbours, it occupied a commanding position for the establishment of contacts between east and west.

After the glories of the Minoan (Bronze) epoch, the tradition remained among the Greeks that the first of all sea-powers had been that of a Cretan autocrat Minos, the son of Zeus and Europa, who according to the *Odyssey* had ruled by the dispensation of his father – and continues to reign among the dead. Poseidon (or according to another version Aphrodite) caused Minos' wife Pasiphae, the daughter of Helios, to fall in love with a bull sent by Poseidon for sacrifice. Disguised as a cow by the help of the legendary craftsman Daedalus, she made love to the animal and gave birth to the Minotaur, half man and half bull. Daedalus constructed a maze, the labyrinth, for its concealment, and Minos confined his annual tribute of Athenian youths and maidens in the labyrinth together with the monster, which was killed, however, by the Athenian hero Theseus. This he achieved with the help of a clue of thread given him by Minos' daughter Ariadne so that he could find his way out; and they fled the island together, though Theseus left her abandoned on Naxos, until the god Dionysus came to her rescue.

During the dawning period of Iron Age Greek history, after the arrival of Dorian invaders or immigrants, Crete, unlike most other Aegean lands, remained prosperous, enjoying a Mycenaean twilight in which many earlier, Bronze Age traditions managed to survive.[1] According to the *Iliad*, the island contained ninety cities. The *Odyssey*, on the other hand, mentions a hundred – and speaks of four other racial elements, besides the Dorians, among the inhabitants, and a no less complex (although probably not quite corresponding) mixture of tongues,[2] although the resultant amalgam seemed to later Greek authors homogeneous enough for 'Cretan' affairs and customs to be written about in generic terms.

According to a story which evidently echoes and reflects population movements of the time, the Cretans were described as the founders of Apollo's cult at Delphi (Chapter 4, section 2). During the ninth and eighth centuries the island was still probably the richest of all Aegean territories. This wealth was due not only to the unusual preservation of so much of the material past but also to piracy, for which the Cretans possessed a formidable reputation. Odysseus implicitly referred to this aspect of their lives when, telling a mendacious story about his origins, he identified himself as a Cretan who had turned pirate.[3]

Nevertheless, the cities of the island also operated a stable agrarian system. Their aristocratic ruling classes dominated a subject population including chattel slaves, acquired by loot or by purchase, as well as Helot-like serfs (*klerotai, mnoitai, oikeis*; cf. Chapter 1, note 62), who enjoyed certain limited rights, owning their own houses and tools, and doing what they liked with the harvest – once they had paid the rent – but forbidden the use of arms (and, later, excluded from gymnasia).

Other Greeks, interested in Cretan institutions, noted that this serf class recalled the practices of Crete's fellow Dorians at Sparta. So did many other features in the life of the island's cities. For example, their civil officials (*kosmoi*) resembled the Spartan ephors (except that they did not coexist with kingships, but had supposedly replaced them). Communal organization and education likewise presented similarities.

Aware of these resemblances, both Spartans and Cretans took trouble to assert that the two peoples remained alike in each having more regard for character than for bodily beauty. Plato, on the other hand, sharing a widespread (and probably erroneous) view that homosexual love was a Dorian invention, commented, with greater accuracy, that Crete and Sparta shared a particularly entrenched and institutionalized form of the practice.[4] Timaeus expressed the view that pederasty was invented by the Cretans, a view embodied in Ephorus' account of ritualized homosexual rape in Crete, and expressed mythologically by a Cretan historian Echemenes who argued that it had not been Zeus who carried off the beautiful youth Ganymede, but Minos of Crete. Aristotle, too, stresses Cretan homosexuality, commenting that it was designed to prevent over-population.[5] These (with the possible exception of Echemenes) are all later authorities, and cannot be cited with confidence as witnesses for what happened in early times. But they all imply that at least one of Sparta's customs, its attitude to homosexuality, was imitated from Crete.

And the same process of borrowing was attributed to other institutions as well. It was believed that many aspects of the life of the Spartans – notably their tripartite tribal organization, and their lawgiver Lycurgus – were directly influenced by and modelled upon Crete. But these various resemblances – accompanied, it should be added, by a good many differences – were more probably owed, not to any direct borrowing by one from the other, but to the common descent of the conservative Cretan and Spartan ruling classes from Dorian tribal immigrants. Certainly, between cousins of similar outlook, a certain amount of borrowing may well have occurred – in both directions. Thus whereas, for example, *paians* (hymns to Apollo) were said to have been introduced by Sparta from Crete, the Cretan town of Lyttus, on the other hand, was a Spartan colony.

The city of Cnossus lay in the northern part of the island, on the west bank of the River Kairatos. After its unequalled Bronze Age magnificence – abolished, before 1350, by major destruction followed by impoverished partial occupation – the city was rebuilt by the Dorian immigrants beside the demolished Minoan palace. This revived settlement reasserted and retained its position as the leading centre of the island (a place it occupies in the Homeric poems).[6] It controlled harbours at Amnisus (now Karteros, reputedly the port of the legendary Minos) and Heraclion (Herakleion, the modern capital of Crete), and was stated by Pseudo-Scymnus to have colonized the Aegean islands of Peparethos and Icos.[7]

Cnossus also remained a natural channel of communications with the east, and was one of the first Greek territories to feel the impact of the orientalizing artistic style. For the late ninth century had already witnessed the arrival in Crete of a group or guild of metalworkers from northern Syria or Phoenicia who precociously reawakened the visual arts of the island. Granulation, filigree and inlay were among the techniques that they introduced, and they were also skilled in bronze-work and the cutting of hard stones. Moreover, Cnossus has recently yielded discoveries of ninth-century vases (notably bell-craters) with every sort of freehand curvilinear motif and unexpectedly early figure-scenes. Finds of unmarked gold, silver and electrum lumps or 'dumps' – precursors of coinage – seem to date from not later than 800. In the century that followed, the Cretan school of jewellery maintained its lead (though rivalled now by Corinth and Athens), and another product was armour, in which the island's specialities included a form of helmet (*mitra*) and a belly-plate.

The greater part of Crete consists of mountain ranges. They form four principal groups, the White Mountains in the west, Psiloriti in the centre, and Lasithi and Sitia in the east. Rising to the highest point of Psiloriti was Mount Ida – south-west of Cnossus – around which were clustered the principal cities of the island.

According to Greek mythology it was in a cave upon this mountain that Zeus was born to Rhea, and that the nymph Ida, daughter of Melisseus, helped her sister Adrasteia (served by wizards known as the Idaean Dactyls – meaning Fingers, because they were ten [or five] in number) to nurse the divine baby on the milk of the goat Amaltheia,[8] while the half-divine Curetes (of Minoan origin) concealed the infant's presence from his murderous father by dancing around his cradle and clashing their weapons so that his cries should not be heard.[9] In addition, Zeus' tomb was pointed out in Crete: upon Mount Iouktas, above Arkhanes between Ida and Cnossus. But the islanders largely owed their widespread reputation as liars[10] to these claims to his birthplace and burial-place, which other Greeks rejected. Historically speaking, the various stories about the connection of Zeus, the Indo-European sky-god, with the island reflect his partial, incomplete merger with other deities worshipped earlier in Crete. One of these Cretan divine figures was a young male, consort of the earth-goddess, and a power of fertility who dies and is reborn. He was still venerated, in the sixth century, by the semi-legendary Cretan wonder-worker Epimenides (resembling a shaman – Appendix 2), who brought this blend of ideas to Athens.

The other antique Cretan divinity with whom the Indo-European Zeus became identified was a god worshipped in caverns. Bronze Age remains and early votive offerings relating to his cult have been found in two caves on Mount Ida. Discoveries of somewhat later date, but still before 700, have also come to light. They include large, conical, highly decorated bronze shields, displaying animal-headed bosses and embossed reliefs of animals and monsters. These shields were imported by north Syrian or Phoenician craftsmen – or, more probably, made in Crete itself by immigrants from these areas – for dedication in the sacred place; and *tympana* (tambourines) made for the same purpose have also been found. Such objects, blending Syrian (and farther eastern) and native Cretan elements, might be the products of a second school of immigrant artists, separate from those who came to Cnossus, but the evidence is not conclusive. This resplendent bronze-work may have inspired the makers of the massive bronze cauldrons of the same material, more or less eastern in appearance but originating from various centres, which were dedicated in large numbers at Olympia, Delphi and other sanctuaries, and exported to Etruria and Latium, or imitated there (Appendix 3). Once again, however, no firm decision regarding the extent of this influence, if any, can be reached; the extent to which Crete was the intermediary in Greek orientalization is not yet certain.

However, the north Syrian or Phoenician influence evident in these and other early Cretan works of art is noteworthy for another reason. For Cretan inscriptions of *c.*500 (as well as others from Teos and Mytilene, and passages in Herodotus) describe the alphabet of the Greeks as *phoinikeia*.[11] This recognizes the North Semitic origins of the lettering they had adopted (Appendix 1), and the Syrians and Phoenicians could have brought this script to Crete along with their decorated metal-work, or along with the men who made it or taught Cretans how to employ and adapt its letters. Some have gone further, and conjectured that the Greek alphabet originated from Crete, where the letters (like the related scripts of Thera and Melos; cf. Chapter 1, note 35) are close to those of the Phoenicians. This origin, however, seems unlikely, since the claims of Euboea – in close contact with the north Syrian ports (section 4 below) – are more convincing; and it looks as if the alphabet came to the Greeks through a single channel. But the cities of Crete, all the same (together with those of Cyprus), even if not the earliest of all, were *among* the earliest to receive and make use of this Syro-Phoenician importation.

The perpetual rival of Cnossus, Gortyna, lay in the interior of the island south-south-west of Cnossus, on both banks of the River Lethaeus (Ieropotamos, Mitropolitanos), strategically located at the northern tip of the fertile Mesara plain, where it succeeded Bronze Age (Minoan) Phaestus as the principal centre of the area. Epic references suggest that Gortyna, like Cnossus, may already have been a walled settlement in the Bronze Age, or at least in the early Iron Age. Greek traditions variously ascribed its foundation to the Cretan monarch Minos or to Laconian colonists, whose town Amyclae is recalled by the Gortynian cult-name Amyklaios. Yet another version indicated the arrival of settlers from Tegea in Arcadia, where the name Gortys still survived in later times.

A fairly substantial temple at Gortyna, containing large stone reliefs, a central slab-lined sacrificial pit and at least three interior compartments, has been ascribed to very early dates, but an attribution to the seventh century now seems more probable. This would also appear to have been the epoch when a Cretan sculptor, Daedalus, lived and worked – the earliest sculptor in Greek tradition. His very existence has been doubted, since his name was that of the mythical architect of the labyrinth, but the existence of the sculptor may nevertheless be accepted. He seems to have lived in the seventh century; the place of his birth is not clearly stated, but Pausanias quoted a report that he 'took a wife from Gortyna',[12] so that whether himself a Gortynian or not, he evidently possessed a close connection with the place.

A distinctive and historic stylistic phase, represented by wooden, terracotta, bronze, ivory and stone statuettes and reliefs, has been named after him; and in due course larger images with similar characteristics followed, notably the 'Auxerre Girl' and an over-life-size marble dedication to Artemis offered by the Naxian Nicandre at Delos (*c*.650). Daedalus learned, it was said, how to endow his figures with expressive eyes and legs and arms.[13] But the typical feature of the 'Daedalic' style is a rectangular, wig-like block of hair framing a triangular face tapering down to a pointed chin. This hairstyle is north Syrian, but the Greek sculptors imposed their own disciplined formula, analogous to designs on orientalizing vases. Daedalic terracottas, in particular, are found in numerous centres (mostly but not entirely Doric) including the towns and shrines of Crete, to which the origin of the style – together with the pioneer adoption of moulds for producing statuettes in this material – can be attributed.

If so, then these Cretan works are the precursors of almost all early Greek art. Indeed, Dipoenus and Scyllis – who were 'the very first men', according to Pliny the elder, 'to make a name as sculptors in marble',[14] and migrated to Sicyon – had been born on the island, and were even asserted by some to have been Daedalus' sons.[15] An attractive stone relief of a female figure, of late-seventh-century date, was found on the doorway of a shrine at Prinias, between Cnossus and Gortyna.[16]

Thaletas, a famous, legendary Cretan writer of songs and paeans, was said to have belonged to the same period. He was supposedly born at Gortyna (or, according to other accounts, at Elyrus or Cnossus in the same island), from which he emigrated to Sparta. The aristocratic choral lyrics composed by Thaletas exhorted his fellow citizens to be law-abiding, and he himself was reputed to have been a law-giver. Indeed, he was stated, by a source known to Aristotle, to have taught other pioneer practitioners of the same skills, Lycurgus of Sparta and Zaleucus of Locri Epizephyrii.[17]

In this field of law, however, the reputation of Gortyna is pre-eminent for another reason, because of the massive monument known as the Gortyna Code.[18] These twelve columns, nine feet high, incised with 17,000 letters, date from as late as 480/450 BC, but are nevertheless relevant to preceding epochs since many of these enactments, blending primitive with progressive attitudes, must belong to dates preceding, by as much as 200 years, the period when the inscriptions were incised. Indeed, they constitute our most important source for the whole of early as well as classical Greek legislation.

The document embodies a series of laws which form a kind of unsystematic codification and revision. They divide the population into 'free men' (belonging to men's clubs, from whom the state recruited its officials), and the *klerotai* (serfs, Helots) also described, pejoratively, as *apetairoi* ('without comrades'). Debtors are harshly treated, but less harshly than was so often the case elsewhere (avoiding reduction to chattel slavery, for example). And the laws also deal with family matters, including property rights – in which women fare better than they did, for example, at Athens. Thus, at Gortyna, if a wife divorces, she can keep the property she had when she got married – plus half the produce derived from it, and half of whatever textiles or garments she had woven for the household – provided that the divorce was caused by her husband; if he denied responsibility the judge would decide whether his excuse was justified or not. There is also legislation about *epikleroi*, or as Gortyna called them *patroiouchoi*, women who had no brothers. Here again they receive more liberal treatment than among the Athenians, since if there were no claimants for such a woman 'as prescribed', she could marry anyone in her civic tribe, and if no one in her tribe wanted her she was then at liberty to choose her own husband. The matrimonial arrangements of serfs and slaves, too, are included in this relatively advanced treatment, since their marriages to people of different social status obtain an unusual degree of recognition.

Drerus was situated in north-eastern Crete, upon one of the spurs of Mount Kadiston (a northern outcrop of Lasithi), west of the Gulf of Mirabello. Although small, it possessed two citadels, and was one of the most important city-states of the island from the eighth to the sixth centuries BC.

Its site has provided evidence for one of the earliest-known temples of the Iron Age, of which the construction was begun in 725–700. The remains have survived because the material employed for the building, even at that remote date, was not wood, but rough stone-work. The small rectangular shrine was probably dedicated to Apollo Delphinios, who together with Athena Poliouchos was the principal deity of the place.

The investigation of the building was prompted by the discovery of three statues made of hammered bronze-plates (originally designed as facings for wooden surfaces) which seem to represent Apollo, Artemis and Leto, and have a claim to be the earliest-known cult-images from

Greek lands. Moreover, in a hollow between Drerus' pair of citadels lie the remains of the most ancient civic meeting place (*agora*) that has so far come to light in the Greek world. Enclosed by an extensive stepped area (inspired by the theatre-like structures in Minoan palaces), it evidently served as a setting for public assemblies, both religious and political, and provided a precedent for the theatres and council-houses of later Greek towns. This *agora* was clearly contemporary with the temple, since they were constructed on the same alignment (and linked by two uphill paths).

A group of inscriptions from Drerus, of the later seventh century, include some of the oldest-known regulations concerning Greek constitutional law; and they are also the most antique examples of alphabetic writing mobilized to serve the state. Here, too, is the first clear mention of the *polis* as a strictly political entity. Illegitimate prolongations of office by the city's oligarchic rulers (*kosmoi*) are forbidden, in order to provide safeguards against the establishment of a dictatorship: the same man could not become a *kosmos* twice in three years.[19] The Drerus laws, together with the more traditional among the enactments in the Gortyna Code, seem to confirm the tradition that Crete may have been the first part of the Greek world to codify legislation in writing, as was appropriate in the island which, according to myth, was the home of the archetypal legal figure, Minos, judge of the dead, and had then produced the pioneer law-giver Thaletas. Cretan laws were believed to be excellent, and received extensive study at other Greek centres. In this field, as in the sphere of art, it is possible to detect the influence of north Syrian and Phoenician cities, of which the advanced legal codes were available as models.

This eastern part of Crete was dominated by Mount Dicte, which contested with Ida its claim to be the birthplace of Zeus. Dicte has been variously identified with Lasithi (south-east of Cnossus) or (more probably) Mount Modi, part of the Sitia range in the extreme east of the island, overlooking a shrine of Dictaean Zeus (on the site of the Minoan town at Paleokastro) which provides remains dating back to the seventh and sixth centuries BC. It was here that a later *Hymn to Dictaean Zeus* was discovered.[20] This tradition regarding the god's birthplace, followed by Apollodorus, indicated that he was born in a cave (identified with a sanctuary at Psychro), although this detail may be due to confusion with the other story ascribing the event to a cave on Mount Ida.

Despite its Bronze Age efflorescence and subsequent distinction during the early Iron Age, Crete later remained detached from the mainstream of Greek history, and exercised little influence upon its developments, except through the exportation of numerous pirates and a certain number of colonists,[21] and, in particular, through the availability of a large quantity of mercenary soldiers (specialists in slinging and archery), who were eager to obtain better economic prospects than those provided by the island.

2 CYPRUS: SALAMIS, PAPHOS

Cyprus lies about fifty miles south of Cilicia (south-eastern Asia Minor). The largest island in the eastern Mediterranean, it is 60 miles wide at its maximum breadth, and 140 miles long, about one-third constituting the Dinaretum (Karpas) promontory that extends to the north-east. Between mountains, the central plain of Mesaoria was thickly wooded, providing timber for the construction of ships (although natural harbours are scarce) and for the smelting of the local copper, which was more abundant than anywhere else in the Mediterranean area, so that the Romans later named the best quality metal *aes Cyprium* after the island.

After housing significant Mycenaean settlements in the later Bronze Age, when it served as an important entrepôt between the Levant and regions farther to the west, Cyprus, like Crete, subsequently offered exceptional continuity with the past Mycenaean world. For it retained a population of Achaean (Mycenaean) stock. Moreover, these people – despite influxes of Greek refugees from Pylos and elsewhere on the Greek mainland, and more or less uninterrupted communications with undestroyed Athens and Euboea (Lefkandi) – continued to speak their old dialect of Greek, which was related to a similar conservative linguistic enclave in Arcadia, so that the two forms of speech are grouped together as Arcado-Cypriot.[22] The continued employment, for writing down this language, of a (not very suitable) late Bronze Age script, consisting of the fifty-six or fifty-seven characters of the classical Cypriot syllabary – arbitrarily selected from the 200 characters of Mycenaean Linear B – is further confirmation of this link with the past. Cyprus, unlike the Greek mainland, did not go through a prolonged period of illiteracy. Moreover, its various city-states, among which Salamis and Paphos were pre-eminent, carried on. Their monarchies, too, still existed, not giving way to aristocratic systems of government, as in other parts of the Greek world.

However, from *c*.1000, Cyprus was already becoming the object of increasing Syrian penetration, and before *c*.800 Phoenician colonists had settled important sections of the island. This was an eastern parallel to the joint occupation of Sicily by Phoenicians (Carthaginians) and Greeks. On Cyprus, the largest of several Phoenician city-states was

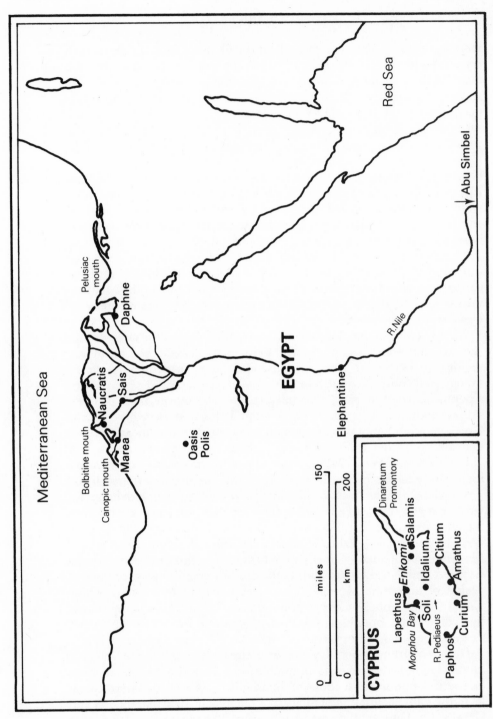

Mediterranean Sea

Red Sea

Pelusiac mouth

Daphne

Bolbitine mouth

Canopic mouth

Naucratis

Sais

Marea

Oasis Polis

EGYPT

Elephantine

R.Nile

Abu Simbel

CYPRUS

Dinaretum Promontory

Lapethus

Morphou Bay

Enkomi

Salamis

Soli

Idalium

R.Pediaeus

Citium

Paphos

Curium

Amathus

miles
0   150

km
0   200

7 Egypt and Cyprus

the kingdom of Citium (Qart Hadasht) near Larnaca in the south-east, where the Mycenaean and other refugees were reduced to subjection. Early in the ninth century, the first Phoenician inscriptions appear in these communities, and it was from Cyprus, according to one suggestion, that the Syro-Phoenician alphabet came to the Greeks, and was thus available for their own adaptation. This theory, one of a good many (Chapter 1, note 35), has been supported by inscriptions (and passages of Herodotus) describing the Greek alphabet as *phoinikeia*. But one of the centres in which these inscriptions were found was the island of Crete, which might likewise be the centre of transference – though on the whole it still seems most likely that this role was fulfilled by the cities of Euboea, through their access to markets on the north Syrian coast (section 4 below).

A period of Assyrian suzerainty over Cyprus followed from c.709 (its men served in Esarhaddon's invasion of Egypt in 681). Under this regime the seventh century was a euphoric period of prosperity and craftsmanship on the island. Its art during the period continued to absorb abundant near-eastern influences without, however, losing its own particular identity (which still went back in part to the Mycenaean tradition); so that in this sense Cyprus – not altogether unlike Crete – acted as a forerunner of artistic movements in other Greek lands. According to one theory, the 'Aeolic' column-capital came from Cyprus, although Phoenicia has been suggested as an alternative place of origin; and the source of Greek gem-engraving has also been traced to the Cypriots, who were familiar with the Phoenician techniques involved.

After the downfall of Assyria (612), the city-states of Cyprus momentarily resumed their independence, but then fell subject to Egypt in the early 560s. During the short subsequent period of Egyptian suzerainty the island reached the climax of its cultural development. While ancient traditions continued to be maintained, not least in the religious sphere, Cypriot civilization prospered amid active overseas exchanges with near-eastern and Aegean centres. In c.545, however, as Egyptian power dwindled, the Cypriots were obliged to submit to the Persians. Despite the abandonment, at this time, of certain sites on the island, their ships and soldiers assisted in a series of campaigns against Caria and Babylonia and then against Egypt as well.

From c.520 the kings of the cities of Cyprus began to issue their own coinage. The monarchs of Citium and another Semitic-speaking city, Lapethus, in the north, employed the Phoenician language to inscribe these pieces, but six other states began by using the local syllabary: Salamis (north-east), Paphos (west), Amathus (south), Idalium (centre) and Marium (north-west). Greek lettering, however, soon appeared on these coinages instead. For whereas the Persians scarcely affected Cypriot culture, the influence of the Ionian Greeks became increasingly active and widespread on the island, which acquired a Cypro-Greek school of sculpture, accompanied by the importation (and sometimes imitation) of East Greek and Attic vases, and Greek terracotta statuettes. In the years before 500 the various Cypriot centres became sharply divided between pro-Persian and pro-Greek factions. During the Ionian revolt against the Persians, the Phoenician cities of the island remained loyal to Persia, but their Greek counterparts attempted a rising, which was crushed (499 – 497), as will be seen further in connection with the individual states concerned.

During the Mycenaean epoch a town had existed at Enkomi on the east coast of Cyprus (five miles from the modern Famagusta), linked to the estuary of the River Pediaeus (Pedias) by a navigable channel. But in about 1075 BC Enkomi was succeeded by nearby Salamis. Its acropolis stood on a plateau overlooking a broad sandy bay beside the river-mouth, which provided a natural harbour.

According to Greek myth, the city's founder was Teucer, son of Telamon, king of that other, earlier Salamis off the coast of Attica (Chapter 2, note 15). The first settlers were believed to have been refugees from the collapse of Mycenaean civilization in the Greek homeland, though they no doubt intermarried with the Mycenaean population whom they found at their new home. The persistence of these links with the Bronze Age past, common to so many parts of Cyprus, is confirmed by archaeological discoveries.

Rich finds from the tombs of local kings, flourishing vassals of Assyria – dating from c.750 and continuing into the seventh century – recall complex burial descriptions in the Homeric poems; indeed they may even owe this resemblance, in part, to a knowledge of the *Iliad* that was spreading among Greek communities during these years. And there was also an eleven-book eighth-century epic the *Cypria*, attributed variously to Homer or (with greater probability) to Stasinus of Cyprus or Hegesias of Cypriot Salamis, which dealt with the preliminaries to the Trojan War.

A ruler of Salamis, Euelthon (c.560–525), while acquiescing first in Egyptian and then in Persian suzerainty, cherished political ambitions of his own. Salamis was, in his time, the leading city-state in Cyprus, as Queen Pheretime of Cyrene acknowledged, when she asked Euelthon for military assistance (530). Indeed, he claimed to be regarded as king of the whole of his island. This is shown by Salaminian coinage, which he seems to have been the first Cypriot monarch to issue, perhaps in the early 520s. For these pieces, although they employ the Persian monetary standard (and show the Egyptian *ankh*, a T-cross surmounted by a loop), claim the allegiance of the Cypriots as a whole, displaying, in Greek, the first two letters of the islanders' name (ΚΥ). Moreover, Euelthon was eager to maintain his links with Greeks elsewhere, and with this in mind dedicated an incense-burner at Delphi.

Nevertheless, he was well aware that his political strength depended upon the continued favour of his Persian suzerain. Inheriting this knowledge, his great-grandson Gorgus refused to associate himself with the Ionian rebellion against Persian rule. As a result, however, he was overthrown by his younger brother Onesilus, who took the other side, assuming the leading role in Cyprus' contribution to the revolt – which became active after an Eretrian flotilla had defeated the fleet of those Cypriots who sided with Persia. However, in a battle outside his city (498), Onesilus was defeated and killed by the Persians, who were then able to reimpose their control.

At Old Paphos, on the west coast of Cyprus, the shrine of the ancient fertility goddess, whose rituals involved prostitutes and holy doves, goes back to the Mesopotamian (Sumerian) Inanna and the Semitic Ashtoreth-Astarte-Ishtar (Appendix 1), but the cult was identified by the Greeks with the worship of Aphrodite, known as Cypris. It was at Paphos that the Mycenaeans had first encountered this sex-queen, equating her with their own Great Goddess (*wanassa*), and it was from there, too, that Aphrodite became known to Greece. The Paphian holy place became her most famous temple in the Mediterranean world. It stood on the place where, according to local tradition, she had first come ashore after her birth from the foam of the sea, although there were rival claims, notably from the island of Cythera (Kithira), off the southern coast of Laconia.

There were also conflicting traditions about the founder of the temple and city of Paphos. According to one version, he was Agapenor, king of Tegea in Arcadia. Another legend, however, told of foundation by Cinyras, king of Paphos and of the island as a whole, who was stated by the *Iliad* to have presented Agamemnon with a breastplate for the war against Troy; his descendants the Cinyradae formed a dynasty of priest–kings who ruled the city for many hundreds of years.

Excavations have revealed that Paphos existed in the Mycenaean (later Bronze) epoch (*c.*1200), and graves of early Iron Age date have come to light at a nearby village (Skales). A city monarch, Eteandrus, is mentioned in an inscription of the Assyrian ruler Esarhaddon of 673/672 BC.[23] Sections of early fortifications have been unearthed on a 3,000-foot-high hill, and evidence of siege and counter-siege works, including emergency construction material taken from a nearby shrine, has been related to severe fighting which accompanied the participation of the Hellenized cities of Cyprus in the Ionian Revolt, and resulted in the fall of Paphos to the Persians in 498. (Old Paphos was replaced by a new city, ten miles away, towards the end of the fourth century.)

Another Cypriot centre which suffered severely in the Ionian Revolt was Soli. This city (Potamos tou Kambou), beside the River Kambos in Morphou Bay, possessed an acropolis presiding over a lower town which lay close to the harbour. According to one legend, the founder was a hero named Acamas, son of the Athenian king Theseus, accompanied by Phalerus who was also believed to have created Athens' port of Phaleron. Another version placed the establishment of Soli much later, ascribing the initiative to the Athenian statesman Solon (c.594), who allegedly, during a visit to Cyprus at the invitation of King Philocyprus of Aepeia (Vouni), advised him to transfer his town to a more suitable site near the coast, where the monarch duly built a new settlement, naming it Soli after his guest.

These stories, however, are Athenian chauvinistic inventions, for Soli was far more ancient – already existing, as excavations have shown, in the late Bronze Age – and its origins owed nothing to Athens. The place seems to appear in the Assyrian Esarhaddon's inscription of 673/672 BC, under the name of Sillu. Subsequently it came under the control of the Persians, and joined in the unsuccessful Ionian Revolt against them. It held out longer than any other city, but finally succumbed after a five-month siege; its king Aristocyprus, son of Philocyprus, lost his life (497).

Curium, on the south-west coast, fared differently during the revolt. This ancient township, once an opulent Mycenaean centre and later allegedly, according to Herodotus and Strabo, colonized by the Argives,[24] became subject first to the Assyrians and then to the Persians. The Curians joined the Ionian Revolt against them, under their monarch Stasanor, but betrayed the rebel cause by deserting in the decisive sea-battle of Lade (495), which brought about the death of Onesilus of Salamis and sealed the fate of the rebellion.

3 CYRENE

The land of Cyrenaica (also known as Cyrene), in north Africa, was a massive, rounded promontory extending from the Gulf of Syrtis Major (Sirte, Sidra) in the west to the Egyptian border in the east. Because of the deserts, however, which isolated it from Egypt, Cyrenaica was more readily accessible to Greece, and whereas its arid interior was inhabited by Libyan (Berber) tribes, the northern coastal strip, which enjoyed harvests in three different regions at different times, was occupied by a group of Greek colonies.

The earliest of these was Cyrene. Herodotus describes its establishment in great detail, and his version, despite legendary elements, is supported by a detailed inscription, embodying a foundation decree of the mother city.[25] The historian tells how, in the early 630s BC, following the advice of the Delphic oracle, a small party of Greeks was compelled by famine to leave their island of Thera (Santorini) in the Cyclades, which was governed by a narrow aristocracy descended from the first Dorian settlers.[26] These emigrants, including a nucleus of citizens conscripted by lot (an early recorded use of this method – reinforced by the threat of penalties for evaders), and supplemented by a number of volunteers, set sail for the shore of Cyrenaica, a stretch of coast which had not become subject to any of the great powers.

Helped by merchants from Samos, and guided by a purple-dye (*murex*) fisherman, Corobius of Itanus in Crete, the group reached the small island of Platea in the Gulf of Bomba (off the Cyrenaican coast), where they disembarked. In the following year they were joined by a further body of Theran emigrants, under the leadership, it was said (and doubts on this subject seem unjustified), of a certain Aristoteles. These colonists, however, did not fare well, and after two years dispatched a complaint to Delphi, which reminded them they had been instructed to colonize Libya – of which the island of Platea scarcely counted as a part. In pursuance of this injunction, they moved on to the mainland and settled at Aziris (Wadi el Chalig, near Darnis [Derna]), where they remained for six more years.

But then in 632 (if Eusebius' date can be accepted), their Libyan neighbours offered to show them a better location, and guided them to the site of Cyrene, about sixty miles to the west, where they were assured that they would find 'a hole in the sky' – an abundant rainfall. There the immigrants at last settled down, and their founder Aristoteles, assuming kingly power, took the name of Battus (1). This appears to have been a royal Libyan designation, related to a title borne by the pharaohs as kings of Lower Egypt, and its assumption by Aristoteles indicates that there was Libyan participation in the settlement, although at this stage without citizen rights.

The new colony, six miles from the sea, stood on a limestone plateau (the Al Jabal al Akhdar) which rose to a height of 18,000 feet, fronted by orchards and backed by rich fields of grain for consumption and export. The settlement stood on a protruding spur – later the acropolis – protected to the west and south-west by a deep, curving ravine, and on the north-east by a shallower valley. From the southern slopes of this valley gushed the 'fountain of Apollo', whose bride the nature-goddess Cyrene (her name allegedly derived from *kura*, the Libyan word for asphodel) gave the town its name.

In front of the fountain stood a narrow terrace, beneath which extended another, broader terrace containing the city's principal temple and altar, dedicated to Apollo, which dated from the sixth century but was repeatedly rebuilt. Nearby rose a temple and altar of Artemis, of which remains, including a rich and varied foundation deposit, go back to a period almost contemporary with the establishment of the city, though here again numerous reconstructions followed at various times. Around these two principal sanctuaries stood a number of less important shrines. Further away was a holy place containing the tomb of Aristoteles Battus I, the earliest Greek colonial founder whose posthumous worship as a hero (*heros*) is clearly attested.

The city soon exceeded its earliest boundaries, spreading along the main part of the plateau on to another hill below, and down into the valley. Here a Doric column, now re-erected, marks the site of a huge temple of Zeus. Originally dating from the first years of the colony, this shrine, too, required frequent restorations, since it was destroyed by the Persians in c.515 BC (and again by Jewish rebels in AD 115, before its final demolition at the hands of the Christians). In the same neighbourhood (across the Wadi Bel-Gadir), a seventh-century (?) precinct of Demeter and Persephone, rising upon five terraced levels, has also been uncovered.

The city was surrounded by cemeteries, including tombs and rock-cut sarcophagi displaying a variety of shapes. The earliest of these graves, of sixth-century date, line the road to Cyrene's port, twelve miles to the north, at Apollonia (the capital of the country in Byzantine times), where archaeologists have made extensive discoveries, although most of the harbour constructions now lie under the sea.

Apollonia was created by c.600, and at about the same date the Cyreneans dispatched settlers westwards to establish a colony at Euhesperides (Benghazi), upon a promontory overlooking the north bank of a sea lagoon. As a preliminary step to this destination, at an even earlier date, they had sent colonists more than halfway along the same route, to Taucheira (Tocra), where East Greek and Cretan pottery has come to light. These were the enterprises of Aristoteles (Battus I) and his successor Arcesilaus I. The latter also stabilized a form of monarchy at Cyrene, not unlike those of Thessaly and Macedonia, which was supported, or occasionally embarrassed, by an aristocracy of horse-breeding landowners. Under the next king Battus II Eudaemon (c.583–560) the colony was reinforced: with the backing of

Reconstruction of the Ionic Temple of Artemis at Ephesus, rebuilt in *c.* 560–550 BC, entirely of marble, except for the ceilings and roof-beams which were cedar-wood. One of the Seven Wonders of the World.

Doric temple at Posidonia (Paestum) in Lucania (south-western Italy), a colony of Sybaris. It is known as the 'Temple of Ceres' but was probably dedicated to Hera and Athena, *c.* 500 BC.

The mouth of the River Cayster (Küçuk Menderes) in Ionia. In ancient times the river debouched at Ephesus; today, after silt has been washed down throughout the centuries, its estuary is far away.

The peaks of Olympus, home of the gods (on the borders of Macedonia and Thessaly), the highest mountain of the Greek peninsula.

Bronze griffin (with head and neck cast hollow), from the shoulder of one of the many cauldrons dedicated at Olympia, made in Aegina, c. 650 BC. British Museum, London.

Far left: Large bronze statuette dedicated (in two hexameters) by Mantiklos to Apollo, 'the Far Darter of the Silver Bow'. The figure (Apollo?) originally wore a helmet and probably carried a shield and spear, early 7th century BC. Museum of Fine Arts, Boston.

Left: Large marble statue of a youth (*kouros*) from Attica, probably a grave monument, *c*. 625-660 BC. The stance is derived, directly or indirectly, from Egyptian sculpture. Metropolitan Museum of Art, New York.

Terracotta figure of centaur from Lefkandi (Lelantum?) in Euboea, of which excavations have transformed our knowledge of the 'Dark Age', late 10th century BC. Archaeological Museum, Chalcis.

Terracotta group of Demeter and her daughter Persephone (*kore*), the deities of the Eleusinian Mysteries, seated in a cart. Made in Corinth, the bodies are hand-made, but the heads moulded, *c*. 620 BC. British Museum, London.

Limestone relief of a Gorgon from the pediment of the Temple of Artemis at the Corinthian colony of Corcyra (Corfu), *c.* 580 BC. German Archaeological Institute, Athens.

Right: Ivory statuette from the Temple of Artemis at Ephesus, known as the 'hawk-priestess' because the figure forms the handle of a wand surmounted by a hawk, *c.* 560 BC. Archaeological Museum, Istanbul.

Relief of Europa carried off by Zeus in the form of a bull on a panel (metope) from 'Temple Y' (of uncertain location) at Selinus (Selinunte) on the south coast of Sicily, *c.* 560-550 BC. Museo Nazionale Archeologico, Palermo.

Marble statue of a woman (*kore*), found on the Athenian acropolis but made on Naxos and/or Samos: the face is of Naxian and the drapery of Samian style, *c.* 560-550 BC. Acropolis Museum, Athens.

Etruscan terracotta sarcophagus from Caere (Cerveteri), *c*. 500 BC. Ionian styles are strongly influential but modified; and husband and wife recline together on the banqueting couch, according to a non-Greek Etruscan custom. Museo Nazionale di Villa Giulia, Rome.

Terracotta barber from Boeotia, late 6th century BC. Museum of Fine Arts, Boston.

Terracotta relief of Aphrodite holding a sacrificial goat, *c*. 500 BC, from Gela on the south coast of Sicily. Gela had been founded by Cretans and Rhodians, traditionally in 688 BC. Ashmolean Museum, Oxford.

The Etruscan 'Apollo of Veii': terracotta statue of Apulu (Apollo) from the roof of the Portonaccio Temple at Veii. He is moving against Herkle (Heracles) in a dispute over a hind, *c.* 520-500 BC. Museo Nazionale di Villa Giulia, Rome.

Bronze statuette of banqueter. The figure, cast by the 'lost wax' (*cire perdue*) process, was found at Dodona in the sanctuary of Zeus (whom it may represent), but is likely to have been made in the Peloponnese, *c.* 520 BC. British Museum, London.

Neck of large terracotta storage jar found on Myconos–but perhaps made on Tenos–showing the 'Trojan Horse' (wheeled), which, filled with Greek warriors, reputedly enabled their besieging army to capture Troy, *c.* 675–650 BC. Archaeological Museum, Myconos.

Soldiers and chariot on the neck of a bronze mixing-bowl, nearly six feet high and with a capacity of 1200 litres, found in the grave of a Gaulish princess at Vix, Upper Seine (Côte d'Or), France. The bowl was probably made either in Laconia or in southern Italy, *c.* 550–530 BC. Archaeological Museum, Châtillon-sur-Seine.

Cypriot flask found at Lefkandi in Euboea, bearing witness to the resumption of near-eastern overseas contacts.

Vase found at Lefkandi.

Protogeometric amphora, *c.* 950-900 BC. These designs, initiated by the Athenians but subsequently adapted over a wide area, were compass-drawn and painted by a multiple brush, and marked a radical departure from preceding Sub-Mycenaean wares. National Archaeological Museum, Athens.

Geometric jar from Thera (Santorini), 8th century BC. This style developed from the Protogeometric, Athens again taking the initiative. The rectilinear pattern is varied by a small frieze of birds; human scenes were also to appear. National Museum, Copenhagen.

Protocorinthian aryballos, *c.* 720-690 BC. These vases, painted with swirling silhouette designs of Near-Eastern affinities on the whiteish clay of Corinth (burned pale green or buff), played a prominent part in the orientalizing movement in which the Corinthians took the lead. National Museum, Naples.

Earthenware jar with griffin head spout, *c.* 675 BC, found at Aegina but made in one of the Cyclades islands. The head is reminiscent of metallic objects, notably the bronze cauldrons displaying similar designs. British Museum, London.

Wine-jug from Corinth, in the 'Corinthian' style which developed from the Protocorinthian and enjoyed widespread circulation, dominating the Mediterranean area (this jug was found at Rhodes) until Athens superseded Corinth's commercial supremacy, *c.* 625-600 BC. British Museum, London.

Handle of the François vase. Ajax carrying back the body of Achilles, whose death, at the hands of Apollo or Paris (or Apollo in the guise of Paris) was recounted in epic traditions.

The François vase: Protoattic wine mixing-bowl (volute *krater*) found in an Etruscan tomb at Clusium (Chiusi), signed by the potter Ergotimus and the painter Clitias, 575-550 BC. *From top*: dance of Athenian youths and maidens at Cnossus; battle with centaurs; procession of gods at wedding of Peleus and Thetis. Museo Archeologico, Florence.

Handle of the François vase. Artemis the Lady of Wild Things, owing much to Minoan (Cretan) origins. An early example of black-figure pottery, the vase is painted in purple and white, as well as black, on pale orange clay.

Attic black-figure amphora, *c.* 540 BC. Achilles is shown slaying the Amazon Queen Penthesilea. The signature of Exekias seems to indicate that he was not only the potter but the painter (in which capacity he signed other vases). British Museum, London.

Attic black-figure perfume-bottle, decorated by the 'Amasis painter', showing a wedding procession, *c.* 540 BC. Vases often display the bride and groom (especially if they are a divine pair) riding in a chariot. Others show the bride being forcibly led off in a chariot. Metropolitan Museum of Art, New York.

Attic black-figure amphora illustrating the olive-harvest, *c.* 520 BC. The archaic olive-wood image of the goddess Athena in the Erechtheum was the patron of craftsmanship and of the peace that the slow-growing olive-trees needed and symbolized. British Museum, London.

Attic black-figure cup showing 'long ships' (warships) with two levels of oars and 'round ships' (merchantmen), *c.* 520 BC. British Museum, London.

Attic red-figure plate, *c.* 520 BC, signed by the prolific painter Epictetus. A Scythian archer is depicted; the Scythians are well-known among Greeks in this capacity (and provided Athens with its police). British Museum, London.

Left: Attic white-ground perfume-vase signed by Pasiades as potter, *c.* 500 BC. The painting depicts a pair of Maenads (Bacchants), the devotees of the originally Thracian god Dionysus, God of Frenzy and Wine, after whom Euripides' play the *Bacchae* was to be named. British Museum, London.

Attic red-figure cup, *c.* 520–510 BC, signed by the potter Python and the painter Epictetus. Flute-player and dancer. Found at Vulci (Etruria), like very many other Greek vases. British Museum, London.

Attic red-figure amphora by Myson, *c.* 500 BC, showing King Croesus of Lydia preparing to immolate himself on a pyre. There were contradictory stories of his death after his defeat in 546 BC by Cyrus II of Persia. Musée du Louvre, Paris.

Gold ear-ring from Lefkandi in Euboea. Gold quickly became more plentiful in this very early town, suggesting importations or influences from Cyprus and elsewhere in the Near East. Eretria Museum.

Back of a silver-gilt mirror from Kelermes, Kuban district, made for a Scythian patron in artistic styles merging Scythian, Greek and Near-Eastern motifs, 6th century BC. Hermitage Museum, Leningrad.

Bronze tripod-cauldron from Altintepe in eastern Turkey, late 8th century BC. These objects, which probably originated in Syria, have been found throughout Aegean and Near-Eastern lands, and were copied and used by the Greeks as prizes for the great festivals, especially the Olympic Games.

Hoplite (infantry) armour from a warrior's grave at Argos, c. 725-700 BC. The helmet reflects eastern influences; it was surmounted by a horsehair plume which had come to the Greeks from Egyptian chariot-horses, probably through Syrian intermediaries. Argos Museum.

Silver didrachm of Athens. In transition from a series of *Wappenmünzen*, bearing armorial devices interpreted as conciliatory gestures to noble clans by the dictator Pisistratus (546-527 BC), this Gorgon's head may represent not a clan but the nation. Sale catalogue.

Silver didrachm of Thebes: part of a federal Boeotian coinage, defined by the Boeotian shield, later 6th century BC. The *theta* on the reverse is the initial of Thebes, but earlier issues had omitted the letter, hinting at Theban identification with, and control of, the confederacy. Sale catalogue.

Silver didrachm of Thasos, a colony of Paros in the northern Aegean, *c.* 500 BC. The type of a satyr, associated with Dionysus (and here shown amorously carrying off a struggling nymph), recalls the island's pride in its wine. Sale catalogue.

Silver decadrachm of the Macedonian tribe of the Derrones, early 5th century BC. A bearded man is seen driving an ox-cart; above is a Corinthian helmet. The large size of the coins of this area is due to the proximity of the rich Pangaean mines. Sale catalogue.

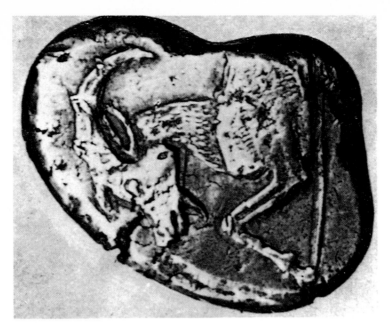

Electrum (pale gold) stater of an Ionian city, perhaps Miletus, showing the forepart of an ibex. One of the earliest Greek coins, *c.* 600 BC. British Museum, London.

Silver didrachm of Aegina depicting a turtle (sacred to Aphrodite). These were the oldest of all coinages on or near the Greek mainland, dating from the early 6th century BC. They circulated widely and established one of the principal monetary standards of the Greeks.

Silver drachm of Croton (Crotone), *c.* 530 BC, an Achaean colony on the toe of Italy, displaying a tripod. These earliest south Italian coins, with their characteristic incuse designs, have been associated with the philosopher-sage Pythagoras, whose father Mnesarchus was a gem-engraver.

Silver tetradrachm of Athens with head of Athena and owl, with a sprig of the sacred olive. This famous coinage, based on a weight standard adopted from the once commercially powerful Euboean cities, began in *c.* 520 BC or a little later.

the Delphic oracle, many new settlers were invited to join its ranks, and a flood of Greeks arrived from the islands (including Crete and Rhodes [Lindus]), while others came from the Peloponnese (c.573).

This expansion, however, alienated the local Libyans. Previously relations had been friendly. The Libyans had found the colonists their site, had joined them as subjects of their ruling Greek dynasty (hence, as we saw, the Libyan title of Battus) and, although themselves partly nomadic, had intermarried with them, so that a mutual exchange of customs took place, and Libyan names made their appearance at Cyrene.

But now the influx of new settlers damaged this amicable relationship, since their arrival involved dispossessing many Libyans of their land. War broke out between the two communities. Apries (Hophra), who had ascended the throne of the Egyptian pharaohs in c.588, came to the help of the Libyans. Since he could not send his Greek mercenaries (the best troops at his disposal), seeing that their loyalty against fellow Greeks would have been uncertain, the native Egyptian force that he dispatched to the scene proved inadequate, and was severely defeated at Irasa (c.570).

In consequence, the Libyans had to submit to Cyrene. But under Arcesilaus II the Cruel (from c.560), although a local poet Eugammon exalted the dynasty in his *Telegonia* – declaring that its members were descended from Odysseus – domestic disputes gave the malcontents another chance. For Arcesilaus II quarrelled so seriously with his younger brothers that they left Cyrene altogether, moved seventy-five miles to the west, and on their own account founded a new city, Barca (Al Marj), situated sixteen miles inland from Taucheira but able to make use of two harbours sheltered by a promontory and offshore islands. In this enterprise assistance was provided by the Libyans, whom the dissident founders of Barca also encouraged to renew their war against Arcesilaus II. In his attempt to reconquer them, he was lured out into the desert and suffered a shattering defeat, losing 7,000 Cyrenean hoplites. Not long afterwards, according to Herodotus, he was succeeded by his brother Haliarchus; but the new monarch soon lost his life to Arcesilaus' widow Eryxo, who secured the throne for her son, Battus III the Lame.[27]

Up to this time of troubles, Cyrene had flourished, deriving a substantial revenue from its abundant grain, oil, horses and wool (of which Arcesilaus II himself is shown supervising the weighing and storage on a Laconian vase).

Another lucrative source of profit was the wild medicinal plant known as silphium, which, although the whole plant, as well as its leaf, seed-vessel or fruit and sprouting bud, is carefully depicted on Cyrene's coinage (inaugurated in $c.560/530$), has eluded attempts at identification. One suggestion is that it may have been laserwort (*laserpitium, latifolium*, related to *assa foetida*). Silphium, which remained a Cyrenean speciality – for it proved resistant to transplanting – was prized throughout the Mediterranean world. Its leaf could be eaten and its root pickled, and it was used as a laxative and an antiseptic. Indeed silphium came to be considered a cure for all troubles, ranging from snake bites to chills. Being ascribed all these varied qualities, silphium no doubt played a part in the school of medicine established at Cyrene during the sixth century, one of the earliest in the Greek world.

During the reign of Arcesilaus II, however, the central power of the Cyrenean state had been undermined, both by dissensions within his own royal house and, above all, by his recent military disaster. So his successor Battus III called in the services of an expert, Demonax of Mantinea in Arcadia, to revise Cyrene's constitutional and legal system, and thus put an end to disputes. Demonax did not propose the abolition of the monarchy, but reduced its prerogatives, limiting them to specific priesthoods and properties. In addition, he divided the population into three tribes, consisting, respectively, of citizens of Theran origin together with 'dwellers round about' (native *perioeci*; cf. Chapter 1, note 61), Peloponnesians (presumably Spartans) and Cretans, and men from other islands.

In this attempt to place the various categories of the local population upon an equal footing – thus removing the privileged position of the original settlers' descendants – the inclusion of *perioeci* in the first-mentioned tribe is noteworthy.[28] For they, in spite of alternative suggestions, were presumably the descendants of the Libyans who had participated in the initial settlement; through the agency of Demonax, they were admitted to full equality with the Greeks. Their enrolment, incidentally, also served to confer numerical respectability on the first of the three new tribes.

However, Battus III's son Arcesilaus III proved dissatisfied with the reduction of the royal powers that had accompanied the reforms of Demonax, and took forcible steps to reverse this move. His attempt failed, and he fled abroad, accompanied by his mother Pheretime. Her efforts to obtain help from Euelthon, the powerful king of Salamis in Cyprus, did not meet with success, but Arcesilaus III mobilized an army of Samians by promises of land, and employed this force to reconquer his kingdom. However, his savage treatment of his defeated opponents made him so many enemies that he had to depart for a second time, leaving his mother to act as his regent at Cyrene, where, enjoying power denied to most Greek women elsewhere at this period, she personally presided over the council. Arcesilaus III, for his part, withdrew to Barca, where he enjoyed the protection, and married the daughter of its king Alazeir (a Libyan name). But the relatives and descendants of the Cyreneans whom Arcesilaus II had banished to Barca incited its people to revolt, and so Arcesilaus III was assassinated.

At this juncture his widow Pheretime, whose father had also lost his life in the same massacre, took refuge in Egypt, appealing to its Persian satrap Aryandes for assistance. Her late husband had duly placed himself under the allegiance of the Persian king Cambyses (525) after the latter's conquest of Egypt, so that the satrap had a good pretext for intervening in favour of the Battiad dynasty, especially as this offered an opportunity to extend Persian influence over Libya in general. He therefore dispatched a powerful land-force under a certain Amasis (not the pharaoh of that name), who following a prolonged siege captured Barca with the help of local traitors (c.515), though Pheretime subsequently recovered the city, and had the leaders of the rebellion put to death. During these convulsions Barca (although not totally destroyed, as Herodotus suggests)[29] suffered grievous damage, and many of its citizens were deported to Bactria in central Asia. Cyrene too was seriously battered.

However, the Persians, while extending their control over most of the habitable and cultivable regions of the country, appointed Battus IV, son of the murdered Cyrenean monarch Arcesilaus III, as king over the whole land, including all four Greek cities, Cyrene, Barca, Taucheira and Euhesperides. Battus IV dreamed of creating, under Persian auspices, a large land empire for himself – a rare ambition among Greeks of the time. When, however, upon his instigation and apparently with the encouragement of the Delphic oracle, a certain Dorieus, son of the Spartan king Anaximandridas and stepbrother of Cleomenes I, attempted a western expansion in Cyrenaica (c.514–512), his attempt to found a colony on the River Cinyps (Oued Oukirre) was frustrated by the Carthaginians, who controlled all lands beyond. Nevertheless, the Battiad dynasty was not replaced by a republican government until c.440, by which time it had lasted for eight generations.

4 MARKET PORTS IN SYRIA AND EGYPT

Although there is some evidence that the Greeks maintained direct contact with the Phoenician city-states,[30] at least three harbour-towns on the north Syrian coast, outside Phoenicia itself, played an even more significant part in their early history, acting as channels through which near-eastern goods of various kinds came to Greek lands. These included objects of an artistic nature, which inspired the creation of the 'orientalizing' phase of Greek art, and included, it would appear, the alphabet as well.

One of these centres, and a leading port for Greek trade during most of the eighth and later centuries, was a commercial harbour-town at Al Mina – its name is unknown – beside the estuary of the River Orontes (Nahr el-Asi), now in the Turkish province of Hatay. An adjacent hill-site (Sabouni) provides signs of late Bronze Age (Mycenaean) occupation and commercial activity, but the principal settlement and trading station began its existence in the last quarter of the ninth century BC.[31] It lay within the sphere of the Aramaean Kingdom of Unqi (Pattin), centred on Kunulua or Caleh (Tell Tayinat?), and adjoined another Aramaean state Guzana (Tell Halaf). The friendship of these north Syrian principalities (Appendix 1) could not be relied on by the Greek merchants, but most of their monarchs were at daggers drawn with one another, and this proved an advantage to the traders, because it saved them from any co-ordinated encroachment.

Phoenicians and Cypriots and perhaps peoples of Asia Minor participated in the business affairs of Al Mina, but the leaders of the enterprise seem to have come from the precocious Greek city-states of Chalcis and Eretria in Euboea, supplemented by Eretrian subsidiaries in the Cyclades and to a lesser extent by the cities of Rhodes and other eastern Greek communities. These businessmen acquired fabrics, ivories, metals (notably gold) and slaves at Al Mina, from which, in the eighth century, they began to dispatch these acquisitions to Greek centres, and these could send wine and oil in exchange.

The recipients included western Greek cities. For there was a channel of communication from Al Mina – employing as intermediaries not only Chalcis and Eretria, but also the initially Eretrian colony of Corcyra (Corfu) – to other Euboean trading posts as far afield as south-west Italy, notably upon the island of Pithecusae (Ischia) and at Cumae on the adjacent Campanian mainland. From these entrepôts contact was made with the Etruscans, whose copper, iron and tin were exchanged, with mutual profit, for the gold and other commodities transported from the Greek markets of Syria.

The alphabet, too, adapted by the Greeks from north Syrian and Phoenician scripts (hence its name *phoinikeia* in Herodotus and inscriptions; note 11) first reached them in all probability, at Chalcis and Eretria in Euboea, coming from Al Mina and other north Syrian ports.[32] Although other Greek centres can make alternative claims (Chapter 1, note 35), and may, indeed, have served as additional subsidiary channels, the Euboeans seem, on epigraphical and historical grounds, to have been the first Greeks to undertake alphabetical writing. Indeed it is at the Chalcidian *emporion* at Pithecusae, as far as our present knowledge goes, that one of the very earliest of all Greek alphabetic inscriptions occurs.

No early epigraphic evidence, it is true, has come to light at Al Mina, despite the extensive pottery, both Greek and non-Greek, which has been found – but that may well be purely accidental. Nor, for that matter, have any signs of Greek tombs or architecture been discovered at Al Mina. There is no evidence, that is to say, indicating that the place was a Greek colony or city. Cities and tribes (*ethne*) were not the only social structures of early Greek communities. There were also trading posts (*emporia*), which, except to a rudimentary extent, lacked the institutions of either. In so far as Al Mina had become Hellenized (for the place must also have been manned by many near easterners as well), it was one of these *emporia*, like Pithecusae and (at first) Cumae at the other extremity of the Greek world.

Al Mina appears to have suffered destruction in *c.*700–675, during a rising by the Cilicians of south-eastern Asia Minor (Appendices, note 2) against Assyrian domination. However, the township was later rebuilt, with a proportionately larger Greek component than before – probably because the Phoenicians were leaving for the west to escape Assyrian pressure. The presence, at this stage, of pottery not only from Corinth (perhaps brought by Aeginetans as well as Corinthians), but also from various eastern Greek cities as well, bears ample witness to this increased Greek stake. The years before 600 witnessed additional construction and reconstruction, perhaps following the establishment of Babylonian suzerainty. During the first half of the sixth century, however, a prolonged archaeological hiatus occurs in the activity of Al Mina. There are two possible explanations for this. Either the conquest of the area by the Babylonians had not, as was suggested just now, brought reconstruction after all, but, on the contrary, had exercised a damaging effect, or perhaps our own knowledge of the site is deficient, owing to changes in the course of the River Orontes.

In any case, however, after Persia had succeeded Babylonia as overlord, a new town came into being (*c.*520), which imported increasing quantities of goods, especially from Athens. Investigations of the site have unearthed single-storeyed warehouses, shops and workshops, built of mud bricks resting on stone foundations and grouped around courtyards.

South of the Orontes, thirteen miles away on the other side of Mount Casius (Musa Dağ) was another Greek trading centre, Posidium (Ras el-Bassit). As recent finds have shown, it had a history of Greek imports not much shorter than Al Mina. The Greeks often gave capes the name of Posidium, after the sea-god Poseidon, and this settlement on the Syrian coast lay beside such a promontory, which is now known as Cape Bassit. The site provides access to an inland route through the hills, leading up to the Orontes valley.

There had been late Bronze Age (Mycenaean) occupation of Posidium, and like Al Mina it served as an *emporion* for Euboean and other Greek traders organizing commercial exchanges with their homelands and with western settlement areas. Few traces of Posidium can be seen today, but in the early years of the last century its remains were still visible.

A third and similar centre was Paltus (Tell Sukas, Bulda), some thirty-two miles to the south of Posidium. Above a mound that offers the customary traces of a Mycenaean presence, there followed a phase of early Iron Age habitation from *c*.850 BC, demonstrated by discoveries of pottery originating, for the most part, from Euboea and the Cyclades. An early temple, of which remains survive, may or may not have been Greek. But Paltus was of particular value to the Greeks as a trading post because, avoiding the not always friendly state of Unqi, it provided communications with the ivory-working centre of Hama, capital of another kingdom, Hamath, in the interior of Syria – until Hamath was destroyed by the Assyrians in *c*.720.

Paltus, too, suffered severe damage in its turn (*c*.675). But the place was rebuilt, and the last years of the century witnessed increased importations from eastern Greek cities (in contrast to Al Mina, which was eclipsed at this time). However, further destructions took place at Paltus in *c*.588, and then, on an even more serious scale, in *c*.552, perhaps at the hands of the Babylonians.

The remains of a temple in the Greek style have come to light, and a Greek woman incised her name on a loom-weight – though it would be wrong to infer that Paltus was actually a Greek city, or the colony of any Greek city-state. It was a marketing centre or *emporion*, like Al Mina and Posidium.

Egypt (Appendix 1) was, in early days, less readily accessible to the Greeks than Syria. But mail-clad Ionian soldiers, together with non-Greek Carians, came to the Nile delta in about 660 BC, either as mercenaries employed by King Gyges of Lydia or bent on their own piratical aims. On arrival, they found employment under the Saite pharaoh Psammetichus (Psamtik) 1 (*c*.663–609), who subsequently posted or settled a considerable number of them not only at his Egyptian garrison towns of Marea (in the west: site conjectured), Daphne (Tell Defenneh, an eastern frontier post) and Elephantine (in the south: they left graffiti on statue-legs at Abu Simbel, c.591),[33] but also at camp-towns (Stratopeda) on both banks of the eastern (Pelusiac) arm of the Nile, where recent excavations have identified their presence (at least at a somewhat later date).

Psammetichus I also posted and settled men from Miletus at the 'Fort of the Milesians' beside the Bolbinitic mouth of the Nile, towards the west of the delta (c.650), and then, after they had defeated an Egyptian pretender Inarus, allowed them to establish a trading post (*emporion*) at Naucratis (Piemro in Egyptian, now Kom Gieif) upon the most westerly (Canopic) arm of the river, where Greek objects dating from the seventh century have been found. Apries (Hophra, 589–570) employed 30,000 Ionian and Carian mercenaries against Amasis (Ahmose), but without success, since Amasis was finally victorious and succeeded him as pharaoh (570–526). A pronouncedly phil-Hellene ruler, who married a Greek girl from Cyrene, he became (for a time) an ally of Polycrates of Samos, and presented gifts to various Greek cities, including Lindus, Cyrene, Samos, Sparta and Delphi.

It was Amasis too – unless Apries had taken the first steps before him – who not only recruited his bodyguard from his Greek and other mercenaries but converted Naucratis into a major treaty-port and commercial link with the west. It became not the colony of any particular Greek city, but an *emporion* like the market ports of Syria that have just been discussed. The internal organization of the Syrian market-towns cannot be reconstructed, but at Naucratis we do know that there was an arrangement involving the joint participation of a number of Greek states. For, as Herodotus records, the walled Naucratite shrine known as the Hellenion was a co-operative enterprise financed by nine such eastern Greek cities, four Ionian (Chios, Clazomenae, Teos and Phocaea), four Dorian (Rhodes, of which the three cities, later amalgamated, acted in unison, Halicarnassus, Cnidus and Phaselis), and one Aeolian (Mytilene).[34]

Miletus and Samos (traditional enemies) on the other hand, as well as Aegina (the only non-East Greek city to secure representation), possessed sanctuaries of their own, dedicated to Apollo, Hera and Zeus respectively; and shrines of the Dioscuri and Aphrodite, presumably shared by the other participants, are also recorded. This is an exceptional example of successful collaboration between a number of independent city-states; and it proved durable. It had been instituted at a time of massive expansion of Greek trade – exemplified by local finds of pottery from various centres – and served as a precedent for the massive enterprises of colonization which followed in other lands and required comparable (though less extensive and formal) inter-city collaboration, since the colonists supplied by mother-cities often had to be supplemented by men from other states.

Naucratis was stated by Herodotus to have become the only port in Egypt where Greek merchants were permitted by the pharaohs to disembark and reside. The multiplication of discoveries in the north-eastern delta, at no less than a dozen sites, suggests that this statement was an over-simplification. Nevertheless, despite all his phil-Hellenism, it was convenient for Amasis not to let the Greeks spread and roam about too freely and widely, and it was hoped that Naucratis would serve as a centre where their efforts could be concentrated, under the control of the pharaohs. The place also served as the port of the Egyptian capital Sais, which was only ten miles away.

The principal commodity sought at Naucratis by its Greek visitors and residents was Egyptian grain (referred to admiringly by Bacchylides).[35] They exported this to their homelands, together with faience and alabaster and manufactured products such as linen (required for clothing and sails), and papyrus (employed as writing material and for the manufacture of ships' ropes). What they brought with them, for bartering purposes, was silver (needed by the pharaohs to pay their mercenaries), together with Greek timber and grain and olive oil (more useful for most purposes, than Egyptian castor oil), and some wine (more palatable than its Egyptian counterparts). Thus Sappho's brother Charaxus, utilizing the Mytilenean representation at Naucratis, brought Lesbian wine to Egypt – and, in the process, he acquired a mistress there, one of the attractive prostitutes for whom, according to Herodotus, the place became famous.[36] Solon, too, was said to have visited the country in the time of Amasis,[37] thus enhancing its reputation among the Greeks as a land of ancient wisdom. He referred, in a poem, to the Canopic mouth of the Nile, which was the approach to the *emporion* of Naucratis.

Other Greek traders who arrived at the place, on the other hand, came to stay, and swelled the number of permanent residents. All the same, a certain time – a period of some centuries, according to the prevalent view – seems to have elapsed before the Egyptian authorities allowed Naucratis to acquire the institutions of a fully fledged city. After the Persians destroyed and took over the Egyptian kingdom (525), the market-town continued to prosper, though on a less considerable scale; and it subsequently became the theme of a poem 'The Foundation of Naucratis' (by Apollonius Rhodius), while a book *On Aphrodite* by Polycharmus, a Naucratite, must likewise have had something to say about local history. Other Naucratite historians were Charon and Philistus. But perhaps the town's greatest claim to fame (shared, presumably, by other Greek settlements in Egypt) was to have acquainted Greeks elsewhere – or reacquainted them, following the long loss of contact since the Bronze Age – with the achievements of Egyptian sculpture and architecture, which they then so rapidly assimilated and improved upon. Greek *kouroi*, it has often been believed (despite doubts) were inspired by the life-size statues of Egypt, and Theodorus of Samos, for example, was stated to have acquired Egyptian techniques,[38] while it was evidently the sight of the country's buildings that provided the stimuli for the first Greek monumental temples.

8 Southern Italy and Sicily

CHAPTER 7

THE WEST

1 CAMPANIA: PITHECUSAE AND CUMAE

The expansion of the Greeks into southern Italy and Sicily, undertaken at an early date, was their most adventurous and far-reaching series of enterprises: within a short space of time there were colonies in Campania, the Gulf of Taras (Taranto), and on the Sicilian Strait (Straits of Messina) and eastern Sicily.

The parts of southern Italy which were thus settled became known as 'Great Greece'. This was perhaps because the continental extent of the region was so unprecedentedly ample and impressive. The country's hot, dry summers and mild winters (especially in the coastal areas) and its characteristic pattern of land and sea and vegetation, offered Greeks a basically familiar and hospitable environment into which they could import their agriculture and other features of their life more or less without change.

Their attention first fell upon Campania on the west coast, the south-eastern neighbour of Latium (Lazio). The volcanic soil of the territory was extremely productive, and this did not escape the notice of the Greeks, but it was for purposes of commerce that the earliest of many Greek settlements were founded.

The first of these was on Pithecusae (Inarime, Aenaria, now Ischia), a fertile island seven miles from the Campanian mainland, offshore from the northern extremity of the Gulf of Cumae or Crater (now the Bay of Naples). Pottery from Greek lands dating back to the late Bronze (Mycenaean) Age (c. 1400 BC) has been unearthed on the steep, defensible promontory of Monte Vico above Heraclion (Lacco Ameno) at the north-western end of the island, where an elevated plateau, adjoining a strip of cultivable territory, is flanked by sheltered harbours on either side.

Subsequently, not later than 775/770 BC (as objects from the local cemetery confirm), a Greek trading station (*emporion*) – not a city – was established on the same site.[1] The men who established this post came from Chalcis and Eretria (in the latter case probably political exiles), the Euboean cities which took the lead in the movement of expansion undertaken by the Greeks at this time. (These merchants were reinforced by a group from Cyme, which is probably not the well-known city in Aeolis [western Asia Minor] bearing that name but a small town in Euboea [now Paleokastri?] which gave its name to the Aeolian city, and later to Cumae). This Euboean connection is confirmed by a cup of c.750 found at Pithecusae, which displays an inscription in the Chalcidian form of the Greek alphabet – our oldest-known example of written verse, consisting of three lines which include a reference to Nestor's cup described in the *Iliad*. Another locally discovered pot offers an early representation of a shipwreck, which illustrates the interest of the Euboeans in sea-voyages.

For their *emporion* at Pithecusae was primarily created in order to effect maritime commercial contact with Etruria – farther up the Tyrrhenian coast, beyond the Tiber – of which the metals, especially iron and copper, were urgently coveted by the Greeks.[2] This link was facilitated by the existence of important Etruscan settlements in Campania itself, notably Capua, which probably acted as an intermediary in the transportation of metals from the Etruscan homeland to Pithecusae. A piece of iron (haematite) discovered in the lowest strata at Pithecusae came from the Etruscan metal-producing island of Ilva (Elba); and Pithecusan sites have also yielded traces of early ironworking, including slag, blooms (lumps of iron squeezed into bars) and the mouthpieces of bellows.

In the transportation of metals there were normally three stages: from the point of extraction to the smelting location, from there to the craftsman's workshop, and from the workshop to the eventual owner. At Pithecusae the second of these stages was dispensed with, since iron foundries and blacksmiths' forges existed side by side. (The same was true at Motya in western Sicily, with whose Phoenician [Carthaginian] merchants the Euboean traders at Pithecusae and elsewhere were deliberately competing – sometimes, it would appear, by going as far as Carthage themselves.)[3]

What prompted the rulers of the Etruscan city-states to provide these Pithecusan businessmen with the iron and copper they wanted was, above all else, the gold that the Etruscans received in return, to which the wealthy eighth-century tombs of the city-states of Etruria testify. The Euboeans had acquired this gold through their *emporia* at Al Mina, Posidium and Paltus in northern Syria (Chapter 6, section 4), and perhaps through market quarters in ports of Phoenicia as well, though where it had been worked up into the jewellery found in Etruscan tombs remains uncertain – this could have been done in Syria or in Pithecusae or in Etruria itself, by immigrant or local craftsmen, or probably both. At all events, the contact of Pithecusae with the east is attested by discoveries of imported scarabs – beetle-shaped gems or seals – designed by Phoenicians, under Egyptian influence (and imitated on the island).

Moreover, an Aramaic inscription appears on an amphora made of Pithecusan clay. Reference has already been made to the appearance of the Chalcidian alphabet on a locally manufactured pot. This has confirmed speculation that the Greeks learned their script from the Phoenicians by way of Al Mina and the other Euboean *emporia* in north Syria. According to this likely hypothesis, the Euboean traders at the Syrian *emporia* not only brought the alphabet to their own native island but also took it much farther west to Pithecusae, from which it spread to the other Greek foundations subsequently established in south Italy and Sicily.

Greek burial arrangements at Pithecusae have attracted interest. The dead were differently treated according to their ages, adults being cremated, but children inhumed. Large stones, however, were placed on the children's coffins to prevent their ghosts from coming back in a state of discontentment, which might otherwise have happened since their exclusion from adult burial was held to have deprived them of a proper afterlife. Slaves were buried with the families to which they belonged.

In about 500 Pithecusae was ruined by a volcanic eruption of Mount Montagnone, a secondary crater of its central mountain Epomaeus (Epomeo), which, though now extinct, was an active volcano during antiquity.

Long before that disaster, however, the Pithecusan market had already lost most of its importance, owing to the Euboeans' establishment of a second *emporion*, later converted into a city, at Cumae (Cyme) on the mainland opposite.

Cumae lay beyond the northern extremity of the Cumaean Gulf (Bay of Naples). Its lofty acropolis looked down upon beaches providing anchorage and upon a protected harbour, at the outlet (which no longer exists) from Lake Lucrinus (Fusaro). This acropolis had been occupied by native inhabitants (Opicans) from shortly after 1000 BC. It was in c.750 that Greek traders moved over from the island of Pithecusae (Ischia) and established a commercial post at Cumae, pacifying the Opicans either by diplomacy or by force. Most of the new arrivals, led by Megasthenes, had originated at Chalcis, but his colleague Hippocleides came from the small Euboean township of Cyme, which gave the Campanian town (like Cyme in Aeolis) its name. The settlers also included some Graioi (from near Tanagra in Boeotia), from whom the word *Graecus*, Greek, originated.

In *c.*730/725 the trading station at Cumae achieved the status of a Greek colony and city, and became independent. The soil of the adjacent plainland was sufficiently productive to enable the Cumaeans to grow enough grain for their own consumption and for exports as well (packed and dispatched, from the early years of the seventh century, in good local copies of Corinthian vases), and it was probably they, too, who introduced Italy to the cultivation of the vine and olive.

Moreover, it seems to have been through their agency that the Greek alphabet, reaching the mainland from Pithecusae (as indicated above), made its way to the Etruscans (Appendix 3), who adapted it to their own needs. For Cumae fulfilled a dominant role in the rapidly growing relationship between the Greeks and the city-states of Etruria, founded on the exchange of Etruscan iron and copper for eastern gold brought to Campania by the Euboeans.

The Cumaeans also derived profits from the fish and shellfish in the adjacent half-salt lakes Avernus and Lucrinus situated within the promontory which formed the northern termination of their gulf. The volcanic crater of Avernus, of which the name was over-imaginatively derived from *aornos*, 'birdless' – owing to the belief that the lakes' mephitic vapours killed any bird that flew over its waters – seemed, according to local tradition, to be the place where Odysseus and Aeneas had descended to the underworld. But the story was also sometimes transferred to Lake Lucrinus (consequently known as Acherusia, the entrance to Acheron in Hades), separated from the sea by a narrow spit, across which – before its penetration by a channel – Heracles was believed to have driven the oxen of Geryon.

Cumae soon became a political power, ambitious to establish control over the Sicilian Strait, which was the channel of communication with the Greek homeland and the near east. According to Thucydides, Cumaean pirates were the first settlers at Zancle (later Messana, now Messina) on these narrows,[4] where they were subsequently joined by colonists arriving directly from Chalcis and other cities of Euboea. This enterprise must have been initiated at an early date, since fragments of pottery found at Zancle date back to *c.*730–720. Later, and much nearer home, Cumaeans founded Dicaearchia (*c.*621; Puteoli, Pozzuoli) and Neapolis (*c.*600; Naples), which subsequently became the metropolis of the region.

Cumae was famous for its Sibyl, one of about ten such prophetesses scattered round the Greek world after the model of the Sibyl of Marpessus in the Troad (claimed also by Erythrae in Ionia). The original holy woman of Cumae, and perhaps her successors there as well, bore the name of Amaltheia. As Virgil described in the *Aeneid*,[5] the Sibyl delivered oracles as the mouthpiece of Apollo (who had succeeded Hera as the principal deity of the place); and on one occasion, according to a legendary tradition, she conducted negotiations with the Etruscan king of Rome, Tarquinius Priscus (*c*.616–579). Within the depths of the acropolis the vaulted chambers, galleries and cisterns cut into the rock of the Sibyl's cavern can still be visited.

But the city of Cumae moved into history, and produced a historical personage for the first time, when its dictator, Aristodemus the Effeminate, found himself at war with certain of the Etruscan city-states which had formerly brought so much profit to Cumae; or the Etruscan warriors who fought against him may have been freelances operating independent bandit groups. At all events an Etruscan army, coming (in part at least) from as far away as Clusium in northern Etruria and even from Spina near the head of the Adriatic, and perhaps invited or supported by Cumae's Etruscan neighbour Capua, undertook the 'long march' to Campania. Joined, *en route*, by other contingents, for example from Ardea in Latium, they clashed with the forces of Aristodemus, who heavily defeated the intruders, though whether he succeeded in expelling them altogether is not recorded. Subsequently, at some date between 506 and 504 BC, he gained the assistance of other Latins who were at odds with the Ardeans, and inflicted a further defeat on Etruscan neighbours or invaders. By these two victories Aristodemus secured and stabilized the position of Cumae against Etruscan threats,[6] until both contestants were swept aside by Samnite tribesmen from central Italy.

2 SYBARIS, CROTON (PYTHAGORAS), LOCRI EPIZEPHYRII

Another area of Greek colonization was the southernmost promontory of Italy. This region was later known as Brettioi (Bruttii), a term which in Oscan meant 'slaves' or 'runaways', referring to the defection of the tribe of that name from another and larger Italic people, the Lucanians, to whom they had formerly been subject. The territory now bears the name of Calabria, somewhat confusingly, since in ancient times Calabria was Italy's heel.

Rhegium (Reggio di Calabria) was founded by the Chalcidians in *c*.730–720, on the strategic southern tip of the peninsula,[7] and a few years later Sybaris was established by the Achaeans upon the 'instep' of

Italy which was formed by the Gulf of Taras (Tarentum, Taranto), an indentation of the Ionian Sea. Under the original name of Lupia, Sybaris was supposedly founded in *c*.720 BC (a few years earlier than Taras,[8] which achieved its fame much later on), and its archaeological record almost goes back to that traditional date of foundation. Under the leadership (according to an imperfectly decipherable passage of Strabo)[9] of a certain Is of Helice, its settlers originated from Achaea in the northern Peloponnese, the home of an otherwise backward people (of Mycenaean origin)[10] who lacked sufficient land and enjoyed few possibilities for trading at home, so that they took a leading initiative in colonizing the extreme south of Italy – including Sybaris. According to Aristotle, a number of additional settlers at the place came from Troezen in the Argolid.[11]

The new foundation occupied an extensive, low-lying site which bordered four miles of sea-coast between the Rivers Sybaris (Coscile) and Crathis (Crati). This shore provided *murex* fisheries; and the settlers were also able to penetrate inland. This was achieved through an agreement with the Serdaioi, a local tribe living nearby, which had escaped extermination from the colonists. With their aid (encouraged by intermarriage), Sybaris expanded its territory across the fertile neighbouring alluvial plain, and thus became able, according to Strabo, to assert its rule over four ethnic groups and no less than twenty-five dependent towns.[12] The design of a bull on the city coins (from *c*.550), while primarily representing the river-god Crathis, at the same time recalled the wealth the Sybarites derived from their livestock, which also included sheep, providing valuable wool. It was not long before they became proverbial for their outstanding riches and luxury.[13]

Sybaris also encouraged a new Achaean foundation at Metapontum, on the gulf to its north.[14] Favoured, too, by oracles from Delphi and Olympia, it sent colonists across the foot of Italy to the western, Tyrrhenian shore at Laus (Lao) and Scidrus.

Moreover, there was another Sybarite settlement, reached by a valley route, farther up the same western coast on an ancient site at Posidonia (Paestum), beside the northern extremity of Lucania (now south-eastern Campania). Pottery finds at Posidonia suggest a foundation date of *c*.625–600 BC, but the site also displays three well-preserved shrines, constituting one of the most impressive groups of Doric temples in the Greek world. The earliest, the so-called 'Basilica' (*c*.550), was probably a sanctuary of Zeus and Hera. To its north stands a building of *c*.500 which is known as the 'Temple of Ceres' but is likely to have been dedicated to Hera and Athena.[15] Beside the Sacred Way stand the remains of an underground shrine (*hypogeum*) for Hera's worship, of approximately the same date; and eight miles to the north-west, at the mouth of the River Silarus (Foce de Sele) was another sanctuary dedicated to the same goddess, where an almost complete series of sandstone metopes of c.575–550, once adorning the temple's treasury, have been found. Although, to judge from its coinage, the colony at Posidonia did not remain politically subjected to the Sybarites, its existence enabled their traders to conduct profitable business with the city-states of Etruria further to the north along the same Tyrrhenian coast, in competition with the Campanian markets of Pithecusae and Cumae which had been established shortly before the foundation of Sybaris.

In addition, the Sybarites, although their only harbour was an open roadstead, made use of their geographical position on the coast of the Ionian Sea to look eastwards as well as westwards for mercantile connections. In this process they established a close link with Miletus, whose textiles both supplemented their own local supplies and passed in transit through their city, handed over by the Sybarites (gathering lucrative dues) to the Etruscans, who took them northwards to Etruria by way of Laus.

In the early sixth century Sybaris was perhaps larger and richer than any other city-state. Within the exceptional six-mile-long perimeter of its walls, it was said to possess a population of 100,000. Roads were shaded and clean and in excellent repair. Crowing cocks and noisy traders were forbidden inside the city limits. Fishers and traders in purple dye were exempted from taxation. Cooks were awarded prizes and patents for inventing new dishes. The Sybarites took steam baths and, like the Etruscans, reclined at meals with their wives, thus incurring shocked censure throughout other Greek lands. Indeed, they lived so softly, their critics claimed, that even rose petals could bring out a blister on their sensitive bodies; and the sight of men at work was said to afflict them with a rupture.

More serious was their addiction to internal strife, due in this case, it was believed, to racial mixture with the local inhabitants which, however diplomatically intended, had the effect of exacerbating the usual Greek scourge of political sedition.

Nevertheless, the Sybarites were stated by Strabo to have attained the capacity, in early times, to place 300,000 men on the battlefield, including 5,000 cavalry.[16] The figure is evidently exaggerated, even if the contributions of allies are taken into account, but a powerful army appeared necessary, because relations with their neighbour to the south, Croton, were poisoned by frequently recurrent hostilities –

a state of affairs which suggests, incidentally, that many of the jeers at Sybarite luxury were Crotoniate propaganda.

At one period during the sixth century, it is true, the two states worked in harmony, for in c.530 they collaborated to destroy Siris, a Colophonian colony of early-seventh-century date which lay between Sybaris and Metapontum (which likewise joined in the destruction). But before long the notorious faction-fighting at Sybaris, where a leader of democratic inclinations named Telys had assumed dictatorial control, gave Croton its chance to strike, under the guise of protecting members of the respectable propertied classes who were in flight from the Sybarite autocrat. With the assistance, therefore, of a Spartan adventurer, the prince Dorieus (already encountered at Cyrene, Chapter 6, section 3), the Crotoniates attacked and captured Sybaris – and then blotted it off the face of the earth (510).

This they did by diverting the course of the River Crathis so that it inundated the city, which remained buried and lost until prolonged searches located its whereabouts twenty years ago. Pumps, drillings and magnetometers have revealed the foundations of sixth-century buildings and brought to light roof-tiles, pots and a pottery kiln of the same period. Ancient Sybaris, however, must also have housed imposing collections of works of art, which have not yet been unearthed. A paved zone beside the anchorage, which is now two miles from the sea, appears to have been a shipyard.

After the obliteration of Sybaris – which was a shocking fate for one Greek state to inflict on another and which caused special mourning among its commercial allies the Milesians[17] – such survivors as there were took refuge in their former colonies, especially Posidonia to which they brought added prosperity. It was not until more than half a century had passed that some of these refugees or their children returned to their former home, where after many vicissitudes they founded the new, international colony of Thurii (443).

Croton (Crotone), the southern neighbour and eventual destroyer of Sybaris, was situated on either side of the mouth of the River Aesarus (Esaro), upon a promontory which flanks a pair of sufficiently sheltered harbours. Its original inhabitants were Messapians, but the place was settled, supposedly in c.710 BC, by Achaean Greeks (compatriots of the people who had recently settled Sybaris farther north), under the leadership of Myscellus of Rhypae (Kunari).

Archaeological discoveries confirm the early date of this foundation: a seventh-century street has been traced, the position of the citadel is identified, the line of the town walls established, and traces of the harbours (imposed by a canal) have come to light as well. Excavations have also revealed the plan of Croton's important shrine of Hera Lacinia, situated on the promontory of Cape Lacinium (Colonna) seven miles to the south-east. The temple already existed before 600 (although the existing remains date from 150 years later).

As the new city of Croton grew and flourished – perhaps by the mining of silver, since argentiferous slag-heaps have been found nearby – it expanded its territory over the productive plains to the south, and founded colonies on its own account, first at Caulonia (c.675/600) in its borderland, and then at Terina across the foot of Italy upon the Tyrrhenian Sea.

The most famous man ever to have lived at Croton was Pythagoras. The son of Mnesarchus of Samos, he had emigrated from that city in c.531 – possibly because of bad relations with the island's autocrat Polycrates – and had moved to south Italy, where Croton became his home. He seems never to have committed his teachings to writing, thus inviting every sort of misunderstanding, taking the form of exaggerated praise and dispraise alike. In particular, the absence of written texts going back to the master himself makes it hard to distinguish what he himself may have said from the assertions attributed to him by subsequent members of his vigorous school.[18] To judge, however, from their quotations of his maxims and enigmatic sayings, and from his much later *Lives* by Porphyry and Iamblichus, the doctrines of Pythagoras formed a disconcertingly heady mixture of religion or superstition, *guru* community guidance, investigation of nature (*historie*), and mathematical and musical theorizing.

To take the more ostensibly scholarly aspects first, he seems to have become convinced that only a numerate, numerical explanation could satisfactorily explain the universe (for which he apparently invented the term *cosmos*, order). That is to say, its nature seemed to him to be interpretable in terms of numbers,[19] of which therefore, as Aristoxenus and Eudemus confirmed, he inaugurated the systematic investigation.[20] This provocative – though divergently interpreted – insight has been hailed as the 'creation of mathematical science', and even if such a claim unduly disregards the earlier contributions of other peoples (notably the Babylonians, by whom he may have been influenced), he clearly advanced such studies in an epoch-making fashion, elevating mathematics to a universal status, so that nature itself became a matter of measurable and countable quantity.

The insights that resulted in these conclusions came to him through his discovery of the numerical ratios determining the principal intervals of the musical scale. But here Pythagoras introduced a characteristically high-flown concept, by identifying the *tetractys* (the first four natural numbers) with the harmonious Song of the Sirens – later defined by

Plato (to whom we owe much, perhaps too much, of our information about Pythagoras) as the Music of the Spheres.[21]

This fantastic type of description was not inappropriate for a doctrine of Pythagoras, since his scientific or quasi-scientific enquiries were blended inextricably with imaginative concoctions which, despite the exercise of a certain weird logic, were unrelated to any scientific method. Thus he gained a reputation as an occultist and miracle-worker, and claimed (and perhaps possessed) exceptional psychic powers. One of the aspects of his teaching which caused shock and distaste was its ample percentage of conjurer's magical ideas (invested with moralistic interpretations), combined with irrational, primitive taboos, which Pythagoras apparently presented to the public wearing a melodramatic costume of white robe and trousers and gold coronet. Much of this strange hotch-potch was devised piecemeal by his followers of various dates, but other features evidently go back to his own pronouncements.

Moreover, the doctrine of opposites, which had seemed fruitful when put forward by Anaximander of Miletus and Heraclitus of Ephesus, was invested by Pythagoras with anti-feminist features as crack-brained as anything in Hesiod or Semonides. Men, he declared, although 'limited', are right and light and good, whereas women are unlimited (in their dangerous potentialities, when out of control) and left, dark and bad. Or, at least, that is what Aristotle declared that he said.[22] Perhaps, however, the true nature of Pythagoras' expositions on the subject was, in reality, somewhat more complex, since we are also told, contradictorily, that he had a large following of women, who were admitted to his fellowship on equal terms.

More incontrovertible were Pythagoras' teachings about the human soul, which he was one of the first Greek thinkers, following up hints from Anaximenes and Heraclitus, to treat explicitly as something of ethical importance, thus heralding the shift of philosophical studies from the universe to man, carried so much further in the following centuries by Socrates and Plato. Pythagoras envisaged the soul both as the harmonizing principle in a human being and as the microcosm corresponding to the macrocosm of the living universe, since he saw both alike as related to the numerical ratios of a mathematical scale – a link that appealed greatly to Plato.

But Pythagoras also, and for this we can rely on the evidence of his (highly critical) contemporary Xenophanes,[23] believed that the soul is a fallen, polluted divinity imprisoned within the body, as in a tomb, and destined to a cycle of reincarnations (*metempsychosis*) within human beings or animals or plants, from which, however, it can gain release by the elaborate practice of ritual purity. The doctrine seems to have been inspired, in its general lines, not by Egypt (a view quoted by Herodotus – Appendix 1, note 27), but rather, like certain beliefs encountered among Milesian thinkers, by the teachings of the Indian Upanishads, transmitted, presumably, through Persia.

This ritual purging, accompanied by ascetic abstinence, was associated with the worship of Apollo, of whom Pythagoras was a devotee, so that the Crotoniates, who shared his dedication to the cult – in the god's capacity as 'the purifier' – actually identified him with Apollo Hyperboreios, 'the northerner'. This northern link has to be seen in connection with Pythagoras' concept (attested by Aristotle) of the indestructible soul as temporarily detachable from the body, since this theory of 'bilocation' was derived from shamanistic faiths – often described as Orphic – current in Scythia and Thrace (Appendix 2).[24] From those peripheral countries such ideas somehow or other found their way to the far west, where Pythagoras may have been the first to give them expression, or at least to earn them widespread attention, reputedly circulating poems of his own under Orpheus' name.[25]

This redemptive purification, he maintained, would enable the soul to achieve harmony not only with itself and the world, but also with the unchanging, eternal pattern of truth and of the good, which corresponded with the proportion and order of the universe. The individual, insisted Pythagoras, could attain such personal harmony by pure thought, which he regarded as the highest activity of which human beings are capable. Men and women could reach their goal, that is to say, by devoting themselves to intellectual training and study. When he called himself a 'lover of wisdom' (*philosophos*), people agreed that he was the archetype of a sage, able to expound what human existence and death truly meant; and Plato was right to say that he taught an entire 'way of life'. For the Pythagorean design for living amounted to nothing less than a whole new religion.

It was practised at Croton by an ascetic society linked by social and religious bonds (including shared devotion to the cult of the Muses). The group soon obtained such extensive political influence in the city that 300 of its young adherents, 'bound to each other in oath like a brotherhood, and living segregated from the rest of the citizens', conspired to take over the government, and were triumphantly successful.[26] These developments, apparently, occurred under the personal direction and guidance of Pythagoras himself, who then adopted the role of a law-giver. In his old age, however, a Crotoniate aristocrat named Cylon, who had been rejected for admission to the society (allegedly because of his turbulent character), led a hostile movement which compelled the sage to withdraw to Metapontum, where he died – though Pythagoreanism continued to flourish without him.

The chronology of this series of events is uncertain, but both before and after Pythagoras' time Croton continued to rise to a position of great power in southern Italy. Its ascent became all the more impressive when it extended the network of secret Pythagorean societies to a number of other city-states, which Croton thus dominated. These freemason-like ruling juntas, organized, according to Polybius, in 'club-houses',[27] provided early and conspicuous examples of oligarchies based exclusively, in practice as well as theory, on election rather than on family allegiance and tradition, though it is not clear to what extent wealthy candidates were favoured.

Croton's successes, however, had not been uninterrupted. In a disgraceful military reverse on the River Sagra (Sagriano or Turbolo) – perhaps attributable to c.540, though the date is quite uncertain – 10,000 soldiers from Locri Epizephyrii and Rhegium were said to have defeated 130,000 Crotoniates. Yet this proved merely a temporary setback. For in c.530, as we saw – shortly after the arrival of Pythagoras, who according to tradition revived its people's morale – Croton collaborated with its northern rival Sybaris and with Metapontum to destroy Siris. Then in c.510, with the assistance of the Spartan freelance Dorieus (earlier encountered at Cyrene), the Crotoniates launched their victorious attack upon Sybaris itself, in response to an appeal from its exiled oligarchs, thus becoming, for a time, the leading power in southern Italy.

Their success in this onslaught was said to have been due to the martial prowess of Milo, Croton's most famous son. One of the disciples of Pythagoras,[28] whose Panhellenistic attitude encouraged inter-state competitions, he was the best-known Greek athlete of all time, and made a huge contribution to his city's unique record of victories in the Olympiads. This mountainous, half-legendary personage boasted that no one had ever brought him to his knees. He won the boys' wrestling at Olympia in 540, and then the adult contests at five successive Olympic Games, as well as gaining six, nine and ten similar victories at the Pythian, Nemean and Isthmian festivals respectively.

It was only in much later days that the cult of athleticism, personified in Milo, began to lose its appeal, when Cicero pictured the old wrestler weeping for his lost strength – commenting that his nobility came not from himself, but from his trunk and his arms – and the physician Galen, in the second century AD, observed that the bull Milo carried around and then ate up on a single day (perhaps in obedience to some Pythagorean dietetic programme) was no more of a blockhead than the athlete himself.[29]

Milo's daughter married Democedes, a member of Croton's school of physicians (which was under Pythagorean influence, and constituted one of the earliest of such schools – Chapter 1, note 56). Democedes went abroad to practise at Aegina, Athens, Samos and the court of Darius I. Then he returned to his native city, from which, however, for political reasons, he subsequently fled once again.

His chronology is obscure, and so is that of an even more eminent Crotoniate doctor, Alcmaeon. Alcmaeon may have worked in the later sixth century, or some time after 500. He wrote a book (now lost) on natural science, in which he seems to have stood up for 'rationalistic' methods against the magical cures and dreams in which temple doctors placed their faith. Despite this distaste for magic, however, he was, like Democedes, in touch with Pythagorean thought. Thus he compared the immortality of the soul to the endless circling of the heavenly bodies. And he ascribed conditions of the human body to the Pythagorean interplay of opposites, becoming the first, perhaps, to apply this idea to medical matters, and to add the deduction that health depends on harmony, being based on an *isonomia* ('equal rights') of opposites, in contrast to disease, which he described as a *monarchia*, synonymous with evil tyranny (*tyrannis*). Alcmaeon also maintained that the human body contains passages or ducts linking the sense-organs with the brain (which, followed by Plato but not by Aristotle, he recognized as the central organ of perception). Moreover, he founded such assertions not only on the theoretical sort of argument which so many Greek scientific thinkers tended to favour – nor even on the principle of inference, though he stressed the validity of such a method – but on surgical practice. For in bold pioneer fashion he conducted the dissection of animals (thus developing embryology); and he undertook operations on the human eye, which enabled him to discover the role of the optic nerve.

To Pythagoreans Croton remained a holy city, dedicated to sound minds by way of its philosophical and religious doctrines, and to healthy bodies by means of its medical experts and athletic victories. On the political level, however, the local Pythagorean junta finally succumbed to a more democratically inclined regime. Its leader was said to have been a certain Theages, himself a former member of the movement. But his dating (and even his existence) is disputable. His *coup* may have had something to do with the second departure of Democedes. What is clear, however, is that once the Pythagorean hold on Croton was loosened, bloody class conflicts persisted in the city to a degree which was rare even in Greek city-states.

Locri Epizephyrii (Locri in the West) stood on the Ionian Sea near the southern extremity of the toe of Italy. The city was established by

Greek settlers, according to Eusebius, in 679 or 673 BC, a view confirmed by local finds of Protocorinthian pottery. The colonists, led by
Euanthes, came from the insignificant, backward and divided territory of Locris on the central Greek mainland. They consisted for the
most part of Opuntians (East Locrians), with an additional element
of Ozolians (West Locrians, probably backed by Corinth) – as well as
a contingent, it was asserted, of Laconian slaves who had seduced
aristocratic Spartan matrons while their husbands were away fighting
the First Messenian War, although this story was sometimes rejected
as an anti-Spartan propaganda myth.

After three or four years at a location that proved unsatisfactory
(possibly the Zephyrian promontory [Cape Brazzano], though this
attribution may only have been deduced from the colony's second
name), the settlers moved twelve miles farther north to a site nearer
the coast (Gerace Marina, now renamed Locri), where earlier native
Oenotrian inhabitants (i.e. Sicels – note 32) – who seem, from
archaeological evidence, already to have been in touch with Euboean
traders – were treacherously ejected by the settlers, despite a prior
agreement, although what happened is obscured by romantic
anecdotes.

The earliest Greek settlement at the new centre has not been
located, but it probably stood in hilly country where an acropolis was
later to be seen. The colony possessed no satisfactory natural harbour, but a town grew up beside the anchorage, because of the value
of the site: for Locri Epizephyrii was the last continental port for
voyagers from south Italy to Sicily. Remains of a shrine going back to
the seventh century (and reconstructed in the fifth) can be seen at
Marasa, and votive objects and dedicatory inscriptions testify to a
temple of Persephone, which became important after 600 – and can
be identified, it seems, with a building on the top of the Mannella
hill.

Locri Epizephyrii is above all notable for Zaleucus, who can be
claimed as the earliest historical Greek law-giver of western Greek
lands. Legend shrouds his name and story, but there is no good
reason to reject the date of c.663 given by Eusebius, which places him
at the very beginning of the colony. When, however, his written code
was described as the first in the entire Greek world, this neglected the
prior claims of Drerus and other cities of Crete (Chapter 6, section 1),
which had taken the lead in this respect owing to the early presence of
Phoenician traders, familiar with such codes. And indeed Zaleucus
was described as a pupil of the Cretan Thaletas, though Ephorus,
mistakenly, ascribes models for the Locrian laws not only to Crete but

to Athens and Sparta as well (whose legendary Lycurgus was also described as Thaletas' pupil).[30]

Zaleucus' laws, in so far as we can reconstruct them, mirrored the disciplinary requirements of Locri's aristocratic constitution, based on the rule of the Hundred Houses, and allocating sovereign power to a thousand leading men. His measures were notorious for their severity; they included the principle of retaliation (*lex talionis*), and the spelling out of exact penalties for any and every crime. He was also said to have discouraged legal changes.

And yet Zaleucus also became, paradoxically, famous as a conciliator of social classes. Indeed, the very fact that his measures were written down at all meant that people could now at least see where they stood. This codification process, it is worth noting, first occurred in one of the western colonies – these being cities which were probably impelled to publish codes in order to calm political strife, deriving from current, local ethnic and other frictions, as well as from earlier injustices in the motherland which had prompted emigration and must not be repeated in the emigrants' new home. Moreover, legislation was easier at a recent foundation which lacked deadening traditions – and enactments of various kinds also seemed urgently required in order to keep up the number of settlers, which was why Zaleucus reputedly forbade sales of land.

For the same sort of reasons, similar legal codifications proliferated elsewhere in Greek south Italy and Sicily as well, the earliest codifier after Zaleucus being Charondas of the Chalcidian colony of Catana (sixth century BC?),[31] while Androdamas performed a similar function at another Chalcidian settlement, Locri's neighbour Rhegium.

Locri Epizephyrii profited from its position on the peninsula's narrow toe to found colonies on its opposite Tyrrhenian shore. These included Hipponium (*c.*650, where Vibo Valentia was later established), Medma or Mesma (now Rosarno; where the earliest archaeological discoveries are of *c.*625–600), Taurianum (near Monte Traviano; *c.*600–550), and Mataurus or Metaurus (where a Locrian colony of *c.*550 succeeded a Zanclean foundation).

The land portage of goods from Locri to these colonies multiplied its revenues, which were also derived from the agriculture of its fertile, though narrow, coastal plain. At some indeterminable date, perhaps *c.*540 (as we saw earlier) the Locrians won a victory on the River Sagra over much superior forces of Croton, allegedly with the miraculous help of the Dioscuri, Castor and Polydeuces.

3 EASTERN SICILY: SYRACUSE

Sicily, separated from the Italian mainland by the narrow Sicilian Strait (Straits of Messina), is the largest island in the Mediterranean, measuring over 160 miles across and nearly 100 miles (in its eastern region) from north to south. It was originally known as Thrinacia (from *thrinax*, a trident), and later as Trinacria, referring to its triangular shape. Ancient writers distinguish between three principal pre-Greek peoples occupying the island, Elymians (believed to be of Trojan origin) in the north-west, Sicans (from whom Sicily's name in the *Odyssey*, Sicania, was derived) in the south-west, and Sicels (Siculi, who gave the island its permanent name) in the east.[32]

During the late Bronze Age (later second millennium BC), Mycenaean merchants visited Sicily and the adjacent Lipara (Lipari) islands (also known as Aeolian, after the wind-god Aeolus). Then, from the eighth century onwards, the coastal regions of the island were occupied, at selected points, by the Phoenicians and Greeks. Our surviving literary tradition, however, is fragmentary, and remains in this unsatisfactory state for centuries to come. Thucydides assigned chronological priority to the Phoenicians, stating that, before the Greeks arrived, they extensively settled the headlands and offshore islands of Sicily for purposes of trade. But the coming of the Greeks in large numbers, especially to the eastern part of the island – which most closely resembles the coasts of the Aegean, and offers agricultural land – compelled the Phoenicians to withdraw (not necessarily at a very early date) into three cities in the west. These were Motya (Mozia), Soloeis (Soluntum, Solunto) and Panormus (Palermo), all of which later became linked, though by what administrative arrangements we do not know, with the leading Phoenician foundation of Carthage in North Africa.[33] As regards the origins, however, of these and other Phoenician settlements on the island, archaeological evidence does not so far confirm Thucydides' view that they antedated the Greeks. Whether it was Greek or Phoenician sailors who first revived the Mycenaean practice of navigating the Sicilian Strait we do not know. But the Greeks seem to have been engaged in such activity a good deal before the establishment of their first colony. At first, relations between the two immigrant peoples were not, perhaps, unfriendly. This became the case, it is true, in the sixth century, but the same state of affairs need not necessarily have existed at an earlier date.

The Greek colonies received luxury goods from their homeland and from eastern Greece, and also received consignments of marble, since the local rock was too soft to provide first-rate building stone. Presumably they sent back, in exchange, mainly wheat – in which the island abounded – together, perhaps, with some vegetables, fruit, timber, olive oil and wine, though not a great deal of these additional products, since Greece possessed enough of its own. By the fifth century, at least, Sicilian wine was exported to Carthage, but we do not know when trading with this and other Phoenician centres first began to develop.

The earliest Greek colony in Sicily, according to tradition, was Naxos (Giardini Naxos) beneath Mount Etna on the east coast,[34] reputedly established in 734 by settlers from Chalcis in Euboea and Naxos in the Cyclades. Syracuse (Siracusa), further south on the same coast, was said to have been founded a year later, on the site of a former Mycenaean trading post. The colonists of the new settlement, under a certain Archias – reputedly in flight after committing a crime – were Corinthians (or rather farmers from the inland village of Tenea, near Corinth). And in the very same year, according to the record, other Corinthians (replacing Eretrians and Illyrians) colonized Corcyra (Corfu), a natural staging point between Sicily and the Greek homeland.

This double colonization was rightly seen as a decisive step in the process that made Corinth powerful. Throughout the initial century after the foundation of Syracuse, virtually all the pottery it imported – serving as a general distribution point for other parts of Sicily – was Corinthian (subsequently superseded by Athenian wares); and it was Corinth that negotiated the treaties which gained these cargoes right of way through the strait. Yet Syracuse, like Corcyra, resisted or evaded the Corinthians' desire to control the colonies they had founded, although, unlike Corcyra, it remained on friendly terms with its mother-city.

The original Corinthian colony at Syracuse was established on the offshore island of Ortygia, which had been inhabited since the Palaeolithic epoch. Ortygia's situation, right up against the Sicilian coast, created two excellent natural ports, of which one, the spacious Great Harbour, was the finest on the entire east coast of the island. Ortygia also possessed an ample fresh-water spring, taking its name of Arethusa (identified with Artemis Ortygia) from a nymph who, according to Greek mythology, had fled there from Greece in order to evade the amorous advances of the river-god Alpheus. Her attempt to take refuge in Sicily, however, proved useless, since the god flowed through the Ionian Sea and she could not escape his attention.

On Ortygia the traces of rectangular houses erected by the first generation of Corinthian colonists have now come to light, directly on top of the Sicel village they superseded. The smallness of these earliest

Greek dwellings, and their limitation to a single room, indicate that the famous later wealth of Syracuse was not yet to be seen. However, before the eighth century was over, as recent excavations have demonstrated, this habitation centre had begun to expand on to the mainland, where, beyond the agora, the mainland quarters of Syracuse gradually came into being, namely Achradina (commercial and governmental), Neapolis and Tyche (north-west, north-east; both residential) and finally the heights of Epipolae. Two miles to the south-west of Achradina was the Olympieum, dedicated to Olympian Zeus in about the middle of the sixth century. It stood just beyond the River Anapus, of which the plain, beyond an estuary marshland, produced an abundant cereal crop. They enriched the aristocratic ruling class of the city, who were known as the *gamoroi*, 'those who divide the land', and formed an assembly 600 strong.[35]

This ruling class also gained control of a wider surrounding territory, expelling some of its native Sicel inhabitants (so that the major Sicel sites of Pantalica and Finocchito were abandoned at about the time of the colony's foundation), and reducing others to the status of Helot–serfs (*Kyllyrioi*) or tribute-paying dependants.[36] In addition, the Syracusans established new colonies of their own, at Helorus (Eloro) lower down the east coast of the island (traditionally in *c*.700), Acrae (Palazzo Acreide) on a steep, defensible hill in the interior (*c*.663) and Casmenae upon an even loftier site (*c*.643).

These last two locations, in mountainous country high up the valley of the Anapus, were chosen with a military aim. For all around were dense populations of Sicels, who found themselves, in effect, concentrated in a reservation in this corner of the island, and enjoyed, on the whole, less friendly relations with Corinthian than with Chalcidian colonists (section 4 below). West of Casmenae, however, was a Syracusan coastal settlement, Camarina (*c*.598), which established a better relationship with its Sicel neighbours – and asserted its independence from the Syracusans by a revolt (*c*.550). But they, unusually, succeeded in maintaining direct control over their other colonies, which were near enough for this to be possible. Thus the city acquired a substantial territory, and effectively dominated almost the entire south-eastern region of Sicily.

The increasing importance of Syracuse at this time was signalized by the construction, upon Ortygia, of a temple dedicated to Apollo (*c*.575?), which may have been larger than any known predecessor elsewhere in the Greek world, and displayed the first-known Doric entablature of stone (unless the Temple of Artemis at Corcyra [Chapter 8, section 1], another Corinthian colony, is older).[37] At the end of the sixth century many people would have pronounced Syracuse (in succession to Sybaris) the greatest city in the entire Greek world. At about this time, too, its rulers inaugurated their long-lived and magnificent coinage, which had not been needed before, since they had relied on the currency of their trading partner Corinth, but which now – issued, incidentally, on the Euboic-Attic and not the Corinthian standard – proved useful for the payment of the abundant mercenary troops the government of Syracuse needed to employ in order to maintain its power. The silver from which the coins were made was no doubt paid for out of taxation at home and from the sale of subject Sicels into slavery.

During the first decade of the fifth century, however, Syracuse began, for a short time, to be overshadowed by Hippocrates, the dictator of Gela (section 5 below) – the western neighbour of Camarina – who after seizing power in his own city in c.498 severely defeated the Syracusans beside the River Helorus some six years later. He was restrained by Corinthian and Corcyraean diplomatic intervention from occupying Syracuse itself. Yet it was at this stage, in all probability, that the ruling Syracusan aristocracy, thus discredited, was expelled in a democratic revolution. If so, this was a forerunner of countless disturbances in the city during the centuries to come, which, despite its riches and triumphs, prevented the civic rulers from ever attaining the unchallengeably supreme position to which they aspired.

One factor which contributed to these continual convulsions was the settlement pattern. For examination of the territory has suggested that while the rich plainland became the property of the first colonists and their descendants the *gamoroi* 'who divided the land', later arrivals and others of inferior status had to live, grumbling, in the peripheral hill-country. Syracuse, presenting all the problems of a multi-racial society, shared with Croton and Cumae the unhappy distinction of suffering not merely from factional strife but from authentic class conflict as well, so that its achievements appear against a background of almost unceasing, cruelly conducted, internal struggles.

The comic poet and dramatist Epicharmus was a resident and probably a native of Syracuse (though other cities, including Cos, claimed to be his birthplace). He apparently inaugurated his activity in the later sixth century BC, since Aristotle stated that he lived a 'good while before' the Athenians Chionides and Magnes,[38] who won victories in 486 and 472 respectively (he survived, however, right down to the reign of Hiero I [478–467/466], with whom various anecdotes associate him). Although only a few fragments of his plays are still extant, he was a writer of distinction – as Plato emphasized,[39] as well as imitating for his own purposes Epicharmus' witty and graceful dramatic technique of question and answer.

Thirty-seven titles of his works, written in the Sicilian Doric dialect, have come down to us, and bear witness to an extremely varied output. These plays may have been staged at local festivals of Artemis and Demeter – an interpretation with which, since the Greeks liked to mix grave with gay, the burlesquing of mythology, detectable in more than half his known plays, does not conflict. One of his favourite personages was Odysseus, portrayed both as shipwrecked sailor (*Nauagos*) and as the shirker (*Automolos*) who tried to evade the dangerous leadership of a spying expedition to Troy. Another prominent 'hero' is Heracles, represented as a prodigious sexual athlete and a heavy, noisy eater. Epicharmus also wrote a comedy on the grim topic of the murderous Medea, and another which, although called *Mr Argument and His Wife* (*Logos and Logina*), is shown by recently discovered fragments to have dealt with yet another mythological theme.

Prometheus and Pyrrha contained a dialogue between Pyrrha and Deucalion (survivors of the Flood) about their Ark. An examination of this dialogue (in conjunction with a fragment from another piece) has led to the conjecture that Epicharmus brought three actors on the stage (like Aeschylus [d.456] in his later plays at Athens).[40] Employment of a chorus, too, may be suggested by a number of the Sicilian dramatist's titles, which resemble those of the great Attic tragedians, with the implication that he is parodying their plays, or rather, in most cases, earlier Attic plays (now vanished) on the same subjects.[41] The employment of stock characters such as braggarts, parasites and rustics (the *Agroikos*) offers analogies with the fifth-century Attic comedy of Aristophanes, and Aristotle's view that this owed debts to his plots,[42] though unprovable, cannot be discounted.

As for the forerunners of Epicharmus, this is a complicated subject since he employed a variety of different styles and tones (as well as metres). Epic themes are, of course, called upon, and his ribald presentation of Heracles probably owes something to previous Doric Sicilian farces and mimes; Epicharmus himself indicates his debt to Aristoxenus of Selinus, inheritor of farcical conventions from Megara. He also indulges freely in moralizing epigrams (later collected together, with the addition of forgeries). They provide evidence of an interest in philosophy. Thus he agrees with Heraclitus' postulation of an eternal world order, and Plutarch records that he became a Pythagorean,[43] though that may not be true.

4 NORTHERN SICILY: ZANCLE AND HIMERA

The Euboean city of Chalcis, which played a leading part in the establishment of markets (*emporia*) at the Campanian centres of Pithecusae
(*c.*775/770 BC) and Cumae (*c.*750) – in the latter case followed by a
colony, some twenty years afterwards – was no less prominent, and no
less prompt, in sending settlements to Sicily. Indeed Chalcidian Naxos
on the east coast was reputedly the first Greek colony on the island
(734), slightly earlier even than Syracuse.

It was not surprising, then, that within the same space of years
Chalcis also took the lead in colonizing the shores of the uniquely
strategic Sicilian Strait separating the island from Italy. For it was
there that Zancle (later Messana, and Messina) was founded, on the
site of a Bronze Age – and even earlier – centre, during the decade
(archaeological discoveries suggest) between 730 and 720, although in
later generations the foundation of the place, for patriotic reasons, was
dated still earlier and even ascribed to the mythical nymph Pelorias.
After her, the hills on one side of the colony's narrow plain were called
the Peloritan mountains; and on the other flank of the plain was a long,
curved spit or sandbar likewise known by the nymph's name. It was
this natural mole that gave the place its name Zancle, from *zanklon*,
meaning a sickle in the language of the Sicels whom the colonists
dispossessed.

According to Thucydides,[44] these settlers were Greek pirates (of
Chalcidian or other Euboean origin) from Cumae, who were joined by
other immigrants from the same Euboean cities. Their leaders were
Perieres of Cumae and Crataemenes of Chalcis. Portions of the original
colony – traceable at the point where the 'sickle' joins the mainland –
show that the early habitation area was unexpectedly substantial.
Remains of a temple of eighth- or seventh-century date have been
uncovered at the tip of the Pelorias spit itself.

We do not know to whom this shrine was dedicated, but the city's
coinage (which did not begin before the late sixth century) show that its
principal deities were Pan and Poseidon. The coins also honour a local
hero and legendary ruler Pheraemon, son of Aeolus, and depict the
armed god Adranus, worshipped in a temple on the western slopes of
Mount Aetna (Etna) (beside the Sicel settlement of Adranus [now
Aderno], within a sacred enclosure where more than a thousand guide-
dogs were kept). The founder-nymph Pelorias, too, was held to deserve
numismatic attention. The spit named after her contained three volcanic lakes which helped to bring Zancle its prosperity, owing to their
abundant provision of fish (as well as game round their banks). This was
fortunate, since the city's territory was small. But the principal source

of its power and wealth was its key position on the narrows, where its rulers could control the traffic passing through, and exact tolls.

Zancle also founded the only two Greek cities on the north coast of Sicily. First it sent colonists westwards to fertile Mylae (Milazzo, c.717/716), to make good its own deficiency in cultivable land. And then another batch of settlers was dispatched still further west, in order to establish a colony at Himera (Imera, c.648). This, too, possessed a productive territory, and opened up commercial contacts both with the island's interior through the valley of the River Himeras and with Elymians and Phoenicians farther west. For Himera was the remotest Greek outpost in the northern part of Sicily, as Selinus was in the south (section 5 below).

Thucydides wrote that the place was colonized by Chalcidians from Zancle, in association with the Myletidae – a clan who had been banished from Syracuse – and that the community spoke a mixture of Dorian and Chalcidian but followed Chalcidian customs and laws.[45] Strabo, on the other hand, describes the founders of Himera as Zancleans from Mylae.[46] Perhaps the Myletidae clan took their name from Mylae because they had lived there for a time after leaving Syracuse, and before migrating to Himera.

The latter city comprised, as recent excavations have shown, a defensible upper town on the rim of the hills overlooking the mouth of the Himeras, and a lower town beside the estuary and the harbour. Even if the tradition ascribing the foundation of Rhegium, just across the Sicilian Strait, to Zancle may be anachronistic, a smaller Greek settlement at Mataurus or Metaurus (c.650?), a little way up the Tyrrhenian coast, is likely to have been another Zanclean colony, as Solinus indicates[47] – although there is also evidence (as we saw in section 2) of participation by Locri Epizephyrii, apparently a century later.

The link between Mataurus and Zancle seems to be confirmed by the tradition that the former city was the birthplace of the poet Stesichorus but that, except when engaged on his travels (including a visit to Sparta, and exile in Arcadia), he became a resident of Zancle's other colony Himera.[48] He was probably born in the third quarter of the seventh century and died at an advanced age in the middle of the sixth. The name by which he was, and is, generally known meant 'choirmaster', but he originally bore the name of Tisias.

Although only fragments of his works survive today, in ancient times he enjoyed renown throughout the Greek world, being regarded as one of the outstanding figures in the formative period of lyric poetry. Moreover it was he who put the western Greeks on the cultural map, so that they were not merely squatters in distant, uncivilized outposts, but could claim to be authentic participants and indeed joint leaders in the Hellenic tradition. He was revered as a canonical authority on the whole range of Greek mythology, and critics had much more to say about him as well. Dionysius of Halicarnassus praised his plots and characterizations for their nobility, and Quintilian, too, admired the *dignitas*, moral elevation, with which he invested his heroes and heroines, describing him as the successor of the epic poets, whose myths and legends Stesichorus continued to embroider, adapting their heroic narratives to the musical charm of lyric metres.[49] Most of his subjects, in fact, are taken from the sequels to the *Iliad* and *Odyssey* known collectively as the Epic Cycle. Indeed, he himself contributed to the cycle, by the composition of a *Sack of Troy (Iliu Persis)*, including an account of the Wooden Horse constructed by Epeus; and he was also one of the writers of *Nostoi*, returns of Greek heroes from the Trojan War.

In his *Helen* Stesichorus followed the usual version indicating the heroine's willingness to be seduced by Paris, and describing her subsequent departure for Troy. But in his famous *Palinode* that followed he went back on this account, declaring himself prompted by Helen herself to pronounce it untrue: she had never gone to Troy at all, and the pretence that she had done so was the fault of Homer (in a second *Palinode* the blame was laid on Hesiod). This retraction by Stesichorus, while reflecting the masculine view that such a great war could not have been fought about a woman, may also have been prompted by a desire to take even fuller advantage of a topic which had already brought him success. Or he may have hoped to cease offending those who worshipped Helen as a goddess. Among such people, for example, were the citizens of Sparta whom Stesichorus' *Oresteia* complimented by attributing the death of Agamemnon to their city. This may also have been the first work to inbue the event with the terrible moral significance later emphasized by Aeschylus. Perhaps the piece was written for singing at a spring festival – although it has now been questioned whether he wrote for such choirs, and the suggestion has been made that instead he recited his poems himself.

In his *Europa*, Stesichorus turned to the Epic Cycle of Thebes in Boeotia, describing that city's mythical foundation and narrating the myth of Eriphyle, the disloyal wife of Amphiaraus, who was killed by their son Alcmaeon. The poet seemed to have explored the tragic consequences of love with unprecedented fullness and skills. And while, as we have seen, he could be described as the continuator of epic, heroic, narrative themes, he endowed them with a fresh inventive vigour, which led the way to the Athenian tragedians of later generations.

Stesichorus' *Funeral Games of Pelias* drew on the story of the Argonauts, displaying an awareness of the Black Sea, the scene of their legendary voyages, and a knowledge of current maritime enterprises. Local affairs, however, apparently lay behind his fable of the horse which, driven off its pasturage by a stag, appealed to a man for help but then was unable to get rid of him: for this was said to be a warning to contemporary Himerans not to call in Phalaris, whom he had tried to prevent from seizing autocratic power at Acragas (*c.*570–554/549; note 64), for assistance against their non-Greek neighbours.

The poet also revealed that he had heard of the silver mines of Tartessus in south-west Spain. This emerges from a passage in his *Geryoneis*, which was one of a number of his poems devoted to Heracles, and appears to have offered the earliest full-scale treatment of the hero's mythical visit to north-western Sicily (to perform his tenth Labour, the winning of the arms of Geryon). Stesichorus' interest in the theme may represent a preliminary stage in the ambition of the Greek colonists to seize that region from the Phoenicians and Carthaginians, a desire which was subsequently to lead to so much warfare (cf. note 63).

The poetic philosopher or theologian or idiosyncratic critical sage Xenophanes provides an argument against the geographical pattern of this book because he travelled so widely from place to place and country to country (cf. Chapter 1, note 4). 'As Xenophanes himself somewhere says,' records Diogenes Laertius,[50] '"Already there are seven and sixty years tossing my thought up and down the land of Greece; and from my birth there were another twenty-five to add to these, if I know how to speak truly about these things."'

He was in his prime, adds Diogenes, during the 60th Olympiad (540–537 BC); perhaps he lived from *c.*570 to *c.*475 BC. Born at Colophon in Ionia, he was expelled from his mother-city (probably at the time of its capture by the Persians in *c.*546–545), and thereafter 'passed his time at Zancle and Catana in Sicily'.[51] Although, that is to say, he lived a wandering life, he spent a great deal, or most, of his time at those Sicilian centres, so that the historian of Sicily, Timaeus, gave him attention,[52] and Xenophanes became the poet of the Ionian intellectual enlightenment in the west.

One of his elegies outlined the rules of behaviour for a symposium,[53] suggesting that he received an honourable reception in noble households and clubs (*hetaireiai*), and recited his poems at such gatherings. His tastes seem to have been simple but fastidious, favouring moderate indulgence in social pleasures. However, he denounced the accepted standards of aristocratic, militaristic behaviour, which, with the approval of other poets, lavished such exaggerated approval upon wrestlers, charioteers and boxers. In Xenophanes' opinion, a state derived more benefit from intellectual exploits – such as his own.

The surviving fragments of his verses are mostly in the elegiac metre or in hexameters, although occasional iambic occurs. Certain of these poems were classified as *silloi* ('squints'), a satirical genre which was made famous nearly three centuries later by Timon of Phlius in the Argolid, who recognized Xenophanes as his literary ancestor.

As a theologian, Xenophanes' principal achievement was the ruthless demolition (for all his Ionian background) of the pictures of the gods presented in the Homeric epics, as well as in the poems of Hesiod. In the first place, he declares, such a depiction of the deities as immoral and criminal must be wrong. Secondly, their presentation in human form is equally unacceptable. They had only been shown in this anthropomorphic guise, he suggests, because it was humankind that was describing them; and in this connection he makes the further, relativistic point that different peoples endow their deities with their own ethnic characteristics, the Thracians seeing their gods as red-haired and blue-eyed, and the Aethiopes (Ethiopians) envisaging them as snub-nosed and black. If (he goes on to observe) cattle and horses and lions had hands and were able to make images of the gods, it would be as cattle and horses and lions that they would represent them.[54]

Xenophanes, for his part, does not deny that a divine power exists. But he understands it quite differently, and endows it with an unfamiliar brand of spirituality: as an eternal consciousness, without motion (thus anticipating the Unmoved Mover of Aristotle), which 'shakes all things by the thought of its mind'.[55] That is to say, it governs the world by the power of spirit and reasoning. He had introduced the idea of a divine intelligence pervading and regulating everything that is and happens. Such a divinity, according to Xenophanes, can be 'in no way similar to mortals either in body or in thinking'.[56] He himself, it is true, also writes of 'gods', in what seem to be polytheistic terms.[57] But this may be little more than a conventional poetic device, or a concession to popular terminology; and it remains likely that Xenophanes thought in basically monotheistic terms – maybe under the influence of Persian ideas, which had reached Ionia before his departure for the west.

Be that as it may, his sophisticated definition of the divine authority marks a step forward in the intellectual history of Greece, and, in particular, of the Sicilian city-states in which Xenophanes lived. However, it was also an isolated approach ahead of its time, fitting into no known category, so that his views inevitably provoked misconceptions, prompting Plato, for example, followed by Aristotle, to see their author as the founder of the Eleatic school of philosophy in the following century[58] because Xenophanes' all-pervading, motionless deity seemed to foreshadow the motionless Sphere of Being described by Parmenides of Elea.[59] In fact, however, the two men's concepts are entirely different; and stories that related Xenophanes to Elea – suggesting that he wrote a poem on its foundation, and died at the place – are probably inventions derived from this fictitious attempt to discern a link.

Perhaps indebted, as we have seen, to Persian monotheistic traditions, Xenophanes also did not forget the interest in natural phenomena shown by earlier Ionian thinkers (Thales, Anaximander and Anaximenes of Miletus).[60] In this field, despite his acceptance of naïve views – such as the belief that the earth was of infinite length, breadth and depth – he displayed an unusual gift for scientific observation, as opposed to the mainly theoretical arguments preferred by so many Greek thinkers (although the Milesians had, at times, moved beyond these). Thus the discovery of shells and fossils of sea-creatures in rocks inspired him to move right away from mythological interpretations of the world's origins, and to deduce instead that the land had once been covered by the sea – a conclusion which led to his further belief that the earth had originally evolved through an alternation between flooding and drying.

But perhaps the most impressive of Xenophanes' contributions was his warning about the inevitable defectiveness of human knowledge:

No man knows, or will ever know, the truth about the gods and all that I speak about. For even if someone happened to tell the complete truth, yet oneself does not know it; but all things are matters of opinion. . . . Let what I say be interpreted as resembling the truth. . . . The gods have not revealed all things to men from the beginning; but by searching out men find out better in time.[61]

This may not quite amount to the complete and total scepticism that was later seen in the passage. On the contrary, what Xenophanes seems to be trying to do is to stress, once again, the omnipotence of the divinity (as he understood the term), by pointing out its total contrast with the limitations of human beings.

Moreover, in the course of making this point, he also stresses a distinction between what one has seen for oneself or established at first hand and what can merely be the subject of inference – because, for all the inevitable defects a man must possess, he believed that arduous, first-hand investigation can nevertheless achieve rewarding results, and confer a special state of insight, provided that the investigator is someone who knows how to set about this task. And he felt that he himself was such a man.

As for wild, uncorroborated theories such as the doctrine of reincarnation preached by his Ionian fellow emigrant Pythagoras, he made fun of them (despite some strange beliefs of his own) by telling ludicrous anecdotes.[62] And he regarded Orphic priests (Appendix 2) as impostors.

5 SOUTHERN SICILY: GELA AND SELINUS

The most important Greek cities on this coast, from east to west, were Camarina, Gela, Acragas and Selinus. Camarina has been mentioned in connection with Syracuse, which was its founder. To the west of it, just beyond the sacred River Gelas, was Gela, the earliest colony dispatched to the southern shores of the island.

Situated upon a long, narrow, steep, sandy elevation, which had already been occupied by Sicans during the Bronze Age, the Greek city of Gela can be dated to c.690/688, as tradition reported (discoveries of late-eighth-century pottery do not justify an earlier date). Its founders were colonists from Rhodes and Crete, under the leadership of Antiphemus and Entimus respectively, who received the blessing of Delphi for the site they had chosen, in an oracle that has been preserved. After prolonged warfare against Sican hillmen for the domination of the inland plain – which possessed fertile arable land, and provided grazing for first-class cavalry horses – the Geloans pushed further into the interior, where they brought a number of the native settlements under their control, including Mactorium (Monte Bubbona) and Omphace (Butera). Moreover, expanding some forty miles westwards along the coast, they established, or joined other Rhodians in establishing, a colony at Acragas (Agrigento, c.580), which in the hands of a notorious tyrant Phalaris (c.570–554/549) gained substantial wealth and power on its own account.[63]

At Gela, in about the same period, a temple, dedicated to Athena, was built on the acropolis, and decorated with polychrome terracotta ornaments, for which Gela was famous. There was also a sanctuary of Demeter Thesmophoros at Bitalemi, near the mouth of the Gelas, where numerous objects have recently came to light.

However, the aristocratic government of Gela eventually succumbed to the cult of athleticism. One of its leading citizens, Pantares, was owner–victor in the four-horse chariot race at the Olympic Games in 512 or 508, thus becoming the first, as far as we know, of a long series of Sicilian notables and princes who competed successfully in this most prestigious and expensive of all contests. Taking advantage of the renown gained by this victory, Pantares' son Cleander seized control of the city. There had already been trouble in Gela before, at some uncertain earlier date, when party strife caused a number of its citizens to seek refuge at Mactorium in the neighbouring hills. But now Cleander abolished the aristocratic constitution altogether, and set himself up as dictator (505), a post he occupied until he succumbed to murderers seven year later.

He was succeeded by his brother Hippocrates, who during the seven years of his reign, by single-minded ruthlessness, momentarily made Gela the greatest power in the island. Excavations suggest that Hippocrates (perhaps following in his brother's footsteps) established the groundwork for this success by constructing fortifications on the northern rim of hills above Gela. He also reinforced his army, with special attention to the cavalry which its plainland so excellently bred. Then, his home base secured, he moved against the island's Chalcidian colonies of Naxos, Zancle and Leontini, seizing booty and installing local puppet despots.[64]

After some delay in sorting out the tangles that these appointments created, Hippocrates next went for the greatest prize of all, which was Syracuse. This was not an easy task, because he had no fleet, since Gela possessed no harbour, other than a shelving beach, and consequently disposed of no docks or other facilities for building ships. And that, indeed, was one of the principal reasons for his attack, because he was eager not only to acquire the immeasurable riches of Syracuse but also to obtain access to its excellent port. So he moved by land, with his strengthened army, against the city of the Syracusans, and when they tried to stop him, inflicted a resounding defeat on their forces beside the River Helorus (see also above, section 2).

Then he approached the temple of Zeus, just outside Syracuse, and was prevented from assaulting and sacking the city itself only by the good offices of the Corinthians and Corcyraeans, who negotiated a truce. By the terms of this agreement, if not earlier, Hippocrates took over from Syracuse its sovereignty over the region's Sicel inhabitants. But he made the mistake of treating them roughly, and trying to compel them to accept Hellenization. In the continued fighting against recalcitrant Sicels that followed, he met his death during a battle at Hybla (c.491/490), whereupon his cavalry-commander Gelon dispossessed the late ruler's sons – of whom he had been made, or made himself, the guardian – and seized the dictatorship for himself, becoming founder of the spectacular Deinomenid dynasty.

To the west of Gela, beyond Acragas, was Selinus (Selinunte). It lay towards the south-western extremity of Sicily, centred upon a promontory jutting out into the sea between two rivers, the Selinus (Modione) to the west and the Galici (now the Gorgo di Cottone depression) to the east. The estuaries of the two streams, although surrounded by swampland, provided valuable, even if diminutive, harbours, and their valleys offered penetration into a fertile inland plain. Selinus was settled either in c.650 (Diodorus, Eusebius) or, more probably, in c.628 (Thucydides), by colonists from Megara Hyblaea, just north of Syracuse, under the leadership of Pamillus or Pammilus, who came with that purpose from Megara in Greece, the mother-city of the Hyblaean Megarans.

Selinus was the westernmost Greek city of the island, bordering on the region inhabited by the native Elymi (resistant, like some of the Sicels, to Hellenizing endeavours) and immediately adjoining the area colonized by the Phoenicians, who were in close touch with Carthage across the narrow neck of the central Mediterranean. With both these communities the Selinuntines generally contrived to maintain peaceful relations, although a lapse occurred in c.580 when they abetted an encroachment upon the Phoenician zone by an unsuccessful Cnidian and Rhodian move to settle Lilybaeum (Marsala), accompanied by hostilities against the Elymian town of Segesta.[65]

Nevertheless, the Selinuntines controlled territory as far west as the River Mazarus (Mazaro), and extended their territory eastwards to the Halycus (Platani), their boundary with Acragas. On the farther bank of the Halycus, too, they founded an outpost at Minoa (a name which may recall a late Bronze Age 'Minoan' township – unless it was merely a mythological fiction). This was presumably part of an attempt to check Acragantine expansion, though the seizure of Minoa in c.500 by a Spartan colonizer Euryleon (who gave the place the additional name of Heraclea) eliminated this influence of Selinus.

All the same, Selinus became extremely prosperous, and to this end its good relations with the Phoenicians proved invaluable, since the riches of the Selinuntines mainly came from the export of wine and olive-oil to Carthage.[66] Following the initiative of Syracuse, this wealth was illustrated by one of the most remarkable displays of architectural and sculptural expenditure to be found anywhere in the Greek world, described by Swinburne as 'the most extraordinary assemblage of ruins in Europe'. On the acropolis a primitive sanctuary (now known as the 'megaron') was followed by two additional shrines of sixth-century date, one perhaps dedicated to Apollo and the second to Athena, although the attributions of all these buildings to one deity or another remain conjectural. The temple ascribed to Apollo was adorned by friezes of *c*.550–530 BC depicting Apollo and Artemis and Leto in a quadriga, Heracles and his goblin enemies the Cercopes, and Europa carried off by Zeus in the guise of a bull. These friezes, which, like other Selinuntine sculptures, have been removed to the museum at Palermo, remain unique, because no other Sicilian city seems to have developed its own school of sculpture. The temple itself was reconstructed in AD 1925–6.

A further group of sacred buildings stood on another hill to the east of the city and acropolis, beyond the River Galici. One of these shrines, perhaps dedicated to Dionysus, is of mid-sixth-century date and was decorated with metope reliefs representing duels between gods and giants. Nearby was a monumental edifice which seems to have been dedicated to Olympian Zeus. It was one of the largest temples in the entire Greek world, so immense that its central nave can never have been roofed. Work was begun on this Olympieum, if that is what it was, in the later sixth century, but when the city was devastated by the Carthaginians in 409 it still remained unfinished, and at some unknown later date was demolished by an earthquake, leaving débris of gigantic dimensions.

The town-plan of Selinus is one of a number of such designs that confirm the employment, by early colonial foundations, of the sort of right-angled, grid-iron urban lay-out which was subsequently given the name of the fifth-century architect Hippodamus of Miletus. The residential area, on Manuzza hill, lay behind the acropolis, which was protected by the most formidable fortifications in the whole of Greek Sicily, first devised in *c*.500, but often replanned and strengthened thereafter.

At Gaggara to the west, across the River Selinus, stood a sactuary of the fertility goddess Demeter Malophoros, the 'apple-bearer'. It goes back to the beginnings of the colony, originating from an open-air altar which was replaced in the late seventh century by a temple surrounded by high walls. But this, too, was redesigned, first in *c*.580 and then frequently afterwards, developing into an elaborate architectural complex. The precinct, frequented by members of other Greek and non-Greek communities in the region, has yielded abundant finds of early Corinthian pottery, and more than 12,000 terracotta statuettes representing female donors or goddesses (and often made from the same mould). Adjoining the main shrine were areas dedicated both to three-headed Hecate Trimorphos (goddess of the underworld, of crossroads and of women) and to Zeus Milichius (protector of his devotees) – both deities who were venerated at the colonists' mother-city of Megara in Greece. Large cemeteries, containing masses of pottery from the seventh century onwards, have come to light on either bank of the River Selinus.

6 MASSALIA

Massalia (Massilia, Marseille) was a port-city upon the southern, Mediterranean coast of Transalpine Gaul, in the Gallic Gulf (Golfe du Lion). Already in the seventh century BC some pre-colonial trading operations may have been conducted in the area by Greeks, perhaps from the cities of Rhodes, though this has been doubted, since the Greek finds of the period are not extensive. At the same time, however, there were larger imports of Etruscan pottery and wine (or oil), apparently carried on ships provided by the city-states of Etruria (Appendix 3).

The Greek colony at Massalia was founded by men from Phocaea in Ionia in c.600. An alternative tradition dates the foundation to c.545, but archaeological evidence supports the earlier chronology; perhaps the later date coincided with the arrival of a second draft of colonists, refugees from Phocaea when the mother-city was attacked by the Persians. According to a romantic story which Justin probably derived from Timaeus, the site of the colony was acquired from King Nannus, of the Ligurian tribe of the Segobrigii,[67] whose daughter Gyptis became the wife of Phocis, the leader of the Greek colonists[68] – and other inter-marriages followed.

The settlers set up their new homes within a small area, only a mile and a half in circumference, upon a rocky spur comprising three low hills near the sea. Traces of the earliest foundation have been found at the Église de la Mayor and the Fort S. Jean, where Rhodian, Ionian, Corinthian and Attic pottery has come to light in successive strata. The site was protected by a marsh and flanked by streams. Behind it was a small plain of which, as Strabo observes, the soil was less suitable for grain than for vines and olives,[69] which were introduced at an early date from Greek lands (or by the Etruscans, who had themselves learned their cultivation from the Greeks) and subsequently spread from Massalia to the rest of Gaul.

Strabo adds that the location was selected not for any agricultural advantages but because of the facilities it offered for maritime enterprises – the new colony was rightly ascribed to Phocaean commercial ambitions. For it overlooked a deeply recessed inlet which contained the spacious and well-protected harbour of Lacydon (Vieux Port), in easy reach of the Rhodanus (Rhône) estuary but beyond the range of its silting. The possession of this harbour enabled the city to exercise control over the sea-routes leading to the west.

Thus, in the course of the sixth century, Massalia founded a colony at Agathe Tyche ('Good Fortune', now Agde) in Languedoc, near the mouth of the River Aramis (Hérault), halfway to the Spanish border;[70]

and the earliest archaeological evidence for Emporiae (Ampurias), at the end of the Gulf of Rosas on the Costa Brava in Catalonia (north-eastern Spain), dates from *c*.600–575. During this period Phocaean Greeks occupied the island of Palaia Polis or Palaeopolis, 'Old City' (San Martin d'Ampurias, now attached to the mainland), where they established a trading post (*emporion*) and erected a temple of Ephesian Artemis, which had also become the principal divinity of Phocaea's Gallic colony Massalia. Later in the sixth century a new batch of Massalians arrived at Emporiae and settled upon a mainland promontory just across the strait, employing the mouth of the river later known as the Clodianus (now Muga) as a harbour. With ready access to the great Spanish coast-road, Emporiae soon attained independent city-status on its own account. On the other hand assumptions of early Phocaean–Massalian settlements or trading posts further down the Mediterranean coast of Spain seem to be anachronistic, being based on the erroneous belief that the *Ora Maritima* of Avienus was founded on a sailing manual of the sixth century BC. The Massalian colonies east of the mother-city, too, on the French Riviera adjoining the border with Italy, were likewise not founded until a later date.

Nevertheless, the early Massalians, even without such intermediaries, assiduously maintained their relations not only with Phocaea but with other Aegean and mainland Greek centres as well. The adoption of Artemis of Ephesus and Apollo of Delphi as their principal deities ensured contact with the sanctuaries of those cities, and Massalia maintained its own treasury at Delphi. Furthermore, it co-operated in the Phocaean foundation of a colony at Alalia in Corsica, while the evacuation of that settlement after the battle named after it (*c*.540/535) correspondingly weakened Massalian influence on the island.

This setback was brought about by an alliance between Etruscan Caere (Appendix 3) and Carthage (note 33).[71] Massalia had already, in previous years, employed its fleet against the Carthaginians, but it had also – despite an obvious element of competitiveness – maintained trading associations with the city-states of Etruria. This is confirmed by the discovery of an Etruscan wreck of *c*.570–560 off Antipolis (subsequently a Massalian settlement [cf. note 70]; now Antibes) and by the appearance of abundant Etruscan imitations of Corinthian wares at the fortified centre of Saint-Blaise (Bouches-du-Rhône). But as the sixth century drew on, the proportion of Greek (as against Etruscan) pots at Massalia increases – many of them from Chios and other eastern Greek regions, as well as from Athens, of which the imports to this area reached their peak in *c*.525. And a substantial amount of pottery, too, continued to be manufactured locally.

This did not, however, necessarily mean that the Massalians lost their interest in the Etruscans; and they may well have possessed a link with early Rome. Massalia's later relationship with the Romans became famous – it enabled them to store their votive offerings at Delphi in Massalia's Delphic Treasury – and there was a tradition that this went right back to the period of Rome's Etruscan monarchy in the sixth century BC. Such assertions, it is true, often antedate reality. Nevertheless, Massalia's keen interest in Italy makes this early connection seem plausible.

The Romans, for their part, subsequently expressed admiration for the stability of the Massalian constitution. This was at first based on a narrowly aristocratic system. Before long, however, an attempt was made to diminish the great families' influence by insisting that, if a man belonged to the Council, his son could not, and if an elder brother was a member, his younger brother was excluded. Such specific provisions may have lapsed, but the tendency they represented gained force, and gradually, as elsewhere, the aristocratic regime developed into an oligarchic system, based on wealth. This government, according to Strabo,[72] was directed by a Council of Six Hundred, of which the members had to be able to claim citizen descent for three generations, or, alternatively, had to possess children – though a passage in Aristotle suggests that the list was revised from time to time.[73] This Council of Six Hundred elected a steering committee of fifteen (*timouchoi*) from its ranks, under three presidents. A peculiar feature of the Massalian system was that a criminal condemned to death was maintained at the public expense for a year, after which he was executed as a *pharmakos*, or purification of the city.

When Midacritus the Phocaean passed through the Pillars of Hercules (Straits of Gibraltar) to collect tin, at about the date of Massalia's foundation, he became the pioneer of other Greek explorations, starting from Massalia itself. For, although the evidence is cryptic, it appears to have been in about the mid-sixth century that Euthymenes of Massalia likewise sailed through the straits and then moved southwards along the African coast, where he claimed to have seen a river of which the waters were being driven back by offshore wind. When he saw crocodiles in the river, he identified it with the Nile – which confirms the supposition of a sixth-century date, since that was a time when the Nile figured largely in Greek geographical speculations. But what Euthymenes evidently saw was not the Nile – which was on the the the other side of the continent – but the River Senegal. This exploratory voyage by a Greek was a rarity in comparison with the much more extensive opening up of the African coast by the

Phoenicians. Nevertheless it testified to the wide horizons of Massalia's enterprise.

The city also developed a unique commercial relationship with the Celtic peoples in the interior of Gaul. The Rhône itself was not easily navigable above its delta, but an extensive traffic passed by road up the river-valley from Massalia to the north. By this means Massalian salt and Greek luxury goods and especially cups and mixing bowls found their way to far-distant settlements and graves belonging to the later phases of the 'Hallstatt culture',[74] and became status symbols of a revolution in upper-class Gaulish drinking habits.

The most spectacular of these discoveries were made at Vix, the cemetery of Mont Lassois overlooking the Seine. Among them was a very large mid-sixth-century bronze mixing bowl (*crater*).[75] Such pieces were no doubt presents to gain the favour of local rulers. Moreover, plenty of other objects have been found at Vix, including wine cups and drinking vessels from Massalia, although Justin's reference to a Hellenization of Gaul[76] could not be applied to this period without exaggeration. Artefacts from Etruscan city-states, too, have come to light in the tombs of Vix.

There has been a good deal of speculation about what the Greeks received in return. Grain and amber have been suggested, and a traffic in slaves is likely. Tin from the Cassiterides in Cornwall (Chapter 5, note 51), also, may have moved across the Channel and then down the land- and river-routes of Gaul (by way of the Somme, Oise and Seine) through the initiative of the Massalians into whose hands the metal then passed.

Yet, according to the archaeological evidence, these contacts between the Celtic rulers and the Mediterranean seem to have terminated abruptly by c.500. It may be that Massalia fell into temporary economic decline at this epoch, its influence weakened by the Phocaean withdrawal from Corsica and, in general, by increasingly successful competition on the part of the Carthaginians, who since the Massalians had blocked their land-route to the British tin mines were developing an all-sea route of their own through the Straits of Gibraltar.

CHAPTER 8

THE NORTH

1 THE ADRIATIC: CORCYRA, ATRIA, SPINA

In ancient times the designations 'Adriatic' and 'Ionian Seas' were employed more or less interchangeably to denote the waters between Italy and the Balkan peninsula, which form a prolonged indentation with an average width of 110 miles. Later, the northern and southern sectors of this gulf came to be described as the Adriatic and Ionian Seas respectively, with their division at the Straits of Otranto, although the rugged Adriatic coast north of that point became known, by an extension, as the Ionian Gulf. The first Greek settlement of these shores was intended to provide halfway houses to markets and colonies at Pithecusae and Cumae in Campania, by Euboeans from Chalcis and Eretria, and Syracuse in Sicily.

The scene of the initial colonizing venture in this area was Corcyra (Kerkyra, Corfu). This is the northernmost island of the Ionian archipelago, in the sea of the same name off the north-west coast of Greece, separated by a narrow channel from the mainland (now Albania). Rainfall supplies a more flourishing vegetation than is to be found on the other islands of the group. Thucydides recorded the tradition that Corcyra was Homer's Scheria, the home of the Phaeacians,[1] although it had not, in fact, been the poet's design to identify Scheria with any real geographical location.

Corcyra was originally populated, it would seem, by people related to the Epirotes on the mainland opposite,[2] and Apulians from southeast Italy were among the other inhabitants. In the early years of the eighth century BC, however, the Euboean city of Eretria created a commercial post upon a peninsula jutting out from the island's eastern shore. This market, at first named Drepane (reaping-hook, because Demeter was said to have taught Titans to reap corn on the island), was served by two harbours, one upon the sea and the other in a deep-water lagoon. In addition, the settlers or visitors possessed a foothold upon the mainland opposite, so that they were able to dominate the Straits – and control the traffic to Italy and Sicily.

In c.733, however (though a later date of c.706 has also been proposed), Corinthian migrants, too, made their way to Corcyra, under the leadership of a certain Chersicrates, and expelled the Eretrians. The new arrivals established a colony at the port, under the name of Palaepolis (just north of the modern city), protected by an acropolis (Analepsis). The new colonists claimed that the designation Corcyra (Kerkyra) itself was of Corinthian derivation, explaining it as a corrupt version of 'Gorgo' (Gorgon), the monstrous Medusa who was struck down by Corinth's hero Bellerophon, but who symbolized the warding off of evil – although the name may, in fact, be of non-Greek origin, derived from the Illyrians who inhabited the hinterland of the northwest Balkan region.[3]

In keeping with the unusually determined desire of the Corinthians to keep their colonies in a dependent status, it has been suggested Corcyra, too, was originally in such a situation. That is not certain, but at first the two communities did remain closely related. Yet not much time elapsed, all the same, before the island colony became involved in fierce fighting against its mother-city, whose fleet it defeated heavily off the Sybota islands, in the first recorded naval engagement between Greek states. The battle has been attributed to c.664, but it may have been somewhat later.

While Cypselus was dictator of Corinth, the two cities collaborated in the foundation of Epidamnus (Dyrrhachium, Durrës) up the Illyrian coast. The Corcyraeans were the principal participants, although other colonists of the place, including its founder, came from Corinth (c.627; the original tribal leaders [phylarchoi] were later replaced by a council). Corcyra also probably collaborated in Cypselus' colonies at Ambracia (Arta) and Anactorium, and on the island of Leucas. The first coins of Apollonia in Illyria, too, suggest a joint foundation. They are datable to c.600; and it was during this period that, although the Corcyraeans received the assistance of Cnidus (which itself colonized the island of Black Corcyra [Korčula], so-called because of its dark pine forests), Cypselus' son and successor Periander (c.625–585) established (or re-established?) political control over Corcyra itself, exercising this domination through one of his sons.[4]

Later, however, the island reasserted its independence. When this happened is uncertain, but the architects and sculptors of its temple of Artemis, erected in c.580 (or a little later?), still seem to have been Corinthians. This has been claimed as the first stone temple of the Greeks (though the material was also employed for the entablature at Apollo's temple at Syracuse, another Corinthian colony, at about the same epoch). The Corcyraean shrine contained the earliest-known example of a limestone pediment, adorned by sculptures, which represent a huge Gorgon – the city's symbol – flanked by panthers. Moreover, since this pediment and the roof behind it needed heavier supports than wood could provide, the columns, too, were made of stone.

In the following century we learn from Herodotus that Corcyra could man sixty triremes, a form of warship which, according to Thucydides, this was (outside Sicily) the first Greek state to employ in substantial numbers, during the later sixth century BC.[5] Herodotus indicates this fact in relation to the Persian Wars, in which the Corcyraeans could not be persuaded to help the Greek cause at the battle of Salamis, because they were convinced that the Persians were going to win.

On the opposite shore of the Adriatic, with its unsatisfactory harbours and menacing populations, the Greek city-states did not attempt a similar programme of expansion. Indeed, in marked contrast to the southern and south-western shores of the Italian peninsula, this coast experienced no Greek colonization at all. Nevertheless, Greek penetration was by no means lacking, since the northern extremity of the Adriatic coast, by the end of the period discussed in this book, witnessed the development of two communities, Atria and Spina, in which Greeks and Etruscans lived and traded together, utilizing sea- and land-routes and the river passage of the Eridanus (Padus, Po) in order to develop extensive commercial contacts with their compatriots elsewhere, and with non-Greeks in central and northern Europe as well.

Atria (now Adria) was a market town (*emporion*) to the north of the Po delta, between that river and the Atesis (Adige). It was important enough to give its name to the Adriatic Sea, which lay only a few miles away. Foundation myths offer deviating stories, in which leading parts are variously assigned to the Etruscans or to the Greek hero Diomedes – during his journeyings after the Trojan War, and as part of his alleged foundations of many Italian cities. But a different people altogether, the Illyrian (?) Veneti (Eneti) who lived round the top of the Adriatic, should be identified as the earliest settlers of Atria.[6]

Thereafter, however, Greeks and Etruscans – while maintaining a connection with the Veneti (see also Spina below) – shared the site, constructing a town upon a complex arrangement of wooden piles. Which of these two elements of the population was predominant among its settlers or traders is not entirely clear. The Greek vases found on the site, however – notably Corinthian and East Greek wares – go back as early as the 560s BC, whereas the inscriptions and graffiti that principally bear witness to the Etruscan presence are relatively late, so that Atria can be identified, with some probability, as a port primarily utilized by the Greeks – to facilitate their contacts with Italy and remoter Europe – but also possessing an Etruscan quarter. We cannot identify the cities of Etruria from which these Etruscans came. But epigraphic evidence suggests that the Greek founders were from the island of Aegina (Chapter 2, section 6).

Linked to Atria by a canal, Spina lay a little to its south – four miles west of the modern town of Comacchio – where a branch of the Po delta debouched into a sea-lagoon providing a harbour. First of all, villages were constructed on piles, as at Atria; and then later, in the sixth century, these hamlets were amalgamated to form the township and port of Spina. It was built round a long, broad canal, detected by air photography, which also served to widen the channel linking the sea to the lagoon. Criss-crossed by a network of bridged canals or ditches (foreshadowing Venice, not far away), Spina covered an extent of more than 700 acres. The town comprised systematically planned blocks of approximately rectangular houses, built of stakes, clay and twigs, and this habitation area was flanked by richly furnished cemeteries lying along what was at this time the coastline.

The name of Spina has been thought to derive from the Indo-European, Italic dialect of the Umbrians, whose main centres lay in central Italy. But the place was subsequently occupied by both Greeks and Etruscans, as a blend of foundation myths, no less complex than those of Atria, testifies. Once again, a Greek version ascribes the beginnings of the settlement to the hero Diomedes (another account tells vaguely of 'Pelasgi', a people coming from Dodona in Epirus and invading Italy via the northern Adriatic on their way to Umbria).

Spina apparently came into existence a generation or two later than Atria, in c.525/520. At first sight the Greeks might again seem to have been the predominant partners, since a large quantity of Attic pottery has been found in 3,000 local graves, beginning in the later sixth century and culminating in the second quarter of the fifth. Moreover, inscriptions in the Ionic–Attic alphabet have come to light – referring to cults of Apollo, Dionysus and Hermes – and Spina, according to Pliny the elder, possessed its own treasury at Delphi[7] (in which it lodged the plunder derived from its maritime enterprises). However, another Italian centre, Caere, which possessed the same distinction, was not Greek but Etruscan (Appendix 3). Despite the Greek pots at Spina, epigraphic evidence – notably inscribed territorial boundary markers – and the nature of the urban plan, as well as the presence of bronzes imported from Etruria, suggest that this may have been primarily a town of the Etruscans, which possessed, however, a Greek trading quarter, thus displaying the reverse process to Atria, but resembling, in this respect, a number of cities of the Etruscan homeland (including Caere). While both these *emporia*, then, were co-operative Greco-Etruscan ventures, Atria seems to have served as the principal Greek port in the upper Adriatic, while at Spina the dominant role fell to Etruscans.

The Etruscan businessmen of Spina were no doubt primarily concerned with furnishing overseas supplies to the principal Etruscan city of northern Italy, Felsina (Bononia, Bologna), although it is likely that Spina was not politically dependent on Felsina or any other centre, but remained an autonomous entity, like Greek *emporia* in Campania, Syria and Egypt.

Probably imitating an example set by Atria, Spina also worked together with the Veneti in providing a transportation route for Venetian horses and Baltic amber, exchanged for exports (discovered in German finds), which it then passed on to Greek and Etruscan city-states. The Veneti again collaborated with the two *emporia* in another of their principal tasks, very welcome to other Greek centres around the Adriatic, which was to police the waters of that sea against native rivals, whom they designated as pirates – although the latter, for their part, no doubt likewise described the fleets of Spina and Atria as piratical.[8]

The Greeks and Etruscans achieved this local partnership in Atria and Spina at precisely the time when, in Campania, their compatriots' rivalry had broken out into open warfare, in which Cumae and Capua were the leading opponents. And indeed the Etruscan elements in Atria and Spina, too, may eventually have been drawn into these conflicts, since Dionysius of Halicarnassus,[9] alluding to the years 525–524 BC, tells of a 'long march' against Cumae undertaken by a mixed force led by 'the Tyrrhenians (Etruscans) who had inhabited the country near the Ionian Gulf' – the name for the northern sector of the Adriatic Sea.

These men could have come, as adventurers or mercenaries, from Atria and Spina, in which case the binational co-operation in the two places may already, at that time, have collapsed, at least temporarily. On the other hand, Dionysius' chronology is cast into doubt by his further assertion that these people had been chased out of their homes by the Gauls – whose gradual infiltrations in Italy, however, do not appear (despite Livy's statement to the contrary)[10] to have started much before 400. During the fourth century Atria and Spina, like the rest of northern Italy, fell under Gaulish control.

2 THE NORTHERN AEGEAN AND BLACK SEA APPROACHES

North of Greece proper, in the limited sense of the continental homeland, lay the kingdom of Macedonia. Its nucleus was the fertile Macedonian plain, formed by the Haliacmon, Lydias and Axius – large, permanently flowing rivers of continental type – at the head of the Thermaic Gulf (Gulf of Salonica). All around was a double horse-shoe of mountains, inhabited by wild tribes and clans of mixed Illyrian, Thracian and Greek affinities, under their own chieftains and princes. Macedonia's barrier to the south was Olympus, the only mountain in Greece exceeding 10,000 feet in height.

The Bronze Age culture of the country, according to Herodotus, had been succeeded and superseded by an influx of Phrygians (*c.*1150; Appendix 1).[11] Later, however, these people left for the territory in Asia Minor that took their name, under pressure from a second wave of

9 The Northern Aegean

invaders, who may be identified with the Dorians. It was the descendants of these Dorians, mixed with various other peoples but speaking a language close to Greek (perhaps a primitive Aeolic dialect), who formed the upper class among the Macedonians of subsequent epochs. They do not appear in the Homeric epics, but Hesiod records a Greek myth tracing their origins back to Macedon, the son of Zeus and of Thyia, daughter of Deucalion, the survivor of the Flood.[12]

Although there were conflicting traditions of their subsequent descent, the monarchs of Macedonia claimed to derive their origins from Heracles and the name of their dynasty from Argos, so that they called themselves Argeads and boasted pure Greek descent. Confronted by the dubious reactions of Greeks elsewhere, they were more assertively and self-consciously Greek than their subjects troubled to be. The court religion, for example, was manifestly Hellenic, including the cults of Zeus Hetairides (who presided over the king's relationship with his aristocratic companions) and Heracles Kynagidas (patron of hunting, an activity to which the ruling class was devoted).

The earliest Macedonian state was a small and struggling principality in the hilly country above the upper and middle Haliacmon valley, with its capital, we are told, at Lebaea, though this place has not been located. In c.640, however, King Perdiccas I, the first historically identifiable Argead monarch, pushed eastwards, occupied Eordaea to the west of the Thermaic Gulf, and overran the Macedonian (Emathian) plain and part of its coastland, moving his capital to Aegae (Palatitsa, Vergina), though this did not become a city (*polis*) in the Greek sense, since Macedonia, like certain other political units, remained an *ethnos*, without an urban centre (cf. Chapter 1, note 11). Subsequent kings, embodying the state in their own person, enforcing their wills by a well-disciplined infantry force, and deriving profits from stock-raising, expanded these dominions still further. In c.512, however, Amyntas I, as a result of Darius I's Balkan expedition and annexation of Thrace, felt obliged to become a Persian vassal.

However, even before the seventh-century monarch Perdiccas I penetrated to the coastland, this region had become a target for colonization by the Greek city-states. Here the object was simply the acquisition of land, in what happened to be the nearest non-Greek (though partly Hellenized) area available to their mariners. Moreover, the early Greek colonists derived revenue from exporting Macedonian animal products and timber, during an epoch when the kingdom was not well organized enough to undertake or monopolize these processes itself. Here, as elsewhere, the lead was taken by the cities of Euboea, and it was said that already before 700 Eretrians, who had been expelled from Corcyra by its new Corinthian settlers, came to found Methone, on the western shore of the Thermaic Gulf.

But Eretria's fellow Euboeans from Chalcis were even more active, as the name of the Chalcidice bears witness. This is a peninsula to the east of the Thermaic Gulf, which extends southwards into the three promontories of Pallene (Cassandra), Sithonia (Longos) and Acte (Athos). The Chalcidice offered attractions to seafarers, because of its long indented coastline and proximity to the gold and silver mines of Mount Pangaeum, and it received a considerable number of colonies from Chalcis, of which the most important was Torone, towards the southern extremity of the central (Sithonia) promontory. Situated on the slope of a rocky cape, Torone possessed a useful harbour (Porto Koufo). Cremation and (less numerous) inhumation burials indicate habitation since the early first millennium BC. Chalcidian settlement followed soon after 700, and was later backed up by the efforts of a law-giver, Androdamas of Rhegium, whose legislation regarding murder and *epikleroi* (women without brothers) was esteemed.[13] In c.655 Andros, an island under Euboean influence, was helped by Chalcis and its offshoots to colonize Acanthus, situated on the isthmus leading to Acte, the eastern promontory of Chalcidice; and there were three other Andrian colonies nearby.

A rare intrusion into this region dominated by Euboeans and their dependent islanders was Potidaea, founded by Corinth in c.600 upon the isthmus of the third and westernmost prong of Chalcidice, namely Pallene. The colony at this strategic location was established by the Corinthian dictator Periander, under the leadership of one of his sons, in order to dominate the Macedonian terminal of the trans-Balkan route to Illyria and the Adriatic. And since the settlement looked both ways it was able to obtain metals from Pangaeum and to engage in trade with the north-east as well. When Potidaea started issuing coins, in about 500, they depicted Poseidon, after whom the city took its name. He is shown carrying a trident – and riding on a Thracian horse. Through their intercourse with these Chalcidic colonies and Methone, the Macedonians gradually adopted a more Hellenized way of life.

East of Chalcidice, Thasos, five miles offshore from the mouth of the River Nestus, was to become the foremost Greek colony of the northern Aegean. Sixteen miles in diameter, it was a mountainous island, but contained fertile valleys and possessed a supply of water. Before the arrival of the Greeks it had been occupied, under the name of Odonis, by a Thracian tribe known as the Sintes, whose habitations (together with those of earlier Neolithic peoples) have been traced at a site upon Mount Kastri (the medieval capital, near Theologos, in the south of the island), as well as beneath the city founded by the Greeks, which lay on the northern coast. Its colonists were men from the island of Paros, under the leadership of the aristocratic Telesicles (*c*.650 BC?), whose initiative received the approval of a surviving Delphic oracle. The Parian poet Archilochus was one of the original, or early, settlers on Thasos.

They quickly gained control over the entire island, and within twenty or thirty years, as finds of pottery reveal, they or their sons had also, on their own account, planted townships on the mainland opposite (the Thracian Peraea), at Neapolis (Kavalla), Oesyme and Galepsus. The profitable purpose of these enterprises, apparently undertaken in friendly collaboration with the local tribes, was, once again, to dominate the adjacent gold and silver mines of Mount Pangaeum, which the Thracian tribe of the Satres had previously allowed Phoenicians to exploit. The tradition that gold mines also existed on Thasos itself has been doubted, but its possession of silver and iron and copper mines is attested. In a more easterly sector of the mainland coast, opposite another island, Samothrace – settled by the Samians and famous for its cult of the twin Cabiri, of Phrygian origin (gods of the underworld subsequently believed to protect sailors) – the Thasians disputed the control of their own colony Stryme with Maronea (founded by Chios before 650).[14]

Thasos was a bulwark of Hellenism against the mainland Thracians, whose town on the island itself, upon Mount Kastri, was abandoned or destroyed, although a grave in the *agora* of the Greek city of Thasos set up by 'the sons of Bendis' bears witness to the survival of a Thracian element in its population. The sixth century witnessed the beginning of the island's greatest prosperity, when it exported timber for ship construction and began to export also a famous wine. The mines on the mainland to which it enjoyed access had by now become extremely profitable, and from *c*.500 the silver available on Thasos itself enabled its government to issue a local coinage. This depicted a sexually aroused satyr, a follower of the wine-god Dionysus, carrying off a nymph.

The principal temple of Thasos, which eventually became a five-roomed building, was dedicated to the cult of Heracles, who may have been a successor of the Phoenician Melkart. This shrine stood in the lower town, where there were also sanctuaries of various other foreign deities (reflecting the inhabitants' various races), as well as of Dionysus, Poseidon and Artemis, near whose altar votive objects of *c*.500 came to light. Residential quarters have also been unearthed.

The Thasians possessed a useful fleet, but in 491 were forced to place it at the disposal of the Persian invaders of Europe (on their way to the battle of Marathon). Nevertheless, the fortifications of their city, enclosing one of its harbours, were destroyed, a misfortune that was to befall them on two further occasions before the century was over.

On the mainland of Thrace (Appendix 2) stood the Greek city of Abdera, nearly opposite Thasos and eleven miles north-east of the River Nestus.[15] Despite a mythical tradition that its establishment went back to Heracles, the first attempt to found a Greek colony was made in c.654 by Timesias (or Tynisias) of Clazomenae in Ionia, but it failed owing to Thracian opposition. In 545 emigrants from another Ionian city, Teos, finding Persian domination unendurable, settled on the site; among them was the poet Anacreon. Although careful to protect their territory from incursions by Thracians from the interior, these Abderans nevertheless traded extensively with this native population. Indeed, at each of these Greek centres, relations with the huge concatenation of Thracian tribes was a dominant factor. As a result of such contacts, important elements in Thracian religion, especially relating to the worships of Dionysus and Orpheus, gradually passed into Greek cult.

Greek cities a little farther to the east played a similar part in this process of transmission. One of them was Aenus, jointly settled by Lesbos and by Cyme in Aeolis;[16] and another was Cardia, similarly colonized by Miletus and Clazomenae. Cardia lay on the Bulair isthmus linking the mainland to the Thracian Chersonese (Gallipoli peninsula), which extended southwards to the Hellespont (Dardanelles): the first of three maritime passages (the others being the Propontis [Sea of Marmara] and the Thracian Bosphorus) leading to the commercially vital Black Sea.

The Hellespont was named after the mythical Helle, the daughter of Athamas and Nephele, who was believed to have fallen into the strait after escaping upon a flying ram in the company of her brother Phrixus (whom their stepmother Ino had been about to sacrifice to the gods). Its tortuous and forbidding channel, forty miles long and averaging only about a mile in width, contains numerous rocks and seethes with currents, which surge in from the Black Sea at a speed of four or five miles an hour, and are endowed with increasing malevolence, during nine months of the year, by an unremitting north-easterly wind.

In consequence, Greek vessels, after struggling up the Aegean – and there too they had had to face these gales – found it hard even to enter the narrows at all, not to speak of the difficulty of fighting their way through once inside. Accordingly, they were often glad to disembark their cargoes on the Asian coast just before the strait began, to be carried overland to a re-embarkation point farther on.

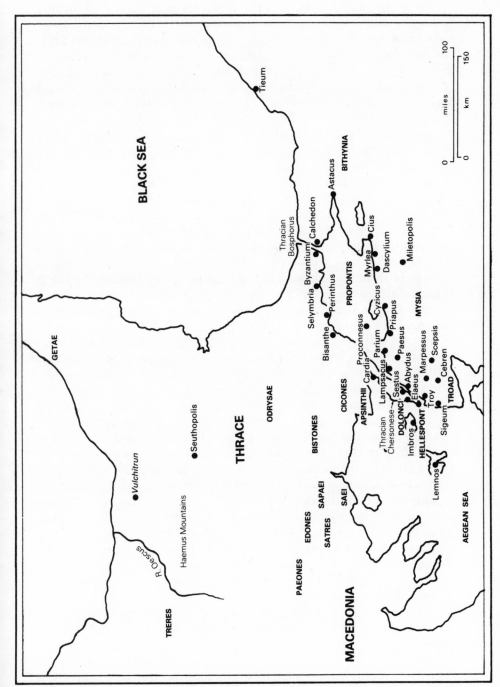

10 The Black Sea Approaches and Thrace

The southern, Asian bank of the Hellespont, which offered friendly inshore shallow water, presented greater attraction than the more forbidding northern European shore – which was partly why Troy, commanding this Asian shore, had become so significant during the Bronze Age. In the historical period, too, Greek colonies were founded on this southern coast at Abydus (c.680–652), Lampsacus (c.654) and Sigeum (c.600/590), by Miletus, Phocaea and Athens respectively.[17] Nevertheless, beside the more difficult northern shore as well, the Ionian city of Teos managed to establish a colony at Elaeus (c.600) upon the southern extremity of the Thracian Chersonese, and Sestus was colonized by the Lesbians.

Athens, too, extended its interest from the south to the north of the strait, and in c.555, with the sanction of a Delphic oracle, the entire Chersonese was occupied by Miltiades the elder, an Athenian nobleman of the Philaid family, who ruled it as an independent state – but with the support of Pisistratus (preparing for a second *coup d'état* at Athens – Chapter 1, section 4). Miltiades also gained the backing of nearby Thracians (Dolonci), whom he obliged by defeating their hostile compatriots the Apsinthii.[18] Next he proceeded to fortify the Bulair isthmus linking the Chersonese with the mainland, and took over the Athenian settlement at Sigeum (c.546).

In c.516 his nephew Miltiades the younger, who had served as archon at Athens, was sent by Pisistratus' son and successor Hippias to safeguard Athenian influence in the peninsula.[19] The younger Miltiades, while issuing coins of his own, found it diplomatic, or necessary, to become a vassal of Darius I of Persia and accompany him on his Scythian expedition of c.513–512 (Appendix 1). But his later claim to have suggested the destruction of Darius' Hellespont bridge in order to cut off the Persians' return (a plan frustrated by the dictators of other Greek cities in the area) is disproved by the fact that the monarch left him in power, as he would not have done after such a disloyal proposal.

This second Miltiades ruled over the native Thracians of the Chersonese; and he married Hegesipyle, daughter of the Thracian (Sapaean) king Olorus,[20] so that after a brief exile necessitated by a Scythian invasion it was the Thracians who brought him back (496). Subsequently he did venture to turn against King Darius and, liberating the island of Lemnos from his rule, took part in the Ionian revolt. After the collapse of the rebellion (494), he returned to Athens, where he survived a trial for exercising 'tyranny' in the Chersonese – and became the principal architect of the historic victory at Marathon (490).

The Hellespont led through to a more open stretch of water, the

Propontis, 'Before the Pontus', a name it owed to its location as the ante-chamber to a larger sea, the Pontus Euxinus (Black Sea). The Propontis, now the Sea of Marmara, is 175 miles long and 40 miles wide at its greatest breadth. Its strategic position provoked avid competition between the maritime, colonizing Greek states, as emerges from a list of the principal settlements they planted on its opposite shores.[21]

As on the Hellespont, the south coast was the more welcoming of the two, and it was here that the most important of its centres was located. This was the Milesian colony of Cyzicus (Balkız, Belkis). Its site occupied part of the hilly, broad-headed, offshore Arctonnesus (Bears' Island, off the mouth of the River Aesepus), which was transformed into a peninsula, containing part of the Greek city, by the construction of two parallel dykes shored up by accumulated sand. In Greek mythology its king had given hospitality to the Argonauts, who nevertheless killed him. When we come to historical events, however, the earlier of two foundation dates given by Eusebius (c.756) is not verifiable (though the temporary existence of a colony at that time, swept away, perhaps, by the Cimmerian invaders of Phrygia [c.695], cannot be excluded). But even the second date he proposes, 679, to which there can be no such objection, gives Cyzicus an early place among the settlements of the Milesians.

The place was served by two major lines of land communication. But its site was, rather, selected for other reasons – defensibility, and access to two good flanking harbours, subsequently linked to one another by a canal. These harbours enabled Cyzicus to become a port of call for ships passing between the two seas. In consequence, there were stories linking the place with the distant Scythians, who lived beyond the Black Sea (Appendix 2). One of them, Anacharsis, was said to have taught his own people Cyzicene rituals (though they put him to death for doing so); and another half-legendary figure Aristeas, a Greek from Proconnesus (an island of Cyzicus), who was believed to have made a supernatural appearance in that city after his death, had written about Scythia and its customs.

The government of the Cyzicenes, well known for its efficiency, derived lucrative profits from catching the tunny (whose presence provided a reason for the foundation of many Greek colonies), and the fish appeared as a city badge on its electrum (pale gold) coinage. This may have been inaugurated before 600, and in the course of the next century became the most important currency of the eastern Greek world.

Cyzicus did not, however, manage to maintain its political independence throughout this period, falling under the control first of the Lydians and then of the Persians, whose monarch Darius I the Cyzicene dictator Aristagoras, according to Herodotus, refused to betray during the Persian invasion of Europe (c.513–512).[22] In the subsequent Ionian revolt (499–494), an initial impulse to join the rebels was quenched by the approach of the Persians' Phoenician fleet, which impelled Cyzicus to come to terms with Oebares, the Persian satrap resident at Dascylium.

The strait which terminates the Propontis to the west, the Hellespont, is paralleled by a second funnel, the Thracian Bosphorus, to the east. The currents surging through the Bosphorus, like those of the Helles-pont, are hazardous, zig-zagging seven times from shore to shore under the lash of the winds. However, they had to be faced, because the narrows stood at the shortest crossing point between Europe and Asia, and because they led to the Black Sea. An additional attraction was an abundance of migratory fish, seasonally passing to and from that sea. Thus dolphins, which figure in numerous myths as the friends of humankind, are among the coin-types of the two most important cities on the strait, Calchedon (Kadıköy) on the Asian bank, near the southern extremity of the narrows, and Byzantium (Constantinople, Istanbul) nearly opposite on the European shore. Standing upon the dolphin on the issues of Calchedon is an ear of corn, but at Byzantium this corn-ear is replaced by a cow, referring to the wanderings of Io, the mythical daughter of Inachus and priestess of Hera at Argos, who was transformed by Zeus, so that she could escape Hera's jealousy, into the form of that animal. It was Io's crossing of the strait that gave the Bosphorus its name, 'cow's ford'.

Calchedon, of which the site has yielded prehistoric remains, may originally have been a Thracian settlement, but was later colonized by Megara, traditionally in 685 BC. Darius I's general Megabyzus, Her-odotus remarks, described its founders as blind, because they missed the superb site of Byzantium on the opposite coast, which was only settled some seventeen years later.[23] But the first voyagers from Megara, in all probability, did not feel strong enough to plant a settle-ment among the Thracians on the European side of the strait (who were more numerous and menacing than the tribesmen on its southern bank). Moreover, Calchedon, although its port was vulnerable to currents, possessed good grain-land – as the ear of corn on its local coins indicates – and derived revenue from the copper mines and semi-precious stones of the adjoining island of Chalcitis (Heybeliada), whose name, derived from *chalkos*, copper, led to the alternative spell-ing of Calchedon as Chalcedon (the true derivation of the city's original name is unknown).

Its lawyer Phaleas (fifth century BC?) laid down, or confirmed, rules providing for a citizen body of limited dimensions, and insisted on equality of property among them, with a view to the avoidance of internal strife. However, Calchedon's subsequent association with the Ionian revolt earned it destruction at the hands of the Persians (494). Thereupon the survivors took refuge at Mesembria (Nessebur) up the Black Sea coast, which had been jointly colonized a decade or so earlier by Megara, Calchedon and Byzantium.

The foundation date of Byzantium was variously ascribed to 668, 659 and 657 BC. Its settlers once again came from Megara, although emigrants from other places in central Greece and the Peloponnese may also have taken part. They subjugated a local Thracian population and reduced it to serf (Helot-like) status under the designation of Prounikoi (bearers of burdens).

Compared by a medieval chronicler to a three-cornered sail bellying in the wind, the Megarian settlement at Byzantium occupied a headland at the western extremity of the Bosphorus, overlooking the Propontis to the south, and the elongated natural harbour of the Chrysokeras (Golden Horn) to the north. This Golden Horn was a riverless and therefore silt-free breakwater, sheltered by hills from northern gales. It had already served as a ferry-station in previous centuries, and was a providential halting-point for vessels which were preparing to tackle, or had just finished tackling, the perilous waters of the Bosphorus. Moreover, the winds that caused those difficulties also filled the Horn with the abundance of fish to which its adjective 'Golden' may be owed.

Ariston, the dictator of Byzantium, joined Aristagoras of Cyzicus in refusing to act against Darius I of Persia when the latter was returning from his invasion of Europe (c.513–512). During the Ionian revolt, however, many Byzantines fled before the Persians' Phoenician fleet to their colony at Mesembria, in company with the Calchedonians with whom they had shared its foundation.

Yet the future of Byzantium remained secure. It was easily defensible, its walls coming to be regarded as the strongest in any Greek land. Moreover, 'it commands the mouth of the Black Sea so securely', as Polybius later remarked, 'that no trader can sail in or out without its consent. And since the Black Sea contains many of the commodities required by other peoples for their way of life, the Byzantines enjoy complete control over all these supplies.'[24] Polybius was writing in the second century BC. Thenceforward, during the millennium and more that lay ahead of that time, the many other advantages of Byzantium came to the surface as well; and as the bridge between Europe and Asia, the city became, under the name of Constantinople, the capital of the western world.

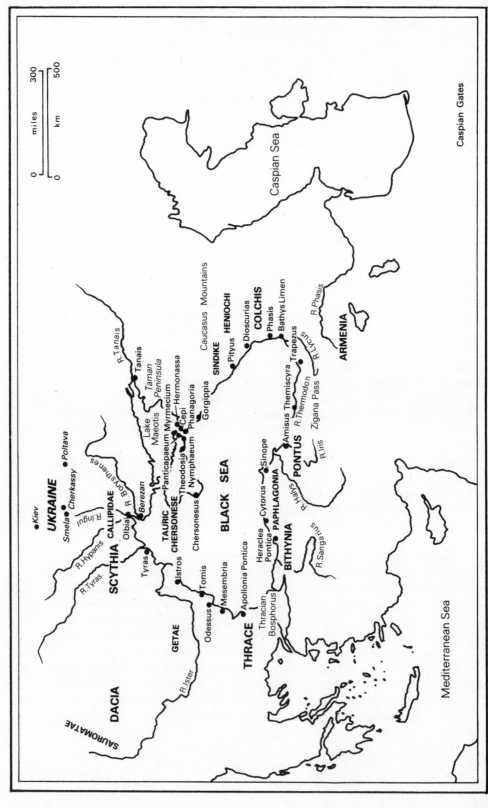

The Black Sea

3 THE BLACK SEA: SINOPE, ISTRUS, OLBIA

The Greeks called the Black Sea the 'Euxine', a term meaning 'friendly to travellers', although this was supposedly a euphemistic variation of an early name Axeinos – which meant the reverse – unless, as seems possible, the new designation was a corruption of a non-Greek word signifying 'dark' or 'north'. In mythology, the sea was famous for the story of the Argonauts, told in the Hellenistic epic poem of Apollonius Rhodius but reflecting maritime explorations (in search of copper?) that dated as far back as the second millennium BC.

By 800, Ionians and other eastern Greeks knew something of the tribes and customs of the coastlands of the sea, and the Homeric poems display an imprecise acquaintance with its southern sea-board. But it was not until the seventh century that first-hand information became available. In that period the Milesians converted the Black Sea into what was virtually a private lake of their own (Chapter 5, section 2).

The waters into which they first ventured, on entering the sea, seem to have been beside its southern shore – which they found accessible because the current sets eastward along that coast. The maritime strips of northern Asia Minor that they thus proceeded to colonize were backed by the hinterland of Pontus, inhabited by a multi-lingual non-Greek population grouped around large, autonomous temple communities under the rule of priests served by sacred slaves. Well watered and fertile, Pontus enjoyed a mild climate along the lower valleys of the Rivers Halys (Kızıl Irmak) and Iris (Yeşil Irmak), and in the coastal plains. These produced abundant grain, a variety of fruits and nuts, and fertile pastureland. The nearest of the parallel mountain ranges in the interior also provided extensive timber for shipbuilding; and their slopes were rich in iron, mined by the Chalybes, said to have been the world's first workers in the metal.[25]

At the central point of this coast, the Milesians came to Sinope (Sinop). The site, occupying a peninsula or promontory, had been inhabited by a native Pontic people, the Paphlagonians, together, perhaps, with some Phrygians (Appendix 1). Ancient writers, however, are divided on an important point: did the Milesians arrive at Sinope, did they, that is to say, begin the colonization of the Black Sea coastlands, in c.756 or c.631? The evidence is complex – Eusebius offers both dates to choose from – but the probability is that certain Greeks, all or some of them perhaps from Miletus, established a trading post (like those in Campania and Syria) at the earlier of those two dates. They arrived under the leadership, it was said, of a certain Habrondas. But that *emporion*, if it ever existed, was later destroyed by the

Cimmerians (Appendix 1), whereupon a group of men from Miletus, led by the exiles Coes and Cretines, established a colony in *c.*631.

Sinope was well supplied with water, and could grow its own olives – unlike any other Pontic city, except Amisus. It also had access to agricultural resources and timber, and to the silver and iron mines of the interior. These close relations with inland Asia Minor are confirmed by local finds of Phrygian vases. Moreover, the place became famous for *miltos* – 'Sinopic earth', brown–red ochre or red-oxide of iron, employed for painting ships – which was brought from Cappadocia for shipment, though how early this traffic was inaugurated is not clear.

But, in any case, none of these land-communications were easy, and Sinope's strength lay in its two deep-water harbours. From these ports, much the best for many miles around, the Sinopitans engaged in profitable tunny fishing. Moreover, their colony stood at the point where the distance from the opposite, northern side of the Black Sea is narrowest, so that they could dominate sailings across its waters.

For its exports in this and other directions Sinope produced numerous amphoras, which have recently (like local inscriptions) been studied in detail. The pots found in local graves come mostly from eastern Greek cities, but there is some Corinthian pottery too, of early-sixth-century date. In the literary field, also, connections with Greek culture were cherished, since Homeric studies flourished in at least some periods of Sinopitan history.[26]

Trapezus (Trebizond, Trabzon), at a more easterly point of the same coast, stood on a coastal ridge at the foot of the Paryadres mountains. Its establishment – like that of its founder Sinope, according to one of Eusebius' versions – dated back to *c.*756, so that this place, too, may again have been an eighth-century *emporion*, which later became a city on its own account, although in the early fourth century BC its citizens were still paying tribute to their mother-city Sinope.[27] Trapezus, situated upon a plateau (*trapeza*, table), was equidistant between Sinope and the far end of the north coast, in an area inhabited by the non-Greek tribe of the Mossynoeci, who adorned themselves with floral tattoos, ate boiled chestnuts and offered monstrously fat boys for sale.

Otherwise excluded, perhaps, from the new colony, the Mossynoeci remained unfriendly neighbours, and the poor harbour of Trapezus proved another obstacle to development. Nevertheless, the city enjoyed a defensible location, flanked on either side by cliffs overlooking gullies. It was also favourably located for trading with the iron-producing Chalybes – and served as the northern terminal of a major land-route leading over the Zigana Pass to Armenia and Mesopotamia.

The Milesians and Phocaeans jointly founded Amisus (Kara Samsun) in c.564, in a rare, olive-growing region like that of Sinope. Situated to the east of that city and to the west of Trapezus, between the deltas of the Iris and the Lycus, this colony, like Trapezus, stood at the head of a trade-route into the interior (as finds of Phrygian vases at Ak Alan ten miles inland testify), and it shared the ability of the Trapezuntines to obtain iron from the Chalybes and export it to the Greek world. Moreover, like Trapezus once more, Amisus enjoyed a defensible location, upon a peninsula which, being bounded on two sides by the sea and almost cut off from the mainland by a ravine, was practically an island.

Then in c.560–558, on the same coast, far to the west of these three cities, the Megarians, under the leadership of Gnesilochus, established another new colony, with the help of a Boeotian contingent and perhaps with Milesian connivance. This was Heraclea Pontica (Ereğli), named after Heracles, who was believed to have descended to the underworld through a cavern on the adjoining Acherusian promontory (Baba Burnu). The site, shaped like a theatre, has been thought capable of accommodating a maximum population of 10,000. The colonists reduced the previous non-Greek inhabitants, members of the tribe of the Mariandyni, to serfdom, but agreed, in return, that none of them should be sold into slavery outside their homeland.

Aristotle tells us, unusually, of early constitutional developments in the colony.[28] Its initial rulers, the 'notables' (gnorimoi), found themselves almost immediately driven into banishment, and a democratically inclined system was set up in its stead. But the exiles returned, overthrew this administration, and re-established oligarchic government, based on an assembly of 600.

Prospering from rich agricultural territory and profitable sea-fishing, Heraclea soon controlled the coast as far east as Cytorus (Kidros), a township that had been mentioned in the Iliad.[29]

At an early date, traditionally in 657 BC, the Milesians sailed far up the west coast of the Black Sea as well, and founded a colony at Istrus (Histria) in what is now the Rumanian Dobrogea (Dobruja), just south of the delta of the Danube (Istros, Ister, which gave the place its name), and less than fifty miles from the river's great curve before it approaches the sea.

The new foundation stood on a low hill at the extremity of an island or peninsula – within a gulf that later became the Sinoe sea-lagoon, and is now a landlocked lake. The colonists succeeded to a settlement of the Getae (Appendix 2), and were governed, as Aristotle records, by a narrow group which was then, however, dislodged by a group of wealthy men hitherto excluded from office.[30]

At first Istrus was only a little settlement of one-room stone houses, situated on foundations intended to stabilize the marshy land near the ancient anchorage, so that a livelihood could be gained from the fisheries of the Danube delta. But the colony soon began to assume a more ambitious appearance. For excavations beside the lagoon, extending downwards to a depth of thirteen feet beneath the present land-surface, have uncovered a varied collection of religious buildings, including an early temple of Aphrodite. Moreover, Istrus began to trade with eastern Greek centres. (A potter named Istrocles, working at Smyrna in c.650, provides evidence of such activity.) These commercial operations were assisted by Miletus' foundation of further colonies on the sea-route from the Thracian Bosphorus. One of these was Apollonia Pontica, traditionally in c.610, a staging point encircled by hostile Thracian forts (and liable to internal strife due to a corrupt oligarchy).[31] Odessus was founded at about the same date – and subsequently, a little before 500, Tomis (Constanța), Ovid's place of exile more than half a millennium later, much to his disgust. The Istrians also established a number of small markets (*emporia*), notably Istrian Harbour, much farther up the coast of the Black Sea, not far from Olbia (see below).

At the same time, however, Istrus maintained an active relationship with its non-Greek neighbours. For the existence of a suburb of mud-brick houses, interpreted as native dwellings, suggests cohabitation with the previous Getic inhabitants, and an understanding with these and other tribes in the grain-growing hinterland – a conclusion confirmed by excavations at the native settlement of Tariverde, eleven miles to the south-west, a prosperous market by the early sixth century. This Greek relationship with the surrounding population took the form of exporting wine and oil (in locally manufactured pots), as well as furniture and weapons, into the continental interior of Europe, while in return slaves and farm produce and hides were acquired and sent to the coast. Moreover, proximity to the Danube, where an advanced depot or *emporion* was established at the river's bend (near Braila), facilitated access to gold and silver in the mountains beyond the opposite bank.

These enterprises, however, did not prove lasting, since shortly before 500 the city of Istrus was sacked by Scythian invaders or raiders (Appendix 2). Nevertheless, it recovered, and indeed greatly expanded its trading links in the following century, although three further catastrophic destructions were to ensue before the end of antiquity.

Only ten years after their establishment of Istrus, so it was said – and archaeological evidence now seems to discount a later dating – a group of enterprising Milesians, joined by people from other Greek cities, had moved a much greater distance to the north, in order to establish the colony of Olbia (Olvia, near Parutino) at the farthest extremity of the Black Sea.

Founded under the patronage of Apollo, whose Delphic oracle signified approval of the venture, the location selected for the settlement was on the right (west) bank of the River Hypanis (Bug), near the entrance of its large estuary gulf (*liman*), twenty-three miles west of the Borysthenes – later Danapris, now Dnieper – which at first gave its name to the new colony (until it came to be called Olbia, after *olbos*, happiness). The chosen site, although not previously occupied by any sedentary population, was well placed to dominate the traffic of these inland rivers, two of the massive up-country waterways which form such a characteristic feature of southern Russia.

This new foundation comprised a lower town bordering the Hypanis *liman*, overlooked by an upper town on a plateau 120 feet above the sea. The lower town is now partially under water, owing to a rise in the sea-level, but four zones in this sector have lately been excavated, indicating that the population increased before long from an original total of 6,000 to approximately 10,000. The public buildings of the upper town appear to date from the years 550–500. Sacred precincts of Zeus and Apollo Delphinios stood beside the *agora*, to the north of which large merchants' houses with storage areas were erected, on a scale still rare in mainland Greece, contrasting with some forty huts of lower economic status which have also come to light. Another early residential district has been identified at the western extremity of the city, overlooking the Hare's Ravine (Zayach'ya Balka), and traces of workshops are also to be seen. Tombs round the city assume a variety of forms.

The colony emphasized its Greekness by the stimulation of Homeric studies. A similar phenomenon has been noted at Sinope, but the home of such studies was, of course, Ionia, and Olbia was especially designed to be a faithful reflex or adaptation of the Ionian mother-city Miletus, to whose citizens it granted equal rights, or, perhaps, freedom from taxation.[32] It also imitated the Milesian list and sequence of the months of the year, and provided accommodation, temporary or permanent, to Milesian goldsmiths.

However, the magnificent gold-work they produced was largely intended for the Scythian peoples of the hinterland, too, with whom Olbia maintained a close relationship. This is reflected by the many anecdotes told by Herodotus (who visited the place, and knew the course of the Hypanis, too, for many days' journey upstream).[33] There seems to have been a good deal of intermarriage, and at least one nomadic Scythian people, the Callipidae, became sedentary under Olbian influence.

These contacts have prompted the reasonable supposition that, from its earliest years, Olbia – which, although walled, was not easily defensible – owed its existence to the protection of its Scythian neighbours, although the theory that they formed an important part of the Olbian ruling class, supposedly supported by Herodotus' account of the pro-Greek Scythian Scyles (Appendix 2, note 50), remains unproved. Archaeological evidence, too, tells a similar story of close connections. For example the Gute Maritzyn warriors' grave of c.490 shows a complete cultural fusion: the abundant Greek artefacts were buried in a tomb of Scythian design. Moreover, the grave was found to contain 377 bronze arrow-heads, all of a socketed type introduced to the Greeks by the Scythians.

Literary sources, although describing Black Sea trade at later periods, have nothing to say about commercial exchanges in the period before 500. But archaeological evidence hints at the character of these dealings. As to land communications, Olbia's main trade-route to the forest steppe evidently ran due northwards through the valley of the River Ingul (which debouched into the same *liman* as the Hypanis) to Smela and Cherkassy. However, the city traded up the Hypanis as well, for a distance of at least 200 miles, for East Greek vases of the late seventh century have been found as far as Nemirov.

With regard to sea-routes, stones of Aegean origin discovered at Jagorlik and Berezan (see below) evidently came as ships' ballast, indicating a lighter outward cargo (wine, oil) which needed this additional weight, but was followed by a heavier return cargo (grain) that enabled the ballast to be left behind. In the sixth century Miletus facilitated such inter-Greek contacts by establishing a further colony, Tyras (Belgorod Dniestrovsky), on the *liman* of the River Tyras (Dniester), between Olbia and Istrus, which itself, as was mentioned above, founded an *emporion* of its own at Istrian Harbour, near Olbia.

The Olbians became the rulers or suzerains of a considerable number of Greek Black Sea settlements or trading posts, and were in direct control of a substantial territory, thirty miles deep and forty miles across. This piece of land contained numerous inhabitants, who resided, as recent investigations have shown, in no less than seventy communities, linked by an elaborate intercommunications system. The neglect of this vast complex of Hellenism in most Greek history books (explainable on the grounds that Russian excavation results are not easily read) creates a serious unbalance.

There proved to be good material reasons for naming the city 'happiness'. Herodotus praises the lower reaches of the River Borysthenes for its fine pastures and varied, abundant products.[34] Fish swarmed multitudinously in the Scythian river-mouths, including giant sturgeon as well as the Mediterranean tunny and mackerel; and salt was available to preserve these various fishes in dried and smoked and pickled form.

But grain was the major clue to the existence of Olbia, as of other Black Sea colonies – and it also formed the principal basis of their relations with the Scythian hinterland. Ancient writers tell us of the huge quantities of grain obtained from the inexhaustibly fertile 'Black Earth' region of the Ukrainian and Moldavian plains; and some evidence of the part Olbia played in this traffic can be seen at Shirokaya Balka, a mile south of the city, where twelve large storage pits have come to light, in addition to an oven, employed perhaps for drying the grain.

Yet that was not the only product of the hinterland. Polybius later adds cattle, honey and wax;[35] and there were also furs, timber from forests in the interior, metals brought by river from Transylvania – and considerable numbers of slaves, who were exported from Olbia and other Black Sea ports to other Greek lands, and carried, for the most part, by Milesian vessels. In exchange, the Greek ships calling at Black Sea ports brought consignments of wine and olive-oil not only for the Greek settlers, who wanted to drink and eat like their compatriots elsewhere, but for non-Greek populations over a huge area of northern and central Europe and central Asia. This traffic, it may be inferred, had already begun to travel in both directions as early as the sixth century.

The most important site in the area under Olbia's control was Berezan, of which the Greek name is unknown. The place was situated on what was probably a peninsula but is now an island, controlling the outlets of the Rivers Borysthenes (joined near its mouth by the Ingul) and Hypanis, which flowed together at this point to form the largest of the Black Sea estuaries or *limans*. The suggestion that the foundation of Berezan preceded the establishment of Olbia has become hard to support. The latter, probably, was established first, and the former soon afterwards.

The houses of Berezan were single-roomed, thatch-roofed buildings, mostly rectangular but in some cases round, measuring 6 by 9 feet or 9 by 12. They were set low in the ground, for protection from winter cold, and possessed fireplaces. Pits for storage or refuse are also to be seen. The island on which Berezan is now located (including the landing-place on its eastern shore) has yielded many finds of widely different periods, including, now, a small group of sixth-century electrum (pale gold) coins.

In the crack of a wall was found a private letter of c.500, written on lead and rolled into a scroll.[36] This early example of Greek commercial correspondence illustrates the existence of a professional class of traders. The letter, composed in the Ionic dialect, is obscure and allusive, but according to one reconstruction Achillodorus, the writer, is engaged upon a business journey on behalf of a certain Anaxagores when a third party, Matasys, seizes his cargo and attempts to reduce him to slavery. Matasys may be endeavouring to exercise the right of personal reprisal against the property of Anaxagores, according to a practice whereby the member of one city, if labouring under a grievance, exercised this right against the member of another. For Matasys asserts that Anaxagores has deprived him of a possession, and claims that Achillodorus, as a slave of Anaxagores, is liable to seizure in compensation for this wrong. Achillodorus urges his son Protagoras to report to Anaxagores what is happening, and takes the opportunity to explain that he is a free man and no slave, and is not, therefore, liable to seizure.

The Scythian expedition of Darius I in c.513–512 (Appendices 1 and 2) must have caused anxiety to merchants such as these, and indeed to people at Olbia and Berezan in general. For one thing, it probably cut off their access to one of their commercial outlets, the mining country of Transylvania; and it meant that the Black Sea was in danger of becoming a Persian lake.

South-east of Olbia lay the peninsula of the Tauric Chersonese (Crimea), of which the mountainous interior and its fierce inhabitants were discouraging to Greek seamen. However, the eastern extremity of the peninsula, facing the Cimmerian Bosphorus (Kerch promontory), proved attractive to colonists – especially from Miletus – because the strait led into Lake Maeotis (the Sea of Azov), which although stormy contained a huge wealth of fish.

Moreover, the lake extended northwards to the River Tanais (Don), at the mouth of which the Milesians (if it was they, as seems probable) founded the most remote of all their colonies (c.625–600, or a little earlier), named after the river, which provided communications into the Scythian interior. Strabo described a major Greek market-city of Tanais, a common *emporion* of European and Asian nomads,[37] which has been identified with the modern Nedvigovka, but the earlier settlement does not seem to have been on the same site. It may have been at Taganrog instead – where Greek pottery going back to the seventh century has been found under water – or on the island of Elizaveto-vskaya (alternatively believed to have been the ancient Alopecia), beside the main southern branch of the River Tanais' delta.

At the southern end of Lake Maeotis, a number of Greek colonies clustered round the Cimmerian Bosphorus, upon both its banks. The most important of them was Panticapaeum (Kerch) on the western shore, founded by colonists from Miletus in c.600. It stood on the site of an earlier Scythian settlement (Panti Kapa), which had conducted trade with visiting Greek merchants: a royal Scythian burial at Temir Gora, two miles from the township, was found to contain a Greek wine-jar of c.640–620.[38] Apparently maintaining a close relationship between the ethnic groups, Panticapaeum owed its importance to a favourable location, protected by a defensible acropolis (Mount Mithridates); and the citizens exploited their proximity to the best grain-lands of the Tauric Chersonese.

The hereditary rulers (*archontes*) of the city belonged to the Milesian family of the Archaeanactids. A decade or two after the termination of the period covered by this book, they consolidated their power and inaugurated the long-lasting kingdom of the Cimmerian Bosphorus, which exercised control over a number of native peoples, displaying various degrees of Hellenization. By that time, other Greek colonies, too, had been founded near Panticapaeum.[39]

The eastern, Kuban shore of the Cimmerian Bosphorus (the Taman peninsula, terminating in the Taman gulf) was extensively penetrated by Panticapaeum, which showed a keen interest in the metals of the Caucasian hinterland. On this eastern side of the strait, the earliest identifiable Greek foundation can be attributed (like Panticapaeum itself) to the Milesians. This is Hermonassa (Tamansk). Standing at the southern entrance to the narrows, Hermonassa was well placed to exploit their commercial and strategic importance. It could also make use of the estuary of the River Anticites (Kuban),[40] of which the principal channel, in those times, flowed into the Black Sea just to the south of the city (not into the Sea of Azov as today). Recent excavations at Hermonassa have uncovered a series of buildings, streets and tombs, dating from the early years of the sixth century, when the city seems to have been founded. Other colonies in the area date from about the same period.[41] The river-valley ensured Greek communications with tribal centres of the hinterland, including a small fortified enclave left behind by the expelled Cimmerians (Appendices, note 2), although some of these peoples liked to capture Ionian sailors, and sacrifice them to the Great Goddess (Tabiti).

But the principal Greek colony on this eastern side of the narrows was Phanagoria, a little to the north (near Sennaya), on an island bordering upon Lakes Maeotis and Corocondamitis and a branch of the Anticites. Unlike most Black Sea foundations, this was not a Milesian foundation, but the colonists came instead from another Ionian city, Teos. Their settlement extended over two terraces, of which one formed the acropolis and the other a lower town. Most of the latter has now been submerged to a distance of between three and thirty feet beneath the sea, by a geological process known as the 'Phanagorean regression'. But remains of four early dwellings on the upper terrace have now been unearthed, including one that is attributable to the initial epoch of the colony's life. A necropolis in the suburbs indicates the predominance of Ionian pottery during that period, superseded by the products of Attic and Thasian workshops; and from the sixth century onwards various Greek wares began to be imitated locally. To the south-west and west of the city impressive chamber graves were erected. Their contents included lavish funeral gifts, including saddles and harnesses made of gold and of gilded bronze.

Thus within the span of a century the entire western and northern coasts of the Black Sea came to be studded with Greek towns, fulfilling a joint role as trading posts and agricultural settlements. Moreover, down the east coast of the sea, within its recess beneath the Caucasus, lay several other Milesian townships of sixth-century date, though it is uncertain whether they ranked as cities (*poleis*) or were marketing posts (*emporia*) without civic status.

The northernmost of these places was Pityus (Pitzunda, Bichvint), in the tribal territory of the Heniochi, upon whom the Greek settlers or traders may have been to some extent dependent (this area now forms part of the Abkhazian Autonomous Republic attached to the Soviet Republic of Georgia). Next came Dioscurias (Sukhumi, the capital of Abkhazia), near the mouth of the small River Besletka, replacing or joining a native settlement dating back to the second millennium BC. Despite its remoteness, this market-town gradually developed the importation of products from many parts of Greece, and the export of local salt and of Caucasian wood, linen and hemp. Seventy languages, it was said, could be heard in the bazaar of Dioscurias, or according to another account 300, though Strabo queried this higher figure.[42]

A third and more southerly Milesian *emporion* was Phasis, somewhere near the mouth of the river of the same name (now the Rioni, in Georgia). Silting has made its identification problematical, but a possible site is

Simagre eleven miles up the river, where traces of sixth-century build-ings upon a mound have been unearthed. The upper valley of the River Phasis, before it reached the feverish marshy lowlands, provided the same Caucasian products as those sold at Dioscurias, in addition to iron from the country of the Chalybes (note 25). This fertile region formed the nucleus of the kingdom of Colchis, which, succeeding to the dominions of a principality of Colha or Qulha – destroyed in c.720 BC – may have come into existence in the course of the sixth century,[43] although an alternative view does not see Colchis as an organized state before 300.

Be that as it may, its prominence in Greek mythology had gone back to very early dates – perhaps in the second millennium BC, or in any case during the earliest years of Milesian exploration. The land of the Colchians was regarded as a magical land of wealth, to which the Argonauts sailed in order to seize the Golden Fleece from Aeetes, named after his kingdom Aea – the land of the Rising Sun – which was generally identified with Colchis, although the Taman peninsula has also been suggested as a rival possibility.

The Argonauts were reputedly led by Jason, whom Pelias, the usurper of Iolcus in Thessaly, had tricked into setting out to capture the Fleece before he could lay claim to the throne of Iolcus. Passing through the Thracian Bosphorus into the Black Sea, by way of the Clashing Rocks (having tested their passage by dispatching a dove before them), the crew of the *Argo*, it was said, received entertainment by the tribe of the Mariandyni. Later, after stopping briefly at Sinope, they came to Aea or Colchis, where they put into the mouth of the River Phasis, beside which stood the royal city. With the aid of the king's daughter Medea, Jason performed a task set by Aeetes: that he should yoke a pair of fire-breath-ing bulls, plough a field, sow it with the teeth of a dragon or snake (slain by Cadmus) and overcome the warriors who would sprout up from those teeth. Then, still helped by Medea, Jason took the Golden Fleece and fled. His return journey to Greece was the subject of many variant versions, and indeed, at all points, the story contained a great con-glomeration of sagas and fairy-tales. But it also, in mythological form, mirrored early Greek travels and explorations along the Black Sea coasts.

The farther shores of the sea, or even regions beyond, are also associated with another fundamental Greek myth, the story of the Amazons. They were located at Themiscyra on the River Thermodon in northern Asia Minor, east of Amisus and the River Iris[44] (from which region, however, Strabo said they had been driven[45] – a statement perhaps based on the absence of any local trace of their existence). Alternatively, they were said to have lived far away to the north-east by the mouths of the River Tanais,[46] or an even greater distance to the east by the Caspian Gates, south of the sea of that name.[47]

The point was that they were always placed on the very borders of the known world. This was because they represented the reversal of the natural order of things (exemplifying a well-known type of folktale, applied by Herodotus, for example, to Egyptian customs).[48] For the Amazons were women, and yet they were also warriors, a match for men, *antianeirai* as Homer twice called them.[49] Thus they stood for a state of affairs in which everything had gone wrong – fighting being the business of men. And no one could feel that more strongly than the Greeks, who believed, with few exceptions, that the position of women was quite different from, and below, the position of men.

As for the Amazons, not only were they like men, a match for men, but they fought against men. In particular, Arctinus, an eighth-century Milesian, told in his *Aethiopis* (or *Amazonis*) how the Amazon queen Penthesilea had come to the aid of Troy in the Trojan War[50] (in the *Iliad* she had earlier been an enemy of the Trojans),[51] fighting a duel against Achilles. He struck her down and killed her, as Amazons were always defeated when they fought against males (not only Achilles, but Heracles and Theseus and Bellerophon as well). For their monstrous assertion of masculine status had to be resisted. But their claim, nevertheless, is illustrated by frequent artistic juxtapositions of battles against Centaurs with battles against Amazons – an implied comparison designed to stress that both peoples alike, though one was male and lustful and the other female and chaste, were equally in opposition to the correct and decorous established order. These portrayals of Amazons occur from the seventh century onwards; they are depicted in short tunics, and sometimes in Scythian or eastern trousers.

But the extraordinary, outrageous behaviour which mythology thus ascribed to these formidable women had so greatly taken hold of the Greek imagination that they crop up in a variety of places and roles, not only, and most obviously, as an object lesson justifying sexual polarity and male chauvinism, but even as the founders of important cities in western Asia Minor, including Cyme and Ephesus (whose Artemis was not always the immobile image of her temple but sometimes, also, an Amazon-like figure). Herodotus was indeed unusual when he struck a blow for greater equality between the sexes by marrying the Amazons off to the Scythian-related Sauromatae or Sarmatae, north of the River Tanais,[52] in a fictitious society which arranged relations between the sexes, and laid down their respective appropriate functions, in a mutually satisfactory manner, allowing neither the one nor the other to be wholly dominant.

CHAPTER 9

AFTERMATH

The half-millennium described in this book had started with the almost complete collapse that accompanied and followed the downfall of the Mycenaean palaces. An attempt has here been made to chart the gradual recoveries from that collapse achieved in one region and place after another. In every sphere – political, economic, social, poetical, philosophical, scientific, artistic – and in many different city-states and regions, the developments that occurred were varied, profound and creative.

They laid the foundations for a brilliant future. In the political field the demarcation between what had gone before and what was to follow, during the 'classical' period, is clear. For immediately after the latest events that have formed our theme came the Persian Wars. They formed a turning-point, marked by the engagements of Marathon (490), Thermopylae, Artemisium and Salamis (480), and Plataea and Mycale (479). The Greeks won, and thus not only earned the survival of their independent city-states but gained a source of pride for evermore.

But it was a close-run thing. We have seen, throughout this study, a continuing contrast and counterpoint between the Panhellenic spirit, represented by common race, language and religion, and the centrifugal trends involved in the divisive relationships between one city-state and another. Now, faced with a Persian threat to all, unity just managed to prevail against disunity. By no means every state of the Greek mainland resisted the Persians – some felt obliged, or inclined, to take their side, and others remained neutral – but those that did fight stood firm and prevailed. Their leaders (despite friction and quarrelling) were Sparta and Athens; though in what proportion those two states should be acclaimed the principal authors of the victory was disputed for many years to come.

It was widely felt, after the Persian Wars were over, that the precarious Greek collaboration which had made the success possible should somehow be preserved. In practical terms, however, it could only be maintained by recognizing Athens or Sparta as the dominant power. The Spartans, however, as very soon became clear, lacked the competence or the will, or both, to assume this role. So Athens formed its 'Delian League', which became an empire (under the guidance of Pericles). But this process, inevitably, aroused the jealousy of Sparta's Peloponnesian League, supported by Corinth and Thebes.

The outcome (through whose fault has been endlessly discussed) was the Peloponnesian War or Wars (431–421, 416–404), immortalized by Thucydides. The final losers were the Athenians, primarily because they had, gratuitously, intervened to help a rebel movement against the Persians in Asia Minor. A little earlier, too, they had launched an expedition against Syracuse in far-off Sicily, which ended in disaster; and subsequently they executed a team of generals who had won them a victory (at Arginusae), because human lives had been lost in a storm after the battle.

The success of Syracuse reminds us that although, in the homeland, Athens and Sparta by that time held an unquestioned pre-eminence not existent in earlier times, other cities in the Greek world were still enjoying flourishing careers too easily forgotten among the dramas of the Persian and Peloponnesian Wars. At the time of Salamis, Syracuse and Gela had repelled the Carthaginians – and Syracuse remained thereafter a major power. Its story, however, during the fifth century, comes to us almost by chance, when it happened to impinge upon the picture of the Athenian homeland so concentratedly presented by Thucydides. In the far west, too, Massalia was still important, and Greek life on the northern shores of the Black Sea retained its significance, though not so much expressed through independent city-states, as in earlier times, as in the story of the Archaeanactid kingdom of the Cimmerian (Crimean) Bosphorus whose grain-trade became the life-line of Athenian survival.

This fifth century, the age of the Persian and Peloponnesian Wars, produced a unique concentration of intellectual and artistic talent in which all the earlier trends described in this book bore fruit more or less simultaneously in the composite, contemporary, short-lived, 'classical' phenomenon that has never been equalled.

But whereas the achievements of the earlier period were diffused over extensive areas of the Greek world, and whereas this diffusion still continued to a certain, not inconsiderable extent, the 'classical' efflorescence was concentrated to an outstanding degree at Athens. And this is not merely due to the Athenian bias of our sources, which tends to neglect the political history of other states, for Greek cultural life was now, truly, centred upon Athens. Thinkers and writers came and worked there far more extensively than hitherto: the popular philosophers or 'sophists', and the historian Herodotus; his successor Thucydides, too, was an Athenian; and Athens was the home of many other literary genres as well, such as tragedy, comedy and the sort of inward-looking, dialectical philosophy carried by Socrates, as far as we can reconstruct his thinking, to hitherto unimaginable lengths. As to the visual arts, the murals of the age (like those of the preceding epoch) have been lost, but many paintings on Athenian red-figure pottery have survived, and we can see that they continued to explore new areas of artistry and naturalism. At the same time the Parthenon (*c*.447) and its statue and reliefs by Pheidias demonstrate how Athens had taken the lead in architecture and sculpture.

An insistent question becomes inevitable: why, in the fifth century BC, was there this unique concentration of talent at Athens? To answer that it came about because the Athenians had by now developed the system inherited from Cleisthenes (Chapter 2, section 5) into a mature democracy cannot be regarded as a sufficiently justifiable conclusion, because wonderful things, as we have seen, had been done by the Greeks before democracy existed at all. The answer rather appears to be – and Thucydides was not unaware of it – that empire brought the Athenians enough money to pay for the leisure which enabled people to think and write to the height of their remarkable gifts and to pay architects and sculptors for masterpieces of comparable quality.

Whether the democracy initiated by Cleisthenes, and imitated or adapted by many other Greek communities, should be regarded as a success has been widely discussed and disputed. On the credit side, its institutions enabled citizens to participate personally in their states' workings to an extent never paralleled before or since. On the debit side, this mass participation, accentuated by the levelling use of the lot, caused many serious mistakes to be made.

And, indeed, the errors that lost the Athenians the Peloponnesian War continued during the fourth century, as they tried to revive their empire, at a time when their greatest living thinker, Plato, was, ironically, a man who deeply disapproved of democracy (although rebuffed by the dictatorial regime of Syracuse). Yet it was not only democrats who were to blame. The government of Sparta, too, which, although theoretically directing a body of equals, was not a democracy in any sense of the word that would be regarded as valid today, had already by that same time, under the shadow of Persia, failed no less abysmally to set up its own commanding group of Greek-states – leaving it to Thebes to try, briefly and unsuccessfully, to do the same.

Philip II of Macedonia (361–336) put an end to all such endeavours.

Hitherto his autocratically ruled and backward country (Chapter 8, section 1) had not attained much distinction. But despite the attempts of an Athenian oratorical genius, Demosthenes, to whip up a coalition against him, Philip, overhauling his kingdom, made it much more than a match for the whole of mainland Greece put together, and at the battle of Chaeronea (338) reduced the autonomy of its city-states to a shadow. Then his son Alexander III the Great (336–323), sweeping the Persian empire away in one of the outstanding military feats of all time, brought about an expansion of the Greek world that rivalled the age of colonization 300 to 400 years earlier.

The 'Hellenistic' world which, after a period of confusion (the age of the Diadochi or Successors), inherited Alexander's work was largely a world of kingdoms: his own continuing state of Macedonia (later re-organized by the Antigonids), the Egypt of the Ptolemies (with its capital at the conqueror's foundation, Alexandria), and the huge Seleucid dominions of the near and middle east (ruled from new metropolitan cities at Antioch in Syria and Seleucia by the Tigris). Moreover, other kingdoms, too, survived or were created, notably at Sparta (where a series of reforming or revolutionary monarchs emerged); at Syracuse (still tormented by political convulsions); upon the Cimmerian Bosphorus (now under a new Spartocid dynasty); across huge tracts of Asia Minor (already at Halicarnassus, and now in Pontus, Bithynia, Cappadocia and Pergamum); and as far eastwards as India (Bactria and the Indo-Greek principalities, as well as non-Greek Parthia).

Yet in Hellenistic times there were still city-states as well, under non-monarchic rule: Athens, Rhodes (where three states had amalgamated in the fifth century) and Taras in south Italy were particularly prosperous. Moreover, the federal experiments of which, during the earlier period, we have already seen evidence in Boeotia (Chapter 4, section 4) were carried further by the Achaean and Aetolian Leagues, both occupying regions where urbanization and city-state development had hitherto been weak.

The New Comedy of Menander (d.293/289) flourished at Athens, and the same city was still the philosophical centre of the Greek world, under Aristotle of Stagirus in Thrace (d.322) and his successors Zeno (from Citium in Cyprus) and Epicurus (from Samos), who founded the Stoic and Epicurean schools respectively. But Alexandria proved more than a rival in the poetical field, attracting Callimachus, Apollonius and Theocritus, from Cyrene, Rhodes and Syracuse respectively. Science and medicine, too, centred upon Alexandria, though the outstanding scientist of the age, Archimedes, was another Syracusan. The wonders of Hellenistic sculpture, blending new, baroque ideas with ancient traditions, were to be seen in many centres, among which Pergamum and Rhodes were especially notable.

But the Hellenistic kingdoms fell to quarrelling with the rising power of Republican Rome (which had absorbed the Greek-influenced city-states of the Etruscans – Appendix 3), whether from their own shortsightedness or the aggressive designs of some Romans, or because of a fatal blend of the two. The Greeks did not join forces against Rome as successfully as some of the city-states, centuries earlier, had momentarily united against the Persians, and one after another the Hellenistic kingdoms went down, until the annexation of Cleopatra VII's Egypt by Octavian (Augustus) in 30 BC proved a tame, though romantically presented, conclusion to a long-drawn-out process. An Indo-Greek principality seems to have survived for a few years longer, but we know little about its final phase.

Its conquerors were not Romans; but by now the rest of the Greek world formed more than half of the Roman empire – yet its political role, under Roman rule, was insignificant. It began to get its revenge when Constantine I the Great (AD 306 – 37) converted Byzantium (Chapter 8, section 1) into a new foundation, Constantinople, which became the capital first, briefly, of the Roman empire, and then, for a millennium, of its east Roman and Byzantine successor. And as time went on Greek replaced Latin as the official language of the Byzantine state.

RELATIONS WITH OTHER PEOPLES

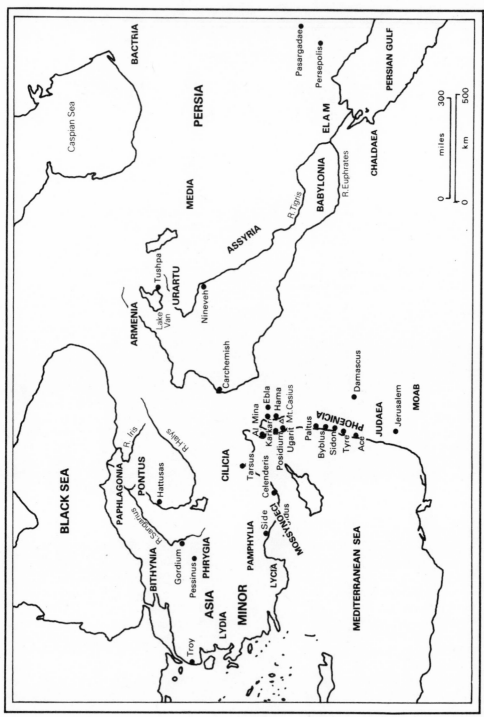

12 The Near and Middle East

COUNTRIES INFLUENCING THE GREEKS:
THE NEAR AND MIDDLE EAST

Phrygia formed a large part of the central plateau and internal western flank of Asia Minor. The country was occupied, during the widespread convulsive migrations of the thirteenth and twelfth centuries BC, by the Indo-European-speaking but non-Greek Phryges, a horse-rearing aristocracy. According to tradition, they came from Thrace, where they were known as the Bryges. It may have been pressure from coastal Mycenaean settlements in southern Macedonia that caused them to leave for Asia Minor.

Arriving there, they helped to overwhelm the Hittites (note 19), and founded a large kingdom associated in Greek legend with traditions regarding kings Midas and Gordius. The latter gave his name to the capital Gordium, in the valley of the Sangarius (Sakarya) which Homer mentions as the scene of the earliest Phrygian advance.[1] Remnants of the architecture, sculpture, metal-work and wood-work (in at least eight woods) of the Phrygians survive, and they were said to have been the inventors of animal fables.

Another, historical king Midas, ruled from c.738 to c.696 BC. In Assyrian records, he appears as Mita of Muski, who joined a coalition against King Sargon II (715) and shortly after 700 seized Cilicia (Khilakku) in south-eastern Asia Minor (probably with the help of a Greek contingent from Ionia),[2] but was driven back to his homeland and became an Assyrian vassal. In c.676 (?), however, he reputedly committed suicide, when the Phrygian empire was overthrown (and several Greek cities beyond its western borders ravaged) by Cimmerian migrants from beyond the Caucasus under a king known as Lygdamis to the Greeks and as Dugdamme to the Assyrians.[3]

Although the Phrygians blocked the eastern, landward expansion of the Ionian city-states – notably Miletus – they quickly took over the Greek alphabet (unless the similarity between the two scripts is owed to a common source instead). Bronze belts and brooches and painted pottery found at Gordium have a Greek appearance, and King Midas not only became the first non-Greek monarch to send gifts to Delphi (where they were lodged in the Corinthian treasury), but married the daughter of the king of Greek Cyme in Aeolis, Agamemnon. The Greeks, for their part, acquired Phrygian textiles and slaves.

But above all they owed the Phrygians important debts in the field of religion. Ancient writers report that Dionysus (Appendix 2) came to them from Thrace or Phrygia – which owed its creation, as we saw, to a Thracian tribe. The Phrygians knew the god as Diounsis, a deity of vegetation. By the eighth or seventh century, too, the great mother-goddess of Asia Minor, whose principal sanctuary was at Pessinus on the border of Phrygia, had come to Greece under the name of Cybele (Kubila and Agdistis to the Phrygians). The Great Gods (Cabiri) of the north Aegean island of Samothrace (colonized by Samos – Chapter 8, section 2), who were at first underworld (fertility) deities, also seem to have originated in Phrygia.

The musicians of that land, too, exercised much influence on the Greeks, who credited them with the invention of cymbals, flutes, triangles, the Pan-pipe, and the Phrygian 'mode' (cf. Chapter 1, note 40), accepted, by implication, by Plato as a sufficiently virile and sober type of music, but rejected by Aristotle.[4]

Lydia was an inland territory in the west of Asia Minor, centred on the lower Hermus and Cayster valleys. According to more or less legendary stories, the country was ruled in early times by royal families which, although not of Greek race, claimed, or were ascribed, descent from the mythical Greek Atys (whose family was wrongly believed to have colonized Etruria – Appendix 3) and from Heracles (perhaps identified with the Lydian lion-taming god Sandon).

The last monarch of the so-called Heraclid line of Lydian monarchs, Candaules, was killed by Gyges (c.685–657), founder of the Mermnad dynasty ('House of the Hawk'), with its capital at Sardis on the River Hermus, at the edge of a well-watered plain. Gyges married his predecessor's widow, and earned the first-known mention, by Archilochus, of the term *tyrannos* (dictator), whether this is a Lydian word or not (cf. Chapter 1, and note 48).

Although, like Midas of Phrygia before him, Gyges sought the favour of the Greeks by presenting six golden bowls to Delphi (where the Corinthian treasury once again housed them), he employed his cavalry to break Colophon, the strongest Ionian power of the day (Chapter 5, note 31). The Milesian colony at Abydus on the Hellespont was evidently founded with his agreement. Later, however, he came into conflict with Miletus, but despite military victories he failed to overthrow the city, and finally admitted it into alliance. Nevertheless, the Ionians felt harassed by Lydia, which presented an obstacle to their landward expansion, and this contributed to their desire to get away and establish colonies elsewhere. Gyges asked the Assyrians (whose monarch Ashurbanipal claimed him as a subject) for assistance against Cimmerian raids (note 3), but forfeited this favour by supporting their enemy Psammetichus I from Egypt – and the Cimmerians killed him.

However, his great-grandson Alyattes (c.617–560), son of Sadyattes (625–615) the son of Ardys (652–625), drove the last Cimmerians out. Extending his dominions eastwards to the Halys, and thus founding the Lydian empire – despite hostilities with Cyaxares the Mede – he also moved west, captured Smyrna, and married his daughter to Melas, the dictator of Ephesus. Clazomenae and Miletus foiled him, but Alyattes (like Gyges before him) conciliated the Milesians, assisting in the reconstruction of their sanctuary at

Didyma. Once more following the example of Gyges, he presented gifts to Delphi, including gold objects and an iron stand made by Glaucus of Chios. He was sent a gift of 300 noble youths of Corcyra by Periander of Corinth, so that he could employ them as eunuchs.

Alyattes' son Croesus (c.560–546), of legendary wealth, yet again showed generosity to Delphi,[5] and under his rule Lydian contacts with the Greeks became even more far-reaching and intricate. This particularly applied to Ephesus, where Croesus helped to reconstruct the Artemisium (and borrowed money from its priests). Indeed, Ephesus virtually became his dependency, and as time went on he obtained control of nearly all the other Greek coastal cities as well, which thus had their fears of Lydian encroachment all too amply confirmed – and became the first Greeks to experience subjection to a non-Greek state.

Various Greek sages (following the example of Solon of Athens) visited Croesus' court, as well as engineers, bankers, businessmen and political refugees; and Sardis became the financial capital of the near-eastern world. But the rise of the Persian empire caused Croesus' downfall. For in 546, despite appeals to Greek cities and to Egypt, Sardis was conquered by the Persian monarch Cyrus II the Great. The Lydian kingdom was extinguished, and Sardis became the capital of a Persian satrapy (suffering briefly from devastation by the rebels during the Ionian Revolt [498]).

The Lydians had learned from Phrygia, and developed further, its religious rites (notably those in honour of the Great Mother Cybele, which they transmitted to Greece). They had likewise inherited Phrygia's textile industries, and produced gaily patterned fabrics, purple rugs and smart hats. Jewellery and excellent cooking were among their other specialities. All this earned them a reputation, among the Greeks, for enervating luxury. However, Herodotus observes that their customs were not basically so different from those of Greece – except that their girls engaged in prostitution.[6] He also describes the men of Lydia as the earliest retailers (kapeloi), which meant that at Sardis, for the first time, the Greeks saw permanent shops.

The historian adds (confirming an earlier testimony ascribed to Xenophanes) that the Lydians were the first to strike and employ coins of gold and silver,[7] a statement which prolonged modern research has confirmed, except that the initial metal has been found not to be gold or silver but electrum (pale gold) washed down the Rivers Pactolus and Hermus; and with regard to the stamping of the first designs – which was an integral feature of this creation of coinage – the forepart of a lion, with gaping jaws, on Lydian coinage cannot be regarded, with absolute certainty, as earlier than other animals' heads on Greek (Ionian) coins.

However, it was the Lydians who invented this practice of issuing these pieces of regulated weight, stamped with some mark of authority, in place of the various sorts of lumps, bars and spits of metal which had served similar purposes before. This innovation is now ascribed, on evidence derived from finds at the Ephesian Artemisium and elsewhere, to the years c.625–610, during the reigns of Sadyattes or Alyattes. The principal denominations were too high for ordinary day-to-day commerce, or for the retail trading mentioned by Herodotus: the commonest Lydian pieces were worth twelve sheep each – a year's or half a year's salary – and must have served primarily as a unit of accounting. Their initial purpose was probably the payment of mercenary soldiers.[8] ·

However, the institution of coinage, with its joint merits of durability and portability, was soon adapted to every sort of commercial purpose, and spread to the Greek cities of the coastal districts and islands, and from there to the mainland (Chapter 1), forming the most important Lydian contribution to Greek civilization.

In music, too, like their mentors the Phrygians before them, the Lydians taught the Greeks a great deal. For example, the seven-stringed lyre was said to have been brought from Lydia by Terpander of the Lesbian city Antissa, and Greek elegy was probably influenced by Lydia (in addition, perhaps, to Phrygia).[9] Plato, while approving, as we have seen, the Phrygian musical mode, condemns Lydian styles as effeminate (like those of the Ionians) and plaintive.[10] The possible role of Sardis in transmitting Babylonian cosmogony and astronomy will be mentioned later in this Appendix (cf. note 15).

The millennial earlier history of the lands of Mesopotamia (Iraq) between and around the Rivers Tigris and Euphrates cannot have failed to exert some influence on Greek thought and art. But that influence was largely indirect, being owed to the temporarily successful efforts of the empires of Babylonia (the southern plain between Baghdad and the Persian Gulf) and Assyria (in the region around Mosul) to gain control of northern Syria and Phoenicia, the major sources of the orientalizing processes experienced by the Greeks (see below). On the whole, Babylonia, and its capital Babylon, remained the cultural centre of this Land of the Two Rivers until its conquest by the Persians in 539. But political power, while shifting back and forth, had often been in the hands of the Assyrians instead, whose military and administrative capability was outstanding.

It was fortunate for the little states of northern Syria and Phoenicia that after the death of the powerfully expansionist Tiglath-Pileser I (c.1116–1076 BC) Assyrian power declined, while Babylonia, too, had become ineffective at this period. But Assyrian imperialism was revived by Ashur-nasirpal II (884–859) who compelled these Syrian princes to pay tribute, and his son and successor Shalmaneser (859–824), in the course of a campaign including the famous but apparently indecisive battle of Karkar (853), wore down their new coalition (which Israel had joined). After subsequent temporary decline, a new Assyrian empire was formed by the usurper Tiglath-Pileser III (745–727). A fresh coalition of north Syrian rulers, under the king of Urartu,[11] was again defeated and all their principalities reduced to submission, so that the Greek trading ports of north Syria now had a major power on their doorsteps.

Sargon II (722–705), ruling Babylonia as well as Assyria in a personal union, fought numerous wars, during the course of which most of the small north Syrian states, already much diminished, came to an end altogether, and the Greek cities of Cyprus, too, recognized Assyrian supremacy. In a

Cilician revolt Sargon II had to contend with Greek (Ionian) mercenary troops, and so did Sennacherib when the Cilicians rebelled again (note 2). In his reign an uprising of the Elamites (south-west Iran) resulted in the destruction of Babylon (689). Esarhaddon (681–669) was gravely threatened by the Cimmerians (note 3), and in order to secure help against them gave his daughter in marriage to the Scythian king Bartatua (Protothyas).

Egypt fell to the Assyrians (671), but in the reign of Ashurbanipal (669–630) became independent again under Psammetichus I. Then, in 612, the Chaldaean Nabopolassar, who had captured Babylon in the previous decade, took and destroyed Nineveh (in alliance with the Medes), thus becoming heir to the Assyrian empire and founding a Neo-Babylonian empire in its place. His son Nebuchadrezzar II, who had played a large part in these victories, conquered 'all of Hatti', that is to say Syria, which he continued to 'pacify' during the early part of his reign (605–562).[12]

This process may have brought a temporary revival to Greek *emporia* such as Al Mina – although it is also possible that the contrary was the case, and that Babylonian influence exercised a destructive effect. In any case, under Nabonidus (556–539), this Neo-Babylonian state succumbed to the Persian king Cyrus II the Great. Cyrus then proceeded to annex Babylonia and Syria, combining them in a single provincial satrapy, in which, however, although revolts were suppressed, the conquerors did nothing to discourage local traditions and cultures.

During the earlier centuries of this troubled period numerous Assyrian artistic motifs and themes had filtered through into the art of the Greeks, by indirect transmission, through northern Syria and Phoenicia (see below). Thus cut-out plaques in Crete are derived from Assyrian models, and lead discs from Sparta and Chios recall Assyrian pendants. The lions on Corinthian vases, after first looking Syrian, then adopt an Assyrian appearance,[13] while Homer's *Iliad* endows Hera with triple-bossed, berry-shaped earrings of an Assyrian type,[14] and a heavy helmet of c.725–700 found in a warrior's grave at Argos reflects a similar origin. The cylindrical form of one of the earliest large-scale Greek statues, the Samian image of Hera dedicated by Cheramyes (c.575–570), likewise goes back to Mesopotamian models.

Babylonian literature and thought also influenced the Greeks. It is Hesiod who shows these effects most clearly. Not only does his poem the *Works and Days* reflect Mesopotamian Wisdom Texts, but the *Theogony* shows unmistakable resemblances to the Babylonian creation epic, the *Enuma Elish* (originating from the Akkadians, named after the Mesopotamian city of Agade), which indeed, indirectly, forms one of the poem's main sources (second only to the Hurrian–Hittite *Epic of Kumarbi* – note 19). Although surviving in cuneiform tablets of seventh-century date – whose existence recalls Ashurbanipal's careful copying and collection of Babylonian literature – the *Enuma Elish* goes back as far as Sumerian stories of c.3000 BC, reflecting in its stories of convulsive divine conflicts the unpredictable, perilous weather and river conditions of the Mesopotamian plain. How the contents of the *Enuma Elish* became known to Hesiod remains uncertain. Perhaps the north Syrian and Phoenician centres were once again the points of transmission.

Other themes of Greek religion and mythology betray a similar Mesopotamian origin. The goddess Aphrodite, as worshipped at Paphos in Cyprus, is close to the Sumerian Inanna, who became the Akkadian Ishtar and then the Levantine Ashtoreth–Astarte. Homer's Councils of the Gods mirror a Mesopotamian conception. There are also many Homeric echoes of the *Epic of Gilgamesh*. Like Gilgamesh, Achilles is of divine extraction but doomed to die, and he mourns Patroclus as Gilgamesh lamented for Enkidu. Odysseus, too, follows the example of Gilgamesh when he visits the dead; Calypso recalls Siduri, to whose abode Gilgamesh comes; and Odysseus' encounter with Circe echoes the catalogue, recited by Gilgamesh, of Ishtar's lovers whom she has metamorphosed into animals. Another Homeric idea, that of the ocean as a river encircling the world, could be either Babylonian or Egyptian. The story of Demeter and Persephone (Chapter 2, section 2) reflects many Mesopotamian and other near-eastern tales of disappearing fertility deities. The wondrous birth ascribed to Cypselus of Corinth resembles analogous stories about the third-millennium Sargon, legendary founder of Agade. Furthermore, the fable of Deucalion, survivor of the Flood – like the story of Noah in the Old Testament – is reminiscent of Mesopotamian traditions and circumstances.

The Milesian cosmologist Thales, known as the first Pre-Socratic philosopher, derived much of his astronomical knowledge from Babylonian records. According to Herodotus, 'the Greeks learned from the Babylonians of the celestial sphere and the gnomon (a set square or any vertical rod whose shadow indicates the sun's direction or height) and the twelve parts of the day'.[15] It is likely that this information was available to the historian at Sardis.

Yet, as the foregoing summary has suggested, the most important points of transmission of near-eastern culture to the Greeks were the ports of north Syria, including Phoenicia.[16] The Phoenicians were, by origin, Canaanites,[17] who had evaded subjection to the Aramaeans,[18] though the latter (followed by Philistines and Israelites) had occupied the remaining three-quarters of what had been Canaanite land. The Phoenician maritime city-states, led by Sidon and its colony Tyre (which subsequently outshone it), began from the turn of the millennium to fill the vacuum left by the Mycenaean collapse, re-establishing the trade of the Mediterranean and maintaining, for as long as possible, their own political freedom.

They used the local *murex* sea-shells (now almost extinct in the area) to make purple dye; the *murex*, dead, putrefied and stinking, secreted a yellowish liquid which provided tones ranging from rose to dark violet. In addition, employing wood from the Lebanon range as fuel, the Phoenicians worked and exported silver from Cilicia (note 2), and gold from Cyprus and probably Nubia and other near-eastern and middle-eastern lands to which the Mycenaeans had already, indirectly, possessed access. Cyprus contained Phoenician settlements, notably at Citium (Qart Hadasht – Chapter 6, section 2) and Idalium. Others were in north Africa (first Carthage, traditionally 814 BC), western Sicily (Motya, Panormus – Chapter 7, sections 3–5), and Sardinia (Nora, Tharros).

Meanwhile, on the Syrian coast – a little to the north of the Phoenician city-states – the Greeks had established their own trading posts (*emporia*) at Al Mina, Posidium and Paltus (Chapter 6, section 4). Benefiting from the inland valley routes of the Rivers Orontes (Nahr el Asi) and Leontes (Litani), these *emporia* bordered on the small non-Greek states of Unqi (or Pattin) – presiding over the fertile Amik plain and centred on Kunulua or Caleh (Tell Tayinat?) – and Guzana (Tell Halaf) and Hamath. These were three of the numerous north Syrian principalities intent on guarding their precarious independence against aggressive great powers, which were covetous of the Mediterranean seaboard, and nervous of the possible effects of such an unstable ethnic cauldron boiling over across their own borders.

For these little north Syrian states comprised extraordinary racial, cultural and religious amalgams. The influence of the Aramaeans (note 18) was strong, but so, especially in the north, were 'neo-Hittite' survivals, that is to say heritages of the Hittite civilization of the second millennium BC,[19] which also preserved the traditions of another second-millennium people, the Hurrians.[20] Incidents in Homer's *Odyssey*, therefore, such as the visit to the underworld resembling a similar happening in the *Epic of Gilgamesh* (of Babylonian origin, but current in the Hittite and Hurrian languages), and the shooting of the suitors (which is like a feat of the Hittite king Gurpanzah) probably came to the Greeks from the same north Syrian region.

And above all the same seems to be true of the Creation Myths in Hesiod's *Theogony*, of which the *Epic of Kumarbi* and *Song of Ullikummi* (of Hurrian origin but found in the royal archives of Hittite Hattusas [Boğazkale, Boğazköy]) are the principal sources, providing models for his tales substituting one deity by another (Anu – Kumarbi – storm-god; Kronus – Zeus).[21] Moreover, one of Zeus' enemies, according to Hesiod's account, was the monster Typhoeus, who was associated with Mount Casius (Akra) in northern Syria, and therefore once again may have become known to the poet through the Greek *emporia* on this coast. For these *emporia* were in close touch with Greece and particularly with the cities of Euboea, visited by Hesiod and close to his Boeotian home, although he might, alternatively, have derived his knowledge from Cyme in Asia Minor – his father's homeland – which could have retained traditions from Hittite Asia Minor.

Be that as it may, it was from the Greek coastal markets of Syria, Al Mina, Posidium and Paltus – together, no doubt, with additional Greek trading quarters, of which we know little, at Tyre and other Phoenician centres – that there was a massive transmission of cultural influences to the Greeks. They adopted these influences, with revolutionary effect, so as to push their whole process of civilization decisively forward during the eighth and seventh centuries BC (a process begun earlier, when faience [bluish or greenish glass after Egyptian models], exported by way of Syria, and gold brought there from various near-eastern lands, had already come to Euboea in the years around 1000).

The bronze 'Argive' cauldrons, too, distributed in many Greek lands and presented as offerings to Delphi and Olympia, are now regarded as north Syrian in origin rather than Urartian (note 11). The 'Daedalic' statuettes of Greece, displaying wig-like hairstyles, likewise recall the styles of Syria (with characteristic Greek amendments and refinements) and it was from that country, also, that the Greeks learned how to make such figures from shallow, one-piece moulds.

But the most conspicuous example of Syro-Phoenician influence is provided by the whole 'orientalizing' artistic movement led by Corinth. Thus Proto-corinthian and Corinthian vases make very heavy borrowings (once again with Greek modifications) from the animal, monster and vegetable motifs that played such a part in the reliefs and figurines and textiles of north Syria and Phoenicia. But there were many other influences from those lands at work on early Greek art.[22] Moreover, Corinthian and other shipbuilders owed a lot to Phoenician instruction.

To specify the exact zone or city within this Levantine territory from which each influence originated is impossible, because the art of the whole region was a multiple amalgam of Aramaean, neo-Hittite, Mesopotamian, Assyrian, Urartian and Egyptian (and later Persian) elements, of which the deviations from one Syrian or Phoenician locality to another (in so far as they existed) generally elude us – all the more so because people from every part of the Levant continued to flock westwards to escape great-power pressures, and successively, but untraceably, added their various influences to the already complex Greek orientalizing picture.

Thus only occasionally can we say, for example, that the ivory-working which played a large part in this artistic activity (adapted, notably, on Samos, Rhodes and Crete, and by the Athenians) had been centred upon the Syrian city of Hamath, which specialized in figures of Ashtoreth–Astarte and enjoyed access to the ivory of Syrian elephants (the Mycenaeans had obtained their ivory from Ugarit [Ras Shamra] on this same coast). As for the gold which was likewise dispatched from these shores, eventually gracing Etruscan tombs in lavish quantities (Chapter 7, section 1, and Appendix 3), it had reached north Syria and Phoenicia from a variety of near-eastern and middle-eastern sources, from which the richer states of the time had been at pains to acquire it.

The Phoenicians, with their city-state structures, perhaps attracted more fellow feeling in similarly organized Greece than the frequent derogatory references to their 'piracy', inspired by commercial competition, would seem to suggest. Thus the presence of Phoenician craftsmen in Crete (Chapter 6, section 1) may explain the presence of the earliest Greek legal codes in the island's cities, since such codification had long been familiar to Semitic-speaking peoples.

It was writing that made these collections of laws possible, and the greatest debt of all that the Greeks, and the world, owed to this Levantine coast was the alphabet, which they took over in c.750, half a millennium after their own Linear B (Mycenaean) script (Chapter 1, note 2) had gone out of use for ever. The Phoenicians had completed a spectacular transformation and simplification of earlier syllabic scripts (such as Akkadian with 285 signs, Linear B with 88, Cypriot with 56) into a standardized alphabetic lettering of only 22 characters (seen, for example, on the early-tenth-century sarcophagus of King Ahiram of the Phoenician city of Byblus). They were thus able, as Josephus asserts, to make more extensive use of writing than any people before them,[23] though how far the practice was still restricted to their scribal class remains unclear.

The Greeks reduced this number of letters to twenty-two, contriving, however, to include a few new letters of their own, and, above all, altering four (with the addition of one more) so as to achieve an independent representation of vowel sounds, with which the Phoenician alphabet, designed for a Semitic language, had dispensed. Once more, the exact nature and channel of the transmission is not certain. According to one view, it was a north Syrian (Early Canaanite) and not a Phoenician script that was originally taken over, and the Phoenician influence only came slightly later – though Greeks themselves called the letters *phoinikeia*, and a basic Phoenician origin seems unmistakable.

As for the Greeks who first borrowed the alphabet, this fateful act seems to have taken place at a single Greek centre, since the alphabet which they adopted, despite regional differences, everywhere shares basic essential, mature uniformities (such as the inclusion of the four or more vowels) which appear to exclude a process of multiple diffusion. The Greeks believed that Cadmus, the legendary Phoenician founder of Thebes, introduced writing to Greece,[24] but that claim may merely rest upon that city's preservation, during the early Iron Age, of Mycenaean tablets which were no longer understood (Mesopotamian cylinder-seals have likewise been found at Thebes). It seems necessary to find another region, in which Greeks and north Syrians lived closely enough together for the adaptation to take root and be perfected on the spot.

By thinking along these lines, the introduction of Phoenician writing to the Greeks has been claimed in favour of a variety of Greek centres (Chapter 1, note 35). On the whole, however, on epigraphic and historical grounds alike, it seems most likely that the transmission was effected by those Euboeans who took the initiative in establishing Greek markets at Al Mina, Posidium and Paltus. It was they, on this hypothesis, who learned of the alphabet, adapted it to their own needs, and took it back to the leading mercantile cities on their own native island (Chapter 4, section 1).

From there, it would appear, the advantages of this medium for communication, culture, commerce and indeed almost every aspect of life were rapidly seen and exploited, and use of the alphabet soon spread throughout all Greek lands, enormously contributing to their evolution. Moreover, modified to suit the needs of different languages, similar lettering systems were brought into use, for their own needs, by the Phrygians (unless, as we saw above, the resemblance between the two scripts is due to a shared origin rather than to transmission from the Greeks) as well as by the Etruscans and then the Romans. The Roman version is employed by the western world today – except in Slavonic lands, where a further evolution produced the Cyrillic lettering, and among the modern Greeks themselves, whose alphabet is still the script their forerunners borrowed from the Phoenicians over two and a half millennia ago.

Subsequently, when the Lydian institution of coinage spread via the Greek states of Ionia to the Greek homeland, both the principal weight-standards employed there, the Aeginetan and Euboic–Attic, were based on the Syrian pattern of fifty shekels to one *mina*.

When widespread convulsions swept away the Hittite and Mycenaean worlds, they menaced Egypt as well, in the form of confederacies of Libyan tribesmen and seaborne invaders from the north ('Sea Peoples'). These attacks were repelled (*c.*1218, *c.*1182), but Egypt did not fully recover, and its unity suffered. In *c.*1080, at the end of the 20th Dynasty, this fragmentation took the form of a recognized division of rule, and then, during the four centuries that followed, partial control of the country was successively assumed by Libyans (or men of Libyan descent) and Nubians and Assyrians. The armies of Assyria reached Egypt in *c.*734 and *c.*720,[25] its kings Esarhaddon and Ashurbanipal sacked Memphis (*c.*671) and the Upper Egyptian city of Thebes (*c.*663/661) respectively, and installed local governors.

At the head of these governors under Ashurbanipal stood Necho II, who was ruler of Sais and Memphis. He then became independent (610–575), and is regarded as the founder of the 26th or Saite Egyptian dynasty, comprising six rulers. In 600 he dedicated the armour from a victorious Syrian campaign at Apollo's sanctuary at Didyma, thus acknowledging the help of Greek mercenaries; and the triremes that served as his warships were probably built for him by Greeks. His son Psammetichus (Psamtik) I expelled the last Assyrian garrison, and declared himself pharaoh of all Egypt. The Saite epoch has been hailed as an Egyptian Renaissance, but the dynasty continued to depend on Greek mercenaries and businessmen. The Corinthian dictator Periander named his nephew and successor after his Egyptian ally Psammetichus II.

This contact with Egypt, in which Naucratis played an intermediary part (Chapter 6, section 4), exercised a decisive influence on the art of the Greeks, in several ways. It taught them large-scale, monumental stone architecture, exemplified by the Heraeum at Samos and the Artemisium of Ephesus, with its close-packed columns reminiscent of Egyptian buildings. Palm capitals, and patterns of alternating lotus buds and flowers, are likewise of Egyptian derivation. Egypt also showed the Greeks how to design architectural complexes, such as the group of buildings round the lions' avenue at Delos.

In addition, the country showed Greek visitors its mural paintings, which influenced their own artists, working on walls and vases alike. Egyptian bronzes came to the Cretans and Samians, and taught them the hollow casting of bronze griffins. Theodorus of Samos – to judge from a doubtful passage of Diodorus Siculus – perhaps acquired his canon of human proportions from the same source,[26] and the full-sized stone sculpture of *kouroi* and *korai* may have been learned by the Greeks from the Egyptians, reappearing first, it would seem, on islands such as Naxos and Paros where marble could be quarried. This, too, has been contested, but at the very least information about Egyptian art familiarized the Greeks with the idea of large-scale sculpture.

It has also been argued that the Thracian and Greek Mysteries of Dionysus were based on the Mysteries of the Egyptian god Osiris. The old Homeric idea of the Ocean encircling the world could likewise be of Egyptian origin – if it is not Babylonian. Hesiod's *Theogony* shows a debt to Egyptian royal accession hymns, in which the creation miracle is repeated with the arrival of each new monarch, and his vituperative account of women comes indirectly from ancient Egyptian folklore. Stories indicating that Thales of Miletus visited Egypt, and brought geometry from it to Greek lands, are suspect. But his belief that the earth floats on water may be Egyptian.[27]

A disastrous expedition sent by Apries (Hophra, 588–569) to help the Libyans against the Greek colony at Cyrene provoked the anger of the Egyptian soldiery against privileged treatment supposedly accorded by the monarch to his Greek mercenaries, and Apries died at the hands of his own people.[28] Nevertheless, Amasis II (569–526) persisted in the employment of numerous Greeks and arranged alliances with the dictators of their cities. But the rising power of Persia filled him with alarm; and indeed his son Psammetichus III was dethroned by the Persian king Cambyses II, who reduced Egypt and Cyrenaica to subjection (525). Cambyses and his successors became Egyptian pharaohs, ruling more beneficently than Herodotus supposed[29] (Darius I [522–486] visited the country and promoted its religion) and permitting Greeks and Carians to maintain their distinct ethnic entities, but imposing a heavy tribute and mobilizing many Egyptians (as well as Phoenicians and Cypriots) as sailors.

Throughout the early part of the first millennium BC, Medes, Persians and other Iranian groups, speaking versions of an Indo-European language, gradually moved into the western half of the Iranian plateau and became the dominant powers in the region. Under Cyaxares the Mede (c.625–585), his people was pre-eminent, driving Scythian invaders or immigrants back to south Russia. Marching into the Assyrian empire, he formed an alliance with Nabopolassar of Babylon, and their combined armies sacked Nineveh (612). During the 580s Cyaxares was fighting against Alyattes of Lydia.

In 550, however, his son Astyages was captured by Cyrus II the Great (559–530), who substituted Persian for Median suzerainty throughout the region, and laid the foundations of the most formidable empire that the near east had ever known. His conquest of Lydia in 546 meant that Sardis became a major Persian staging point upon the Royal Road from Susa to the Mediterranean. This ancient route now assumed a new strategic significance, since Harpagus, the Persian satrap installed at Sardis, employed the town as a base from which he could conquer the Greek city-states on and off the western seaboard of Asia Minor (with the exception of favoured Miletus). In consequence, a large part of the population of Phocaea and Teos, and many artists and writers from other Ionian cities as well, fled to the west. The city-states of Cyprus and Syria–Phoenicia were also reduced to subjection. Babylon fell to the Persians in 539, and Cambyses II conquered Egypt in 525. A Persian satrap Oroetes lured Polycrates of Samos to his death (c.522); but Darius I executed the satrap for acting too independently.

In this period, stimulated by the famous issues of Persian gold coins, named 'darics' after Darius, who first issued them in western Asia Minor, contacts with the Greeks developed considerably. In Syria, for example, the Greek market at Al Mina was allowed to revive (and received substantial imports from Athens). But Persian intervention at Cyrene (c.515) resulted in the destruction of its temple of Zeus. Moreover, Darius' invasion of Thrace (which he annexed) and Scythia (which he failed to subdue) in c.513–512 brought the Persian empire into Europe and dangerously close to the Greek homeland (Appendix 2).

The subsequent massive revolt of the Ionian cities against Persia (499) was defeated off Lade (495). The satrap Mardonius reassuringly established democracies rather than dictatorships in the defeated mainland cities. Nevertheless, the fate of Miletus, destroyed by the Persians, horrified the entire Greek world – with good reason, since Darius, who had given refuge to the expelled Athenian autocrat Hippias, cited the ships and men provided to the Ionian rebels from Athens and Eretria as justification for the invasions of Greece that were about to follow (490, 480).

The principal Persian sites of the imperial period were: Pasargadae, begun by Cyrus II the Great, who employed Lydian and Greek masons (559–550); Persepolis, Darius I's spring capital, in the creation of which the role of Greek architects and sculptors is disputed; and Susa, the winter capital and administrative centre, where, as a foundation tablet records, Darius employed skilled craftsmen from a wide range of peoples – including the Greeks. Although the layout of these buildings remains fundamentally Assyrian and Babylonian (with some Egyptian influences), numerous Greek elements can be detected in their construction. A famous sculptor named Telephanes of Phocis (or Phocaea or Sicyon?) worked for Darius I and Xerxes I.

Conversely – and this was more significant – the monotheistic, Zoroastrian religion of the Persians gradually influenced Greek thought. It has been noted, for example, in the theological poetry of Pherecydes of Syros (c.550), and Pythagoras was said to have visited Zoroaster in Babylon. That is a myth, but his doctrine of reincarnation seems to echo comparable beliefs described in the Indian Upanishads, which could penetrate to Greek thinkers through Persian, Zoroastrian intermediaries. Pythagoras' own receptivity to these influences presumably went back to his early days at Samos.

Heraclitus' picture of souls rising upwards into the air after death indicates a similar Indian or Persian origin, and Milesian thinkers too, notably Anaximander and Anaximenes,[30] likewise present views reminiscent of Upanishadic and Zoroastrian thought. It was not, however, until the fifth century that such religious views became widely known to the Greeks from Persian sources.

RECIPROCAL INFLUENCES:
THRACIANS AND SCYTHIANS

The Thracians spoke an Indo-European language. However, although stories were concocted to claim that their mythical king Tereus (alternatively described as the ruler of Daulis in Phocis) had married Procne, daughter of Pandion the king of Athens, they were not Greeks. They had no script or literature of their own, so that they are known to us only through Greek writers. These descriptions are fragmentary, pejorative and restricted to matters of Greek interest. But they are now supplemented, to a limited extent, by excavations.

More than fifty tribes could later be identified in Thrace. Out of these, the *Iliad* (listing contingents that helped the Trojans) mentions three,[31] the 'Thracians' beside the Hellespont, the Cicones between the mouths of the Rivers Hebrus (Maritsa) and Nestus (Mesta), and the Paeones, an originally Illyrian (?) tribe, who were later partially integrated with the Thracians and lived on what came to be regarded as Macedonian soil, beside the middle reaches of the Strymon (Struma) and Axius (Vardar). Homer also refers to a people at Sestus in the Thracian Chersonese (Gallipoli peninsula).

Finds at Vulchitrun in northern Thrace (northern Bulgaria) confirm significant developments in the later Bronze Age. In the south-eastern part of the country, too, megalithic graves and dolmens ranging in date between the twelfth and sixth centuries BC reveal a materially advanced civilization. Moreover, Thracians preceded the Greeks in some of the most important islands of the northern, central, western and eastern Aegean (Thasos, Samothrace, Imbros, Lemnos; Euboea; Naxos; Lesbos, Chios).[32]

The sixth century ushered in a new, flourishing epoch in which the Thracian tribes strengthened their organization, and a revival of the arts began to be apparent. Several south-western tribes (in what was subsequently Macedonia) issued their own coins, including the Edoni. Their king is described as Getas, a royal designation which was also the tribal name of the Getae, the northernmost of the groups of Thracian peoples in the hinterland of the Greek colonies of the western Black Sea coast. The Getae were confused by Greek writers with their relatives the Dacians, but Herodotus implicitly recognized their Thracian character when, supplementing his own researches from Ionian geographers, he enlarged the frontiers of Thracian habitation northwards as far as the River Istros (Danube).[33] The twelve tribes that he mentions include the Dolonci in the Thracian Chersonese. These people had quarrelled with their northern neighbours the Apsinthii in *c*.560/555, and appealed to the Athenian Miltiades the elder, who proceeded to occupy the peninsula.

Herodotus noted the numerous inhabitants of the country, and its massive but ineffective potential power. 'The population of Thrace', he wrote,

> is greater than that of any country in the world except India. If the Thracians could be united under a single ruler in a homogeneous whole, they would be the most powerful nation on earth, and no one could cope with them. That, at any rate, is my own opinion. But in point of fact such a thing is impossible: there is no way of its ever being realized, and the result is that they are weak.[34]

Herodotus may have been exaggerating about the size of the Thracian population (for example, Thucydides described their cavalry as less numerous than that of the Scythians). Nevertheless, his words contain much that is relevant, not only to the historian's own fifth century, but to earlier periods as well. The revenues of the princes of Thrace, including the gifts they received from ingratiating Greek states, were enormous. They ruled over a warrior race, and their armies were large and impressive; the southern coastal plain encouraged horse-breeding. But they did not ally themselves effectively with one another, or fight together. Joint action by the various principalities had so far failed to emerge. The Thracians, it is true, shared a common race, religion and culture, and in some places enjoyed conspicuous wealth – exemplified by fifty burial mounds near Douvanli (Plovdiv), culminating in the sixth and fifth centuries BC. But politically they had not yet risen beyond the fragmented tribal stage, and in remoter areas had not even achieved tribal unity, living in separate, uncontrolled villages.[35]

Despite, however, the ferocious character of these inhabitants of the hinterland, the Thracian seaboard was planted with Greek colonies: beside the northern Aegean; along the Thracian Chersonese; upon the north coasts of the Propontis (Sea of Marmara) and Thracian Bosphorus; and on the western shore of the Black Sea (Chapter 8, section 2). In addition to inevitable hostilities, there was a good deal of collaboration and cohabitation between these Greeks and the Thracian tribesmen. This meant, in due course, a substantial influx of Thracians – especially archers and slaves – into the Greek city-states.[36]

But the principal effect of this relationship was the diffusion of Thracian religious ideas in Greek lands. The deities of the Thracians included: the Great Mother of the Gods, from whom their kings claimed descent; Bendis, goddess of the chase and of fertility, identified with the Greek Artemis; a war-god, equated with Ares; Zalmoxis, a god of the dead – especially revered by the Getae – to whom the ideas of the Pythagorean community at Croton were said to be related; the Great Gods or Cabiri, likewise divinities of the underworld, whose famous sanctuary was on the island of Samothrace (Chapter 8, section 2); a widely worshipped Rider-God like the Dioscuri (Castor and Polydeuces), sometimes described as 'the lord Hero'; and many others.

But another Thracian god became of outstanding significance to the Greeks. This was the deity they called Dionysus. In his Thracian homeland he stood for vegetation and fertility, and his rites were uninhibited and orgiastic, involving the tearing apart and eating of the raw flesh of hunted animals. Under the name of Diounsis – connected with Dio(s), the sky-god – he was worshipped not only in Thrace but among the Phrygians of Asia Minor, who had migrated there from Thrace (Appendix 1).

The Thracians probably brought the cult of Dionysus to Greece at about the beginning of the first millennium BC, although it had not been altogether unknown there at an earlier date, since his name appears in late Bronze Age Linear B tablets of Mycenaean Pylos. Homer had heard of his wild rites,[37] and of how King Lycurgus was driven mad for attacking him. The *Iliad* locates the event on Nysa, a legendary mountain, placed in a variety of countries by different authors, but Lycurgus was later identified as a Thracian (Edonian).

Although Dionysus had been known among the Bronze Age Greeks, their later compatriots were still eager to emphasize that he was a stranger. This was partly because of the wild, shocking irresponsibility which he offered to women, personified by his Maenads (Bacchants), whose Dionysiac emancipation from all normal conventions was uniquely alien to Greek religion and life, and a thing apart. Thus according to one famous myth, recounted in Euripides' disquieting *Bacchants*, Pentheus, king of Thebes, paid the penalty for his rejection of Dionysus by being torn limb from limb by these frenzied females. Such stories reveal the extent to which the god's ecstatic, miracle-working cult seized the fancy of the Greeks.

In historical times, 'orgies' continued to be celebrated on Mount Parnassus by an official feminine association, but by then the Delphic oracle had toned down the ungovernable excitements of earlier proceedings, admitting Dionysus to a more decorous partnership with Apollo. Dionysus first appears in Greek art in the early sixth century, and thereafter he is to be seen with great frequency, and in a variety of guises, especially on vase paintings; and his revelling Maenads, too, are often depicted. The Athenian Lenaea and Anthesteria were festivals of Dionysus, and Iacchus, sometimes regarded as his son, was revered at Eleusis (Chapter 2, note 12). The Sileni and satyrs who surround Dionysus are daemons of fertility, and in choral dances men disguised themselves as animals to assimilate themselves to the god and take on some of his strength. A phallus, the symbol of this fertility, was carried in Dionysiac processions; but wine, with which he was later universally identified, played little part in his earlier worship.

How many of the vast accretions of Dionysiac cult go right back to its Thracian origins is hard to determine. But most of these manifestations, at least in their more primitive forms, appear derivable from a Thracian source, and came to Greece through the medium of the Greek colonies in the Thracian coastlands.

The second major element in Greek religion that seems to have been transmitted to Greece by the Thracians was the cult of the singer Orpheus, believed to have been the son of a Thracian river-god Oeagrus (unless Apollo was his father) and of a Muse, who taught him singing. The object of diverse interpretations, he, like Pentheus, was said to have been killed and torn to pieces by Thracian Maenads; Attic vase-painters depict the scene.

There were strong, though contradictory, traditions locating the origins of Orpheus in southern Thrace, where his abode was variously stated to be beside the Hellespont, or (according to the more usual version) in the land of the Cicones (where Mysteries in his honour, for warriors only, were linked with those of Dionysus[38] – which Orpheus was said to have founded).[39] Or alternatively, his origin was attributed to a more westerly region of Thrace, between the Rivers Axius (Vardar) and Strymon (Struma). Medicines were said to have been prescribed on Thracian tablets by Orpheus, for the country was renowned for its healers. And, above all, he was believed to have been able to charm trees, wild beasts and even stones with his song.

But the principal importance of the cult to the Greeks was its latent or expressed promise of immortality. For it was probably this that prompted the later development of similar ideas in Greek lands, inspiring, for example, the teachings of Pythagoras, who appealed to the authority of Orpheus and was asserted (though perhaps not accurately) to have circulated his own poems under Orpheus' name.

This doctrine of immortality was linked with the role of Orpheus not only as a god of the underworld, but as capable of dissociating his soul from his body. This shamanistic concept of bilocation had come south from Scythia (see below) and taken root in Thrace, where it was associated not only with Orpheus but with that other Thracian underworld deity Zalmoxis. Herodotus reported a legend that Zalmoxis had been Pythagoras' slave.[40] But it was to the name of Orpheus, above all, that Greek ideas of immortality were attached. One product of this way of thinking was a series of accounts of his *Descents into the Underworld*, incorporated in the famous myth recounting his failure to bring his wife Eurydice back to the earth.

However, the task of assessing Orpheus' early Thracian and Greek cults is complicated by the emergence of an 'Orphic' religious movement, which spread very widely indeed, so that gold plates inscribed with its doctrines have been found as widely apart as south Italy, Crete and Thessaly. Orphism's chief contribution to religious thought was an account of the origins of humankind which sought, like the Old Testament Book of Job, to explain the problem of evil. It had come into existence, these writings maintained, because wicked Titans ate the infant Dionysus, and were burned up by Zeus: the smoke gave birth to human beings, who are therefore evil in substance, but tempered by a tiny portion of the divine soul-stuff.[41] Whether this particular set of doctrines originated in Thrace, or developed during the subsequent spread of Orphism throughout the Greek world cannot be determined.

The same, too, has to be said of the so-called Orphic poems. Some of them were collected, and in certain cases apparently forged, by Onomacritus of Athens, a literary personage at the court of Pisistratus.[42] Such poems repeated that humankind is guilty and polluted by Titanic wickedness, and must purge its guilt by purifications, to secure deliverance in the afterlife (the fifth-century vase-painter Polygnotus depicts Orpheus surrounded both by happy dead and by their tormented counterparts, who have not won salvation).

All this represented a potent Orphic counter-culture, a sub-rational, personal movement of dissent from the main currents of Greek civic religion, offering a relief from psychological tensions, such as the less emotional Olympian religion was unable to provide.

The disorderly world of the small Thracian princedoms was overturned when Darius I of Persia launched his first attack on Europe, by way of their country, in c.513–512 (with the help of a fleet mobilized among the eastern Greeks). Crossing the Thracian Bosphorus on a pontoon bridge constructed by the Samian engineer Mandrocles, he received the submission of many Thracian tribes, and converted the country into a Persian satrapy, which was in convenient reach of the gold and silver mines of Mount Pangaeum, and influenced the Macedonian kingdom that lay on the other side of the mountain.

Towards the north, his invasion of Scythia, as we shall see, did not prove equally successful, but at least the new Thracian province was able to maintain contact with a number of tribal units north of the Danube. Moreover, its creation was a perilously significant turning point for the Greeks, since this European beach-head in the hands of Darius, providing him with a land-route towards their homeland, brought the Persian Wars much closer.

When they became menacingly imminent, in 492/491, Mardonius reorganized the satrapy (shaken by a Scythian raid that had perhaps taken place some three years earlier). He subjugated the last Greek holdings (destined for liberation, once the Persian Wars were over), and delegated authority to selected, friendly Thracian tribes, notably the Odrysae, who reached the zenith of their power later in the same century (note 35).

Scythia was the vague designation given by the Greeks to the entire, huge, east European territory which extended between the Carpathian mountains and the River Tanais (Don). It was inhabited by a mixed conglomeration of peoples and groups of peoples, originally nomads from central Asia, who had begun to penetrate westwards early in the second millennium BC. Their various ethnic affinities have remained speculative, but most of the population probably spoke an Indo-European, basically Iranian tongue, though the intrusion of Ugro-Altaian (Ural-Altaic) elements is also likely. We have to be content, however, to employ the terms 'Scythia' and 'Scythian' loosely, reflecting not only the geographical vagueness of Herodotus and others, but also their confusion between ruling classes (which were small, and composed of people who could be strictly regarded as Scythians) and subject peoples (who were many, and diversified).

When the Scythians and their dependants reached eastern Europe and the Caucasian region from central Asia, they clashed with the Cimmerians (note 2), with the result that many Scythians moved southwards across the Caucasus into north-western Persia and its border-lands. There they first raided the Assyrian empire (Appendix 1) but subsequently allied themselves with its rulers, one of whom, Esarhaddon (c.681–669), gave his daughter in marriage to the Scythian king Bartatua (Protothyas). Before long, these Scythian immigrants dominated the central Asian lands into which they had moved. After twenty-eight years, however, during and after the collapse of Assyrian rule, they were expelled by Cyaxares, king of the Medes (Appendix 1), and once again gradually returned north across the Caucasus, resuming their occupation of the southern regions of what is now the Soviet Union.

Peoples related to them migrated as far to the west as Prussia and Hungary, and moved into Rumania and Bulgaria (where the Dobrogea [Dobruja] came to be known as 'Lesser Scythia'). Others trekked as far to the east as the Altai mountains (the scene of fifth-century discoveries at Pazaryk, in the High Altai). But the core of Scythia was the hinterland of the northern Ukrainian shores of the Black Sea, from the lower Borysthenes (Dnieper) to the Tanais (Don), with additional territory in the Kuban and certain parts of the Tauric Chersonese (Crimea).

In the interior, between the two great rivers, was the kingdom of the Royal Scyths, 'the best and most numerous of the Scythian peoples', according to Herodotus.[43] Their homeland was divided into four districts (or three for military purposes), each under a governor; and they ruled or presided over an enormous but loose confederation.

Many of their subjects were farmers, but others, like the Royal Scyth leaders themselves, maintained their traditional nomad customs, 'living not by tilling the soil but on their cattle – their waggons the only houses they own', although the excavation of Kamienskoye, a trading post near the Borysthenes, qualifies Herodotus' further assertion that they possessed no fortified towns.[44] However, he was right to stress that their strength lay in their mobility, the asset that enabled them to control their vast lands.[45] Although turbulent by nature, they achieved this control by effective organization and discipline, reinforced by the possession of numerous horses, of which they had been among the earliest riders; the numbers of horses interred in their burials run into hundreds. They also boasted expert archers – who were depicted on Athenian pottery of c.570 (the François Vase) and c.540 (Exekias) – and came to be employed by Athens, in the following century, as mercenaries and policemen.

In describing their picturesque way of life (confirmed at unexpected points by archaeology), Herodotus pointed out that this was, in many respects, the antithesis of the practices of the Greeks.[46] Attic vase-painters, too, show their non-Greek beards and long hair, swept back from the forehead, and their deep-set eyes, pronounced noses and heavy brow-ridges.[47]

No less un-Greek, too, in its original spirit was the Scythians' 'animal' style of art, owing debts to Assyria and Iran and the steppes, and found on numerous portable objects (the possessions of people on the move) which finally came to rest in the tombs of south Russia from the last years of the seventh century onwards, as also in many other parts of the vast areas to which Scythian influence extended. The animals thus depicted – stags above all (which 'Saca', the Iranian name for the Scythians, probably means), but also horses, ibexes, boars, wolves, Siberian snow leopards, eagles and fishes – possessed a religious significance, relating, it may well be, to animal ancestors or spirits, for ancestor worship was prominent in Scythia, under the auspices of the Great Goddess Tabiti, patron of beasts as well as of fire. Moreover, these spiritually potent animal designs served as badges of the mounted warriors' tribes and clans.[48]

The best of the Scythian works of art display a penetrating, lucid rhythmical balance, in which multiple contortions resolve themselves into graceful curvilinear patterns. Here is an advanced community culture, and in the absence of literacy it is upon the art of the Scythians (supplemented by the writings of foreign visitors, such as Herodotus) that we depend for our knowledge of what they were like. Iranian and central Asian themes are detectable and indeed dominant, but what is relevant to the present study is the secondary, but growing, influence of Greek artistic tendencies.

Even at first there had been an obvious analogy between Scythian art and the animal styles similarly favoured by orientalizing Greek vase-painters. But at this early stage the resemblance was coincidental, bearing witness not to any debt by one people to the other, but to the debts of both schools alike to older eastern traditions. From the later seventh century onwards, however, Greek artists deliberately made objects for Scythian notables, probably operating for the most part from the colonies of the Black Sea littoral. During the sixth and fifth centuries this process accelerated. At first a few Ionian artists, and especially metal-workers, moving out of reach of Lydia and Persia, made their way to this remote coast, and then they and their children worked for the chieftains of the hinterland – adapting their themes to include, for example, scenes of nomad life which were depicted in the Greek manner but could only be of interest to the tribal chiefs.

What attracted these Greek artists was the hope of gaining a share of the wealth of Scythia, rightly stressed by Herodotus and others. Its grain, and many other products too – fish, salt, skins, furs, timber, slaves, cattle, horses – gradually assumed great importance for the Greeks (Chapter 8, section 3); and the riches that this trade showered upon the Scythian chieftains enabled them to acquire quantities of gold, presumably from north-east of the Urals and the Altai mines. How they paid for the gold, unless they just seized it, we cannot tell. But its acquisition is demonstrated by the lavish quantities of the metal employed to decorate the harnesses, plaques for armour and shields, and other equipment found in their tombs. Greek artists from Olbia and other Black Sea colonies, originating no doubt, in many cases, from Miletus, decorated these objects with reliefs, thus providing the finest gold-work that the Greeks ever produced, since gold was scarce in their own homeland (cf. Chapter 1, note 50).

Most of this Greco-Scythian gold-work belonged to the fifth and later centuries BC, but not all, since certain objects precede those dates. The most costly Kuban burials, for example, date from c.600 or c.550; they belong to the earliest group of Scythian notables who were able to indulge their love of opulence. A silver-gilt mirror from Kelermes, in the Krasnodar region, is notably multi-cultural, since its reliefs combine a far-eastern (Siberian or Chinese) shape with near-eastern and Scythian and Greek motifs; a Great Goddess (Tabiti), who is depicted, resembles the Cybele of Asia Minor, men fighting a griffin are Scythians, but a winged Artemis has a Greek (Ionian) appearance – and not only she, for more than one Ionian model was employed for these figures.

Another burial in the same region, at Kostromskaya, belonging to a slightly later date, offers a chased gold statuette of a recumbent stag. Found lying upon an iron shield, to which it must originally have been attached, it displays a bevelled surface, reflecting a wood or bone model. The stag is a Greek essay in the Scythian animal style, and its body is covered with small relief animals that again present a Greek appearance; a fully classical Greco-Scythian art is now seen to be emerging. Similar blends can be detected in other seventh- and sixth-century burials on either shore of the Cimmerian Bosphorus (Strait of Kerch), as well as near Kiev and even as far afield as Prussian sites.[49]

Herodotus tells of a Scythian king Scyles of his own day, who was thoroughly phil-Hellenic.[50] But in earlier times, apart from the taste for Greek artistic workmanship, direct cultural (or matrimonial) interchanges seem to have been rare. An exception was Anacharsis (brother of another Scythian monarch Saulius), who reputedly visited Athens in c.592/589 as Solon's guest, and was hailed as a model of 'Scythian eloquence'.[51] He did not, it was said, much care for the Greeks, but even so his contacts with them allegedly earned him execution on his return home, for attempting to introduce Hellenic rites learned at Cyzicus into the Scythian cult of the Great Goddess Tabiti. Anacharsis became a legendary figure, one of the Seven Sages, and a specimen 'noble savage'.

Another contribution made by the Scythians to the Greeks, and transmitted, no doubt, through their Black Sea colonies, was the range of beliefs and emotions covered by the term shamanism. Although the word itself, of Tungus origin,[52] was not known to the Greek's, they became receptive to these ideas from an early date. The essential feature of such doctrines is the conviction that the souls of certain men are able to leave their bodies, so as to travel to distant parts, and, indeed, to the realm of the spirits; and from this capacity for dissociation (bilocation), already mentioned above in connection with its Thracian transmitters to Greece, the shaman – singer, prophet and healer – derived miraculous curative skills, and the power to escort the souls of the dead to the other world.

Ideas of this kind were widespread, finding their completest expression in Siberia but also deeply rooted in Scythia, where they came to the knowledge of the Greeks. The result was the appearance of Greek *iatromanteis* – shamanistic seers, magical healers and religious teachers – some of whom are specifically associated with these northern lands. One such semi-legendary figure was Abaris, who supposedly lived in the third quarter of the sixth century, and came out of the north riding upon an arrow. Abaris, it was said, banished plagues, foretold earthquakes, wrote religious poems, taught the worship of his northern god (translated by the Greeks as Hyperborean Apollo), and dissociated himself so effectively from the body that he could manage without human food altogether.

Another wonder-worker, Aristeas, likewise ascribed to the mid-sixth century BC (if not earlier), was again credited with the separation of his soul from his body, seeming to be dead at his home Proconnesus (in the Propontis) and yet making an appearance at the same time in Cyzicus, and many years later in Metapontum as well. He, too, possessed a Scythian connection, for he was said to have written a poem about legendary one-eyed northerners, the Arimaspians, containing extensive information about savage tribes north and east of the Caspian, based on a mixture of travellers' tales (derived from his own journeys?) and folklore. Other similar reputed examples of psychic excursion were recorded; and it has also been suggested that Pythagoras' belief in repeated incarnations and bilocation (and his identification with the Hyperborean Apollo – Chapter 7, section 2) may be derived from the same distant regions with which these other miracle-men were associated, since not only was he described as the slave-master of the Thracian Zalmoxis but also (though at how early a date we cannot say) as the teacher or pupil of the Scythian Abaris.

Evidence of a more material kind for Greco-Scythian contacts is provided by the Gute Maritzyn tomb outside Olbia (in which the two cultures are inextricably intermingled – Chapter 8, section 3) and by commercial objects[53] including Athenian vases depicting Scythian slaves serving as archers (and police). The Scythians also performed a political role as protectors of Greek Black Sea colonies. There were mixed tribes, such as the increasingly sedentary, farming, grain-trading Callipidae behind Olbia, whom Herodotus describes as 'Helleno-Scythians' or Scythian Greeks. The Geloni, too, centred upon Belskoye in the land of the Boudini (the wooded steppe area north of Poltava), had originally been Greeks from the trading posts (*emporia*), and spoke a language that was partly Scythian and partly Greek.[54] In a later period people of this dual origin could be known as *Mixellenes*, half-Greeks.[55] But all was not sweetness and light, for, as we saw earlier, some Scythians, notably in the Taman peninsula, had the habit of capturing Ionian sailors and putting them to death, as sacrifices to Tabiti.

In *c*.513–512 Darius I of Persia launched a major invasion of Scythian territory. His first aim, successfully achieved as we saw, had been to conquer Thrace, a feat which brought Greece, and the Persian Wars, appreciably nearer. But the reasons why he also moved onwards, and crossed the Danube to confront the Scythians – while at the same time ordering his satrap of Cappadocia (Asia Minor) to bring a fleet to attack them across the Black Sea – have invited speculation. He may have had an eye on the mines of Transylvania, thinking it would be convenient to possess a road-head at the mouth of the Danube, to which the metal could be transported. Nor can he have failed to take an interest in the grain of southern Russia: the possibility of cutting off these supplies from the Greeks must have occurred to him. Probably, too, he regarded the Scythians and their nomadic neighbours and kinsmen as presenting a threat all along the northern, Black Sea and Caspian, frontiers of his empire – about which his geographers may have been inadequately informed (confusing the Tanais [Don] and the Jaxartes [Syr-Darya]). Darius was also, no doubt, borne along upon the general psychological momentum of Persian expansion that characterized his reign.

At all events, he advanced from the Danube and penetrated deep into the

Ukraine, without, however, being able to compel Idianthyrsus, commander of one of the three Scythian armies, to meet him in battle. Scorched earth was all Darius found, and he had to withdraw. Although, therefore, his invasion of Thrace had produced positive results, the subsequent advance into Scythia proved unsuccessful, and just as the occupation of Thrace brought the Persian Wars nearer, so the failure in Scythia delayed them for a few years.

Moreover the Scythians, it was said (although this has not been universally believed), planned a massive retaliatory blow: proposing to Sparta a combined operation against the territories of Darius. The Scythians were to invade Media from the Caucasus across the River Phasis, while the Spartans should land at Ephesus and invade Persia's possessions in Asia Minor. But Sparta held back (although its king Cleomenes I, during the negotiations, reputedly learned the Scythian habit of drinking unwatered wine, which drove him mad), and the Scythians had to be content with the sack of the Greek Black Sea port of Istrus (shortly before 500) and a raid on the Thracian Chersonese (c.495?).

INFLUENCED BY THE GREEKS:
THE ETRUSCAN CITY-STATES

Etruria, the land of the Etruscans (Tyrrhenians, Tyrsenians), comprised the modern Tuscany, in western Italy, together with the northern section of Lazio, down to the River Tiber. By processes of comparison and deduction, a considerable number of Etruscan words have been deciphered, but the grammatical structure of the language still eludes identification. It does seem, however, to have been non-Indo-European – like certain other tongues of Italy and its islands[56] – although the Etruscan alphabet was adapted from a Greek model, namely the script of Chalcis in Euboea transmitted by way of the Campanian ports Pithecusae and Cumae (Chapter 7, section 1).

Information about the Etruscans – apart from the extensive evidence provided by excavations and artefacts – is defective, since they left no literature of their own (only, to date, 13,000 inscriptions, mostly brief and formal).[57] We are therefore dependent, for our knowledge, on surviving Greek and Latin literary traditions, which are fragmentary and patchy, concentrating mainly on moments of contact between Romans and Etruscans, and for the most part displaying hostility. The voluminous work of the emperor Claudius (AD 41–54) about the Etruscans, in Greek, has not survived.

The tradition that they originally came from Lydia, reported as a Lydian story by Herodotus,[58] is based on erroneous etymologies, like many other traditions about the origins of 'fringe' peoples of the Greek world. Although the (no doubt numerous) early group movements in and out of Italy, and within its borders, are irretrievably lost, the Etruscans must be regarded as an Italian people. Their archaeological remains reveal a prolonged and varied prehistory before Greek culture ever impinged on the region. This occurred, on a substantial scale, from the eighth century BC onwards, when the Etruscans learned from the Greeks how to make wine and raise olives and press olive-oil, and businessmen and settlers at Pithecusae and Cumae traded gold and other precious objects – imported from Chalcidian markets in Syria, such as Al Mina, Posidium and Paltus – in exchange for the iron of which Etruria possessed an abundance unparalleled in other Mediterranean lands.

The wealth thus acquired by the Etruscans is reflected in lavish burials, made at a time when their habitation centres became city-states, each enjoying independent power (the 'Etruscan League' recorded by ancient writers was mainly limited to religious purposes and meetings, and had little political cohesion or joint activity to its credit).

13 The Etruscan City-States

The influence of Chalcis yielded to that of Corinth (among other cities, including those of the eastern Greeks), and it was the fantastic orientalizing art of the Corinthians (followed by that of the Ionians) which created the specific blend of Greek and native styles notable in the mature Etruscan art of the sixth century. (In the later artistic achievements of classical Greece, on the other hand, these people, with their taste for the bizarre, showed little interest.)

Tarquinii (the Etruscan Tarchnal, now Tarquinia), situated in south-western Etruria (now Lazio) – upon hill-spurs five miles from the Tyrrhenian Sea – was founded, according to legend, by Tarchon the brother of Tyrsenus (and

Tages was said to have risen from its soil to teach the people their religion). As further tradition recounted, it was the earliest Etruscan locality to become a unified, prosperous centre. The villages on the site had begun to flourish in pre-urban times, before and after 900 BC, when their inhabitants were already exploiting the metals of Mount Tolfa. In the eighth century these villages coalesced into the new city of Tarquinii, under the stimulus of the demand for iron from Greek Campania. As a result, large tombs, covered with mounds of earth, began to appear soon after 700.

One of the men buried in its seventh-century graves was called Rutile Hipukrates; his first name was Etruscan and his second Greek (Hippocrates), probably taken from his mother and father respectively. Another man of Tarquinii, Lars Pulenas, describes his great-grandfather as Creices, the Greek.[59] The paintings on a local form of seventh-century pottery echo the Corinthian style which apparently became known to these artists from Cumae, so that the wares are known as Cumano-Etruscan.

In the same period a Greek, Demaratus, emigrating from Corinth, was said to have come and settled at Tarquinii (Chapter 3, section 2), accompanied by three *fictores* (terracotta sculptors), as well as by his own entire family, including two sons, one of whom he brought up with a Greek and one with an Etruscan education. The latter subsequently moved to Rome, where he became one of its kings, Tarquinius Priscus (c.616–579).

The Hellenization of Tarquinii had now reached a more advanced stage; and from the middle of the sixth century many of the tombs beside the city were decorated by a unique series of wall-paintings. Greece has nothing comparable to them – their earliest surviving counterparts in Greek lands, at Aegae (Vergina) in Macedonia are 200 years later – and yet they reflect various successive Greek influences upon Etruscan art, while at the same time preserving inherited native Italian features (in religion, the same blend is perceptible, with local traditions of Etruria to the fore). Thus paintings in the Tomb of the Bulls (c.550–540), which inaugurates the series, show a curious amalgam of local motifs and Corinthian and other Greek and near-eastern analogies. The Tomb of the Augurs (c.530) displays an Ionian style, and the Tomb of the Baron (c.500) reflects a novel impact of Attic vases (at the time of transition from black to red figure), combined both with colourful Ionian idiosyncrasies and with Italian traditions.

Despite the elimination of certain satellite townships, Tarquinii controlled a number of other centres in various parts of its surrounding inland territory. It also possessed three sea-ports, in which it kept a fleet that took the lead in Etruscan maritime power, as a series of inscriptions (*elogia*) relating to the Spurinna family suggests.[60] From c.600–580 one of these ports, Graviscae (Porto San Clementino), included a quarter occupied by Greek traders, who established a sanctuary dedicated to Aphrodite (the Etruscan Turan) and subsequently, about forty years later, added shrines of Hera (Uni) and Demeter, containing Greek dedications and cult lamps respectively.

An inscription found at this Tarquinian port of Graniscae, written in c.570 in the script of the island of Aegina (Chapter 2, section 6) reads: 'I belong to the Aeginetan Apollo; Sostratus had me made' (the name of a well-known trader mentioned by Herodotus, though not necessarily the same man).[61]

Caere (the Etruscan Cisra or Chaisr[i]e), now Cerveteri, extending over spurs three and a half miles from the Tyrrhenian Sea, became urbanized only a little later than its south-eastern neighbour Tarquinii, whose economic and political supremacy it soon challenged, apparently by taking over control, for the most part, of the metals of Mount Tolfa. Caere's huge mound tombs (from the years before 600), sometimes designed to imitate domestic interiors, were equipped with pieces of jewellery imported from Pithecusae or Cumae, which had brought from Syria the gold of which they were made. It is also likely that the Etruscan alphabet first appeared at Caere, after adaptation from the script of the Cumaeans. Pottery was imported from Corinth in quantities rivalled only by Vulci (see below); and fine pots were manufactured and painted at Caere itself, by Greek immigrants (notably Aristonothus, from Euboea, in the later seventh century; and Corinthian artists), as well as by their Etruscan pupils. Caere also became the principal producer of the distinctive Etruscan type of ceramics, black *bucchero*, in its fine or thin-walled form (from *c*.650).[62]

In addition to Tolfa, the Caeritans annexed a hinterland containing picturesque rock-tombs. They also overtook Tarquinii as a sea-power, and joined forces with Carthage to halt the encroachment of Greek colonists from Phocaea and Massalia and Alalia (Aleria in Corsica). In *c*.540/535 the two sides clashed in the naval 'battle of Alalia', by which the Phocaeans, though victorious, were too severely weakened to retain their Alalian colony.[63]

Caere's coastline was studded by five or more ports. One of them was Punicum – to which the Romans later gave this name, presumably because it contained a settlement of Carthaginian traders. Another Caeritan port was Pyrgi (Santa Severa), which possessed a sanctuary of Hera. A Samian is recorded as worshipping her under this Greek name – the designation of his own city-goddess – and not as Uni, her Etruscan equivalent. Ionian artists flocked to Caere and its ports because of the Persian threat to their own country. One Ionian workshop in the city, familiar with Corinthian in addition to its own native pottery, produced a series of water jars (*hydriae*) painted in polychrome by two (?) talented artists in racy and humorous styles, paying unusual attention to human physiognomy (*c*.525–505).

And, above all, it was by a comparable exploitation of Greek influence that Caere developed its school of terracotta sculpture, rivalled only by contemporary Veii. The Married Couple, reclining on a sarcophagus, in Rome's Villa Giulia Museum, epitomizes, with masterly skill, the characteristic Etruscan blend of native and Ionian motifs and ideas. Local sculptors of the time also made fine reliefs, notably a frieze of *c*.525–485 from the Pyrgi sanctuary depicting the battle between the Gods and the Giants in a style somewhat reminiscent of painted Attic vases.

However, the government of Caere was by no means wholly orientated towards the Greeks, since further discoveries at Pyrgi have included three sheets of gold leaf with bilingual Punic and Etruscan inscriptions (*c*.500), recording a dedication by the Caeritan ruler Thefarie Velianas to the Carthaginian (Phoenician and Syrian) goddess Astarte.[64] Hostile relations with Veii later threw his successors into the arms of Rome (see below), whose friendship helped them to establish powerful spheres of influence in Latium and Campania.[65]

Vulci (the Etruscan Velcha) lay north-west of Caere, upon a hill protected by steep cliffs, standing above a loop made by the River Armenta (Fiora) and two of its tributaries six miles from the sea. Flourishing villages united to form a single city in c.700. The Armenta valley provided a route to Mount Amiata and its metals, which provided Vulci with most of its wealth.

The dimensions of these resources are displayed by a huge and prolonged influx of Greek vases, including a quantity of Protocorinthian and Corinthian wares equalled only by Caere. Numerous local imitations were made, and the later sixth century witnessed the establishment of an original school of Caeritan pottery (misnamed 'Pontic'), painted with Greek mythological scenes by Ionian refugees from the Persian occupation of their country. Vulci also produced stone statuary – a fairly rare activity in Etruria, where suitable stone is not abundant – and utilized the Amiata mines to develop the most active bronze-working industry in the country, exporting more of its products to Spina on the Adriatic than any other city of the Etruscan homeland (Chapter 8, section 1). Prosperous towns in the hinterland, dependent on the Vulcentines, proved short-lived, but they possessed a port at Regae or Regis-villa (Le Murelle), not far from the mouth of the Armenta; and it presumably controlled the well-protected trading harbour at Orbetello, now identified as the ancient Calusium.

The Cucumella (c.560–550) outside Vulci, the largest mound-grave in Etruria (measuring over 200 feet in diameter), testifies to the grandeur of the city; and wall-paintings from the François Tomb (c.300) in the Torlonia Museum at Rome offer a glimpse of an entire heroic tradition relating to the city's past. The depiction on this mural frieze, of a Tarquin, slain by a warrior of Vulci, even hints at a time – perhaps in the late sixth century – when soldiers or adventurers from that city may have briefly seized control of Rome. Moreover, Vulci appears to have been the centre of the cult of Aeneas, which passed, directly or indirectly, to the Romans (so that he became the hero of Virgil's epic). Men from Vulci also seem to have played a prominent part in the Etruscan expansion into Campania – employing Rome, perhaps, as a staging point. However, when Etruscan influence in Campania was destroyed by the Samnites in the later fifth century BC, the Vulcentines did not allow this setback to suppress their expansionist enterprises, transferring these to northern Italy instead, where much of the bronze-work and jewellery found in the later stages of the life of Spina came from Vulci or copied its techniques.

Veii (Veio), in south-eastern Etruria (now Lazio), stood on a broad plateau consisting of two ridges and a southern outcrop (the acropolis), protected by steep cliffs rising above the River Cremera (Valchetta) and one of its tributaries. The Cremera, which flowed into the Tiber, was still navigable in ancient times. Early in the first millennium BC the site housed several villages, which coalesced to form a city and city-state during the second half of the eighth century. Veii's location as the southern point of entrance into Etruria, emphasized by an elaborate system of routes radiating outwards from its seven principal gates, prompted the Greek traders at Campanian centres such as Pithecusae and Cumae to utilize the place as an intermediary with other Etruscan cities further north, whose metals the Greeks coveted.[66] Veii did not produce metals on its own account, but no doubt profited from their transit. A substantial revenue was also derived from agricultural production, augmented by skilful irrigation still to be seen in numerous artificial channels (*cuniculi*). A large income also came from the beds of salt (rare in other parts of Etruria) at the mouth of the Tiber.

With the backing of these resources, Veii became, in the course of the sixth century, one of the most important non-Greek centres of Italy. In addition to cemeteries,[67] remains of its residential area (including modest sections) have come to light on an unusual scale. Five temples, too, have been identified; the most impressive of them is a threefold shrine dedicated to Menrva (Athena, Minerva) in the extramural Portonaccio sanctuary (*c*.520–500). Upon the central ridge of its roof were perched large terracotta statues, including the Apulo (Apollo) of Veii, now in the Villa Giulia Museum at Rome. This masterpiece was based on Ionian–Attic artistic models.[68] Like all the best Etruscan statuary, however, it injects an element of its own, alien to Hellenism – an almost brutally dramatic, Etruscan feeling of power and movement, together with a tense roughness that is the sculptor's personal contribution. The statue was perhaps the work of a famous Veientine sculptor, Vulca, or members of his school.

Vulca may also have been active at Rome; and during the Romans' regal period their relations with Veii remained friendly – although the two cities were only twelve miles apart. But after the fall of Rome's Etruscan monarchy (*c*.510/507) competing claims to salt-pans and commercial markets soon led to serious friction, exacerbated by Veii's establishment of an outpost, Fidenae, on the left bank of the Tiber, near the outskirts of Rome itself.

We now come to the more northerly regions of Etruria. Vetulonia (the Etruscan Vetluna or Vatluna), forty-five miles to the north-west of Vulci, stood on hill-spurs rising to 1,130 feet above sea-level, protected by steep cliffs on three sides, and overlooking a bend of the River Bruna and its tributaries. In ancient times, Lake Prilius – now drained, but then a navigable sea-lagoon into which the Bruna and Umbro (Ombrone) discharged – came up close to the walls of Vetulonia. Two separate villages had stood on the site, drawing wealth from their proximity to a fertile territory and, above all, to the copper- and iron-bearing zone of the Massetano, so that the villages, as their resources grew, amalgamated into a city in the seventh century. By that time, when imports from the Greek markets and colonies of Campania were arriving, Vetulonia had developed its own form of circle graves grouped within rings of stones, and subsequently covered with earth mounds. Remains of the habitation centre have come to light, including terracottas from a sixth-century frieze or pediment. Like Vulci, Vetulonia also had its own stone sculpture. But its outstanding art was gold jewellery (displaying a special form of granulation), perhaps partly imported from Pithecusae and Cumae but partly, also, of local fabrication.

The city-state of Vetulonia not only possessed mainland dependencies (for example Marsiliana and Ghiaccio Forte, which did not however outlive the sixth century), but also enjoyed a vigorous maritime existence, fostering contacts with Sardinia, in particular, from an early date through a series of harbours on Lake Prilius. Before 500, however, the place seems to have been partially eclipsed by Rusellae.

Rusellae (Resala in Umbrian; the modern Roselle) stood on a plateau which in ancient times overlooked Lake Prilius – nine miles away from Vetulonia, on the opposite bank – and presided over the fertile valley of the River Umbro (Ombrone) which debouched into the lagoon. The original villages on the spurs were amalgamated on a new site before 600. This settlement was protected by a stone wall, one of the oldest in Etruria, but it was supplemented and replaced, soon afterwards, by more impressive fortifications. Traces of the residential area have also come to light on an unusual scale for an Etruscan city, including dwellings which provide even more evidence than those of Veii for the lives of the poor.

The initial urbanization of Rusellae was probably instigated not by Vulci (despite suggestions to that effect) but by Vetulonia, nine miles away on the other side of the lake. In the later sixth century, however, as we saw, that city may have been outshone (perhaps partly destroyed?) by the people of Rusellae. Even before this, the Rusellans had no doubt exploited the Massetano mining district, and the eclipse of Vetulonia may have placed the metals of the Campigliese under their control.[69] Rusellae possessed one or more harbours on Lake Prilius, at or near Terme di Roselle, in addition to other ports (including, probably, Telamon [Talamone]), as well as dependencies farther away.

Populonia (the Etruscan Fuflun or Pupluna), a coastal town to the north of Vetulonia, was situated on and around a defensible acropolis-promontory which was at that time a peninsula and virtually an island. Two early villages, which had amalgamated before 700, made use of a harbour in a spacious bay (Porto Baratti).

Chamber-tombs of various forms, drawing upon Sardinian models, had appeared by 800 or even earlier. Then, after c.600, came large graves covered by mounds. These contained objects of an increasingly wealthy nature, acquired from the Greek merchants of Pithecusae and Cumae in exchange for the abundant metals of the adjacent Campigliese zone and the island of Ilva (Aethalia, Elba; perhaps Vetalu or Aitale in Etruscan), smelted at Populonia from at least c.750. The interest shown by these traders soon made the Populonians the largest importers of Greek artefacts in the area. The Etruscan deity Fufluns, however (identified with Dionysus), from which the place derived its name, seems to have come from the city of Byblus in Phoenicia, with which Populonia evidently possessed direct or indirect connections.

For a long time the place did not become a city-state on its own account, probably depending not, as a passage of Servius would suggest, on Volaterrae (see below),[70] but on adjacent (and culturally related) Vetulonia. However, Populonia seems to have been one of the first Etruscan centres to issue coinage, though not before 500.

Volaterrae (the Etruscan Velathri, now Volterra) was an inland city farther to the north, situated on a precipitous hill between the Rivers Era – a southern tributary of the Arnus (Arno) – and Caecina (Ceicna in Etruscan, now Cecina). The valley of the Caecina was rich in metals; and it was no doubt the availability of this source of wealth that encouraged a group of villages (already notable for the manufacture of small bronzes) to amalgamate into a single city, at some date before 600. A massive landslide (Le Balze) has destroyed most of the evidence for the early life of the town. But a relief on a gravestone (c.500?) displays a warrior chief Avle Tite, wearing an elaborate coiffure in the near-eastern fashion and carrying a long spear and bow and short sword.

Among a number of other harbours, Volaterrae probably had a port at or near the mouth of the River Caecina. More than most Etruscan cities, however, it tended to look inland, expanding down the valley of the Era and another tributary of the Arnus, the Elsa, and along the Arnus itself (to Faesulae, the Etruscan Vizul, now Fiesole), and beyond its other bank as far north as the basin of the Eridanus (Padus, Po) and Felsina (Bononia, Bologna). Gravestones at Felsina in the form of horseshoes are inscribed with the name of the Ceicna (Caecina) clan, which evidently originated from Volaterrae, since it was named after the Volaterran river and is known to have owned claypits and salt-beds nearby.

Clusium (the Etruscan Clevsin, now Chiusi) lay far in the interior of north-eastern Etruria, situated upon a volcanic plateau above the River Clanis (Chiana; now vanished), of which the valley was cleared and fertilized by extensive drainage. In c.700 these hill villages and others in the neighbour-hood (inhabited by an Italic people, the Umbrians) amalgamated to form a single city. Although Clusium, by reason of its location, was comparatively remote from Greek influences – depending for its prosperity on local agriculture rather than on metals – it became, within a century, the richest and most powerful city-state of the region.

Clusian potters developed a peculiar art form, consisting of large terracotta cremation urns with lids that bore generalized, but arresting, representations of human heads. An early bust of a woman echoes a bizarre mixture of Syrian-influenced Greek prototypes. Clusium also, in the later sixth century, produced distinctive funeral reliefs, adapted loosely from Ionian and then Attic models. In addition, it evolved its own school of black *bucchero* pottery, thick-walled or 'heavy', in contrast to the thin-walled pots of Caere.

The people of Clusium reached the height of their activity and power in the later sixth century, under Lars Porsenna, whose tomb (described in portentous terms by Varro)[71] has not so far been found. Lars Porsenna (whose real name is unknown; both of these designations appear to be titles) was described as 'King of Clusium and Volsinii', an appellation emphasizing his control over the Shrine of Voltumna (near the latter city), which was the religious centre of the Etruscan League.

Volsinii (now Orvieto), Arretium (Arezzo), Cortona (the Etruscan Kurtun) and Perusia (Perugia) all seem to have been established by colonists from Clusium, despite their later pretensions, after each had become an agriculturally prosperous independent state, to impressive, though contradictory, foundation legends invoking heroic Greek origins.[72] A number of these colonizing enterprises can be tentatively attributed to Lars Porsenna, who must have been one of the first rulers to exploit the arrival or manufacture of hoplite arms and armour – after the Greek fashion – in Etruria, where sixth-century archaeological evidence attests their presence.

It was also due, probably, to the initiative of Lars Porsenna that the influence of Clusium achieved an unparalleled twofold expansion, to the north beyond the Apennines and to the south into Campania and Latium.

From an early date certain (unidentifiable) Etruscan city-states, or individuals or groups acting for them or breaking away from their control, had extended their commercial, artistic and perhaps on some occasions political dominance to those fertile and wealthy areas of Italy. In the north, the nucleus of an extensive Etruscan presence had long been Felsina (the Roman Bononia, now Bologna), where a group of villages already existed at the end of the tenth century BC. They prospered owing to their proximity to supplies of iron, and derived profits, also, from contacts with bronze-working areas beyond the Alps, and as far afield as Slovenia.

Influences from the Etruscan homeland were already apparent at Felsina before 700, becoming predominant as the villages amalgamated into a city, which presumably became an independent state. It controlled the Renus (Reno) valley, and its dependency Casalecchio presided over the point where the valley opens out on to the plain. Upon this route to Etruria, late in the sixth century, an additional *emporion* was established at Misa (Marzabotto), in order to supervise the trade moving through the Apennine passes. Other towns in which Etruscans figured prominently included Mantua (Mantova), whose mixed population is illuminatingly analysed in Virgil's *Aeneid*.[73] All these communities conducted trade with two market-towns on the Adriatic coast, Atria and Spina, which were collaborative enterprises of the Etruscans and Greeks (Chapter 8, section 1).

The trade and power of the city-states of Etruria were also extended to territories lying beyond the southern extremity of their country, the River Tiber.

In fertile Campania the focus of Etruscan expansion was Capua (its Etruscan name was Latinized as Volturnum, now Santa Maria Capua Vetere), strategically situated at a crossing-point of the River Volturnus. Etruscan names found on Capuan inscriptions suggest the commercial or colonizing initiative of Volsinii, though Capua no doubt became an independent city-state on its own account. Recent excavations have also confirmed the importance of another Campanian centre, Cales (Calvi), where the first-known Etruscan ruler has been dated to c.640–620. Further to the south-east, a nucleus of Etruscan activity was located beside the Gulf of Salernum (Salerno), including centres at Fratte di Salerno and Picentia (Pontecagnano). Another ancient town, east of Salernum, seems to owe the name Volci, by which it was known to the Romans, to visitors or colonists from Vulci.[74] Dionysius of Halicarnassus refers to Etruscans from 'near the Ionian Gulf' (Atria, Spina?) invading Greek Campania in 525/524.[75]

In order to maintain their Campanian connections by land as well as by sea, the Etruscans needed to exercise some control over the intervening territories of Latium. Indeed the cultures of the governing classes of Etruria and Latium, at certain times and places, were virtually indistinguishable, except that the Latins, under Etruscan rule, mostly continued to speak their own Indo-European language.

This remained the case, for example, at Rome, which nevertheless, for part of the seventh century, and almost the whole of the sixth, came under the rule of the Etruscans, and was Etruscanized to a considerable extent. King Tarquinius Priscus (traditionally 616–579) appears to have come from Tarquinii, in which his Greek father Demaratus had settled on arrival from Corinth as a political refugee.[76] Priscus evidently governed Rome as an independent state. The expulsion of his son or grandson Tarquinius Superbus was said to have been the event that inaugurated the Roman Republic (c.510/507), although short periods of control by Vulci and Clusium cannot be excluded.

Throughout this time, however, Greek as well as Etruscan pottery and other artistic influences continued to reach Rome, partly, no doubt, by way of Etruscan intermediaries, but also through Latian (Latin) and Phoenician middle-men, and by direct trading as well. Thus shrines at S. Omobono near the river, dating from c.600–575 but rebuilt in c.500, have yielded finds of Euboean, Pithecusan, Corinthian and Cycladic pottery of eighth-century date.[77] The architectural terracottas of the temples, which were dedicated (at least later) to Fortuna and Mater Matuta; are of the east Greek style, and Greek artists, merchants and artisans probably resided around the city's river-port. Moreover, the temple of Diana on the Aventine Hill, which overlooked the wharves, and reputedly owed its construction to King Servius Tullius (c.578–535), was apparently inaugurated under the influence of Massalia, and contained – from what date we do not know – a statue resembling the image of Ephesian Artemis, whom the Massalians revered. Likewise, Hercules Victor, worshipped at his ancient altar (Ara Maxima) below the northern end of the Aventine, was an Italian version of the Greek Heracles, god of traders, who may have become known via the Latian city of Tibur (Tivoli).

There is a strong case for believing that, after the fall of Rome's Etruscan monarchy, further cults that appeared during the first decade of the fifth century were borrowed, directly or indirectly, from the Greeks, but now without Etruscan intermediaries. Thus a shrine of Ceres, Liber and Libera (c.493) was said to have been decorated by the Greek sculptors and painters Damophon and Gorgasus[78] and this divine triad represented the Greek deities

Demeter, Iacchus and Kore, and not an Etruscan trinity. Further Greek imports to Rome included Mercury (Hermes – god of merchants like Hercules, introduced at a time of grain shortage); and Saturn (worshipped with head uncovered like the Greek Cronus). Castor and Pollux (Polydeuces), too – reputedly worshipped (from c.484?) as a thanksgiving for victory over the Latins at Lake Regillus (c.496) – are described on an inscription from Lavinium, of about that period, by the Greek designation of *quroi* (*kouroi* – the *Dios kouroi*, sons of Zeus).[79]

Similar Greek contacts could be listed at other Latian cities as well. And yet in these centres, as at Rome, Etruria, too, exercised a strong influence during the same period. The considerable number of sites which display such connections include Alba Longa, Ardea and Politorium. And at Praeneste (Palestrina), in particular, an initial burst of wealth before 700 was followed by tombs of the following century containing artefacts which cannot be distinguished, in style, from grave-finds in the city-states of Etruria itself.

There and elsewhere in Latium the leading part among those states of the Etruscan homeland, in promoting commercial and cultural contact and perhaps undertaking actual colonization, seems to have been played by Caere, whose king Mezentius was reported, according to tradition, to have reduced the people of the territory to tributary status;[80] although it cannot be excluded that Lars Porsenna of Clusium, too, if he took Rome, may have exercised control over other Latian towns as well.

The Etruscan city-states, as independent powers, were already declining at the end of the sixth century. After Aristodemus of Cumae had destroyed an Etruscan invasion of Campania in c.525/524, Lars Porsenna's son Arruns was killed at Aricia (Ariccia) by a coalition of Latins and Campanian Greeks (c.505). The fifth and fourth centuries witnessed the successive collapses of the various nuclei of Etruscan power.[81]

CHRONOLOGICAL TABLES*

1 THE GREEK LANDS

CENTRAL AND NORTHERN GREECE (*Chapters 2, 4*)

12th-early 9th cent.	Lefkandi (Lelantum) flourished
1050	Cremation becomes common
1050/1025–700	Athenian Protogeometric and Geometric pottery in lead
900(?)	Unification of much of Attica
8th cent.	Colonization by Chalcis in west and market at Al Mina (later colonies in Chalcidice); Phoenician alphabet borrowed
late 8th cent.	Hesiod
late 8th or 7th cent.	Delphi's Panhellenic fame
700	Lelantine war between Chalcis and Euboea
683/682 or 682/681(?)	Annual archonships at Athens
mid-7th cent.	Hymn to Apollo (Delphi, Delos)
675	Subjection of Eleusis to Athens
632	*Coup* of Cylon at Athens
late 7th cent.	Athenian black-figure pottery in lead
late 7th cent.(?)	Aleuads of Larissa become *tagoi* of Thessalian League
end 7th cent.	Phrynon seizes Sigeum for Athens
595/590	Aegina's turtle coinage
595–583	First Sacred War (Delphi)
586/585 or 582/581	Pythian Games at Delphi
6th cent.	Solon, Pisistratids and Cleisthenes at Athens
555	Miltiades the elder (Athenian) in Thracian Chersonese
540/530	Final subjection of Salamis to Athens
540	Boeotians (Thebans) defeat Thessalians
534	First Attic tragedy: Thespis
530	Athenian red-figure pottery in lead
520	First Athena-owl coinage at Athens

*Very many dates are approximate

576	Miltiades the younger (Athenian) in Thracian Chersonese
519	Athenians and Boeotians at war over Plataea
506	Athenians defeat Boeotians and Chalcidians; then 'Heraldless War' against Aegina
499–498	Athens and Eretria help Ionian revolt
493	Themistocles archon at Athens

THE PELOPONNESE (*Chapter 3*)

1075/1050	Dorian invasions and immigrations at height
9th–8th cent.	Argos the earliest centre of power in Peloponnese
776	Olympic Games
747	Corinthian monarchy ends
740/730–720/710	Sparta's First Messenian War
733	Corinthians colonize Corcyra and Syracuse
8th cent.	Biremes at Corinth
725/700	Hoplite armour at Argos
late 8th cent.–550	Protocorinthian and Corinthian pottery in lead
7th cent.(?)	Triremes at Corinth
early 7th cent.(?)	Pheidon of Argos
685–657	Megarians colonize Calchedon and Byzantium
669	Argives defeat Spartans at Hysiae
664 or later	Corinthians defeated by Corcyraeans off Sybota
658–581	Cypselid dictatorship ('tyranny') at Corinth
655–555	Orthagorid dictatorship at Megara
650–620	Sparta's Second Messenian War
7th cent.(?)	Sparta's politico-social system (*agoge*)
590/580	Tegeans defeat Spartans
581	Isthmian Games
573	Nemean Games of Panhellenic status
572	Elis takes over Olympic Games from Pisa
570	Corinth's 'colt' coinage
560–550	Laconian (Spartan) vase-paintings at height
556/555	Chilon ephor at Sparta
by mid 6th cent.	Peloponnesian league under Sparta
546	Battle of Champions between Sparta and Argos at Thyrea
519–490/488	King Cleomenes I at Sparta
494	Spartans defeat Argives at Sepeia

THE EASTERN AND CENTRAL AEGEAN (*Chapter 5*)

1150–after 1000	Migrants settle in Cyclades, Ionia and Aeolis
10th cent.	Settlement of Smyrna (wall by 850)
900	Dorians found three cities on Rhodes (also Pentapolis in Asia Minor)
750/700	Homer

734	Naxians colonize Naxos, earliest Greek colony in Sicily
700	Temple of Artemis at Delos rebuilt
675/650	Cimmerians plunder Artemisium at Ephesus
660	Samian Heraeum rebuilt
7th cent.–550	Delos under Naxian control
7th–6th cent.	Large-scale statues at Naxos and Paros
mid 7th cent.	Hymn to Apollo (Delos, Delphi)
mid 7th cent.	Parians colonize Thasos
mid 7th cent.	Archilochus of Paros
7th cent.	Semonides of Amorgos (from Samos)
640/638	Colaeus of Samos at Tartessus
600(?) and 560–550	Artemisium at Ephesus rebuilt
600	Thrasybulus dictator of Miletus
early 6th cent.(?)	Mimnermus of Colophon
590	Pittacus 'arbitrator' at Mitylene; Alcaeus and Sappho
6th cent.	Thales, Anaximander, Anaximenes at Miletus; Heraclitus at Ephesus
565	Phocaeans colonize Alalia (Corsica)
mid-6th cent.	Expedition of Midacritus (probably Phocaean) to west
546	Ionia under Persian control; Xenophanes and Pythagoras leave Colophon (545) and Samos (531) respectively
540/535	Battle of Alalia: Phocaeans against Carthaginians and Caeretans
540–522	Polycrates dictator of Samos
500	Hecataeus at Miletus
499–494	Ionian revolt: battle of Lade 495, sack of Miletus 494, destruction of Naxos 490

THE SOUTH AND EAST* (*Chapter 6*)

1000–800	Syro-Phoenician settlement of Cyprus
850/800	Greek trading stations at Al Mina, Posidium, Paltus
late 9th cent.	Metal-workers from north Syria and Phoenicia in Crete
8th cent.	*Iliad* and *Odyssey* indicate 90 – 100 cities in Crete: Cnossus and Gortyna in lead
725–700	Temple at Drerus in Crete
709–612	Cyprus under Assyrian control
700–675	Destruction of Al Mina
7th cent.	Cretan sculptor Daedalus and poet and law giver Thaletas

*For eastern kingdoms and empires see the second Chronological Table

660	Ionian soldiers in Nile delta: settle at Naucratis and elsewhere
632	Therans colonize Cyrene under Aristoteles Battus I
later 7th cent.	Laws of Drerus in Crete
by 600	Cyrenaeans colonize Apollonia and Euhesperides
early 6th cent.	Al Mina rebuilt
588, 552	Paltus destroyed
583, 552	Baltus II Eudaemon enlarges Cyrene, defeats Apries at Irasa 570
570/526	Naucratis becomes major treaty port
from 560	Arcesilaus II the Cruel at Cyrene: defeated and killed by Libyans
early 560s, 545	Cyprus under Egyptian then Persian control
560–525	Euelthon king of Salamis in Cyprus
535/530	Arcesilaus III at Cyrene, murdered 520/515, widow Pheretime recovers Barca from Egypt
520	New town at Al Mina under Persian suzerainty
520	Cypriot city-kings initiate coinage
514–512	Western expedition of Dorieus from Cyrene fails
499–497	Cypriot risings to support Ionian revolt
480/450	Gortyna code (Crete) embodying earlier laws

THE WEST* (*Chapter 7*)

775–770	Trading station at Pithecusae (Euboeans), then Cumae (750)
8th cent.	Greeks and Phoenicians in Sicily
750/725	Cumaeans and Euboeans colonize Zande
734/733	Chalcidians colonize Naxos (Sicily) and Corinthians colonize Syracuse
730/710	Chalcidians colonize Rhegium and Achaeans colonize Sybaris, then Croton
706	Spartans colonize Taras
690/688	Rhodians and Cretans colonize Gela
679 or 673	Locrians colonize Locri Epizephyrii
663	Law-giver Zaleucus at Locri Epizephyrii
648	Zancleans colonize Himera
628	Megaran Hyblaeans colonize Selinus
625/600	Sybarites colonize Posidonia
600	Phocaeans colonize Massalia (Marseille)
600	Cumaeans colonize Neapolis (Naples)
600/575	Massalians colonize Emporiae
early 6th cent.	Stesichorus at Himera
575	Temple of Apollo at Syracuse
570–554/549	Phalaris dictator ('tyrant') at Akragas

*For the Etruscans see Appendix 3

565	Phocaeans colonize Alalia (Corsica)
mid-6th cent.	Bronze Vix crater (M. Lassois, Seine)
545	Xenophanes moves to Zancle and Catana from Colophon
540(?)	Locrians and Rhegians defeat Crotoniates on R. Sagra
540/535	Battle of Alalia
531	Pythagoras moves to Croton from Samos
525/524	'Long March' by Etruscans and others against Cumae
515	Birth of Parmenides at Elea
510	Crotoniates destroy Sybaris
later 6th cent.	Earliest work of Epicharmus of Syracuse
later 6th cent.	Construction of Temple of Olympian Zeus initiated at Selinus
later 6th cent. or after 500	Physician Alcmaeon at Croton
498–491/490	Hippocrates dictator at Gela, 492 defeats Syracuse on R. Helorus

THE NORTH (*Chapter 8*)

756	Trading-post at Sinope founded by Milesians
733	Corcyra colonized by Corinthians
early 7th cent.	Torone and Acanthus 655, (with others) colonized by Chalcidians
685, 657	Calchedon and Byzantium colonized by Megarians
680/652	Abydus and Cyzicus (679) and Istrus (657) colonized by Milesians
664 or later	Corcyraeans defeat Corinthians off Sybota
654	Lampsacus colonized by Phocaeans
before 650	Maronea colonized by Chians
650	Thasos colonized by Parians
647	Olbia (later Berezan) colonized by Milesians, etc
640	Perdiccas I of Macedonia moves capital from Lebaea to Aegae
631	Sinope colonized by Milesians
625	Epidamnus colonized by Corinthians and Corcyraeans
625/600	Tanais(?) and Panticapaeum colonized by Milesians
	Potidaea colonized by Corinthians
end 7th cent.	Sigeum seized by Phrynon for Athens
early 6th cent.	Hermonassa colonized by Milesians
580	Temple of Artemis at Corcyra
560/558	Heraclea Pontica colonized by Megarians, Boeotians and Milesians(?)

326

560s, 525/520	Greco-Etruscan settlements at Atria and Spina (N. E. Italy)
555	Thracian Chersonese occupied by Miltiades the elder (Athenian)
545	Abdera recolonized and Phanagoria colonized by Teians
6th cent.	Pitys, Dioscurias, Phasis colonized or given trading stations by Milesians
520	Thracian Chersonese occupied by Miltiades the younger (Athenian)
513–512	Thracian–Scythian expedition of Darius I of Persia
512	Amyntas I of Macedonia becomes Persian vassal
494	Calchedon destroyed by the Persians

2 THE GREEKS AND THEIR EASTERN NEIGHBOURS

BC

THE GREEKS IN GENERAL

2000–1900	Greece invaded from the North (beginning of Middle Helladic of Middle Bronze Age)
after 1600	Greece increasingly under Cretan (Minoan) influence
1400–1200	Mycenaean civilization at height
1250	Supposed capture of Troy by Greeks
late 13th and early 12th cent.	Destruction of Mycenaean and other civilizations
1100–1050	Sub-Mycenaean pottery
11th cent.	Early Iron Age
1075–1000	Dorian invasions and immigrations
1050–900	Migrations of Ionians, Aeolians and Dorians to western Asia Minor and islands
1025–900	Protogeometric, 900–700 Geometric pottery
900–750	Creation of city-states. Replacement of monarchic by aristocratic governments
776	Traditional date of first Olympic (Panhellenic) Games
750–700	First surviving epic poems
8th–7th cent.	Colonization under way
8th–7th cent.	Orientalizing art
8th cent.	Biremes
750–650	Major development of metallurgy
750	Adoption of alphabet
late 8th cent.	Hoplite revolution
700	Lelantine War between Chalcis and Eretria
700–675	First Doric temples
early 7th cent.	First surviving lyric poems

early 7th cent.	'Daedalic' statuettes
after 700	Samnian Heraeum rebuilt (Ephesian Artemisium after 660)
7th or 6th cent.	Triremes
675–500	Age of dictators ('tyrants'); often replaced by oligarchies
7th cent	First law-givers
shortly before 650	First large-scale statuary
late 7th cent.	First Greek coinages
from late 7th cent.	Black-figure pottery
early/mid-6th cent.	First 'Pre-Socratic philosophers'
mid-6th cent.	Peloponnesian League
from 546	Persian conquest of Ionia (revolt 499–494)
from 530	Red-figure pottery

BABYLONIA AND ASSYRIA

1365–1250	First Assyrian Empire
1116–1076	Tiglath-Pileser I of Assyria
911–745	Assyrian Revival (Ashurnasirpal II 884–859, Shalmaneser III 859–824)
745–612	Second Assyrian Empire (Tiglath-Pileser III 745–727, Sargon II 722–705, defeat of Urartu 714, Sennacherib 705–681, destruction of Babylon 689, Esarhaddon 681–669, conquest of Egypt 671, Ashurbanipal 669–630)
626–539	New Babylonian Empire (Nabopolassar 626–605, destruction of Nineveh 612, Nebuchadrezzar II 605–562, Nabonidus 556–539)
539	Babylonia conquered by the Persians

SYRIA AND PHOENICIA

13th and 12th cent.	Invasions by Peoples of the Sea, Philistines and Hebrews
11th–8th cent.	Aramaeans occupy much of northern Syria
1000	Rise of the Phoenician city-states. (Tyre takes lead over Sidon by 750). Phoenicians transform syllabic scripts into alphabet. Also city-states in northern Syria combining Aramaean, neo-Hittite and Hurrian traditions)
814	Traditional foundation-date of Phoenician colony at Carthage. Also colonies in Cyprus and southern Spain, western Sicily and Sardinia.
9th–8th cent.	Urartu borders upon and dominates the Syrian principalities. Greek coastal markets at Al Mina, Posidium and Paltus.
850–612	Assyrian conquest
605–539	New Babylonian Empire

539–332   Persian conquest

NON-GREEK ASIA MINOR

1450–1200   Hittite empire (Hurrians defeated 1350)
1250   Supposed capture of Troy by Greeks
1200   Phrygians destroy Hittite empire
850–676   Historic Phrygian kingdom (Midas 738–696)
705–637/626   Occupation of Asia Minor by Cimmerians
from 687   Kingdom of Lydia (Gyges 685–657, Ardys 652–625)
625–610   Introduction of coinage by Lydians (under Sadyattes 625–615 or Alyattes 617–560)
560–546   Reign of Croesus in Lydia
546   Conquest of Lydia by Persians

EGYPT

730–715   24th Dynasty (capital at Sais). Kings Tefnakhte and Boccheris (Bakenrenef, 720–715)
730–656   25th Dynasty: Dynasty of Napata or Ethiopian or Cushite Dynasty. Esarhaddon of Assyria captures Memphis 671.
664–525   26th Dynasty: the Saite Age. Necho I, Psammetichus (Psamtik) I, Necho II, Psammetichus II, Apries (Hophra), Amasis (Ahmose) II, Psammetichus III. Use of Greek and other foreign mercenaries and foundation of Naucratis etc
525–404   27th Dynasty: Persian rule after conquest of Egypt by Cambyses

PERSIA

650–550   Kingdom of Media (Cyaxares 625–585). Medes and Persians sack Nineveh 612
550–330   Persian empire
560/559–530   Cyprus II the Great. Conquest of Media, Lydia (546), Ionia and Babylonia (539)
530–522   Cambyses II. Conquest of Egypt (525)
521–486   Darius I. Intervention at Cyrene (515) Thracian–Scythean expedition (513–512), Ionian Revolt (499–494)

NOTES

INTRODUCTION

1 Gellius, *Attic Nights*, XIX, 815.
2 Herodotus, VIII, 144.
3 A modern distinction has been made between wholly Greek lands, substantially Greek lands, and 'non-contiguous Greek dots in an alien world'. But (1) in a number of lands which such a distinction would regard as 'wholly' Greek, i.e. territories of the Greek mainland, there were still large substrata of pre-Greek, non-Greek inhabitants; (2) 'non-contiguous dots' included some of the most important Greek centres ('contiguous' enough by sea if not by land). In this category were the city-states of the northern coast of the Black Sea, gradually becoming known today from Soviet excavation reports. Their significance, like that of 'Great Greece' (south Italy) and Sicily, contradicts any suggestion that the Greek genius can be found only in 'lands washed by the Aegean Sea'.
4 Classification problems are raised by the uncertain origins of a few writers – most notably Homer who, despite famous and ancient doubts, seems to have worked principally on the island of Chios, and certainly belongs to that area. A second difficulty, for the organizer of early Greek history on geographical lines, is presented by the authors and artists who moved from place to place. In dealing with the later, 'classical' period, this would have become so widespread a problem that the material would have to be organized in some different way. But

in this earlier age the problem applies seriously only to about half a dozen of the most significant writers, and I have anchored them to the places where they exercised the greatest impact (e.g. Pythagoras of Samos is described under Croton, Anacreon of Teos and Ibycus of Rhegium under Samos, Alcman of Lydia (?) under Sparta, Xenophanes of Colophon under Zancle). As for sculptors, they may have travelled to the sites of their commissions with a marble block or even a roughed-out statue, but their work usually, at this epoch, continued to reflect the styles of their places of origin.

CHAPTER 1 The Early Greeks

1 These Indo-European-speaking 'proto-Greek' peoples spread in the course of many centuries from their original home between the Caspian and the lower Borysthenes (Dnieper) into India, Iran and Europe. When they entered Greece they were probably accompanied by other immigrants from the Balkans.
2 'Linear B' employed eighty-eight symbols to express the various combinations of consonants and vowels required by the Mycenaean form of what later became the Greek language, together with ideograms designed to help express the sense of the word.
3 The collapse of Mycenae meant the abandonment of communal burials and large chamber tombs in favour of simple individual tombs (in cists,

pits, jars), and the gradual replacement of inhumation by cremation.

4 The later Greeks had no memory of a Dark Age break (or of a Mycenaean civilization different from their own); instead they imagined a thoroughly Greek heroic age, represented by Mycenae and Pylos, as ancestral to themselves.

5 For example, a recent argument suggests that, since various 'Linear B' texts can perhaps be divided between upper-class and lower-class idioms, the Dorians had already been present earlier as the serfs of the Mycenaeans – and that, in consequence, Dorian invasions never took place.

6 They were said to have crossed the Gulf of Corinth from Naupactus to Rhium in Achaea (northern Peloponnese), and then to have divided into different immigrant groups, notably those that settled in the Argolid (Argos) and Laconia (Sparta).

7 One of the three Dorian tribes was known as the Hylleis (after Heracles' son Hyllus). The others were the Dymaneis (a north-western tribal name) and the Pamphyloi ('of mixed tribal groups').

8 The old classification of Greek dialects into Ionian, Doric and Aeolic now requires amendment. Misleadingly linked to supposed sub-divisions of the Greek 'race', it cannot, in fact, represent *pre-existing* racial differences, since distinctions of dialect become perceptible only after 1200 BC, when they are produced by the isolation of small communities separated by mountains and the sea (by the fifth and sixth centuries a sort of racial consciousness separating Dorians and Ionians had been artificially prompted by political, social, religious and linguistic differences).

9 Pottery figures largely in all books that refer to Greek artistic development. That is because (1) so much of it has survived, unlike e.g. sculpture (most of the extant examples of which belong to a later period); (2) Greek pottery was much more important than its counterparts today, fulfilling the combined modern roles of porcelain, glass, wood, leather and basketry; (3) in consequence, it attracted the services of outstanding painters – all early wall-paintings, except in alien but Greek-influenced Etruria (Appendix 3), have vanished. Since Greece was not a luxurious country, these painters were called upon to provide the decoration which no gold or silver vessels were available to supply (except in non-Greek Thrace and Scythia – Appendix 2). These painters enjoyed an artistic freedom denied to convention-bound sculptors, and their choice of themes reflected common ground between the various classes of Greek society.

10 Thucydides, III, 3. Aristotle, *Politics*, I, 7, 1252b, stresses the importance of villages in this evolving structure.

11 Also the Macedonians, Phocians, Locrians, Aetolians, Acarnanians, Achaeans, Arcadians.

12 There may have been eventually 1,500 city-states in the Greek world, of which more than 600 are known. The smallness of some of them can be illustrated by the island of Ceos (Kea). Measuring fifteen miles by eight, it included four such states (three of which eventually issued their own coins). There were three on another small island, Amorgos. Not more than a few dozen cities can have had a population of more than 10,000.

13 It cannot be determined whether the Mycenaeans possessed virtual city-states (as has been argued), or whether Syrian and Phoenician city-states extended citizenship to their free populations. Walled towns of central Europe (such as Heuneburg on the upper Danube) may have possessed certain features characteristic of a city-state.

14 The *oikos* was originally a monogamous nuclear family, but Greek writers tended to identify it with a wider economic unit. The *genos* (not always recognized as an early legal entity) was originally restricted to the nobility, consisting of men who could trace their pedigree back to a

common ancestor, though non-kinsmen, too, were admitted before long. Phratries (perhaps derived from aristocratic warrior bands) included dependants of the *gene*. For these institutions see further under Athens (Chapter 2, section 1).

15 A man who lived in the Attic countryside was as much an 'Athenian' as was a resident of Athens. Citizenship was closely bound up with ownership of land. In considering rural populations, however, the frontiers of city-states, it must be borne in mind, were in many cases not firmly determined until at least the seventh century BC, and not always by then. Each farm, district and region hoped to grow and make nearly all it needed, although this expectation usually proved unrealizable. Greece possessed a modest sufficiency of adequate farming land, producing wheat and especially barley (its staple food, in the form of bread and porridge), supplemented by salted fish, cheese, honey, figs and wine. Vineyards are known in the sixth century and presumably go back to the seventh, and the same applies to olive groves, producing oil which was used for lighting, cleaning, cosmetics, religious rites and subsequently cooking. Yet less than one-fifth of the total surface of the homeland was cultivable, and despite 300 days of sunshine every year the climate is intemperate, offering extremes of heat and cold, and violent winter and summer winds. Greek city-states in other regions, however, often had to endure much harsher climatic conditions.

16 Herodotus, VII, 102, 1.

17 To Aristotle (*Politics*, I, 1, 8, 1252b) man was a *politikon zoon*, a being destined by nature to live in a *polis*. 'The *polis* came into existence for survival; it continues to exist for the good life.'

18 Aristotle, *Politics*, III, 9, 7, 1285b (he believed that Greek civilization had descended from the Mycenaean age by direct continuity – cf. above, note 4). The Homeric picture, which may correspond approximately to

eighth-century practice, is of local single 'kings' (*basileis*) but also occasionally of collective leadership: in Scheria, the mythical land of the Phaeacians, there were other 'sceptred kings' besides Alcinous (Homer, *Odyssey*, VII, 41). Monarchs were not, presumably, liable to any formal institutional restraint from the elders of their council or from their shadowy assembly, but could not neglect the force of convention and custom.

19 E.g. the Neleidae of Miletus – and others in western Asia Minor. The gradual breakdown of royal powers, where these had existed, probably began quite early, in c.1100, and, apart from a few centres, monarchy was rapidly on the wane between the tenth and eighth centuries.

20 Aristotle, *Politics*, IV, 3, 2, 1289b (i.e. states whose strength lay in their cavalry).

21 Homer, *Iliad*, II, 53.

22 Pseudo-Plato, *Epinomis*, 987d.

23 Corinthian wares, like Attic later on, were favoured by traders from other Greek cities as well, because of their high technical and artistic quality.

24 After the smiths of Asia Minor had acquired the (not very easy) techniques of forging iron during the last centuries of the Hittite empire (Appendices, note 19), iron-working was learned by the Greeks in the twelfth or eleventh century, probably from continued contact with Cyprus (shortage of bronze had been the initial incentive; its employment, when available, never flagged). The first iron to be employed by the Greeks was of eastern (not northern) origin (cf. the tradition of the Chalybes – Chapter 8, section 3); Greek sources were Attica (first?), Laconia, Euboea and the Cyclades. Once the techniques had been mastered, iron was cheaper and more abundant than bronze; it was also heavier, though its edges were less sharp, until iron could be tempered into steel (at some date before the fifth century BC).

25 A twofold or threefold or even sevenfold multiplication of population during the eighth century

has been claimed, though doubts are expressed about the highest of these estimates.

26 Cf. Amphis, fragment 17: 'land is the father of life to man: land alone knows how to cover up poverty'.

27 Plato, *Phaedo*, 109B.

28 Sophocles, *Antigone*, 334–7.

29 Aristotle, *Politics*, I, 3, 23, 1258b; Plutarch, *Solon*, 2; Herodotus, II, 167; cf. Thucydides, I, 2, 2; and (for Socrates) Xenophon, *Oeconomicus*, IV, 3.

30 Plato, *Laws*, 626a. In *c*.220 BC the people of the Cretan city-state of Drerus were required to swear an oath that 'they would do all manner of harm to the people of Lyttus', their neighbours. W.Dittenberger, *Sylloge Inscriptionum Graecarum*, 3rd edn., 527.

31 Homer, *Iliad*, XI, 784f.; cf. Chapter 5, section 1.

32 In a late-eighth-century Attic vase a rider is shown wearing the new metal breastplate and leading a second horse behind him, and many seventh- and sixth-century vase-paintings (mainly Attic and Corinthian) show mounted hoplites riding into battle with squires, or depict squires waiting while their masters fought. It is generally believed that pre-hoplite aristocrats rode to battle but dismounted to fight. Some maintain that cavalry was the striking arm in the first recorded struggle between city-states, the Lelantine War fought by Chalcis against Eretria (*c*.700). (Homer no longer understood the Bronze Age military use of the chariot, which he treated as a transport vehicle.)

33 Heavier armour appears from *c*.750, close fighting by *c*.700, full equipment by *c*.700/675 (or some prefer later dates). A few passages of Homer's *Iliad* (IV, 422–43; XIII, 130ff.; XVI, 212ff.) indicate warfare by disciplined infantry forces. The first examples of developed hoplite (phalanx) warfare are in the Peloponnese, e.g. perhaps Argos' defeat of Sparta in 669. Mercenaries trained in phalanx discipline appear in Egypt, *c*.664 – though some, instead, ascribe the earliest use of

these tactics to the Battle of the Champions at Thyrea between the Spartans and Argives, *c*.545. The Spartans became the acknowledged masters of this type of warfare. The dedication of bronze cauldrons at Olympia (note 44 below) came to an end in the seventh century because the metal was needed for hoplite armour. A new type of composite breastplate came into use in *c*.630. (There were also Greek soldiers of the period [notably Cretans – Chapter 6, section 1] who could use the bow, sling and throwing javelin.) On the face of it, a battle formation such as the phalanx seemed at variance with the Greek terrain, since it could prove efficient only on relatively level ground. But it was for such ground that it was intended, i.e. the enemy's level agricultural plain, since few states could endure two years' or even one year's devastation of their crops: to save these a besieged foe, in desperation, would have to come out of its city and fight.

34 Aristotle, *Politics*, III, 5, 3, 1279b.

35 Crete, Cyprus, Melos, Thera, Rhodes, Sparta (Cythera), Thebes and Delphi have also been claimed (besides Euboea) as possible points of transmission. The oldest inscription in the Greek alphabet so far recorded is a hexameter on an Attic vase (the Dipylon *oinochoe*) of *c*.740/725. (There may have been an earlier period in which the Phoenician alphabet was accepted without change – or with preliminary adaptations unknown to us.) The Greeks assigned to each letter not its familiar Semitic sound, but a sound familiar to themselves, by vocalizing the initial with which the name they allotted to the letter began (alpha, beta, etc. – the acrophonic method). Letters derived from Semitic glottal stops, and breathings, were employed to signify vowel sounds, and a few new consonants were also added. Archaic Greek inscriptions often run *boustrophedon* (Pausanias, V, 17, 6), i.e. in cattle-track fashion like a team ploughing, with one line from left to right and the next from right to left (in Thera the oldest inscriptions

are from right to left; others run the other way, or both ways). The Ugaritic language (a north-west Semitic tongue of the late Bronze Age spoken at Ras Shamra) was mostly written from left to right, Phoenician (like Hebrew) in the opposite direction. For other semitic scripts, see Appendices, note 17.

36 Alphabets incised on pottery from the late eighth century indicate the spread of literacy. Previously Greek education, such as it was, had been more physical than intellectual (the *paidotribes*, 'boys' coach', concentrated on sports), and more musical than literary, but the diffusion of the alphabet produced the *grammatistes*, who taught children to read and write.

37 Greek theorists believed that the *polis* had originated from the desire for justice (*dike*), which was needed because individuals are lawless.

38 The 'foot' is derived from the dance with which Greek poetry was intimately connected. A foot consisted of a pattern of long and short syllables, i.e. possessed a quantitative rhythm (in contrast to the stress accent of our own poetry, in which syllables are not long or short, but stressed or unstressed). The accent on ancient Greek words was related to musical tone or pitch, but the relation between pitch and stress is obscure; the accented syllable of a word often seems to have been pitched higher than those that are unaccented. The pitch of the language was seen to relate it closely to music (see also note 40). The dactyl–spondee variation of the Greek hexameter means that it can contain between twelve and seventeen syllables, thus achieving a length and complexity that are unusual in the heroic verse of other literatures.

39 E.g. monody ('Linus Song'); and choral songs including dirge, paean (song to Apollo, said to have been brought to Corinth by the Lesbian Arion, with Dionysus' dithyramb), wedding song, maiden song and mimed song (*hyporchema*).

40 Our understanding of extant parts of Greek lyric poetry is reduced by our ignorance of the complex rhythmical techniques of its accompaniments, music and dance (already imperfectly known in Hellenistic times; only a few specimens of musical notation have survived, although the forms and capacities of instruments are clearer). Ancient Greek music employed a large number of scales or modes (classified, in due course, as Phrygian, Lydian, Lesbian, Dorian, Ionian, etc.), which differed from one another in the sequence of their intervals and probably in the range of their tones. The Greeks invested each mode with its own distinctive emotional and moral associations. There was no harmony. How the music sounded is guesswork; we should have found it unfamiliar.

41 Literally, poetry accompanied by the lyre. We use the term chiefly, instead, for short, personal, intensely felt poems. Plutarch (*Consolation to Apollonius* [*Moralia*, II] 34, 120C, *Whether the Athenians*, etc. [*Moralia*, IV] 5, 348B) employs the term *melic*, which can be applied generally to solo or choral song other than elegiac or iambic.

42 Divination was by clanging pots or gongs, rustling leaves, warbling doves, running waters, and reflecting mirrors. For the procedures at Delphi, and its prestige, see Chapter 4, section 2. The worship of Greek deities was accompanied by the questioning of oracles and prophets, and a soothsayer went with Homer's Greek army to Troy, although city-states often left such enquiries to individuals (such as the founders of colonies and traders). There were many literary anecdotes about the deceptive obscurity of oracles – inscrutable, opaque and understood too late, reflecting the ambiguous bafflement of human contacts with divinity. In many cases, however, the questions that were asked them were practical and down-to-earth, and were answered in a similar vein. Belief in oracles remained widespread.

43 Plato, *Laws*, II, 653d.

44 There were two successive types of these objects: (1) 'tripod' cauldrons on three metal legs (decorated by Geometric, occasionally figure, reliefs), with two large ring-handles often supported by human images and crowned by the figure of a horse, (2) cauldrons on tall, conical, pyramidal stands, with ring-handles held by human-headed birds (sirens), between which protruded long-necked bronze griffin heads (first hammered and then cast). The lively, alert, three-dimensional sirens' faces, and the serpentine elegance of the griffins' heads, point the way towards the Greek sculpture of future epochs. Out of forty-nine noted examples of this type of cauldron, thirty-seven were made in the near east and the remainder were Greek adaptations.

45 The innumerable local shrines of heroes (*heroa*) may have meant more than any of the temples of Olympian deities to individual worshippers, although Homer and Hesiod ignore them. Heracles (see Argos, Chapter 3, section 1) was a universally revered hero, but most were of primarily local concern (including the founders of colonies, who were posthumously elevated to this status). The dead persons or legendary figures thus honoured by shrines were not always heroes known to the *Iliad* and *Odyssey*. Nevertheless, those poems clarified the concept of the hero, and although some such cults may have originated in the earliest Dark Ages or previously, they received a stimulus in the eighth century because (1) at that time the two poems were becoming widely diffused and known, (2) in c.725 Mycenaean graves were reopened and their dead given worship, under the impulse of the poems and of the Epic Cycle in general.

46 For the difference between chthonian (fertility) cults and Olympian religion cf. Plato, *Laws*, IV, 717a (although Dionysus and Demeter belong to both categories). Homer virtually ignored the former (like the local heroic shrines – see last note),

because he was not writing for such parochial, agricultural communities but for a more cosmopolitan aristocracy. There were two kinds of promised immortality: (1) rebirth or reincarnation in a chain or cycle of lives (cf. Pythagoras, Chapter 7, section 2), (2) otherworldly bliss. 'Mystery' comes from *muein*, to keep silent: so as to prevent enemies from learning the secrets of the community's fertility magic. In time the demand for outward ritual purity was extended to inner purity as well. Guilt, sin and suffering figure only in doctrines such as those of Eleusis and the Orphics (Chapter 2, section 2, and Appendix 2).

47 The priest (*hiereus*) was generally just a layman who occupied himself with a public cult (chosen from the noble families, in early days, by vote, because of the 'god-given' political power of the aristocrats). This was a departure from Bronze Age practice, since 'Linear B' tablets had depicted male and female professional priests. The *Iliad* mentions priests on the Trojan but not on the Greek side.

48 Archilochus, fragment 19.

49 Aristotle, *Politics*, v, 8, 4, 1310b.

50 A very early electrum piece showing a stag inscribed 'I am (the badge) of Phanes', found at the Artemisium at Ephesus and probably Ephesian (although it has also been attributed to Halicarnassus in Caria), suggests that the first guarantors may sometimes have been individuals. Coins were produced by the process of striking metal blanks of appropriate size and weight. The instruments were the 'anvil and hammer and well-made pincers' of Homer's goldsmith (*Odyssey*, III, 434f.). To convert this into a coin, a die – made of hardened bronze or iron, and hand-engraved in intaglio (negative) with the obverse type – was fastened in the anvil, and the blank was placed on top of it. The other die, at first a simple punch, and later when designs were required on both sides (but see note 55) engraved with the reverse type, was placed over the blank and hit with the hammer, thus producing the finished

coins. Although so much trouble was competitively taken to produce beautiful and suitable designs, the shapes were then often rounded off inaccurately. The earliest Lydian and Greek coins were thick and bean-shaped. They were of electrum (pale gold – Appendix 1), pure gold being rare in early Greece (though Croesus of Lydia issued coinage in the metal).

51 Aristotle, *Politics*, v, 1303a, 27.

52 Thucydides, III, 84.

53 In the near east these capitals of the type later known as Ionic had appeared only on furniture, and had never been fully incorporated in an architectural order. In Greek lands, the Ionic capital was preceded or accompanied by an 'Aeolic' variety – perhaps derived from Phoenicia via Cyprus and designed originally for free-standing monuments – which directly links the column-shaft and the volutes on either side of its summit. The Ionic capital abandoned this link and instead joined the volutes directly with one another, flattening them out (they had originally branched upwards and outwards) so that they could carry the burden of the architrave.

54 It may have been on Naxos in the Cyclades (or Cyprus or Rhodes?) that the old Minoan–Mycenaean art of gems and sealstones first revived, displaying, at first, influences from Egypt and Phoenicia, as well as the shapes and animal compositions of Mycenaean stones. 'Island' gems, as they are called, of the seventh and early sixth centuries BC are especially found at Melos. In the middle and later sixth century Samos was prominent, but by this time the practice of sealing had become widespread. The usual shape is the scarab, and coloured quartzes are the materials most frequently employed. As in sculpture, attention was devoted to the structure of the human figure, and there was a gradual development from stylization to naturalism. Outstanding among a number of artists of *c.*500 are Epimenes and Semon.

55 South Italian cities at first, in the third quarter of the sixth century, coined incuse pieces on thin, flat flans; on the reverse a design similar to the obverse type appears in negative, the two types being aligned with each other. Cf. also note 50.

56 However, medicine also developed considerably in the course of the sixth century, schools being established at Croton, Rhodes, Cyrene, Cos and Cnidus. The idea of justice (note 37 above) was important to early physicians (cf. Chapter 7, section 2), the 'just law' being identified with the processes of nature.

57 Aristotle, *Politics*, VIII, 2, 4, 1337b.

58 Aristotle, *Rhetoric*, 1367a, 22.

59 Homer, *Odyssey*, XI, 489ff.

60 Numbers of slaves before the classical period cannot even be conjectured. Estimates for fifth-century Athens vary between 20,000 and 400,000, with a preference for 60,000–80,000. Similarly, they have been regarded as forming either a quarter or nearly half the Athenian population. Most slaves were foreigners, relatively cheap to buy. The fifth-century statesman Nicias exceptionally owned a thousand. Sixteen slaves owned by a contemporary included five Thracians, two Carians, two Illyrians, two Syrians, and one each from Colchis, Lydia and Cappadocia. At that period slaves often owned slaves of their own, and received some education: a play of Pherecrates (*c.*430?) was called the *Doulodidaskalos* (*Slaves' School-Teacher*; Athenaeus, *Deipnosophistae*, VI, 262b). Plato complains they were treated too softly. However, this evidence cannot easily be extrapolated to earlier periods. A direct link between slavery and technological stagnation has often been assumed, but is now disputed.

61 E.g. Argos, Crete, Elis, Thessaly, Cyrene had *perioeci*.

62 E.g. there were also Helot-like populations in Argos, Crete, Thessaly, Epidaurus, Sicyon, Corinth, Heraclea Pontica, Byzantium and Syracuse.

63 Plato, *Symposium*, 178e–179a.
64 Xenophon, *Symposium*, 8, 32.
65 Herodotus v, 97. For his words see Chapter 5, section 2 (at note 39).

CHAPTER 2 Athens

1 Plato, *Critias*, 111b.
2 Mimnermus, fragment 12 Diehl.
3 Hecataeus, quoted by Herodotus, VI, 137.
4 The Ionian tribes were the Aigikoreis, Hopletes, Geleontes and Argadeis. Plutarch (Solon, 23) doubted Herodotus' belief (v, 66, 2) that they were named after the sons of Ion.
5 Solon, fragment 4.
6 After 770 inhumation of adults became much more common, and by 750 had largely supplanted cremation in Attica (cremation returned by the end of the century).
7 Homer, *Iliad*, II, 362; cf. IX, 63 on a man not belonging to a phratry.
8 Aristotle, *Constitution of Athens*, 3, 2; he mentions an alternative view that this happened at the conclusion of the reign of Medon.
9 Ibid., 3, 1.
10 R.Meiggs and D.Lewis, *Selection of Greek Historical Inscriptions to the End of the Fifth Century B.C.*, no. 86; for Dracon's 'constitution' see Aristotle, *ibid.*, 1ff.
11 Plutarch, *Solon*, 13.
12 The procession, bringing back to Eleusis the sacred objects that had been taken to Athens, also brought the image of a minor deity Iacchus, variously said to be the son (or consort) of Demeter, or the son of Persephone, or the son of Dionysus (with whom he was especially identified, owing to the resemblance of his name to Dionysus' alternative appellation Bacchus – cf. Appendix 2). There was a theory that iambic verse developed from chants at the Mysteries.
13 Implied by Isocrates, *Panegyricus*, 28; Cicero, *Laws*, II, 14, 36.
14 Pindar, fragment 137 Bergk (102 Boeckh).
15 Salamis is a rocky island of thirty-six square miles, enclosing the wide, lagoon-like bay of Eleusis which is linked with the Saronic Gulf by narrow straits on either side. Neolithic and Bronze (Mycenaean) Age remains have been found. According to Greek mythology Telamon, the brother of Peleus, settled at Salamis, the birthplace of his sons Ajax and Teucer, who subsequently founded Salamis in Cyprus.
16 Solon, fragment 1. According to an alternative view, this is a poem of his old age. Finally ceded to Athens before 527 or in *c*.509, Salamis was still not incorporated in Attica. It was administered by an Athenian governor (Aristotle, *Constitution of Athens*, 54, 8).
17 Diodorus Siculus, IX, 20, 1ff.
18 Solon, fragment 36.
19 Androtion, in Plutarch, *Solon*, 15.
20 Solon, fragments 5, 34.
21 E.g. the Arrhephoria, Skira, Thesmophoria, Lenaea and Adonia.
22 Solon, fragment 25.
23 Plutarch, *Solon*, 25.
24 Ibid., 18.
25 Solon seems to have established two classes of action: (1) *dike*, brought by the aggrieved party in person, (2) *graphe*, written plea brought by any citizen. The lot is not likely to have been introduced for appointment to the Heliaea as early as his time (despite Aristotle, *Politics*, II, 1274a 3; for the Council and archonships and other offices see note 40 below), although the institution was as old as the *Iliad* (VII, 171ff.) and was employed in the seventh century for colonizing purposes at Thera (Chapter 6, section 3). Appeals heard by the Heliaea became so frequent that in the following century magistrates almost ceased to give the verdicts which inevitably led to them. Instead, a system of jury-courts (*dicasteria*) was set up to try cases on behalf of the Assembly. How early this process began is uncertain (it was completed by *c*.462/461; in the latter part of the fifth century juries were usually several hundred strong, but could be as numerous as 6,000). The *dicasteria* were, at least initially, thought of as sub-divisions of the Heliaea (the

latter term was also the name of the largest Athenian courtroom).

26 Plutarch, *Solon*, 18.

27 Solon, fragment 11.

28 Plutarch, *Solon*, 19.

29 Solon, fragment 5.

30 Ibid., fragments 32, 33.

31 The name Amasis is Egyptian and suggests a connection with that country.

32 Why was it called *tragoidia* ('goat-song')? Because of goat-skin-clad satyr dancers? Or was it 'the song of the goat-sacrifice'?

33 Themistius, *Orations*, xxvi, 316d.

34 Diogenes Laertius, iii, 56.

35 Thespis (or a contemporary) divided the fifty-man chorus into four choruses of twelve, with two left over, who could become non-speaking actors.

36 Over 100 buildings have now been identified, and 180,000 objects discovered, in the Athenian *agora*.

37 The inauguration of another genre, satyric drama, was attributed to Pratinas of Phlius (in the Argolid), who participated in the contest of 499/496 at Athens. In addition to eighteen tragedies, he was ascribed thirty-two 'satyr plays', converting a more shapeless kind of entertainment into regular dramatic form. The partly human satyrs – mythological wild country creatures sprouting horses' tails and ears (subsequently a connection with goats prevailed instead) – appear frequently on Athenian vases from *c.*520. Owing to their link with the horse-eared Silenus, regarded as the foster-father of Dionysus, they became associated with Dionysiac cults and festivals. The supposition of Aristotle (*Poetics*, 4) that satyric drama was one of the precursors of tragedy is acceptable in so far as the more formless predecessors of the satyr plays may have been among the numerous forerunners of that genre.

38 Simonides (*c.*556–468) wrote many forms of verse but gained particular renown for his epigrams and epitaphs, and especially for the epitaph he wrote for the men who fell at Marathon (490). By that time he was back at Athens, having left it

after the murder of the co-dictator Hipparchus (514) for Thessaly, where he gained the patronage of Scopas of Crannon and the Aleuadae of Larissa.

39 Herodotus, v, 69 (pejoratively). Pollux, *Onomasticon*, viii, 10, ascribes the inauguration of the system to 507/506.

40 Solon was 'the first champion of the people' – Aristotle, *Constitution of Athens*, 28, 1; and on the lot, ibid., 47, 1, and 8, 1. For the lot in the Heliaea as probably post-Solonian, note 25 above. Despite recent reiterated arguments to the contrary, and although the lot was an ancient procedure (*ibid.*), its use for appointments to archonships and other offices (with *prokrisis*, see text) may also have been post-Solonian, as Aristotle, *Politics*, ii, 1273b 40–1274a 2 against *Constitution of Athens*, 8, 1 (attempts have been made to harmonize these passages). In the same fourth century Demosthenes regarded Solon as the father of the radical democratic movement, as against Isocrates who saw him as the founder of moderate democracy.

41 For Socrates, Xenophon, *Memoirs*, i, 2, 9, iii, 9, 10. Aristotle, *Politics*, iv, 12, 12f., 1300a–b, weighs up the relative 'democratic' qualities of election and the lot.

42 Ibid., vi, 2, 11, 1319b. But Cleisthenes did not, it would appear, challenge Solon's monopoly of political power by the two top census groups.

43 Aristotle, *Constitution of Athens*, 22, 1.

44 Ibid., 20, 1.

45 Aegina backed Megarian colonization in the eighth century (though Megara subsequently took Salamis from Aegina – Chapter 3, section 5). It was the only non-eastern Greek power to be represented at Naucratis, and may have been the founder of Atria in north-eastern Italy (Chapter 6, section 4; Chapter 8, section 1). Its citizen Sostratus was a famous shipmaster, aristocrat and trader, and his name, or that of a synonymous member of his family, appears at Graviscae, a port of

Tarquinii in Etruria (Appendix 3, note 59). Aegina may have been the source of an important group of seventh-century pottery hitherto classified as Protoattic, though this has been queried.

46 Although Aegina was a major distributor of Attic black-figure and red-figure pottery.

47 Pindar, fragment 1 Bergk (4 Boeckh); Herodotus, IV, 91.

48 When the time came, in 490, the Aeginetans remained neutral. Two years later, they won a naval victory against Athens; and at about the same time they constructed a new harbour, for defence against that city as well as for trading. However, they fought well against Xerxes I in 480 and 479. It was not until 459 that the Athenians finally captured Aegina and put an end to its power.

CHAPTER 3 The Peloponnese

1 Heracles (unlikely to have been a historical personage) was allegedly related to King Eurystheus of Argos (his persecutor). His cult may have been introduced from the near east, with elaborations, during the eighth century, when his appearance in Greek art became more frequent. In the sixth century, about one-quarter of all decorated vases depicted him.

2 Epidaurus stood on the rocky hill of a small peninsula (Acte) within a recess of the Saronic Gulf. Participation in the Trojan War: Homer, *Iliad*, II, 561. First occupied, supposedly, by non-Greek Carians and then by Ionian Greeks, the place fell into the hands of Dorian invaders coming from Argos, whereupon the Ionian settlers were believed to have fled and colonized Samos. The Epidaurians paid a religious tax to Argos, but from the eighth (?) century belonged (perhaps to the instigation of Pheidon of Argos) to a religious league (Amphictyony), based on a cult of Poseidon upon the island of Calauria (its other members were Hermione, Aegina, Athens, Prasia, Nauplia and Orchomenus – Strabo, VIII, 6, 14, 374). Epidaurus was later annexed by Periander of Corinth. Its renowned sanctuary of the healing deity Asclepius – located six miles from the city, and the site of four-yearly Panhellenic Games and horse-races – was believed to have been the place of origin of his cult. It superseded a shrine and festival of the god's father Apollo (known locally as Malos or Maleatas) on the adjoining Mount Kynortion, shown by excavations to have been of Mycenaean origin and to have experienced a revival in the seventh century BC.

3 Herodotus, IV, 152.

4 Aristotle, fragment 481 Rose; cf. Ephorus, F.Jacoby, *Fragmente der griechischen Historiker*, IIA, 70 F 115 and 176, and Heracleides of Pontus, in Orion, *Etymologicum*.

5 Pausanias, VI, 22, 2.

6 Aristotle, *Politics*, v, 8, 4, 1310b.

7 Pausanias, VIII, 50, 1; Dionysius of Halicarnassus, IV, 16, 2.

8 Palatine Anthology, XIV, 73.

9 Cleobis and Biton of Argos were brothers who drew the chariot of their mother, a priestess of Hera, to the Argive Heraeum, since its oxen had not arrived in time for the festival. As a reward, she prayed to the goddess to grant her sons the greatest blessing that human beings could receive, and Hera responded by arranging for them to die while sleeping in the temple. According to Herodotus (I, 31), Solon, addressing King Croesus of Lydia, described them as among the happiest of mortals.

10 Pausanias, IV, 24, 4; 35, 2. Sparta instead gave the Nauplians (whom Pausanias believed to have been of Egyptian origin) the town of Mothone in Messenia. Nauplia had at one stage been a member of the Calaurian Amphictyony (note 3 above).

11 Homer, *Iliad*, II, 570.

12 The following list of Corinth's colonies is taken from *Cambridge Ancient History*, III, 3, 2nd edn, pp. 160f. (dates are those from literary sources, A = earliest archaeological material): Ambracia (c.655–625), Anactorium (ditto, with Corcyra: A c.625–600), Apollonia in

Illyria (c.600, with Corcyra), Corcyra (733 or 706), Leucas (c.655–625), Potidaea (c.625–585), Syracuse (733).

13 Strabo, VIII, 6, 20, 378.

14 Pliny the elder, *Natural History*, XXXV, 15f.

15 C.625–620 early, 590–575 middle, 575–560/540 late. True black-figure at Corinth dates from the first half of the seventh century.

16 *Cf.* Gellius, *Attic Nights*, I, 8, 3–6; Lais, in the fifth century BC, charged a very high fee (10,000 drachmas).

17 Corinthian work is also detectable in a temple at Thermum, the cult-centre of backward Aetolia, where the influence of Corinth was dominant. Built over an earlier *megaron* (a hall or house that became a shrine [?], displaying, in its second stage, an exceptionally early peripteral design, i.e. surrounding [wooden] columns), this sanctuary is datable to c.630–620 by its terracotta metopes, which are analogous to Corinthian pottery; the larger scale of the metope paintings, which we see here for the first time in Greek art, enables the drapery patterns to be designed with greater freedom. The existence of these metopes, and the appearance of cornice blocks, bear witness to the new Doric style. Similar fragments have been discovered at the principal Aetolian township, Calydon, famous in mythology for the struggle between Heracles and the river-god Achelous, and for the pursuit of the Calydonian boar, killed by Meleager.

18 At Epidamnus the settlers were mostly Corcyraeans – presumably exiles – but they are joined by Corinthians (who provided the founder) and other Dorians (Thucydides, I, 24, 2).

19 Perhaps by way of the Ionians, whose city Erythrae was credited with the invention of the bireme by the fifth-century historian Damastes of Sigeum (F. Jacoby, *Fragmente der griechischen Historiker*, 5 F 6).

20 Thucydides, I, 13, 3. If Ameinocles' visit to Samos took place in c.704, the ships may have been intended for the Lelantine War between Chalcis and Eretria in Euboea, in which Samos and probably Corinth supported Chalcis.

21 Ibid., 2.

22 Herodotus, I, 23. Suidas, s.v., dubiously ascribes the introduction of spoken verses to Arion. There was also a legend that he invented the *paean* (in honour of Apollo); and a statement that he presented the first tragic drama was ascribed to Solon (Johannes Diaconus, *Commentary on Hermogenes*).

23 Herodotus, III, 50, 52f.

24 *Palatine Anthology*, IX, 151.

25 Thucydides, I, 10.

26 Tyrtaeus, fragment 4 West; Plutarch, *Lycurgus*, 6, 7. The aim of the Rhetra was perhaps to establish the rights of the Assembly in relation to the Council and kings. Plutarch's *Lycurgus* in general offers a glowing and poetically idealized picture of Spartan equality.

27 Aristotle, *Politics*, II, 6, 20, 1271a (for the military basis of the whole system, ibid., 22, 1271b). The origins of the dual Spartan monarchy were explained in different ways. Perhaps it arose from an earlier territorial division (e.g. Sparta and Amyclae).

28 As early as c.750 Timomachus, who captured Amyclae, had a bronze breastplate – Aristotle, fragment 532 Rose.

29 Aristotle, *Politics*, II, 3, 10, 1265b.

30 Herodotus, VII, 104, 4.

31 Cf. Strabo, X, 4, 17, 481ff., against Aristotle, *Politics*, II, 7, 1, 1271b. Herodotus, I, 65 indicates that the Spartans themselves claimed that their system came from Crete.

32 Plutarch, *Lycurgus*, 18, 4.

33 Xenophon, *Constitution of the Laconians*, 2, 13.

34 Theopompus, fragment 225; cf. Plutarch, *Table Talk* (*Moralia*, VIII), 35.

35 Plutarch, *Lycurgus*, 15, 3–5.

36 Plutarch, *Lysander*, 17; *Lycurgus*, 9.

37 Arcadia was the mountainous central area of the Peloponnese, inhabited by people (partly nomadic) who were mainly engaged in pastoralism and stock-raising. The most prosperous parts of the region were its eastern plains, and the valley of the River

Alpheus. Tegea, the leading urban and religious centre, claimed mythical origins and was mentioned in the Catalogue of Homer's *Iliad*. The date at which the villages of the valley basin amalgamated to become a single city is uncertain. Tegea was on the route from the Gulf of Corinth to Sparta, which was eager to assert control of the city, in order to safeguard its own access to the isthmus. The Spartans also coveted Tegea's arable land. (The second major city of Arcadia, Mantinea, was created out of five separate villages in *c*.500.)

38 Bilateral treaties were at some stage replaced by a multilateral agreement, perhaps modelled, to some extent, on the arrangements that Sparta had already formed with its *perioeci*.

39 Herodotus, VI, 84.

40 Homer, *Iliad*, XXIII, 299.

41 According to another tradition, Polybus was king of Corinth. He was also heard of at Argos and Tenea (in the Argolid) and in Boeotia.

42 Pollux, *Onomasticon*, III, 83.

43 Aristotle, *Politics*, V, 9, 21, 1315b.

44 Herodotus, V, 68.

45 Ibid., 67.

46 Themistius, *Orations*, XXVIIa, 337.

47 Suidas, s.v. *Arion* and *Ouden proton Dionyson*; Sicyonian 'phallus-bearers' (or 'wearers'?) may also have been among the precursors of comedy.

48 Pliny the elder, *Natural History*, XXXVI, 9; cf. Pausanius, II, 22.

49 Pliny the elder, *Natural History*, XXXV, 15.

50 Plutarch, *Greek Enquiries* (*Moralia*, IV), 17, 295b.

51 Thucydides, VI, 4, 1.

52 Aristotle, *Politics*, V, 4, 5, 1305a.

53 Plutarch, *Greek Enquiries* (*Moralia*, IV), 18d, 295. When the various convulsions described by Aristotle, *Politics*, IV, 12, 10, 1300a, and V, 4, 3, 1304b took place is uncertain.

54 Aristotle, *Poetics*, 3, 1448a; cf. Ecphantides, fragment 2.

55 Parian Marble (*Marmor Parium*) (F.Jacoby, *Fragmente der griechischen Historiker*, 239), 39.

56 Athenaeus, *Deipnosophistae*, XIV, 659a–c.

57 Cytorus (northern Asia Minor), Callatis (western shore of Black Sea), Chersonesus (Tauric Chersonese).

58 The nucleus of Elis was Hollow Elis, in the basin of the River Peneus. According to tradition the country was settled by Dorians from Aetolia. The controlling oligarchy played little part in Greek politics (no city of Elis was founded until 471) but planted colonies at Buchetium on the Gulf of Ambracia (*c*.700) and in Epirus (660s).

59 Pindar, *Olympians*, 2.3; 3, 11; 6.68; 10.25.

60 Strabo, VIII, 3, 30, 354.

CHAPTER 4 Central and Northern Greece

1 Strabo, X, 1, 10, 447f.

2 Ibid., IX, 2, 6, 403.

3 Aristotle, *Politics*, IV, 3, 2, 1289b. According to Strabo, X, 1, 10, 447, Chalcidian citizens were required to possess a certain amount of property.

4 *Palatine Anthology*, XIV, 73.

5 F.Cairns, *Zeitschrift für Papyrologie und Epigraphik*, LIV, 1984, pp. 145ff. The chief magistrate at Opus (Locris) was also called *archos* (H.Roehl, *Inscriptiones Graecae Antiquissimae*, 132).

6 Plutarch, *Treatise on Love* (*Moralia* IX), 761. (Aristotle, fragment 98); Athenaeus, *Deipnosophistae*, XIII, 601c.

7 Phocis, between Boeotia and Thessaly, included the valley of the River Cephisus (not the Attic river of that name) to the north and the Crisaean plain on the Corinthian Gulf to the south. According to Homer, *Iliad*, II, 517, etc., the Phocians took part in the Trojan War. They were thought to be of Aeolic origin, but their dialect was related to Doric. The wide area over which the country had originally extended was restricted by Boeotian and Thessalian encroachments. Phocis was mainly pastoral and its townships did not become city-states. It owed its importance to Delphi, which it had originally controlled.

8 *Homeric Hymns*, III, 356–62.

9 Ibid., 440–2.

10 According to one theory Delphi played a part in the development of

the Greek alphabet (perhaps in connection with the 'Delphic oracle' of the Spartan Great Rhetra – Chapter 3, section 3 and note 26).

11 Homer, *Iliad*, IX, 404f.

12 *Homeric Hymns*, III, 296.

13 Herodotus, V, 63.

14 Ibid., VI, 77.

15 The Hellenes were originally the people of Hellas, a small tribe in Phthiotis (southern Thessaly; *Iliad*, II, 683f.). The tribe migrated southwards, but we do not know how the name was extended to describe the Greeks as a whole (probably by the eighth century BC). Thucydides (I, 3) states that in the time of Homer, 'the Hellenes were not yet known by one name'. Homer had been familiar with the term 'Panhellene', but as an extended designation of the Thessalian tribe – *Iliad*, II, 530; cf. Hesiod, *Works and Days*, 528.

16 Homer, *Iliad*, II, 711f. Pherae was famous in mythology as the kingdom of Admetus (the husband of Alcestis) and Iolcus as the home of Jason, leader of the Argonauts.

17 Aristotle, *Politics*, II, 6, 2f., 1269a–b.

18 Aristotle, ibid., V, 5, 5, 1305b, however, indicates that principal officials (*politophylakes*) were elected by the people.

19 Herodotus, V, 63. Hippias' father Pisistratus employed Thessalian cavalry as mercenaries (Chapter 2, section 4).

20 Plutarch, *How a Young Man Should Read the Poets* (*Moralia*, I), 15d. Demosthenes called the Thessalians untrustworthy, and Athenaeus described them as lazy and extravagant.

21 Plutarch, *Sayings of Kings and Emperors* (*Moralia*, III), 193e.

22 Homer, *Iliad*, II, 494–510.

23 Thucydides, I, 12 (first settled before the Trojan War).

24 But Herodotus, V, 59, saw tripods inscribed with 'Cadmean' (Mycenaean?) writing in the temple (cf. note 22).

25 The attribution of both works to a single poet was doubted, according to a tradition reported by Pausanias, IX, 31, 4.

26 Hesiod, *Works and Days*, 639f.

27 Ibid., 654f.

28 Thucydides, III, 96. Hesiod was worshipped as a cult-hero at Ascra until the place was obliterated by Thespiae, whereupon Ascran refugees transferred his remains to Orchomenus (see next note).

29 Pausanias, IX, 38, 3.

30 Hesiod, *Works and Days*, 77–82; cf. *Theogony*, 590–612.

31 Hesiod, *Works and Days*, 207.

32 Ibid., 220f.

33 Hesiod, *Theogony*, 27–8.

34 There were Boeotarchs by 479 – Herodotus, IX, 15.

35 Homer, *Iliad*, IX, 381, refers to the wealth of Orchomenus, which remained conscious of its Bronze Age grandeur. Strabo, VIII, 6, 14, 374, unexpectedly describes it as a member of the Amphictyony of Calauria (Poros) in the Argolid (Chapter 3, note 2). This membership perhaps dates from the eighth century and was an anti-Theban move; it may have been prompted by a tradition of early Athenian settlers at Orchomenus (since Athens was a member of the Amphictyony).

36 L.H.Jeffery, *The Local Scripts of Archaic Greece*, p. 93, no. 11. The other three cities named on the federal issues were Mycalessus, Pharae and Acraephia (which had previously coined independently).

37 Aristotle, *Politics*, II, 9.6, 1274a.

38 Hipparchus offered a dedication to Apollo Ptoios at the Ptoion near Acraephia (note 36 above). Fine *kouroi* have been found in the temple, which dates from the same period and was probably likewise a product of Pisistratid initiative.

39 Xenophon, *Constitution of the Laconians*, 2, 12f.; *Symposium*, 8, 32f.; Plato, *Symposium*, 182a–b.

CHAPTER 5 The Eastern and Central Aegean

1 Herodotus, I, 142.

2 There were alternative traditions of foundations by the sons of the Athenian king Codrus, Neleus and Androclus (see Miletus, Ephesus).

3 Pseudo-Herodotus, *Life of Homer*, 23f.; cf. Suidas, s.v. Homerus (b). Homer was said to have died on the island of Ios.

4 Semonides, fragment 29.

5 *Homeric Hymns*, III, 172.

6 Homer, *Iliad*, VIII, 64 (Demodocus); his blindness could have inspired the belief that Homer, too, was blind. The bard Phemius (like the herald Medon) is singled out to be spared by Telemachus, *Odyssey*, XXII, 356.

7 Homer, *Iliad*, II, 493–760.

8 This was reported in the lost *Myrmidons* of Aeschylus (cf. Plato, *Symposium*, 180a).

9 Herodotus, II, 53.

10 Strabo, I, 12, 15.

11 Cf. Homer, *Odyssey*, XVII, 385.

12 *Deltion Archeologikon*, 1889, p. 119.

13 Scholiast to Aristophanes, *Birds*, 574.

14 Thucydides, VIII, 40, 2.

15 Ibid., 24, 4. Chios also possessed a school at least as early as *c*.494 (Herodotus, VI, 27); the island of Astypalaea had one in 496 (Pausanias, VI, 9, 6).

16 C.W.Fornara, *Archaic Times to the End of the Peloponnesian War*, 2nd edn (1978), p. 19, no. 19.

17 The pastoral Carians, speaking a non-Indo-European language, lived mainly in hill-top villages under native dynasties based on sanctuaries, their principal centre being Mylasa (where there was a shrine of Zeus Karios). Sometimes distinguished from, and sometimes confused with, the Leleges, they claimed to be indigenous, although according to a Greek tradition they came originally from the islands. They gained an evil reputation as pirates, but also served as mercenaries, especially in Egypt. After subjection to Croesus of Lydia and then to the Persians, they joined the Ionian revolt against Persian domination (499–494), ambushing an enemy force before their final defeat.

18 The tin of Brittany seems to have been exhausted by historical times. The Greek city-states were able to derive supplies of tin not only from the west (reference in note 51) but from their own homeland and from the near east, although the quantities available are uncertain.

19 For south Spanish copper see Pliny the elder, *Natural History*, XXXIV, 4.

20 Herodotus, IV, 152. Midacritus, probably from Phocaea, appears to have preceded Colaeus (see section 3 and note 51).

21 His allusion to Homer (note 4 above) is the first reference to a literary source in extant Greek writings.

22 It has been suggested that Rhoecus was perhaps the architect of the earlier temple as well.

23 Diodorus Siculus, I, 98, 7–9.

24 Asius in Athenaeus, *Deipnosophistae*, XII, 525e–f (from Duris).

25 Herodotus, III, 122.

26 Ibid., V, 28.

27 Homer, *Iliad*, II, 868.

28 Principal Milesian colonies included the following. *Hellespont and Thracian Chersonese*: Abydus (*c*.680–652), Cardia (with Clazomenae), Limnae, Scepsis. *Propontis*: Cius (627), Cyzicus (756, 659 – see Chapter 8, section 2), Miletopolis, Paesus, Parium (709, with Paros and Erythrae), Priapus, Proconnesus. *Black Sea* (see Chapter 8, section 3): Apollonia Pontica (*c*.610); Odessus (A: *c*.600–575), Tomis (A: *c*.500–475); Cepi (A: *c*.575–550: arch), Hermonassa (?) (A: *c*.600–575: arch), Myrmecium (or from Panticapaeum, A: *c*.600–575), Nymphaeum (?) (A: *c*.600), Olbia (647), Panticapaeum (A: *c*.600), Sindikos Limen (*c*.600), Tanais (?) (A: *c*.625–600), Theodosia (A: *c*.575–500), Tyras (A: *c*.600–500); Amisus (*c*.564, with Phocaea), Sinope (before 716, 631), Tieum; (Phasis). My indebtedness for this list is indicated in Chapter 3, note 12 (again, A = earliest archaeological material). The eighth-century dates are sometimes discounted, or identified with pre-colonial trading enterprises.

29 Thus named because they held their meetings on shipboard, out at sea (Plutarch, *Greek Enquiries* [*Moralia*, IV], 32, 298c).

30 Aristotle, *Politics*, III, 8, 3, 1284a, against Herodotus, V, 92. Miletus

made pottery intended to rival the products of Corinth.

31 Colophon was situated eight miles from the sea at the end of a fertile plain north of Miletus, between Smyrna and Ephesus. According to the poet–musician Mimnermus (section 3) – who originated from Colophon (although his family settled in Smyrna) – its founders came from Pylos in Messenia (fragment 10 Bergk). The Colophonians controlled the nearby sanctuary of Apollo of Claros, and colonized Myrlea (later Apamea) in Bithynia and Siris in southern Italy (c.700 or slightly later). In the seventh century, Polymnestus of Colophon became one of the most famous flute-players of antiquity, introducing a new severe style. The spindle was believed to have been invented at Colophon. But the city, ruled by the rich 'beause they formed a majority' (Aristotle, *Politics*, IV, 3, 8, 1298b), was chiefly renowned for its inhabitants' luxurious way of life. However, in early times they also possessed strong naval and especially cavalry forces. But these did not save them from subjection to the Lydians and then to the Persians.

32 Aristotle, *On the Sky*, II, 3, 294a 28; *Metaphysics*, II, 3, 983b 6.

33 It has been questioned whether Thales was concerned to draw this inference.

34 Aristotle, *On the Soul*, A5, 411a, 7.

35 Simplicius, *On Aristotle's Physics*, 24, 17.

36 Theophrastus, in Simplicius, ibid., 149, 32; Hippolytus, *Refutation of All Heresies*, I, 7, 1. There are certain debts to Thales and Anaximander here. For an alleged, but doubtful, Sythian debt, see Appendices, note 53.

37 Hecataeus, *Histories*, fragment 1.

38 Herodotus, II, 21f.; IV, 36.

39 Ibid., V, 97.

40 Magnesia beside Mount Sipylus had been founded at an early date by the Magnetes of eastern Thessaly, at an important crossroads in the Hermus valley.

41 Heraclitus, fragment 101.

42 Ibid., fragment 12 (Plato, *Cratylus*, 402a).

43 Ibid., fragment 32.

44 Ibid., fragments 118 (dry souls), 44.

45 Ibid., fragment 40.

46 It was said that Homer had at first borne the name of Melesignus, after the River Melas.

47 Smyrna had earlier been devastated by the Cimmerians (Appendices, note 3).

48 Strabo, XIV, 1, 37, 646. In the fourth century the city was reconstructed on a different site, 'New Smyrna', five miles to the south.

49 Phocaea may have had an understanding with the Chalcidians, who controlled the strait.

50 Herodotus, I, 163.

51 Pliny the elder, *Natural History*, VII, 197. 'Midacritus' means 'approved of Midas', indicating a Phrygian connection.

52 The tradition, quoted by Strabo (XIII, 1, 3, 582), that the Aeolian colonization (at first 'under Orestes', the son of Agamemnon) preceded the Ionian settlements by four generations is scarcely acceptable; he was no doubt right to add that the process 'suffered delays and took a longer time'. Mysia was a region of north-western Asia Minor of which the frontiers were variously defined. The non-Greek Mysians, who appear as allies of Troy in the *Iliad* (and reputedly, by virtue of their wealth in gold, silver and lead, and their agricultural resources, contributed to the riches of that city), were believed by Strabo (XII, 3, 541) to have originated from Thrace and to speak a language that was a mixture of Phrygian and Lydian. In the sixth century Mysia passed successively under Lydian and Persian control.

53 Cyme, founded, according to tradition, by an Amazon of that name, occupied twin hills above two streams between the mouths of the rivers Caicus and Hermus. One of its kings, whose name – Agamemnon – was meant to recall the *Iliad*, married the daughter of a king of Phrygia named Midas. When the father of the poet Hesiod migrated to Boeotia in the eighth century it was from Cyme

that he came. The Cymaeans reputedly colonized Cebren in the Troad and Side in Pamphylia (southern Asia Minor), and were believed to have had a share in nearly thirty other settlements as well. They were said to have encouraged trade by refraining from the exaction of harbour dues, so that other Greeks regarded them as stupid and averse to maritime activities. Nevertheless, under Persian rule, they contributed ships to the European expedition of Darius I (513–512).

54 His instrument seems to have been the *barbitos*, a variety of lyre with longer strings and therefore a lower pitch and deeper tone than the *cithara* and *lyra*.

55 Alcaeus, fragment 332 Lobel-Page.

56 Ibid., fragment 428 Lobel-Page.

57 Horace, *Odes*, I, 32, 5, 11f.

58 Sappho, fragments 2, 55, 94, 150 Lobel-Page. Andromeda, whom she disliked (fragment 131), seems to have been the leader of a rival group; also Gorgo.

59 Alcaeus, fragment 130, 132 Lobel-Page. According to Homer, *Iliad*, IX, 129f., Lesbian women constituted an especially valued category of loot.

60 Sappho, fragments 16, 49, 94, 96 Lobel-Page.

61 Naxos may also have taken the lead in gem-making; see Chapter 1, note 54.

62 E.g. Cicero, *Orator*, 4; Quintilian, *Training of an Orator*, x, 1, 60, etc. Writers in the aristocratic tradition such as Heraclitus, Pindar and Critias had dissented.

63 Archilochus, fragment 1.

64 M.Treu, Archilochus (1959). Another Cycladic writer was Pherecydes of Syros (c.550), the author of a mythical cosmogony foreshadowing primitive physics and displaying an interest in ethics. Semonides 'of Amorgos' came from Samos (section 1).

65 Thucydides, I, 8.

66 Scholiast to Pindar, *Nemean Odes*, II, 1.

67 Cults of Anius, Eileithyia, Hecate

and Brizo were likewise legacies from earlier times.

68 Pliny the elder, *Natural History*, XXXIV, 3, 9.

69 Herodotus, I, 64, 2. Rheneia was also the ultimate destination of the dug-up corpses.

CHAPTER 6 The South and East

1 At Karphi c.1100–900 a Mycenaean refugee minority seems to have been ruling over native Cretans. Kato Syme was the site of uninterrupted worship from Minoan to Roman times.

2 Homer, *Iliad*, II, 649; *Odyssey*, XIX, 174: Achaeans, native Cretans, Cydonians, Dorians, Pelasgians.

3 Homer, *Odyssey*, XIV, 229, 232.

4 Plato, *Laws*, VIII, 836b.

5 Timaeus, fragment 104; Ephorus, fragment 1; Echemenes, *Cretica*, fragment 1 (C.Müller, *Fragmenta Historicorum Graecorum*, IV, 103); Aristotle, *Politics*, II, 7, 5, 1272a.

6 Cnossus was the capital of Idomeneus, believed to have been the grandson of Minos.

7 Pseudo-Scymnus, 580ff. Strabo's assertion that Cnossus colonized Brundusium in south-east Italy (VI, 3, 6, 282) must be fictitious.

8 The Dactyls were also attributed to the other Mount Ida, in north-western Asia Minor.

9 The Curetes, of Minoan origin, were credited with the invention of Cretan acrobatic dancing. They were frequently confused, however, with the Corybantes.

10 In his lying account of his past Odysseus had chosen to pose as a Cretan (see note 3). Cf. Plutarch, *Lysander*, 20; *Aemilius Paullus*, 23.

11 L.H.Jeffrey and A.Morpurgo Davies, *Kadmos*, IX, 1970, pp. 118ff.; Herodotus, III, 67, 1; V, 74, 1.

12 Pausanias, II, 15, 1.

13 Diodorus Siculus, IV, 30ff.; cf. Suidas, s.v. *Daidalou poiemata*.

14 Pliny the elder, XXXVI, 9.

15 Pausanias, II, 15, 1.

16 This little temple (representing an attempt to monumentalize old forms) was built over a sacrificial pit, and partly constructed of dressed stone.

It is a century later than the temple at Drerus.

17 Aristotle, *Politics*, II, 9, 5, 1274a ('Thales').

18 *Inscriptiones Creticae*, IV, 72; translations in C.W.Fornara, *Archaic Times to the End of the Peloponnesian War*, 2nd edn, 1983, pp. 86ff., no. 88.

19 R.Meiggs and D.M.Lewis, *A Selection of Greek Historical Inscriptions to the End of the Fifth Century BC*, pp. 2f., no. 2, C.W.Fornara, op. cit. p. 11, no. 11.

20 M.L.West, *Journal of Hellenic Studies*, LXXXV, 1965, pp. 149f. (from a third-century BC original). 'Dictaean' had already appeared on a Mycenaean tablet from Cnossus.

21 Cretans, together with Rhodians, founded Gela in Sicily in c.690/688.

22 The Eteo-Cypriot language, on the other hand, although it was likewise written down, is still undeciphered (cf. the earlier Cypro-Minoan).

23 Translated in *Cambridge Ancient History*, III, 3, 2nd edn, 1982, pp. 57, 59.

24 Herodotus, V, 113; Strabo, XIV, 6, 3, 683.

25 R.Meiggs and D.M.Lewis, op. cit., pp. 5ff., no. 5; C.W.Fornara, op. cit., pp. 18ff., no. 18. It included a pact between the colonists and Therans who remained at home.

26 Herodotus, IV, 151ff.

27 Ibid., 160.

28 These *perioeci* may have been either migrants from the perioecic zone of the island of Thera or descendants of colonists in Libyan territory.

29 Herodotus, IV, 201ff.

30 E.g. excavations at Tyre and potsherds at Kalde from Protogeometric times.

31 Finds at Lefkandi in Euboea suggest the existence of Euboean markets in northern Syria even before Al Mina.

32 For *phoinikeia*, see above, note 11. The legend of Cadmus bringing writing to Greece from Phoenicia (Herodotus, V, 58) reflects this borrowing of the alphabetic script (although it is anachronistically placed in the mythological past).

33 R.Meiggs and D.M.Lewis, op. cit., p. 8, no. 7.

34 Herodotus, II, 178. A large number of vases (from c.600) which have been discovered on the site and were formerly described as Naucratite come from Chios. Additional finds include many vases of Rhodian origin or type. There was also a Cypriot trading factory at Naucratis.

35 Bacchylides, fragment 20b Snell, lines 14–16.

36 Herodotus, II, 135.

37 Ibid., 177.

38 For Theodorus, see Chapter 5, note 23. A Cypriot sculptor Sicon worked at Naucratis, and a statuette from Cyprus was acquired by a merchant of Naucratis. Polycharmus, *On Aphrodite*; F.Jacoby, *Fragmente der griechischen Historiker*, 640 F. The 'Egyptian' Philocles, who according to one tradition invented line-drawing (Pliny the elder, XXXV, 16), may have been a Greek from Naucratis.

CHAPTER 7 The West

1 There was also an Iron Age village two and a half miles to the east, at Castiglione.

2 Greeks were probably not allowed direct access to the Etruscan mines.

3 The place-names Euboea and Pithecusae recur in the Carthage area.

4 Thucydides, VI, 4, 5.

5 Virgil, *Aeneid*, VI, 9–13.

6 A further Etruscan attack was repelled by the Syracusans off Cumae in 474.

7 Rhegium (Reggio di Calabria) stood on a sloping plateau that extended between two ridges and overlooked a harbour near the mouth of the River Apsias. In addition to Chalcidians (under Antimnestus, who according to the historian Antiochus [F.Jacoby, *Fragmente der griechischen Historiker*, 555 F 9] was sent for by the people of Zancle [Messana]), some part was played in the foundation by Messenians, refugees from their first war with Sparta (c.743–720?). Androdamas was a 'law-giver' at Rhegium. In the sixth century it was the birthplace of the lyric poet Ibycus, who left his home town, allegedly because he was unwilling

to become its dictator, and moved to Samos. In *c*.540 additional settlers were sent to Rhegium by the Phocaeans, who subsequently used it as a base for their colonization of Elea. Potters at Rhegium were probably the manufacturers of a group of vases of *c*.550–510 formerly labelled 'Chalcidian'. Anaxilas was dictator of the city from 494 to 476.

8 Taras (Tarentum, Taranto) on the north side of the gulf named after it (opposite Sybaris) had a lengthy prehistory and took its Greek name from the mythical founder of its pre-Greek, native settlement of Messapians (an Illyrian people); his father, the god Poseidon, was believed to have dispatched a dolphin to save his son from shipwreck. The colonists, led by Phalanthus, who arrived, according to Eusebius, in 506 (moving to Taras from a site seven miles to its south-east), were people from Sparta known as Partheniai, 'sons of concubines', supposedly because they were the bastards of Spartan women by Helot fathers, born while their husbands were away fighting – although the story is dubious. There was also a Cretan element in the population. Income was derived from wool, *murex* (purple) dye, and agricultural produce. A late-sixth-century ruler Aristophilides based his kingship on Spartan models. Soon after 500 the Tarantines took steps to repel and suppress adjacent Messapian tribes (inscriptions in their Italic language have been found in the cave-sanctuary of Thaotor [Tutor] near Roca di Gualtieri).

9 Strabo, VI, 1, 13, 263. For Helice, see next note.

10 The name 'Achaea' became attached to this region, although in Homer the 'Achaeans' had been the Greeks of the Trojan War in general, and particularly Achilles' Myrmidons (cf. Achaea Phthiotis in south-eastern Thessaly). Achaea in the northern Peloponnese was divided between twelve small towns forming a loose, mainly religious confederation which met at the sanctuary of Poseidon Heliconius at Helice.

11 Aristotle, *Politics*, V, 2, 10, 1303a: the expulsion of these Troezenians by their Achaean fellow settlers was said to have brought a curse on the city. In mythology, Troezen was the site of Orestes' purification and the birthplace of the Athenian hero Theseus.

12 Strabo, VI, 1, 13, 263. According to an alternative theory the Serdaioi were Sardinians.

13 Herodotus, VI, 127, 1, noted the exceptional wealth of Hippocrates, the son of Smindyrides. The discomfort of Spartan life horrified a Sybarite visitor.

14 Metapontum, which was founded in the later eighth century by Achaeans under Leucippus (or by men from Pylos) on a defensible site – perhaps already occupied by other Greek settlers earlier – between the mouths of the Rivers Bradanus and Casuentus, was intended by the Sybarites to serve as a buffer against Taras. From *c*.550 it issued coins displaying ears of corn, which referred to the fertility of the local farmland. Metapontum possessed its own treasury at Delphi. Towards the end of the century the city was the refuge and burial place of Pythagoras (to whose house Cicero made a pilgrimage – *De Finibus*, V, 2, 4).

15 A third shrine of Posidonia, adjacent to the 'Basilica', is the 'Temple of Poseidon' (in reality dedicated to Hera or Zeus), of *c*.450(?). Paintings of the early fifth century at Posidonia (notably a picture of a diver) suggest analogies with Tarquinii in Etruria.

16 Strabo, VI, 1, 13, 263.

17 Herodotus, VI, 21.

18 Philolaus of Croton or Taras (born *c*.470) and Archytas of Taras (early fourth century) were leaders.

19 Aristotle, *Metaphysics*, I, 6, 986b, 3.

20 Hence Plato's stress on geometry. It is possible that Pythagoras discovered the 'Pythagorean theorem', though not in its form made familiar by Euclid (*c*.300 BC) at Alexandria.

21 Plato, *Republic*, X, 617b.

22 Aristotle, *Metaphysics*, I, 986a 7.

23 Xenophanes, fragment 7.
Xenophanes also scorned
Heraclitus – Diogenes Laertius, IX, I.

24 Aristotle, fragment 191 Rose.
Pythagoras was said to have been the
slave-master of the Thracian
Zalmoxis and to have been in touch
with the 'Hyperborean' Abaris; see
also Appendix 2, note 40.

25 Diogenes Laertius, VIII, 8 (from Ion
of Chios, fragment 12).

26 Pompeius Trogus, *Historiae
Philippicae, Epitome*, XX, 4, 14
(Justin).

27 Polybius, II, 39, 1. The brotherhoods
extended to Rhegium and Taras.
Their abstention from meat and
sacrifice made them unpopular.

28 Strabo, VI, 1, 12, 263.

29 Cicero, *On Old Age*, 9, 27; Galen, *On
the Diagnosis of Pulses*, II (Külm,
Galeni Opera Omnia, VIII, p. 843).

30 Strabo, VI, 1, 8, 260.

31 Charondas was believed to have been
mobile, legislating for a number of
states in Sicily and south Italy. His
provisions regarding the prosecution
of false witnesses were noteworthy.
Aristotle, *Politics*, II, 9, 7, 1274b.

32 Elymians: language uncertain,
believed to have escaped from
defeated Troy to the west. Sicans:
language uncertain, held to have
been displaced from their homes by
Iberians. Sicels: speakers of an
Indo-European language, thought to
have crossed from Italy to Sicily,
from the eastern parts of which they
dislodged the Sicans.

33 For the hypothetical earlier date of
the Phoenician settlements in Sicily,
see Thucydides, VI, 2, 6. Carthage
stood on a peninsula projecting
seaward from the Gulf of Tunis at the
narrow waist of the central
Mediterranean, only seventy-five
miles wide, with a spacious, sheltered
harbour (artificially supplemented),
and easy access to purple (*murex*)
beds. The most important of the
colonies of the Phoenicians
(Appendix 2), the 'New City' (Qart
Hadasht), was established by settlers
from Tyre, traditionally in 814,
though a date some two generations
later is often preferred. The legend of
Queen Dido, narrated in various

forms by Virgil and other writers,
relates to the foundation. During the
seventh century Carthage became
independent of Tyre and gradually
subdued the tribes of north Africa.
Pottery finds suggest that the place
also played a large part in the
Phoenician foundation of Motya; and
it probably likewise contributed to
the establishment of other
Phoenician settlements in western
Sicily. In *c.*535 Carthage and
Etruscan Caere defeated the
Phocaean colonists of Alalia
(Corsica) in a sea-battle named after
that city, and subsequently
confronted the Greeks in Sardinia,
Spain and Sicily.

34 Sicilian Naxos occupied an ancient
habitation site upon a low-lying lava
peninsula beside the mouth of a
stream north of Mount Aetna. It took
its name from the Aegean island of
Naxos, which was an ally of the
colonizing city Chalcis in Euboea.
The leader of the settlers, the
Chalcidian Theocles, established an
altar of Apollo Archegetes the
Founder (to which subsequent
Sicilian travellers to Greece offered
sacrifice before departure). Five
years later Theocles left Sicilian
Naxos to establish a second colony at
Leontini further south, while his
compatriot Euarchus founded a
settlement at Catana.

35 Herodotus, VII, 155.

36 In contrast to the Chalcidian
colonies, which generally maintained
good relations with the natives.

37 The remains of a large Ionic temple
of the second half of the sixth century
have also been recently discovered.

38 Aristotle, *Poetics*, V, 1448a.

39 Plato, *Theaetetus*, 152e.

40 Though it cannot be stated with
certainty that Epicharmus' plays
were performed in a theatre.

41 Epicharmus, *Persians, Bacchants,
Philoctetes*.

42 Aristotle, *Poetics*, V, 1449b.

43 Epicharmus, fragment 1 (probably
genuine; Plato, *Theaetetus*, 160D, saw
him as one of the founders of the
Heraclitean tradition); Plutarch,
Numa, 8.

44 Thucydides, VI, 4, 5.

45 Ibid., 5, 1.
46 Strabo, VI, 2, 6, 272.
47 Solinus, II, 11.
48 But Stesichorus was buried at Catana, where a gate was named after him.
49 Quintilian, *Training of an Orator*, X, 1, 62. But Stesichorus' Homeric imitations are strained, and he can be prolix.
50 Diogenes Laertius, IX, 18.
51 Ibid.
52 Clement of Alexandria, *Stromateis*, I, 64, 2.
53 Xenophanes, fragment 1.
54 Ibid., fragments 16, 15.
55 Ibid., fragments 26, 25.
56 Ibid., fragment 23.
57 Ibid., fragment 170.
58 Plato, *Sophist*, 242d; Aristotle, *Metaphysics*, I, 5, 986b 12.
59 Parmenides of Elea (a Phocaean colony of *c*.540 in south-west Italy, the Roman Velia, now Castellamare di Bruca) was probably born in *c*.515. He supposedly wrote laws for his city, but attached himself for a time to the Pythagorean brotherhood at Croton. His philosophical views were embodied in a short hexameter poem *On Nature*, of which 160 lines are still extant. Parmenides believed that reality has always existed and remains for ever unchangeable and immobile, occupying the whole of space. This view, which sharply contradicted all previous suppositions of the multiplicity of the universe, seemed to Aristotle to have been foreshadowed by Xenophanes (who was thus regarded as 'the first Eleatic'), but the two men's positions were different, since, whereas Xenophanes was reacting against Homeric anthropomorphic polytheism, Parmenides (though claiming divine revelation) believed that his universal picture was based on rigorous logical argument. Plato utilized his analysis in support of his own doctrine of Forms (Ideas), and Aristotle saw Parmenides as one of the principal founders of metaphysics.
60 Xenophanes was criticized by a later Ionian, Heraclitus of Ephesus (Diogenes Laertius, IX, 1).

61 Xenophanes, fragment 34; cf. fragments 35, 18.
62 Ibid., fragment 7.
63 After earlier occupation by Sicans, the Greek colony of Acragas – taking its name from a river adjoining it to the east, while another stream, the Hypsas (Santa Anna), flowed past its western flank – was founded in *c*.580 by settlers from Gela and from the cities of Rhodes. Its ruling aristocracy was overthrown in *c*.571 by the dictator Phalaris, already occupant of a high office (Aristotle, *Politics*, V, 8, 4, 1310b), who became notorious for his cruelty to political opponents but substantially increased the territory of Acragas, overcoming native towns in the interior. Later in the century the city gained wealth from grain production, cattle-breeding and the export of wine and olive-oil to Carthage and elsewhere. (But the great epoch of Acragas, and its astonishing temple-building programme, were inaugurated by Theron [488–472]), victor (with Gelon of Syracuse) over the Carthaginians at Himera (480).
64 Hippocrates also seized Callipolis, a colony of Sicilian Naxos that has not yet been located.
65 Segesta (sometimes Egesta) stood on and below Mount Barbaro, near the River Gaggera, a tributary of the Crimisus. Despite Greek foundation myths the early town was the principal centre of the Elymians (note 32 above). Finds date from *c*.630. After at least *c*.580/576 the dominant theme of Segesta's history was its continual conflict with Selinus. By the fifth century, however, it had become considerably Hellenized, as a variety of discoveries, and one of the noblest of all Doric temples (begun in *c*.430/420), testify.
66 Selinus sided with the Carthaginians against its fellow Greeks in 480 (like Segesta, it may well not have been wholly Greek).
67 The Ligurians are mentioned in a fragment (55) attributed to Hesiod. Whether their name stands for any ethnic or linguistic unity, and if so of what nature, remains uncertain;

Iberian, Greek and especially Celtic influences and infiltrations can be detected. In early times the territories ascribed to the Ligurians extended far behind the modern coastal strip that bears their name (north-west Italy) as well as including large additional areas both of northern Italy and of south-eastern Gaul, where they appeared as neighbours of Massalia. Ancient authors speak of the roughness and toughness of their village life.

68 Justin, XLIII, 3, 5–12.
69 Strabo, IV, 1, 5, 179.
70 Other Massalian colonies on the Mediterranean coast of Gaul (Nicaea, Antipolis, Monoecus) seem to be later.
71 Herodotus, I, 166.
72 Strabo, IV, 1, 5, 179.
73 Aristotle, *Politics*, VI, 4, 6, 1321a.
74 The Hallstatt culture is named after a site in the Austrian Salzkammergut. In central European archaeology it presents successive phases, A (twelfth to eleventh centuries BC), B (tenth to eighth), C or I (seventh) and D or II (sixth). A and B belong to the late Bronze Age of the region, but in C the characteristic weapon was a long iron sword (or bronze copy of this). In D the most advanced centres are found further west, in eastern France, Switzerland and the Rhineland. Waggon burials are prominent, e.g. at Vix (see next note) and Heuneburg. The Hallstatt people are described as pre-Celts or proto-Celts, whereas the population of the La Tène culture which followed – the second period of the continental Iron Age, named after a site on Lake Neuchâtel in Switzerland – can be described as Celtic.
75 The Vix crater (mixing bowl), nearly six feet high, the masterpiece (and largest example) of archaic metal-work, was found in the grave of a Gaulish princess at Vix on the upper reaches of the River Sequana (Seine). The grave is of the late sixth century, but the crater may be somewhat earlier (c.550–530). Its upper rim is decorated with a frieze

of warriors and chariots, a figure of a girl stands on the lid, and the volute handles show Gorgons and lions. These handles and other parts were cast separately and assembled on arrival. The vase was made either (1) in Sparta or elsewhere in Laconia, since its style displays Laconian analogies; or (2) in south Italy, possibly at Locri Epizephyrii.
76 Justin, XLIII, 4, 1–2.

CHAPTER 8 The North

1 Thucydides, I, 25.
2 Epirus, which is now divided between north-western Greece and southern Albania, consisted of four lofty mountain ranges parallel to the coast, enclosing narrow valleys. In the early Iron Age three main groups of Doric-speaking tribes (fourteen in number), partly of Illyrian origin (note 3 below), emerged in the country, the Chaones (north-west), Molossi (in the central region; allegedly conquered by Neoptolemus the son of Achilles, who became their king), and Thesproti (south-west). Apart from the Greek colonies on and off the coast (note 4), the most important centre in the country was the oracular sanctuary of Zeus – known as Naios, and worshipped in conjunction with the goddess Dione – at Dodona, in Molossian territory, which went back at least to 1200 BC and was mentioned by Homer and Hesiod. The *Iliad* (XVI, 234f.) speaks of the Selli, its priests, who 'had unwashed feet and slept on the ground', and Odysseus consulted the oracle in order to learn the will of Zeus from a sacred oak (*Odyssey*, XIV, 327f.). Hesiod (*Catalogues of Women and Eoiai*, fragment 97) writes of doves living in the hollow of an oak (priestesses at Dodona were subsequently known as 'doves'). Later writers asserted that the oracle delivered its messages through the rustling of the oak-leaves, or the murmur of a sacred spring, or on a brazen gong (a gift from Corcyra). Dodona was gradually eclipsed by the oracle of Apollo at Delphi (although it enjoyed a spectacular

Hellenistic revival).

3 The Illyrians occupied the north-western part of the Balkan peninsula, corresponding with (though extending beyond) the modern Yugoslavia and northern Albania. The Illyrian tribes, divided into seven main groups, were of mixed ethnic origins, but mostly spoke dialects of a single Indo-European tongue, which they did not, however, write down in their homeland (although inscriptions of the [Illyrian] Messapians, in south-east Italy, [Chapter 7, note 8], reflect its character). Incursions of Cimmerians and Thracians (*c.*650) proved damaging. By this time, too, the Illyrians' freedom of action was becoming limited by Greek colonization on their coasts and islands, although they also extracted profit from the trading that followed – and the presence of the colonists offered new and tempting fields of action for their natural piratical and warlike tendencies. (For the partly Illyrian origin of the tribes of Epirus, see above, note 1).

4 The founders of all these settlements were sons of Cypselus. One thousand colonists settled at Leucas, where they or their descendants constructed a canal. The earliest graves excavated at Anactorium have yielded pottery from the last quarter of the seventh century. At Ambracia, the trading centre for the timber of central and south-eastern Epirus – reachable by boat up the River Arachthus – the colony's founder Gorgus was succeeded by at least two dictators of the Cypselid house. The second of these rulers, named Periander, was expelled by a coalition of oligarchs and 'people' (*demos*), allegedly as a result of disturbances caused because he had insulted his boyfriend (Aristotle, *Politics*, v, 3, 6, 1304a; and v, 8, 9, 1311a).

5 Herodotus, vii, 168; Thucydides, i, 14.

6 The name 'Veneti' was applied to various peoples of western Europe, but the best known were the inhabitants of north-eastern Italy, which they occupied in *c.*1000–950 BC. Their race is indeterminable, but their language (recorded in 400 brief inscriptions, all later than 500, some in the Latin alphabet and others in a native script) was Indo-European, and seems closer to Latin and to other Italic tongues than to Illyrian (note 3 above). Their principal city was Ateste (Este), overtaken later by Patavium (Padua) – both furnished with mythical Greek foundation accounts. Their horses were famous in the Greek world, and they exercised some control over the Baltic amber trade. Their principal deity was the goddess Rehtia or Reitia, associated with healing and perhaps with childbirth.

7 Pliny the elder, *Natural History*, iii, 120.

8 Lower down the Adriatic, near Ancona, was another important commercial centre, Numana, where Greek traders began to arrive in the seventh century (the place became especially important for Athens 200 years later).

9 Dionysius of Halicarnassus, vii, 3, 1.

10 Livy, v, 33, 5.

11 Herodotus, vii, 73 ('neighbours' of the Macedonians); vii, 20 seemingly gives a contradictory account. There appear to have been iron-using centres in Macedonia as early as the twelfth century BC, when Aegae inaugurated a long period of prosperity.

12 Hesiod, *Catalogues of Women and Eoiae*, fragment 3.

13 Aristotle, *Politics*, ii, 9, 9, 1274b.

14 In the territory of the Cicones, between the Rivers Nestus and Hebrus. Maronea was allegedly named after the legendary Maron, visited by Odysseus.

15 In the territory of the Saei (later Bistones).

16 In the territory of the Apsinthii.

17 Abydus was founded by agreement with King Gyges of Lydia (Strabo, xiii, 1, 22, 590). For Sigeum see Herodotus, v, 95. Periander of Corinth later arbitrated the dispute between the Athenians and Mytileneans, and awarded the place to Athens.

18 Pisistratus also occupied Rhaecelus (later Aenea) on the Thermaic Gulf, i.e. he enjoyed good relations with Macedonia.

19 Pisistratus also established another son, Hegesistratus, at Sigeum across the strait (note 17 above), no doubt with Persian approval.

20 Their son was the fifth-century Athenian statesman Cimon.

21 *South (Asian) shore (from west to east)*: Parium (founded by Paros, Miletus, Erythrae, *c.*709), Cyzicus (Miletus, *c.*756[?] and *c.*679), Cius (Miletus, 627), Astacus (Megara or Calchedon, ?711). Miletus colonized the island of Proconnesus off Cyzicus before 690. *North (European) shore*: Bisanthe-Rhaedestus (Samos), Perinthus (Samos, 602), Selymbria (Megara, before 668).

22 Herodotus, IV, 138.

23 Ibid., 144.

24 Polybius, IV, 38.

25 The Chalybes were variously believed to have lived between Paphlagonia and Colchis – especially south of Trapezus.

26 Sinope later gained fame as the place of origin of Diogenes the Cynic (*c.*400–325).

27 Xenophon, *Anabasis*, v, 5, 10.

28 Aristotle, *Politics*, v, 4, 2f., 1304b; and 5, 2, 1305b. Jurors at Heraclea Pontica were not on the citizen roll.

29 Homer, *Iliad*, II, 853.

30 Aristotle, *Politics*, v, 5, 2, 1305b.

31 Ibid., v, 5, 7, 1306a.

32 M.N.Tod, *Selection of Greek Historical Inscriptions to the End of the Fifth Century B C*, III, 195; W.Dittenberger, *Sylloge Inscriptionum Graecarum*, 3rd edn, 286.

33 Herodotus, IV, 18, 52.

34 Ibid., 53f.

35 Polybius, IV, 38.

36 Translated in M.M.Austin and P.Vidal-Naquet, *Economic and Social History of Ancient Greece*, London, 1977, pp. 221f.

37 Strabo, XI, 2, 3, 493. Parts of a wine-jar of *c.*640–520 were found 125 miles up the Tanais valley at Krivorovija, and another 187 miles inland on the banks of the River Tsuskan.

38 The native centre of Kul Oba ('Mound of Ashes', from early fifth century) was only four miles west of Panticapaeum. Its later gold-work is exceptional.

39 Nymphaeum (near Geroevka), on a small hill eleven miles south of Panticapaeum, occupied the site of an earlier Scythian habitation centre. The founders of the Greek colony, who may have been Milesians, arrived in *c.*600 or soon afterwards. Protected by walls, the settlement enriched itself from an extensive grain trade. Making use, moreover, of local mineral resources, it may have possessed the earliest mint for silver coinage in the region. Its citizens constructed shrines of Demeter and Aphrodite. Finds from burials suggest that Scythian nobles partook actively in the life of the Greek community. Tyritace (Kamysh Burun), another walled town, lay halfway between Nymphaeum and Panticapaeum, which seems to have provided its founders, apparently before *c.*550.

40 The river was also, confusingly, sometimes known as the Hypanis, a name it shared with the Bug (Strabo, XI, 9, 494).

41 Cepi, in the north-western part of the Taman peninsula – at the eastern recess of the bay – was a small colony of the Milesians, datable from local finds (especially in the necropolis) to the first third of the sixth century BC. Sindikos Limen, or Sindike, another Milesian colony – perhaps of approximately the same date – lay to the south-east. It owed its name to the tribe of the Sindi (whose race and character and social development are much disputed). Later the town was known as Gorgippia. The modern Anapa almost covers the ancient site.

42 A cultural layer of sixth- and fifth-century date has been uncovered at Eshevi, half a mile west of Dioscurias.

43 Colha-Qulha is a Urartian name (see Appendices, note 11). At Bathys Limen (Batumi) a Colchian settlement of eighth- and seventh-century date was overlaid by an early sixth-century stratum

containing Chian and other East Greek pottery. At Vani, sixty miles from the coast – sometimes identified as the capital of Aeetes – finds go back to the seventh and sixth centuries, although the place first became wealthy not long before 400.

44 Aeschylus, *Prometheus Bound*, 723–7; Apollodorus, *Library*, II, 5, 9.

45 Strabo, XI, 5, 4, 505.

46 Pliny the elder, *Natural History*, VI, 19.

47 Strabo, op. cit., citing Clearchus.

48 Herodotus, II, 35, 2.

49 Homer, *Iliad*, III, 189; IV, 186. Their name was usually, but imaginatively, interpreted as meaning 'without a breast' – one breast having been removed to facilitate the use of the bow.

50 Proclus, *Chrestomathia*, 175–80.

51 Homer, *Iliad*, III, 189.

52 Herodotus, IV, 113–16.

APPENDICES Relations With Other Peoples

1 Homer, *Iliad*, III, 187.

2 Cilicia, the south-eastern maritime strip of Asia Minor and its hinterland, comprised a wild and mountainous 'Rough' region and a 'Smooth' or 'Level' plain. It was named after the mythical Cilix, son of King Agenor of Troy; though according to another legend it was under the leadership of Mopsus the seer that the Cilices came from the Troad after the Trojan War (Homer, *Iliad*, VI, 397, 415). Their principal city, Tarsus, claimed Heracles, Perseus, Triptolemus and the Argives as its founders. Fragments of Greek pottery earlier than 700 unearthed at Gözlü Kule, have been thought to bear witness to a Greek quarter in the town. After Sargon II's reconquest of Cilicia the country rose again against Sennacherib in 696–695, with Greek participation (Berossus, F.Jacoby, *Fragmente der griechischen Historiker*, 680 F 7 [31]; Abydenus, ibid., 685 F 5 [6]), and the king, after winning a naval victory against the Greeks and putting down the revolt, rebuilt Tarsus on the site of his governor's capital Olymbrus.

3 The Cimmerians appear in the *Odyssey* (XI, 14ff.) – perhaps owing to etymological confusions with 'Cheimerioi' (winter people) – as a people on whom the sun never shines, near the land of the dead. In historical terms, they seem to have been a semi-nomadic people who overran the south Russian steppe from c.1000 BC onwards, breeding cattle and especially horses, and developing a bronze metallurgy. They buried their dead in tombs built like log cabins, and have been identified with what is known as the Late Timber-Grave (Srubnaya) culture of the ninth and eighth centuries. The belief that they were Thracians has not gained acceptance; their speech, or at least that of their upper class, belonged to the Anatolian group of Indo-European languages. After c.750, in flight from the Scythians (Appendix 2), most of their tribal groups evacuated southern Russia and retreated southwards through the Caucasus (though leaving a fortified remnant in the Taman peninsula). Repelled in c.705 by Sargon II of Assyria (who lost his life, however, at their hands) and then in c.679 by a later Assyrian monarch Esarhaddon, they turned aside into Asia Minor, where they and their allies destroyed the kingdom of Phrygia and devastated Lydian Sardis (c.652) and the Greek cities of Smyrna, Ephesus and Magnesia on the Maeander (a colony of the Magnetes of eastern Thessaly). In c.637 (or c.626?), however, after a severe defeat at the hands of Alyattes of Lydia, the Cimmerians dispersed, and vanished from the historical scene. Their remnant perhaps settled in Cappadocia (eastern Asia Minor). Echoes of Caucasian metal-work in Greece, notably openwork bronze pendants and little figures of birds on openwork stands, may have arrived by way of the Cimmerians.

4 Plato, *Republic*, III, 399a. To the Greeks, Olympus was the name of one or more legendary Phrygian musicians, who supposedly introduced the flute and an exciting 'older' form of melody or harmony.

5 This munificence was said to have earned Croesus eternal happiness among the legendary northern race of the Hyperboreans (Appendix 2).

6 Herodotus, I, 94.

7 Ibid., Xenophanes in Pollux, *Onomasticon*, IX, 83. Sennacherib of Assyria claimed to have cast a half-shekel piece (L.W.King, *Cuneiform Texts from Babylonian Tablets*, 1909, Part XXVI; S.Smith, *Numismatic Chronicle*, 1922, pp.176–85); and the Lydo-Milesian group of issues, although varying in weight, followed the Mesopotamian ratio of sixty shekels to one mina (unlike the more usual Syrian 50:1).

8 Croesus, exploiting new metallurgical technology, introduced the first bimetallic (gold and silver) coinage; cf. Herodotus, I, 94.

9 Alcman, who worked at Sparta, seems to have originated either from Lydia or from Greek Ionia.

10 Plato, *Republic*, III, 398e.

11 The name of Urartu, a major imperial power also known as the Haldian (Khaldian) kingdom, had first occurred, as Uruatri, in an early Assyrian inscription, to describe a people inhabiting the Armenian highlands south and south-east of Lake Van, in a country called Nairi by the Assyrians. Their language, typologically similar to Caucasian tongues, has been specifically related to those of the eastern Caucasus, but this is not wholly accepted. In the ninth century the Urartians, united under their king Arame, were defeated by King Shalmaneser III of Assyria, but his Bia dynasty, installing its capital at Tushpa, created, for a short time, the largest state in western Asia, dominating the Syrian principalities until its defeat by the Cimmerians and then by the Assyrian king Sargon II (713). Urartu bordered on the Greek market-towns of northern Syria in the eighth century BC, and the bronze cauldrons dedicated at Olympia and Delphi (Chapter 1, note 44) were at one time said to be of Urartian origin; but they are more appropriately attributable to northern Syria, and it was from there that the Urartians, as well as the Greeks, derived their examples of these objects. Urartian expertise in irrigation, however, did exercise an influence upon the Greeks, as well as upon the Phrygians. Since the Urartians spoke a language related to Hurrian, Hesiod might have derived the close relationship of his Creation myth to the *Epic of Kumarbi* and *Song of Ullikummi* (both of Hurrian origin) from Urartu, but its knowledge probably came to him instead from the small north Syrian states which preserved Hittite and Hurrian traditions (notes 19, 20). Urartu collapsed in 612 under the blows of invading Scythians and Medes.

12 Ration tablets of 595–570 from Babylon indicate the existence of prisoners of many nationalities from western Asia, including Phoenicians, Lydians and 'Ionian' craftsmen (who are likely to have included non-Greeks from Asia Minor).

13 Other motifs of Greek 'orientalizing' pottery seem to echo the textile patterns of Assyrian robes. The half-shekel pieces which Sennacherib claimed to have cast (note 7) may have influenced the Lydian inauguration of coinage.

14 Homer, *Iliad*, XIV, 182f.

15 Herodotus, II, 109. The systematic compilation of astronomical phenomena appears to have started under Nabu-nasir (747–734).

16 Phoenicia corresponds roughly with the modern state of Lebanon, comprising Mounts Libanus (Lebanon) and Anti-Libanus (both rich in shipbuilding timber), the productive Bekaa valley enclosed between the two ranges, and the seaboard between the River Eleutherus (Nahr el Kebir) to the north and Ace (Akko, Acre) to the south. The Phoenicians, who probably arrived in their country in c.3000 BC, were the last surviving independent Canaanites (see next note) – the designation by which they described themselves. The term 'Phoenician' comes from an Egyptian word meaning 'Asiatic', but was interpreted, when it appeared in

Homer, as meaning 'red-skin' (from *phoinos*, red), although the reference may be rather to the local purple dye (*murex*). Greek myth, however, added a new etymological complication, deriving the name instead from Phoenix, father of Cadmus and Europa and king of Tyre or Sidon. Carthage in north Africa (Chapter 7, note 33) was founded by Tyrians.

17 Canaan was the ancient name for a large territory comprising Phoenicia (see last note) and portions of Syria and Judaea (Palestine, Israel). During the middle years of the second millennium BC the Canaanite cities were ruled by separate kings and fortified by massive ramparts. Later, much of their territory came under Philistine and Israelite control. The Canaanite language, of which the older stage is only indirectly known, evolved into Hebrew, Moabitic and Phoenician. (These are part of the north-western family of Semitic languages, to which Ugaritic [possibly a dialect of Canaanite], Amorite and Aramaic also belong.) Three scripts were used in the Semitic languages: Cuneiform, North Semitic and South Semitic. The North Semitic script has two main branches, Canaanite and Aramaic. The Canaanites are the first people, as far as is known, to have employed an alphabet, which they evolved from c.1800 BC onwards. The Phoenician and Early Hebrew alphabets were among its offshoots. All these alphabets express only consonants (it remained for the Greeks to add vowels – Chapter 1, note 35).

18 The Aramaeans, who spoke a north-western Semitic language not unlike Hebrew (see last note), indirectly affected Greek culture, since the Syro-Phoenician artistic amalgam which created the Greek orientalizing style of painting contained Aramaic elements, though they are hard to disentangle. Between the eleventh and eighth centuries BC the Aramaeans occupied large areas both of Mesopotamia and of northern Syria, where they formed numerous small states (of

which the most important was Damascus) incorporating, in various degrees, neo-Hittite elements (see next note) in their population and culture; it was the north Syrian plain (Aram Naharain, Field of the Rivers) that gave them their name. By the ninth century a huge area extending from Babylon to the Mediterranean was in Aramaean hands, but after a series of wars the destruction of Damascus (732) and Hamath (720) by Sargon II of Assyria marked the end of the Syrian principalities; and the three Greek coastal *emporia* (Al Mina, Posidium and Paltus) were probably destroyed in c.700–675, during a revolt of the Cilicians (Khilakku) of south-eastern Asia Minor (note 2). The Aramaeans' most important cultural achievement was to bring the Phoenician alphabet (note 16) into general public and private use. They worshipped Babylonian, Assyrian and Canaanite gods, and after the inclusion of their Syrian states in the New Babylonian empire, the various peoples involved became increasingly hard to distinguish – a process of amalgamation which continued when Syria, Palestine and Cyprus were combined to form a satrapy of the Persians (539), providing the Phoenician sailors who helped them to conquer Egypt in 525. However, the Aramaic tongue became a *lingua franca*, and under Persian rule 'imperial Aramaic' was officially in use over a territory extending from Egypt to India.

19 The Hittites, whose language belonged to the Anatolian branch of the Indo-European group, infiltrated Asia Minor from the north in c.2000 BC. Their Old Kingdom (c.1750–1450) had its capital first at Kussara and then at Hattusas (Boğazkale). The more stable Hittite empire that followed (c.1450–1200) incorporated most of Anatolia and northern Syria, challenging Assyria and Egypt. (During this period the smiths of Asia Minor learned the working of iron.) In c.1200, however, this Hittite state was overwhelmed by the Phrygians in one wave of the

large-scale upheavals, engulfing the whole east Mediterranean region and near east, to which the Trojans and Mycenaeans (with whom the Hittites had been in close touch) also succumbed. The Hittite outposts in northern Syria, however, survived in a 'strange Hittite afterglow' as a chain of Syro-Hittite or Neo-Hittite city-states. These principalities employed a hieroglyphic script invented by the Hittites and adapted to a form of the Luwian language (related to Hittite and formerly spoken in south-western Asia Minor), but underwent varying degrees of Canaanite and Aramaean influence (notes 17, 18).

20 The Hurrians were broad-headed mountaineers whose language was recorded in a syllabic script like those used for Akkadian (of Mesopotamia) and Hittite; apparently agglutinative in nature and dominated by a profusion of suffixes, it seems to have been neither Indo-European nor Semitic. Hurrians can first be traced towards the end of the third millennium BC in Mesopotamia – where Aryan (Indo-European-speaking) dynasts ruled over them. In the next millennium, they spread over Assyria (which for a time they dominated) and northern Syria (where their names and religious texts have been found) and eastern Asia Minor, forming the imperial kingdom of Mitanni, which exercised its power through horses and chariots. Reaching its height in the fifteenth century, this Hurrian kingdom was defeated by the Hittites in c.1350, but carvings at Yazilikaya indicate far-reaching Hurrian influence on Hittite religion, mythology and nomenclature. This influence long survived in the Neo-Hittite principalities of northern Syria (see last note) – and seems to be echoed by references to 'Horites' in the Old Testament. A language closely related to Hurrian was spoken by the Urartians (note 11).

21 The *Phoenician History* of Sanchuniathon, who supposedly lived in the eleventh century BC (fragments of his work are preserved

by Philo of Byblus, of the first century AD), provided similar succession myths.

22 The profusion of Levantine ivories (including many found in Assyria), which, like the textile designs of the area, influenced Greek art, can perhaps be divided into two main groups, Syrian (based on Hama) and Phoenician. The Aeolic capital (Chapter 1, note 53), and Greek gem-carvings, were derived from Phoenicia either directly or by way of Cyprus; while scarabs and scaraboids found in Euboea and Pithecusae are, or copy, Phoenician adaptations of Egyptian originals. Greek metal techniques likewise go back to the *repoussé* and granulation techniques learned by Syrian and Phoenician craftsmen from Egypt, and early Athenian bronze-work contains Syrian elements. The Greeks learned the habit of reclining at banquets from the Levant (cf. Amos, 6, 4).

23 Josephus, *Against Apion*, I, 28.

24 Herodotus, V, 58, 1–2.

25 A seal and faience vase with the name of the XXIVth Dynasty King Bocchoris (Boknrenef, 720–715), found at Tarquinii in Etruria (Appendix 3), is possibly a Phoenician adapation of Egyptian work.

26 Diodorus Siculus, I, 98 (cf. Chapter 5, note 23). The alternative argument is that Greek large-scale sculpture developed directly from the figurines of Corinth, etc. The origin of line-drawing, too, was variously attributed to a Corinthian and Egyptian (Pliny the elder, XXXV, 16), though the latter, Philocles, was probably a Greek resident (Chapter 6, note 38).

27 The view of Herodotus, II, 123, that 'some Greeks' (by whom he probably meant Pythagoras) derived the doctrine of the immortality of the soul from Egypt was probably mistaken.

28 Ibid. II, 169.

29 Ibid., III, 27–38.

30 Anaximenes' heavenly luminaries circling round a northern mountain (Aristotle, *Meteorologica*, II, 1, 354a 28) reflect Persian conceptions.

31 Homer, *Iliad*, II, 844–50.
32 In the seventh century the Treres (probably Thracian), who lived west of the River Oescus (Iskar), joined or followed the Cimmerians (note 2) – which whom they were often confused – in their raids on Sardis and other centres in Asia Minor (Callinus in Strabo, XIII, 4, 8, 627).
33 Thracian remains have recently been identified north-west of the Black Sea, and there are Thracian megalithic chambers in the north-west Caucasus and Taman peninsula. Modern Thrace, in so far as it comprises areas of Turkey and Greece, is greatly shrunken, comprising the south-eastern corner of Europe belonging to the former state, and the north-eastern fringe of the Greek republic. Most modern 'Thracologists', however, return to much wider definitions of the area.
34 Herodotus, V, 3.
35 Thucydides, II, 29, 2. He described their cavalry as less numerous than that of the Scythians.
36 Light-armed troops hired (later at least) by Athens included contingents of Thracian origin.
37 Homer, *Iliad*, VI, 133–5.
38 According to Diodorus Siculus, I, 23, 2, Orpheus ruled the Hellespont by the will of Dionysus. But there were also traditions of Dionysus' hostility to Orpheus, resulting in the latter's death at the hands of the Maenads (Pausanias, IX, 30, 5; cf. Aeschylus' *Bassarids*).
39 Apollodorus, *Library*, I, 3, 2. Orpheus was also said to have initiated the Argonauts into the Mysteries of Samothrace. The inauguration of the Eleusinian Mysteries (Chapter 2, section 2), too, was attributed to a Thracian, namely Eumolpus – Pausanias, I, 38, 3.
40 Herodotus, IV, 95.
41 Or human beings were held to possess a spark of the divine nature of Zagreus, a pre-Greek deity closely associated with Orphism and identified with Dionysus (and related, in addition, to the underworld, to Crete, and to hunting).

42 Whether the Egyptian elements later found in Orphism (cf. Diodorus Siculus, I, 23; I, 96, 4) were already present in the sixth century is uncertain.
43 Herodotus, IV, 20.
44 Ibid., 46; cf. 17, 19.
45 According to Herodotus (ibid., 73) the Scythians were often buried far from their own territories (their kings' funerals being celebrated among the remote Gerrhi – ibid., 71).
46 Herodotus, IV, 76.
47 Some were dolichocephalic and some brachycephalic, the former being more numerous.
48 The combats between animals probably represented conflicts between the divine forces. The limp, dead, passive animals which are sometimes depicted seem to stand for spirits whose power has been put out of action.
49 Smela, Temir Gora and Altin Oba (Panticapaeum), Melgunov (Kirovograd), Kelermes, Kostromskaya, Vettersfelde. For Kul Oba see Chapter 8, note 38. Some prefer to describe sixth-century burials, on either side of the strait, as Sindo-Maeotian – 'Scythian prototypes' rather than Scythian.
50 Herodotus, IV, 78; Scyles may have been exceptional – cf. Chapter 8, section 3.
51 Herodotus, IV, 76.
52 The Tungus are a group of peoples in the sub-Arctic forest of eastern Siberia, speaking an Altaic branch of the Ural–Altaic languages. The central figure of their religion is the shaman.
53 The Scythians taught the felting of woven materials, *pilesis* (Pseudo-Plutarch, *Stromateis*, 3), to the Greeks (though its application to the theories of Anaximenes may be anachronistic).
54 Herodotus, IV, 17, 1; IV, 108, 2.
55 W. Dittenberger, *Sylloge Inscriptionum Graecarum*, 3rd edn, 495.
56 E.g. Ligurian, Sican, Sardinian.
57 The two longest, comprising 1,190 and 300 words respectively, are a liturgical text (the wrapping of an Egyptian mummy in Zagreb

Museum) and, apparently, a prescription for funeral ceremonies (at Perugia).

58 Herodotus, I, 94.

59 M. Pallottino, *Testimonia Linguae Etruscae*, 2nd edn, nos. 155, 131.

60 *Notizie degli Scavi*, 1971, p. 241, fig. 57; Herodotus, IV, 152. The Greeks may have been confined to their own residential quarters at Naucratis (Chapter 6, section 4).

61 M. Torelli, *Elogia Tarquinensia* (1975), pp. 43f.

62 *Bucchero* (from the Spanish term *bucaro*, applied to central and south American pots before the time of Columbus) was made of fine clay – preferably with a manganese content – turned on the wheel and then baked in a slow-burning fire, so that the oxygen reached the clay in insufficient quantities to turn its iron content red, but blackened it instead.

63 The Caeritans, however, subsequently (?) founded a colony known to the Greeks as Nicaea (Victory-Town) in north-eastern Corsica. They were no doubt one of the Etruscan peoples who had close contacts with Massalia (Chapter 7, section 6).

64 M. Pallottino, op. cit., nos. 873–7.

65 Caere and Rome founded joint colonies in Sardinia and Corsica (*c*.378/377, 357/354).

66 Veientine influence also dominated the partly Etruscan civilizations of the Faliscans, whose shrine of Feronia (near Capena) was an important sanctuary. The culture of the Faliscan people displayed a progressive Hellenization, reflected in the growth and urbanization of Falerii Veteres (Civita Castellana), their principal city.

67 The Tomb of the Ducks, of the late seventh century, is the oldest-known painted grave in Etruria.

68 At Athens, in the sixth century, the Nicosthenes workshop and maker of 'Tyrrhenian' amphorae specialized in exports to Etruria.

69 A heap of selected tin has also been found at Rusellae. Fir trees beside the Umbro basin provided charcoal for smelting.

70 Servius of Virgil, *Aeneid*, x, 172.

71 Pliny the elder, *Natural History*, XXXVI, 19, 91ff.

72 Several villages amalgamated during the sixth century to form the city of Arretium, on a plateau overlooking the upper Clanis (Chiana) and the Arnus (Arno). Perusia, formerly inhabited (like Clusium) by Umbrians, rose above the fertile valley of the (then navigable) upper Tiber. Again it boasted pretentious foundation legends. The gravestone of Avle Feluske of Vetulonia (*c*.600?) seems to have been set up by a Perusian comrade-at-arms, Hirumina. Perusia's bronze-work reflects Ionian influence, later deviating into bizarre local elongations. At Volsinii, a city comprising villages amalgamated in *c*.600, the names of the dead, belonging to ninety families buried in the city's rectangular tombs (550–500), show a high proportion of non-Etruscans, including Greeks. Volsinii had close connections with Campania.

73 Virgil, *Aeneid*, x, 200–3.

74 Farther south, the Tomb of the Diver at Posidonia presents Etruscan analogies (cf. Chapter 7, note 15).

75 Dionysius of Halicarnassus, VII, 3, 1.

76 Plinyl the elder, *Natural History*, XXXV, 43, 152. Cf. Chapter 3, section 2.

77 Finds of Attic black-figure and red-figure pottery have also been made in various parts of Rome.

78 Pliny the elder, *Natural History*, XXXV, 154.

79 F. Castagnoli, *Studi e Materiali*, XXX, 1959, pp. 109ff.

80 Cato, *Origins*, fragment 12.

81 In *c*.425 an invading Italic people (the Sabellians) captured Etruscan Capua as well as Greek Cumae. In *c*.396 Veii fell to the Romans, who gradually subordinated the other states of Etruria as well. During the course of the fourth century, Etruscan north Italy succumbed to the Gauls.

BIBLIOGRAPHY

This list names only writers quoted or mentioned in the text.
Those whose work has not survived, or has survived only in fragments,
are marked thus *.

ANCIENT LITERARY SOURCES

GREEK

ABYDENUS, second century AD. Historian of Assyria and Babylonia*
AESCHYLUS, born Eleusis (Attica), 525/524–456 BC.
  Athenian tragic dramatist
ALCAEUS, born Mytilene (Lesbos), c.620 BC. Lyric poet*
ALCMAEON, born Croton (south-east Italy), later fifth century BC.
  Natural scientist and physician*
ANACHARSIS, Scythian prince, sixth century BC.
  Credited with (apocryphal) didactic poems* and letters.
  One of the Seven Sages
ANACREON, born Teos (Ionia), c.570 BC.
  Lyric, elegiac and iambic poet
ANAXIMANDER, born Miletus (Ionia), c.610–after 546 BC.
  Pre-Socratic philosopher*
ANAXIMENES, born Miletus (Ionia), soon after 600–528/525 BC.
  Pre-Socratic philosopher*
ANDRODAMAS, born Rhegium (south-west Italy), seventh century BC (?).
  Law-giver to the cities of Chalcidice (Macedonia)
ANDROTION, born Athens, c.410–340 BC.
  Atthidographer (historian of Attica)*
ANTIOCHUS, born Syracuse (Sicily), fifth century BC.
  Historian*
APOLLODORUS of Athens, born Alexandria (Egypt), c.180 BC.
  Writer on mythology, theology and geography
APOLLONIUS RHODIUS, born Egypt, c.295–c.215 BC.
  Epic poet (*Argonautica*)
ARCHILOCHUS, born Paros, c.710–after 648 BC (?). Poet
ARCHYTAS, born Taras (south-east Italy), first half of fourth century BC.
  Pythagorean philosopher and scientist*

ARCTINUS, born Miletus, eighth century BC (?). Epic poet*

ARION, born Methymna (Lesbos), end of seventh century BC. Poet*

ARISTEAS, born Proconnesus (Propontis), sixth century BC.
Semi-legendary; reputed author of poem on Arimaspeans of Scythia*

ARISTOPHANES, born Athens, 457/445–shortly before 385 BC.
Comic dramatist

ARISTOTLE, born Stagirus (Macedonia), 384–322 BC.
Philosopher and scientist

ARISTOXENUS, born Taras (south-east Italy), c.370 BC.
Writer on music and biographer

ASIUS, born Samos, seventh or sixth century BC. Poet

ATHENAEUS, born Naucratis (Egypt), c.AD 200.
Writer of an encyclopaedic symposium

BACCHYLIDES, born Iulis (Ceos), c.524/521(?)–after 452 BC. Poet

BEROSSUS, priest of Bel, c.290 BC. Historian of Babylon*

CALLIMACHUS, born Cyrene, c.310/305–c.240 BC.
Alexandrian poet and scholar

CALLINUS, born Ephesus, first half of seventh century BC. Elegiac poet*

CHARONDAS, born Catana (Sicily), sixth century BC.
Law-giver for various cities including Rhegium*

CHIONIDES, born Athens, active early fourth century BC. Comic dramatist*

CLEMENT of ALEXANDRIA (St), born Athens (?), c.AD 150–211/216.
Christian theologian

CRITIAS, born Athens, c.460–403 BC.
Politician (one of the Thirty Tyrants), elegiac poet and tragic dramatist*

CYNAETHUS, born Chios, sixth century BC.
Credited with (part of?) the *Homeric Hymn to Apollo*

DAMASTES, born Sigeum (Troad), fifth century BC.
Historian, literary historian, geographer and mythologist*

DEINIAS, born Argos, third century BC. Historian of Argos*

DIODORUS SICULUS, born Agyrium (Sicily), first century BC.
Universal historian

DIOGENES, born Sinope, c.400–c.325 BC.
Founder of Cynic sect. Probable author of dialogues and tragedies*

ECHEMENES, Cretan, of uncertain date. Author of *Cretica*

EPICHARMUS, born Syracuse (?), active early fifth century BC.
Comic dramatist*

EUCLEIDES (Euclid), taught at Alexandria c.300 BC.
Mathematician and musicologist

EURIPIDES, born Phlya (Attica), c.485/480–407/406 BC.
Athenian tragic dramatist

EUSEBIUS, born Caesarea Maritima (Syria Palaestina), c.AD 260–340.
Christian bishop, ecclesiastical historian, biographer

GALEN, born Pergamum (Mysia), c.AD 129–c.199.
Physician, anatomist, physiologist, psychologist, philosopher, critic

HECATAEUS, born Miletus, active c.500 BC.
Geographer, historian, mythologist*

HERACLITUS, born Ephesus, active *c*.500 BC.
  Pre-Socratic philosopher*
HERODOTUS, born Halicarnassus (Caria), *c*.480–*c*.425 BC. Historian
HESIOD, born Cyme (Aeolis), migrated to Ascra (Boeotia), eighth century BC.
  Epic poet
HOMER, probably born Chios and worked in Smyrna, eighth century BC.
  Epic poet
Homeric Hymns, eighth to sixth centuries BC; dedicated to numerous deities
  including Demeter and Apollo (see also Cynaethus). Not by Homer
IAMBLICHUS, born Chalcis beneath Libanus (Syria), *c*.AD 250–306/337.
  Neoplatonist philosopher and writer on supernatural
IBYCUS, born Rhegium (south-west Italy), sixth century BC. Poet*
ISOCRATES, born Athens, 436–338 BC.
  Rhetorician and educationalist
JOSEPHUS, born Jerusalem, AD 37/8–after 94/5.
  Historian of the Jews
Lives of Homer. There are seven, all of Roman imperial times, but perhaps
  going back to an earlier tradition
MAGNES, born Athens, active first half of fifth century BC.
  Comic dramatist*
MELISSUS, born Samos, active 440s BC.
  Fleet commander and Pre-Socratic (Eleatic) philosopher*
MIMNERMUS, born Smyrna or Colophon (Ionia) or Astypalaea (Sporades),
  late seventh century BC. Elegiac poet
ONOMACRITUS, born Athens, active second half of sixth century BC.
  Author or editor of Orphic writings, editor of Homer and oracles
  (suspected of forging them)
ORION, born Thebes (Egypt), fifth century AD.
  Teacher at Alexandria and grammarian
Orphic Poems. Numerous poems circulating from sixth century BC onwards
  under the name of the mythical Orpheus
Palatine Anthology. A collection of 3,700 epigrams collected by an unknown
  Byzantine scholar (or group of scholars) in *c*.AD 980
PARMENIDES, born Elea (south-west Italy), *c*.515 BC.
  Pre-Socratic philosopher
PAUSANIAS, born near Magnesia beside Sipylus (Lydia), second century AD.
  Travel writer
PHALEAS, born Calchedon (opposite Byzantium), probably fifth century BC.
  Political theorist*
PHEIDON, born Corinth, eighth century BC (?). Law-giver*
PHERECYDES, born Syros, active *c*.550 BC.
  Writer of cosmogony*
PHILO of BYBLUS, born Byblus (Phoenicia), AD 64–141.
  Writer on Phoenician religion and customs* (see also Non-Classical
  Sources, s.v. Sanchuniathon)
PHILOLAUS, (1) born Corinth, active *c*.730 BC. Law-giver at Thebes.*
  (2) born Croton or Taras in *c*.470 BC. Pythagorean philosopher*

PHOCYLIDES, born Miletus, active 544/541 BC. Poet*
PHRYNICHUS, born Athens, active 511/508–at least 476 BC.
Tragic dramatist*
PINDAR, born Cynoscephalae (Boeotia), c.518–c.438 BC. Lyric poet
PLATO, born Athens, c.429–347 BC. Philosopher
PLUTARCH, born Chaeronea (Boeotia), before AD 50–after 120.
Philosopher and biographer
POLLUX, born Naucratis (Egypt), later second century AD.
Rhetorician and encyclopaedic scholar
POLYBIUS, born Megalopolis (Arcadia), c.200–after 118 BC. Historian
POLYCHARMUS, born Naucratis (Egypt). Work on Aphrodite*
PORPHYRY, born Tyre (Phoenicia) or Batanea (Syria).
Philosopher and writer on religion
PRATINAS, born Phlius (Argolid), active c.500 BC.
Tragic and satyric dramatist*
PROCLUS (1), second century AD, grammarian.
(2) born Lycia (south Asia Minor), AD 412–85. Neoplatonist philosopher
SCYMNUS, born Chios, active c.185 BC. Geographer;* but the surviving
travel-book (Pseudo-Scymnus) is of c.90 BC.
SEMONIDES, born Samos, but especially associated with Amorgos, seventh to
sixth centuries BC. Iambic and elegiac poet
SIMONIDES, born Iulis (Ceos), c.556–468 BC. Poet
SIMPLICIUS, born Cilicia (south-east Asia Minor), sixth century AD.
Commentator on Aristotle and Epictetus
SOCRATES, born Argos, probably of Hellenistic date. Writer on Argive and
religious subjects* (the Athenian philosopher Socrates left no writings)
SOLON, born Athens, active early sixth century BC.
Statesman and poet
SOPHOCLES, born Colonus (Attica), c.496–406 BC.
Athenian tragic dramatist
STESICHORUS (originally named Tisias), born Matavrus (south Italy) and
lived at Himera (Sicily), c.632/629–556/553 BC (?). Lyric poet
STRABO, born Amasia (Pontus), c.63 BC–at least AD 21.
Geographer and historian
SUIDAS (Suda). A lexicon of the later tenth century AD
THALETAS, born Gortyna (Crete) and lived at Sparta, seventh century BC.
Poet and law-giver
THEMISTIUS, born Paphlagonia (north Asia Minor), c.AD 317–c.388.
Philosopher and rhetorician
THEOGNIS, born Megara, mid-sixth century BC. Elegiac poet
THESPIS, born Attica, active 535/533 BC.
Reputedly the first Athenian tragic dramatist*
THUCYDIDES, born Athens, c.460/455–c.400 BC. Historian
TIMAEUS, born Tauromenium (Sicily), c.356–c.260 BC. Historian*
TIMON, born Phlius (Argolid), c.320–230 BC. Sceptic philosopher*
XENOPHON, born Erchia (Attica), c.428–c.354 BC.
Public figure, soldier, man of letters, historian

ZALEUCUS, born Locri Epizephyrii (south-west Italy), active c.650 BC (?).
Law-giver*
ZENO, born Elea (south-west Italy) in c.490 BC.
Pre-Socratic (Eleatic) philosopher*

LATIN

AVIENUS, born Volsinii (Etruria), fourth century AD. Geographer and poet
CATO THE ELDER ('the Censor'), born Tusculum (Latium), 234–149 BC.
Historian, rhetorician,* writer on agriculture
CICERO, born Arpinum (Latium), 106–43 BC.
Statesman, orator, rhetorician, philosopher, poet, letter-writer
JUSTIN, probably third century AD. Epitomizer of Pompeius Trogus (q.v.)
PLINY THE ELDER, born Comum (north Italy), AD 23/4–79.
Writer on military science, language and history,* and of encyclopaedic
Natural History
POMPEIUS TROGUS, born in territory of Vocontii (south Gaul), active in latter
part of first century BC. Wrote zoological and botanical (?) works and
Universal History (see Justin)*
QUINTILIAN, born Calagurris (north Spain), c.AD 35–c.100.
Educationalist and critic
SERVIUS, born c.AD 360/5 (?). Grammarian and commentator on Virgil
SOLINUS, early third century AD. Encyclopaedic geographer
VIRGIL, born Andes (Mantua, north Italy), 70–19 BC.
Poet (*Aeneid, Georgics, Eclogues*)

NON-CLASSICAL SOURCES

Enuma Elish, Babylonian creation epic which is recorded in its later form in
cuneiform texts of the seventh century BC but goes back to the mid-second
millennium and beyond that to a Sumerian story of c.3000
Gilgamesh, Epic of, relates the story of the best known of all Sumerian heroes.
The fullest of a number of texts (from the early second millennium
onwards) comprises twelve incomplete tablets found in the library of the
Assyrian king Ashurbanibal (669–630 BC) at Nineveh

Kumarbi, Epic of (Kingship in Heaven text). Cosmogonic myth of Hurrian
origin translated or freely adapted into Hittite
Ullikummi, Song of (a stone monster created by Kumarbi). Myth of Hurrian
origin translated or freely adapted into Hittite, and localized in north
Syria and Cilicia

SANCHUNIATHON. A Phoenician writer who probably lived in the eleventh
century BC and whose writings on Phoenician religion and mythology were
translated into Greek in the first or second century AD by Philo of Byblus
(see above, Greek sources)*

Amos, Book of. Book of Hebrew Bible (Old Testament) containing the sayings of Amos, who acted as a prophet in Israel in the eighth century BC but had previously lived at Tekoa in Judah
Job, Book of. Book of Hebrew Bible (Old Testament), datable to the sixth century BC, recounting the sufferings of the Edomite Job

INSCRIPTIONS

M.M.AUSTIN and P.VIDAL NAQUET, *Economic and Social History of Ancient Greece* (1977)
W.DITTENBERGER, *Sylloge Inscriptionum Graecarum*, 3rd edn (1915–24)
C.W.FORNARA, *Archaic Times to the End of the Peloponnesian War* (2nd edn, 1983)
M.GUARDUCCI, *Inscriptiones Creticae* (1935–50)
F.JACOBY, *Fragmente der griechischen Historiker* (1923, reprinted with additions 1957; ii BD no. 239, Marmor Parium)
L.H.JEFFERY, *The Local Scripts of Archaic Greece* (1961)
R.MEIGGS and D.LEWIS, *Selection of Greek Historical Inscriptiones to the End of the Fifth Century BC* (1969)
H.ROEHL, *Inscriptiones Graecae Antiquissimae* (1882)
M.N.TOD, *Selection of Greek Historical Inscriptions* (Vol. I, 2nd edn, 1946; Vol. II, 1948)

T.F.R.G.BRAUN, *Cambridge Ancient History*, Vol. III, Part 3 (2nd edn, 1982) (Assyrian tablets)
L.W.KING, *Cuneiform Texts from Babylonian Tablets* (1909)
M.PALLOTTINO, *Testimonia Linguae Etruscae* (2nd edn, 1968)
M.TORELLI, *Elogia Tarquiniensia* (1975)

COINS

Detailed references to individual coins are not given in the text, but the following books will be found useful.

R.A.G.CARSON, *Coins of Greece and Rome* (2nd edn, 1970)
Catalogues of Greek Coins in the British Museum (1873–1927)
Guide to the Principal Coins of the Greeks from c.700 BC to AD 270 (British Museum, 2nd edn, 1959)
B.V.HEAD, *Historia Numorum* (2nd edn, 1911)
M.HIRMER and C.M.KRAAY, *Greek Coins* (1966)
G.K.JENKINS, *Ancient Greek Coins* (1972)
G.K.JENKINS, *The Coins of Greek Sicily* (2nd edn, 1976)
C.M.KRAAY, *Archaic and Classical Greek Coins* (1976)
M.J.PRICE, E.M.BESLY, D.W.MACDOWALL, M.JONES, W.A.ODDY (eds), *A Survey of Numismatic Research 1978–1984* (1986)
M.J.PRICE and B.L.TRELL, *Coins and Their Cities* (1977)
N.K.RUTTER, *Greek Coinage* (1983)
C.T.SELTMAN, *Greek Coins* (2nd edn, 1955)

SOME MODERN BOOKS

A. W. H. ADKINS and P. WHITE, *The Greek Polis* (Chicago, 1986)

K. ADSHEAD, *The Politics of the Archaic Peloponnese* (Aldershot, 1986)

A. ANDREWES, *Greek Society* (Harmondsworth, 1975)

A. ANDREWES, *The Greek Tyrants* (London, 1956)

M. E. AUBERT, *The Phoenicians and the West* (Cambridge, 1993)

A. BARKER (ed.), *Greek Musical Writings;* Vol. 1, *The Musician and his Art* (Cambridge, 1984)

J. BARNES, *The Presocratic Philosophers* (London, 1979)

J. BARNES (ed.), *Early Greek Philosophy* (Harmondsworth, 1987)

M. BERNAL, *Black Athena: The Afro-Asiatic Roots of Classical Civilization*, Vol. 1, *The Fabrication of Ancient Greece 1785–1885* (London, 1987)

J. BOARDMAN, *Greek Sculpture: The Archaic Period* (London, 1978)

J. BOARDMAN, *The Greek Overseas: Their Early Colonies and Trade* (rev. edn, London, 1980)

J. BOARDMAN (ed.), *Cambridge Ancient History*, Plates to Vol. III (2nd edn, Cambridge, 1984)

J. BOARDMAN, I. E. S. EDWARDS, N. G. L. HAMMOND, E. SOLLBERGER (eds), *Cambridge Ancient History*, Vol. III, Parts 1–3 (2nd edn, Cambridge, 1982)

J. BOARDMAN, J. GRIFFIN, O. MURRAY (eds), *Oxford History of the Classical World* (Oxford, 1986)

R. BROWNING, *The Greek World: Classical, Byzantine and Modern* (London, 1985)

P. BUITRON-OLIVER (ed.), *New Perspectives in Early Greek Art* (Washington, 1991)

W. BURKERT, *Greek Religion: Archaic and Classical* (Oxford, 1985)

A. R. BURN, *The Pelican History of Greece* (rev. edn, Harmondsworth, 1982)

A. R. BURN, *The Warring States of Greece: From Their Rise to the Roman Conquest* (London, 1968)

A. R. BURN (postscript by D. M. LEWIS), *Persia and the Greeks: The Defence of the West c.546–478 BC* (2nd edn, London, 1984)

J. B. BURY and R. MEIGGS, *History of Greece* (4th edn, London, 1983)

P. CARLIER, *La Royauté en Grèce avant Alexandre* (Strasbourg, 1984)

M. CARY, *The Geographical Background of Greek and Roman History* (Oxford, 1949)

M. CARY and E. H. WARMINGTON, *The Ancient Explorers* (rev. edn, Harmondsworth, 1963)

L. CASSON, *Ships and Seamanship in the Ancient World* (with new appendix, Princeton, 1986)

J. N. COLDSTREAM, *Geometric Greece* (London, 1977)

J. N. COLDSTREAM, *The Formation of the Greek Polis: Aristotle and Archaeology* (Wiesbaden, 1984)

J. M. COOK, *The Greeks in Ionia and the East* (London, 1962)

J. M. COOK, *The Persian Empire* (London, 1983)

R. M. COOK, *Greek Art: Its Development, Character and Influence* (London, 1972)

R. M. COOK, *The Greeks Till Alexander* (London, 1961)

M. H. CRAWFORD and D. WHITEHEAD, *Archaic and Classical Greece: A Selection of Ancient Sources in Translation* (Cambridge, 1983)

F. DE POLIGNAC, *Cults, Territory and Origins of the Greek City State* (Chicago, 1994)

V. R. DESBOROUGH, *The Greek Dark Ages* (London, 1972)

I. M. DIAKONOFF, *Early Antiquity* (Chicago, 1991)

B. C. DIETRICH, *Tradition in Greek Religion* (Berlin, 1986)

R. DREWS, *Basileus: The Evidence for Kingship in Geometric Greece* (New Haven, 1983)

R. DREWS (ed.), *The Coming of the Greeks* (Princeton, paperback ed., 1995)

P. E. EASTERLING and B. M. W. KNOX (eds), *Cambridge History of Classical Literature*, Vol. I, *Greek Literature* (Cambridge, 1985)

P. E. EASTERLING and J. V. MUIR, *Greek Religion and Society* (Cambridge, 1985)

I. E. S. EDWARDS, C. J. GADD, N. G. L. HAMMOND, E. SOLLBERGER (eds), *Cambridge Ancient History*, Vol. II, Part 2 (Cambridge, 1975)

H. VAN EFFENTERRE, *La Cité Grecque* (Paris, 1985)

V. EHRENBERG, *From Solon to Socrates: Greek History and Civilization during the Sixth and Fifth Centuries BC* (2nd edn, London, 1973)

V. EHRENBERG, *The Greek State* (2nd edn, London, 1969)

C. J. EMLYN-JONES, *The Ionians and Hellenism* (London, 1980)

C. FARRAR, *The Origins of Democratic Thinking* (Cambridge, 1989)

A. FERRILL, *The Origins of War: From the Stone Age to Alexander the Great* (London, 1985)

M. I. FINLEY, *Early Greece: The Bronze and Archaic Ages* (rev. edn, London, 1981)

M. I. FINLEY (ed., C. DUGGAN), *History of Sicily* (London, 1986)

M. I. FINLEY, *The World of Odysseus* (2nd edn, London, 1977)

M. I. FINLEY (ed.), *The Legacy of Greece: A New Appraisal* (Oxford, 1981)

M. I. FINLEY (ed.), *Slavery in Classical Antiquity* (reprint with supplement, Cambridge, 1968)

C. W. FORNARA (ed.), *Archaic Times to the End of the Peloponnesian War* (2nd edn, Cambridge, 1983)

W. G. FORREST, *The Emergence of Greek Democracy* (London, 1966)

F. J. FROST, *Greek Society* (Lexington, Massachusetts, 1971)

A. FUKS, *Social Conflict in Ancient Greece* (Jerusalem and Leiden, 1984)

M. GAGARIN, *Early Greek Law* (Berkeley, 1987)

P. GARNSEY, K. HOPKINS and C. R. WHITTAKER (eds), *Trade in the Ancient Economy* (London, 1983)

L. GERNET, *The Anthropology of Ancient Greece* (Baltimore, 1981)

M. GRANT (ed.), *Greece and Rome: The Birth of Western Civilization* (2nd edn, London, 1986)

M. GRANT and R. KITZINGER (eds), *Civilization of the Ancient Mediterranean* (New York, 1988)

Grecia, Italia e Sicilia nei VIII e VII secoli a.C. (Atti del Convegno Nazionale, Athens, 1983–4)

P. A. L. GREENHALGH, *Early Greek Warfare* (Cambridge, 1973)

R. HÄGG (ed.), *The Greek Renaissance of the Eighth Century BC: Tradition and Innovation* (Stockholm Symposium, 1981; Stockholm, 1983)

N. G. L. HAMMOND, *History of Greece to 322 BC* (3rd edn, London, 1986)

N. G. L. HAMMOND, *Migration and Invasions in Greece and Adjacent Areas* (Park Ridge, 1976)

V. D. HANSON (ed.), *Hoplites* (London, 1991)

H. A. HARRIS, *Sport in Greece and Rome* (London, 1972)

E. A. HAVELOCK, *The Muse Learns to Write* (New Haven, 1986)

R. J. HOPPER, *The Early Greeks* (London, 1976)

S. C. HUMPHREYS, *Anthropology and the Greeks* (London, 1978)

J. M. HURWIT, *The Art and Culture of Early Greece 1100–480 BC* (Ithaca, 1985)

E. HUSSEY, *The Presocratics* (London, 1972)

L. H. JEFFERY, *Archaic Greece: The City-States c.700–500 BC* (London, 1978)

W. R. JOHNSON, *The Idea of Lyric: Lyric Modes in Ancient and Modern Poetry* (Berkeley, 1982)

G. S. KIRK, J. E. RAVEN and M. SCHOFIELD, *The Presocratic Philosophers* (2nd edn, Cambridge, 1983)

C. KOPCKE and I. TOKUMARU (eds), *Greece Between East and West: 10th–8th Centuries B.C.* (Mainz, 1992)

W. K. LACEY, *The Family in Classical Greece* (London, 1968)

M. R. LEFKOWITZ, *Women in Greek Myth* (London, 1986)

M. R. LEFKOWITZ and M. B. FANT (eds), *Women's Life in Greece and Rome: A Source-Book in Translation* (London, 1982)

A. LESKY, *History of Greek Literature* (London, 1966)

P. LEVI, *History of Greek Literature* (Harmondsworth, 1985)

A. LINTOTT, *Violence, Civil Strife and Revolution in the Classical City 750–330 BC* (London, 1982)

R. J. LITTMAN, *The Great Experiment: Imperialism and Social Conflict 800–400 BC* (London, 1974)

H. LLOYD-JONES, *The Justice of Zeus* (2nd edn, Berkeley, 1984)

C. MEIER, *The Greek Discovery of Politics* (Harvard, 1990)

F. J. MEIJER, *A History of Seafaring in the Classical World* (London, 1986)

S. P. MORRIS, *Daidales and the Origins of Greek Art* (Princeton, 1992)

O. MURRAY, *Early Greece* (London, 1978, 1993)

P. OLIVA, *The Birth of Greek Civilization* (London, 1981)

H. W. PARKE, *Greek Oracles* (London, 1967)

J. J. PERADOTTO and J. P. SULLIVAN, *Women in the Ancient World: The Arethusa Papers* (Albany, 1984)

A. J. PODLECKI, *The Early Greek Poets and their Times* (Vancouver, 1984)

F. DE POLIGNAC, *La Naissance de la cité grecque* (Paris, 1984)

S. B. POMEROY, *Goddesses, Whores, Wives and Slaves: Women in Classical Antiquity* (New York, 1975)

W. K. PRITCHETT, *The Greek State at War*, Parts I–IV (Berkeley, 1971–85)

D. RIDGWAY, *The First Western Greeks* (Cambridge, 1992)

C. ROEBUCK, *Economy and Society in the Early Greek World* (New York, 1979, 1984)

C. ROLLEY, *Greek Bronzes* (London, 1986)

B. RUTKOWSKI, *Cult Places in the Aegean* (New Haven, 1986)

N. K. SANDARS, *The Sea Peoples* (rev. edn, London, 1985)

F. SCHACHERMEYR, *Griechische Frühgeschichte* (Vienna, 1984)

R. SEALEY, *History of the Greek City States c.700–338 BC* (Berkeley, 1976)

A. M. SNODGRASS, *Archaic Greece: The Age of Experiment* (London, 1980)

A. M. SNODGRASS, *Early Greek Armour and Weapons* (Edinburgh, 1964)

C. G. STARR, *The Aristocratic Temper of Greek Civilization* (Oxford, 1992)

C. G. STARR, *The Economic and Social Growth of Early Greece 800–500 BC* (New York, 1977)

C. G. STARR, *The Individual and the Community: The Rise of the Polis 800–500 BC* (Oxford, 1986)

C. G. STARR, *The Origins of Greek Civilization* (London, 1961, 1991)

R. A. TOMLINSON, *Greek Sanctuaries* (London, 1976)

C. A. TRYPANIS, *Greek Poetry from Homer to Seferis* (Chicago, 1981)

E. C. L. VAN DER VLIET, *The Origins of the Greek State* (London, 1987)

J.-P. VERNANT, *Myth and Society in Ancient Greece* (London, 1982)

J.-P. VERNANT, *The Origins of Greek Thought* (London, 1982)

H. G. WALLINGER, *Ships and Sea-Power Before the First Persian Wars* (Leiden, 1993)

L. J. WARLEY, *Hippeis* (San Francisco, 1994)

L. WHIBLEY, *Greek Oligarchies: Their Character and Organization* (London, 1896, reprint Chicago, 1975)

M. R. WRIGHT, *The Presocratics* (Bristol, 1985)

Also regional and local studies, and works on individual writers.

INDEX

Numbers in italics refer to the maps.